CUBA

P9-CBZ-025

2nd edition

Carlos Soldevila
Alexis de Gheldere
Claude-Victor Langlois
Yazid Saïdi

ULYSSES
TRAVEL PUBLICATIONS
Travel better... enjoy more

Authors
Carlos Soldevila
Alexis de Gheldere
Claude-Victor Langlois
Yazid Saïdi

Translation:
Sarah Kresh
Danielle Gauthier
Janet Logan
Stéphanie Lemire
Eric Hamovitch
Tracy Kendrick
Felicity Munn

Proofreading:
Stephanie Heidenreich
Tara Salman

Editor:
Daniel Desjardins
Assistants
Christian Roy
Stéphane Marceau

Production Supervisor:
Pascale Couture

Cartography and Graphics:
André Duchesne
Assistants
Patrick Thivièrge
Isabelle Lalonde
Marc Rigole
François Hénault

Layout:
Christian Roy

Series Director:
Claude Morneau

Ilustrations:
Lorette Pierson
Myriam Gagné

Photographs:
Front Cover
Tibor Bognar

Production *Design:* Patrick
Farei (Atoll Direction);

DISTRIBUTORS

AUSTRALIA: Little Hills Press, 11/37-43 Alexander St., Crows Nest NSW 2065, ☎ (612) 437-6995, Fax: (612) 438-5762

BELGIUM AND LUXEMBOURG: Vander, Vrijwilligerlaan 321, B-1150 Brussel, ☎ (02) 762 98 04, Fax: (02) 762 06 62

CANADA: Ulysses Books & Maps, 4176 Saint-Denis, Montréal, Québec, H2W 2M5, ☎ (514) 843-9882, ext.2232, 800-748-9171, Fax: 514-843-9448, www.ulysses.ca

GERMANY AND AUSTRIA: Brettschneider, Fernreisebedarf, Feldfirchner Strasse 2, D-85551 Heimstetten, München, ☎ 89-99 02 03 30, Fax: 89-99 02 03 31, E-mail: Brettschneider_Fernreisebedarf@t-online.de

GREAT BRITAIN AND IRELAND: World Leisure Marketing, Unit 11, Newmarket Court, Newmartket Drive, Derby DE24 8NW, ☎ 1 332 57 37 37, Fax: 1 332 57 33 99, E-mail: office@wlmsales.co.uk

ITALY: Centro Cartografico del Riccio, Via di Soffiano 164/A, 50143 Firenze, ☎ (055) 71 33 33, Fax: (055) 71 63 50

NETHERLANDS: Nilsson & Lamm, Pampuslaan 212-214, 1380 AD Weesp (NL), ☎ 0294-494949, Fax: 0294-494455, E-mail: nilam@euronet.nl

PORTUGAL: Dinapress, Lg. Dr. Antonio de Sousa de Macedo, 2, Lisboa 1200, ☎ (1) 395 52 70, Fax: (1) 395 03 90

SCANDINAVIA: Scanvik, Esplanaden 8B, 1263 Copenhagen K, DK, ☎ (45) 33.12.77.66, Fax: (45) 33.91.28.82

SPAIN: Altaïr, Balmes 69, E-08007 Barcelona, ☎ 454 29 66, Fax: 451 25 59, altair@globalcom.es

SWITZERLAND: OLF, P.O. Box 1061, CH-1701 Fribourg, ☎ (026) 467.51.11, Fax: (026) 467.54.66

U.S.A.: The Globe Pequot Press, 6 Business Park Road, P.O. Box 833, Old Saybrook, CT 06475, ☎ 1-800-243-0495, Fax: 800-820-2329, sales@globe-pequot.com

Other countries, contact Ulysses Books & Maps (Montréal), Fax: (514) 843-9448

Canadian Cataloguing in Publication Datasee p. 6
© June 1999 Ulysses Travel Publications.
All rights reserved
Printed in Canada
ISBN 2-89464-143-5

"When first in the dim light of early morning I saw the shores of Cuba rise and define themselves from dark-blue horizons, I felt as if I sailed with Captain Silver and first gazed on Treasure Island. Here was a place where real things were going on. Here was a scene of vital action. Here was a place where anything might happen. Here was a place where something would certainly happen. Here I might leave my bones."

My Early Life, Winston Spencer Churchill, 1930

TABLE OF CONTENTS

WRITE TO US

The information contained in this guide was correct at press time. However, mistakes can slip in, omissions are always possible, places can disappear, etc. The authors and publisher hereby disclaim any liability for loss or damage resulting from omissions or errors.

We value your comments, corrections and suggestions, as they allow us to keep each guide up to date. The best contributions will be rewarded with a free book from Ulysses Travel Publications. All you have to do is write us at the following address and indicate which title you would be interested in receiving (see the list at the end of guide).

Ulysses Travel Publications
4176 Rue Saint-Denis
Montréal, Québec
Canada H2W 2M5
www.ulysses.ca
E-mail: guiduly@ulysses.ca

"We acknowledge the financial support of the Government of Canada through the Book Publishing Industry Development Program (BPIDP) for our publishing activities." We would also like to thank SODEC for their financial support.

Canadä

LIST OF MAPS

Canadian Cataloguing in Publication Data

Soldevila, Carlos, 1969-

    Cuba

    2nd ed.
    (Ulysses travel guide)
    Translation of: Cuba
    Includes index.

    ISBN 2-89464-143-5

    1. Cuba - Guidebooks. I. Title. II. Series.

F1754.7.S6413 1999   917.29104'64   C98-941535-X

SYMBOLS

🦑	Ulysses's favourite
☎	Telephone number
⊶	Fax number
≡	Air conditioning
⊗	Ceiling fan
≈	Pool
ℜ	Restaurant
⊛	Whirlpool
ℝ	Refrigerator
K	Kitchenette
◠	Sauna
♿	Wheelchair accessible
☉	Exercise room
tv	Black & white television
ctv	Colour television
pb	Private bathroom
sb	Shared bathroom
½b	Half-board (lodging + 2 meals)
fb	Full board (lodging + 3 meals)
bkfst	Breakfast

ATTRACTION CLASSIFICATION

★	Interesting
★★	Worth a visit
★★★	Not to be missed

HOTEL CLASSIFICATION

Prices in this guide are for one room, double occupancy in high season, unless otherwise indicated.

RESTAURANT CLASSIFICATION

$	under $12 US
$$	$12 to $21 US
$$$	more than $22 US

Prices in this guide are for a meal for one person, not including drinks and tip, unless otherwise indicated.

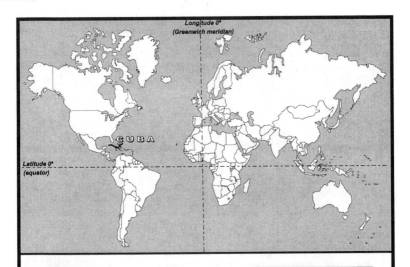

Where is Cuba ?

CUBA
Capital: Havana
Language: Spanish
Population: 11,000,000
Currency: Cuban peso
Area: 110,922 km

Mexico

CUBA

Dominican Republic

Haiti

Puerto Rico

Belize

Jamaica

Honduras

Guatemala

Caribbean Sea

El Salvador

Nicaragua

Costa Rica

Venezuela

Panamá

Pacific Ocean

Colombia

© ULYSSES

Ecuador

Peru

Brazil

PORTRAIT

Cuba entered the world's imagination thanks to Christopher Columbus, who in 1492 described the Caribbean's biggest island in the following terms: "I have never seen a more beautiful country, with palm leaves so big they can roof a house, with thousands of shells on the beach, with such limpid water, and always the same deafening symphony from the songs of birds."

Cuba remains the same wonderful island, replete with breathtaking scenery, idyllic beaches and amazingly fertile land. Mysterious and inscrutable, Cuba would be shaped by human hands in the course of a tumultuous history. If a land can determine the character of a people, it is easy to imagine how this occurred in Cuba. The plains that cover most of its territory would give colonists and slaves alike the docile attitude, the goodness and the human warmth so characteristic of the Cuban people — traits that allowed Spain to

hold onto Cuba long after its other colonies had rebelled. On the other hand, the high mountains, covered with abundant and sometimes impenetrable tropical vegetation, would shape the rebellious side of the Cuban character; the mountains were the refuge of the *mambises*, the 19th-century fighters for independence, and of the *cimarrones*, the black slaves who managed to flee and embrace freedom. It was this rebelliousness that allowed the island's inhabitants to take control once and for all of their homeland's destiny. The *palme real*, or royal palm, the official emblem of the country, symbolizes Cubans' unshakable pride, so often tested but rarely triumphed over.

This naturalist metaphor, of course, is just an abstract of the imagination to describe one of the planet's most fascinating countries. This island would somehow manage to find itself at the centre of historical events again and again, as though destined to serve as a standard-bearer for the utopias of humanity in search of ideals. Venerated by some, despised by others, the political and economic choices of the Cuban people leave hardly anyone indifferent, adding to the enjoyment of travellers as they explore the western world's only socialist country.

GEOGRAPHY

The Cuban Archipelago

Washed by the waters of the Caribbean Sea, the Cuban archipelago skims the tropic of Cancer, just north of the main island, and stretches to the Gulf of Mexico. It is made up of the main island, Cuba, Isla de la Juventud (Isle of Youth), Cayo Romano and close to 1,600 other islands and islets called *cayos*. Situated 148 kilometres south of Florida, 210 kilometres east of Mexico, 140 kilometres north of Jamaica and 77 kilometres west of Haiti, Cuba occupies a geographically strategic position that has earned it the nicknames "Key to the Gulf" and "Crossroads of the Americas".

With a surface area of 11,922 square kilometres, Cuba is the largest island in the Caribbean. Its long, narrow shape – it is 1,200-kilometres long and between 30- and 190-kilometres wide – gives it close to 6,000 kilometres of coastline, including the shores of the other islands and *cayos*. Four large groups of coral reef islets are found around the island of Cuba: Los Colorados to the west, Los Canarreos to the southwest, Los Jardines de la Reina to the south and Sabana-Camagüey to the north. The last one is part of the second-largest coral reef in the world, after Australia's Great Barrier Reef.

Topography

Cuba is a land of fascinating panoramas and extremely varied reliefs. Mountains and hills, lakes and rivers, plains and valleys, beaches and forests succeed each other and form the extraordinary landscape of the "Pearl of the Antilles". The Cuban territory includes three main mountain chains. The most famous of these is the Sierra Maestra in the eastern part of the island, which includes the country's tallest peak, Pico Turquino (1,974 metres). Further east, the Sierra del Escambrey extends over almost 80 kilometres and constitutes a sort of main massif on the island. Finally, the western shores are dominated by the Cordillera de Guaniguanico, formed by the Sierra del Rosario and the Sierra de los Organos, which is famous for its *mogotes*, elevated conical hillocks, in the valley of Viñales The Cuban landscape is also distinguished by its low plateaus and vast plains. Perfect for agriculture and livestock breeding, plains make up three quarters of the country's surface area. The "plain of Cuba", as it is called, is the largest, extending more than 400 kilometres from Pinar del Río in the west to Santa Clara in the centre of the island. In addition to sugarcane, tobacco and coffee plantations, Cuba's lush plains are patterned with citrus orchards, banana farms, rice fields and palm groves.

FLORA

Cuba is endowed with a flora as bountiful as it is varied. It includes no fewer than 6,000 different types of plants, almost half of which are endemic. The vegetation of the coast and the *cayos* is mainly characterized by mangroves, trees with exposed aerial roots that grow in salt water and form literally impenetrable forests. Mangrove trees are also common in swamplands. Beaches are commonly lined with coconut palms and sometimes *uvas caletas*, a grape tree that produces a sweet fruit. The region of Maisi, on the eastern tip of the island, is an arid zone with a great variety of giant cacti.

Red mangrove

Some of the canyons of the Sierra Maestra and the central massif are home to tropical rainforests that favour the growth of the flamboyant, also called the royal poinciana, a tree that boasts brilliant, bright red flowers. Exotic woods such as acanthus, mahogany, ebony and cedar still can still be found in mountainous regions. Although pine and eucalyptus trees are very common, the royal palm, which is practically omnipresent, is most emblematic. Its status as the national tree is incontestable. The other national symbol is the *mariposa*, or white butterfly ginger (*Hedychium coronarium*), a delicate white flower with a subtle fragrance that grows on riverbanks during the rainy season. Cuba is also famous for its more than 200 varieties of orchids.

FAUNA

Like its flora, Cuba's wildlife is remarkably diverse. There are over 350 species of birds, including the *zunzuncito*, or bee hummingbird (*Mellisuga helenae*, the smallest bird in the world, with a body measuring just three centimetres), the tuneful *fermina*, the multicoloured *cartacuba*, the *gallinuela de Santo Tomás*, the swamp-dwelling *cabrerito*, the *cotorras*, or Cuban parrot, and the national bird, the *tocororo*, or Cuban trogon (*Priotelus temnurus*), whose plumage has same colours as the flag. In addition to pelicans, frigate birds, white waders and long-tailed sparrowhawks, Cuba is home to colonies of pink flamingoes that can be seen in the Sabana-Camagüey Archipelago and on the Zapata Peninsula. Crocodiles can also be found on the Zapata Peninsula. Other reptiles in Cuba include iguanas, lizards and non-venomous snakes. There are also the hutia (*Capromys*), a type of diurnal tree rat close to the agouti, stunningly colourful Cuban land snails (*Polymita*), bats, spiders, butterflies and other insects. Mammals include boars and deer, especially in the region of Pinar del Río. In the eastern part of the island, at Cayo Saetía, there are even antelopes and zebras that were imported from Africa.

Iguana

PORTRAIT

The hot, shallow waters of Cuba are teeming with life and colour. Close to 5,000 kinds of fish, molluscs, crustaceans, turtles and coral make up the nation's marine life. Swordfish, barracudas and crayfish swim through a profusion of coral colonies where many species of sponges and exotic fish also live. Starfish and black sea urchins are very common sights on beaches, and manatees occasionally appear on the banks of certain estuaries.

Pelican

HISTORY

Discovery

Before the Spanish arrived, the island of Cuba had been inhabited by the Siboneys, who were hunters and gatherers; by the Taïnos, members of the Arawak family living in the eastern part of the country who probably came here from South America; and also by the Guahanacabibles, who inhabited the western edge of the country on the peninsula that now bears their name. These peoples developed a form of agriculture based on *canucos*, or small landholdings, growing cassava, sweet potato, corn, beans, tobacco, cotton and a variety of fruits, including papaya.

Estimates of the indigenous population at the time of the Spanish arrival in Cuba vary considerably from one historian to another, ranging from one million down to 100,000 people. Fray Bartolomé de Las Casas (see p 184), an ardent defender of the indigenous cause in the 17th century, asserted that the "200,000 Indians inhabiting the island of Cuba vanished, victims of European cruelty." Though he no doubt exaggerated the number of indigenous people, which was probably closer to 100,000, he was nonetheless absolutely correct in stating that the natives were victims of genocide. Decimated by illness, pushed to death by forced labour in the mines and the fields, tortured and sometimes even killed for pleasure, the indigenous people of Cuba virtually ceased to exist a mere half-century after the arrival of Christopher Columbus.

All that remains today of Cuba's indigenous culture are the frescos found in certain grottos on the Isla de la Juventud, some sculptures in the museums, and the names of some regions of the country and of Cuba itself. Only the Baracoa area, in an isolated part of eastern Cuba, still has some people of mixed ancestry.

An extract from the logbook of Christopher Columbus, who arrived from the west in 1492, gives a good idea of the attitude and ignorance of the Spanish toward these peoples. He found "men who had only one eye, and others who had the snout of a dog and who fed on human flesh." Thus was born, from a seafarer's unbridled imagination, the legend of the Carib Indians. In other accounts, Columbus added that these people were rather peaceful, that they were lacking in almost everything, that they were "very gentle and ignorant of what evil was", and that they knew that there was a "God in heaven and were convinced that we came from there."

Confident that he had reached the Chinese continent, the empire of the Great Khan described by Marco Polo, Columbus landed at Gibara (see p 218) on October 28, 1492. Seeing the gold worn by natives, he was certain of his destination, and all the more so when natives assured him that he would find more gold at *Cubanacán* ("centre of Cuba"), a word Columbus took to mean *El Grán Can*. He believed Cuba was the "Province of Mangi", the name Marco Polo gave to all of southern China.

Colonization

Diego Velázquez founded the first Cuban *villa* in 1512 at Baracoa, near the site of Columbus' first landing 20 years earlier. Within a few years Velázquez would found Bayamo, Santiago, Puerto Príncipe, Trinidad, Sancti Spiritus and Havana. The Spanish took over the whole Cuban territory, leaving misery and desolation among the native population in their wake. Colonizing the island turned out to be long and hard for the Spanish. Once the gold reserves were exhausted, the Spanish deserted Cuba little by little, setting out to conquer the continental bounty of Mexico and Peru. Much of this treasure would pass through the ports of Santiago and Havana on its way to Europe.

The departure of the *conquistador* Hernán Cortés for the neighbouring countries left the island in great political disorder, with his friends and adversaries fighting over the territory between 1526 and 1537. Moreover, native groups rebelled several times during

this period, managing to set fire to Baracoa and Puerto Príncipe. Led by Hatuey, one of America's first rebels, the natives reacted to the harsh treatment they suffered in the *encomiendas*, enclaves where they were reduced to slavery and forced labour. After being captured, Hatuey was burnt alive in front of the Baracoa church. According to legend, in the moments before he was executed, he was asked by a priest to atone for his sins if he wished to reach paradise. Hatuey replied that, if there was a Christian god in paradise, he would prefer to go to hell.

The Spaniards' problems would continue during the 16th century. In the depths of misfortune, with the population decreasing, political problems festering, and gold reserves depleting, Cuba was poorly defended against the repeated pirate attacks to which it was subjected. In 1554, the French pirate Jacques de Sores occupied Santiago de Cuba and demanded a heavy ransom for the liberation of the town. The following year, he occupied Havana and set it ablaze.

Sixteenth-century Cuban demography consisted of a small European population, few natives and a steadily growing African population. Around 1570, the country numbered only 270 Spanish families, about 60 of them in Havana. Thanks to its strategic position in the Caribbean, Cuba served almost exclusively as a departure point for the conquest of the continent, supplying the conquerors of the New World with men, livestock and flour. The country's economy in the 16th century was based on livestock raising, along with some copper mining, forestry and the incipient sugar cane industry. But the island remained dependent on the outside world for most finished goods, and contraband trade became not merely significant but essential for the colonists.

To relieve both the economic and defensive problems of the island, a flow of capital was diverted from Mexico to Cuba. This new wealth drew the renewed attention of pirates, and the famous English pirate Francis Drake attacked many Cuban *villas* around 1586 but spared Havana, by then well protected by its new fortifications. In the 17th century, Dutch filibusters would add to the repeated attacks against Spanish strongholds in Cuba.

The 17th century marked the strengthening of colonial society and the establishment of the island's political and economic foundations. Although livestock raising remained the dominant economic activity, the production of sugar cane, introduced in 1548 near Santiago, would gain in importance. Tobacco growing also took hold. Though the Spanish did not find gold in Cuba, they discovered an extraordinarily fertile land, and before long an entire landowning class had become spectacularly wealthy.

Pierre Le Moyne d'Iberville and the Franco-Spanish Alliance

*This section was written by **Jean-Guy Allard**, a journalist and former Havana correspondent.*

On July 9, 1706, a big crowd gathered near the Havana parish church. In the previous hours the news had spread like wildfire: Captain-General Pedro Álvarez de Villarín, newly arrived from Spain, had died suddenly and mysteriously. Even more surprising, Pierre Le Moyne d'Iberville, the Canadian who commanded a powerful French fleet anchored in the harbour and who stood determined to deal a fatal blow to the English presence in America, was felled at the same moment and in the same circumstances by a blazing attack of fever. The sudden deaths of the two men gave rise to rumours. Did the alliance between these two officers, who both saw the British Empire as a threat to the entire continent, cause them to be poisoned stealthily by enemy agents?

The reputation of Pierre Le Moyne d'Iberville had rapidly won over the Cuban capital since his arrival at the head of a powerful fleet. This 44-year-old Canadian, born on St. Paul street in Ville-Marie, New France (now Montreal), lived up to his legend. As a warship commander, d'Iberville attacked and crushed the English enemy with disconcerting accuracy. Not once in the course of countless combats did the enemy from England manage to make him surrender. His exploits had become so well known that Louis XIV, determined the occupy to Mississippi delta, had sent him to take possession of this territory, which became Louisiana. That was where the young hero (he was not yet 40 at the time) had convinced himself of a theory he kept defending with a prophetic tone: "The English have the colonial spirit," he wrote in 1699. "If France does not seize this part of America to possess a colony strong enough to resist that of England, the English colony, which is becoming very substantial, will grow in such a way that, in less than 100 years, it will be strong enough to seize all of America and to push out all the other nations."

In 1706, Philippe d'Anjou, Louis XIV's nephew, was King of Spain. The timing was strategic, and the alliance between Spain and France enabled d'Iberville to deal the English a mortal blow. D'Iberville was placed at the head of an imposing fleet by the French crown and sent straight to the Caribbean. At Nevis, he seized 40 English ships all at once, causing panic in the English islands. The English hardly had time to organize a counter-attack before d'Iberville entered Havana, where he told his hosts of his plans. It was then that the new captain-general, Pedro Álvarez de Villarín, arrived in Havana and was won over by d'Iberville's plans. The Spanish and the French shared with the local elite their anticipation of certain victory.

On July 8, 1706, however, the dream of the two allies ended both abruptly and mysteriously. Both men were struck by a horrible fever that brought them down in a just a few hours. They died on July 9. The event left the population in shock. The auxiliary bishop of Havana, Dionizio Rozino, appeared at the porch of the church in his funeral robes. It was he who pronounced the oration, that beyond the words and the smells of wax and incense, foretold the tragic end of a project with unsuspected consequences. Buried in the crypt of Havana's religious building, along with these two corpses, went the dream of another America.

In 1738, an archivist with the French Navy's hydrographic service would evoke the loss of a hero in brief and enigmatic terms: "He died poisoned by the intrigues of a famous nation that feared a neighbour like him."

White Gold

The capture of Havana by the English in 1762 allowed for the commercial growth of the Cuban capital's port, with exports doubling in 10 years. Havana became one of America's main fortresses and stood out increasingly as the pearl of the Spanish colonies. But it was political events outside the country that really made Cuba one of the most important trading zones in America and once again the world leader in sugar production. The U.S. War of Independence in the 18th century helped open direct trade between Cuba and the new American federation. Added to this, the Haitian slave revolts in the late 18th century and the ensuing destruction of sugar plantations there gave Cuba the opportunity to capture European markets and to grow wealthier in short order thanks to a sharp rise in sugar prices. An exodus of white Haitian landowners to Cuba heralded the beginning of a golden age in sugar production. As sugar plantations extended to the east of the country, there was a doubling in the number of *ingenios* (sugar cane crushing mills), which were equipped with new equipment brought in by the French. White gold sugar crystals became the country's manna and made Cuba one of the richest countries on earth. Although it was a source of fabulous revenues for some people, large-scale sugar production was a true nightmare for others — to harvest the white gold, the Spanish "crushed" the black slaves.

Slavery

To replace the extinct native population, the black slaves trade started early in the Spanish colonial period. The first slaves came mostly from the west coast of Africa, from Guinea to the Congo and Angola. They were brought to work in livestock raising and agriculture, and then increasingly on the sugar plantations. In the mid-18th century, the Cuban sugar boom led to a large-scale forced migration of African slaves. The number of slaves rose from about 40,000 in 1774 to 470,000 in 1840, at a time when the island's population was around one million.

There were times when slavery was cruel in Cuba, but it was never as tyrannical as in the English colonies, where blacks were denied and thus lost their culture. Here the Spanish allowed them to play their drums and to go out into the streets each year at carnival time. In the 18th century, the Catholic Church sanctioned *cabildos*, places where blacks sharing a language or ethnic group could meet to practise their religion as long as they adopted the Virgin, God, Christ or the Holy Ghost as their divinity. It was in this way that the tradition of Afro-Cuban religions was maintained over the centuries (see p 32).

The famous German scientist and explorer, Alexander von Humboldt, born in Berlin in 1769, was regarded almost as the second discoverer of Cuba (in Europe he was seen as a 19th-century Aristotle). While visiting Cuba from 1800 to 1801, he wrote his *Political Essay on the Island of Cuba*. In this little treasure of knowledge about Cuba, the chapter on slavery is especially interesting, revealing much about Cuban slave society at the turn of the 19th century. "The Spanish laws (in Cuba) are completely contrary to the French and English laws since they favour freedom in spectacular ways. The right held by each slave to find a master or to buy his freedom, the religious feelings that inspire numerous masters to grant freedom to slaves in their wills, and the ease with which they can work for themselves are among the reasons that enable so many slaves in the towns to obtain their freedom, passing from enslavement to the state of free men of colour."

Despite this, with slavery being what it is, there were many slave rebellions in the 18th and 19th centuries, although they did not reach the extent they did in Haiti, for example. It was not until 1886 that slavery was finally abolished. But even if the cane cutters were no longer slaves, they were still submitted to harsh conditions on the plantations and since they only worked during the four-month harvest season, they lived in extreme poverty. Right up until the 1959 Revolution, blacks were victims of an insidious racial discrimination that prevented them, through low salaries and segregation, from obtaining good educations and from moving into the liberal professions or the military. Following the abolition of slavery, however, conditions were suitable for a national uprising against the Spanish crown, in which the now free black population played an active role.

The Wars of Independence

By 1825, all that remained of the vast Spanish empire reaching from California to Tierra del Fuego, an empire that had survived more than three centuries, were Cuba and Puerto Rico. "The eternally loyal island" (loyal, that is, to Spanish rule) would see the rise of revolutionaries among its inhabitants who sought the abrogation of foreign rule. The 19th century would be marked by two great wars which would hit the Cuban people and economy hard.

On October 10, 1868, Carlos Manuel de Céspedes, a wealthy landowner and a member of the local elite in the Manzanillo area, freed his slaves and issued the *"Grito de Yara"* (the Call of Yara), a call for freedom that he and a rebel group proclaimed when they took possession of the town of Yara. Céspedes is credited with starting the first war of independence, the Ten Years' War (1868-1878). He attacked Spanish forces using guerrilla tactics; the peasants and slaves found among his ranks knew the territory better than the Spanish. However, the war was directed mostly by the Cuban-born aristocracy, which included the Céspedes and Agramonte families. Ultimately, the pro-independence forces were too divided internally to bring this war to a successful conclusion.

Céspedes himself was killed by the Spanish army in 1874. After 10 years of ferocious struggle, the war left nearly 200,000 dead, and the sugar plantations close to complete destruction. An armistice took effect in 1878 after the signing of the Zanjón Agreement, with the Spanish promising to grant more autonomy to the *Criollos*, Cuban-born people of Spanish descent. Antonio Maceo, a black general, together with Calixto García, continued what was called the "little war", which also ended in Cuban defeat.

The 1880s were marked by fundamental changes, including the abolition of slavery and the start of large-scale U.S. investment in the Cuban economy, particularly in the sugar industry. By 1898, U.S. capital investment had reached a total of nearly $100 million.

The second war of independence (1895-98) was motivated by political ideals very different from those of the Ten Years' War. This time, the Cuban people were led into revolt by Antonio Maceo, by Máximo Gómez, the Dominican-born hero of the Ten Years' War, and by José Martí, the son of a low-ranking Spanish officer. Martí, a brilliant writer, would become the country's ideologue and the greatest of revolutionary heroes. Born in Havana on January 28, 1853 (each year the anniversary of his birth is marked by big celebrations in the Plaza de la Revolución in Havana), José Martí is regarded today as the spiritual leader of the Cuban people. He is one of the most noble martyrs in Latin American history. His writings, filling several volumes, and his political commitment support the cause of the Cuban people as well as social and economic equality for all races. From the age of 16, Martí published a newspaper, *La Patria Libre*. He was accused of treason the same year and condemned to six months of forced labour. He then went into exile in Spain, where he stayed until 1878. Back in Cuba some time later, Martí was again deported to Spain, from where he headed to New York to join the Cuban community in exile there. On April 11, 1895, he landed in the eastern part of Cuba with a group of rebels. He died several months later without realizing his dream of an independent Cuba.

More than anyone else, José Martí showed his anti-Americanism, an attitude that would become the foundation of Cuban political culture in the 20th century. With the Americans eyeing Cuban territory, he wrote a letter on the eve of his death that would prove prophetic: "I live daily in danger of giving my life for my country and for my duty which, as I understand it and achieve it... consists of preventing the United States, when they wish to, extending their power over the Caribbean with the independence of Cuba... What I have done up to this day, and what I shall do, is for that purpose. I have lived inside the monster, and I know its entrails; my slingshot is the slingshot of David." Thus began the political duel which continues to this day between David and Goliath.

The Spanish-Cuban War lasted nearly three years. The Spanish believed the Cuban insurrection would not be able to overcome an army of more than 100,000 men. Toward 1896, Spanish troops numbered close to 200,000, while the entire island had a population of only about 1.8 million. And even so, the insurgents, with the support of the Afro-Cuban population, sought to destabilize Spanish economic interests in Cuba. This is exactly what happened, except that it was not the insurgents who would benefit.

The Spanish-American War

Thanks to similarities between the slave-based economies of Cuba and the southern United States, an annexationist movement developed at the start of the 19th century, many decades before the abolition of slavery in Cuba and before the first wars of independence. Many people in the southern U.S. saw Cuba as belonging naturally to the North American continent. In 1854, Cuba was put up for auction, with the U.S. offering $100 million to acquire the island from the Spanish. But the southern defeat in the U.S. Civil War, along with the end of slavery in Cuba, put an end to that project.

The Americans would get a second chance to grab Cuba. This time, they faced no opposition. Bolstered by increased U.S. investment in the Cuban economy in the late 19th century, and benefiting from the evident inability of the Spanish to hold onto Cuba and of the pro-independence forces to take power, the U.S. Government under President William McKinley became involved in the Spanish-Cuban conflict, pushing the Spanish out of their last territories in the Americas.

U.S. intervention began following the explosion of the American warship *U.S.S. Maine*, anchored in Havana harbour to protect U.S. interests during the Spanish-Cuban war. More than 200 Americans died in the explosion, apparently due to Spanish sabotage or to an accident in the ship's powder magazine. The U.S. press jumped on this event, and the American populace soon envisaged the possibility of a war against Spain. The U.S. Congress insisted that the intention was not to take possession of Cuba but rather to bring peace and to leave the island under the control of a Cuban govern-

ment. After a sham war that lasted three months, culminating in the Spanish-American naval war near Santiago won by the Americans, Spain turned Cuba over to the U.S. Government surreptitiously under the Treaty of Paris of 1898.

With the U.S. triumph, pro-independence Cubans, after fighting against Spain for nearly 30 years, could not take part in the victory parade in the streets of Santiago, and the Cuban army was not even allowed into the city. Calixto García, a Cuban general, was outraged by the attitude of U.S. General William R. Shafter. This affront to the Cuban army was the first, and most symbolic, of a series of U.S. interventions that several generations of Cuban politicians would not forget. Fidel Castro, at the moment of his victory in 1959, paraded in the streets of Santiago, invoking the "confiscated" revolution of 1898: "This time there is no General Shafter here to prevent our victory march."

The American Protectorate and the Vassal Republic

Cuba's 19th-century insurgents saw the American flag replace the Spanish one. A military regime was installed by the United States from 1898 to 1902, to the great discontent of the civilian population. This occupation, however, did involve a vast sanitation campaign which eradicated yellow fever, as well as the construction of a railway between Santiago and Havana. The country's first elections were held in 1901; the first president, Tomás Estrada Palma, took power in 1902.

Cuba's formal independence was granted on May 20, 1902, but a new affront would provoke a wave of protests across the country. The so-called Platt Amendment, imposed as part of the new constitution, gave the U.S. Government a naval base on Cuban territory, in Guantánamo, and conferred upon it the right to intervene militarily in the country and to revise or approve any treaty between Cuba and a third country. The Cuban delegates had no choice but to accept this resolution, or face a continued military occupation. This was the beginning of the vassal republic (which was to last nearly 60 years), with puppet presidents succeeding corrupt dictators.

Between the period of military occupation and the 1929 economic crisis, U.S. companies multiplied their Cuban investments by eight, with the total reaching nearly half a billion dollars, or about 30 per cent of all U.S. investment in Latin America! In 1906, Americans owned 15 per cent of the Cuban sugar industry; by 1929 the U.S. colossus controlled nearly 75 per cent of all production. The United States intervened militarily several times and occupied the island again from 1906 to 1909 following a disputed election. The Platt Amendment was finally deleted from the Cuban Constitution in 1934, but U.S. influence in the country's domestic politics remained a constant, futhermore the Americans held onto their base at Guantánamo.

After the fall of Gerardo Machado's dictatorship on August 10, 1933, the new government led by Grau San Martín lasted only four months, overthrown in its turn by a coup d'état organized by Fulgencio Batista, who would become Cuba's strongman until the Revolution. Though early on the presidency was actually held by Carlos Mendieta, Batista had a firm grip on the reigns of power. Fulgencio's arrival onto the Cuban political stage would be a determining event. This simple yet powerful army colonel, a *mulato*, would not wait long before making himself known. Batista had himself elected

president in 1940. During the early part of his mandate, he gave a proud hand to the labour movement and adopted one of Latin America's most progressive constitutions for that period.

When he left the country in 1944 for Florida, turning the presidency over to Grau San Martín, the country was more stable and more democratic than ever. But Batista's successor would soon land the country in a quagmire of continuous squabbling, allowing the government to be crushed by shameless corruption. In the 1948 election, Grau San Martín was replaced by Carlos Prío Socarrás, who turned out to be just as irresponsible as his predecessor. Batista came back from Florida, convinced that he could win the 1952 election. But a new party, the *Ortodoxos*, promised to clean up the government and attracted the sympathy of the Cuban electorate. Among the leading figures of this new party was a young lawyer named Fidel Castro, who became a congressional candidate in a Havana working-class district. Seeing his hopes for an election victory fading, Batista organized a coup d'état, backed by the Cuban army. Without knowing it, Batista had laid the foundations for an infrastructure that would be blown apart by the Fidelista rebels. Who knows which way Cuban history would have turned if Fidel Castro had won the congressional seat he was up for. Cheated of his electoral hopes, Castro opted instead for armed struggle, the only way to achieve his political aims.

Heading Toward the Revolution

The fact that a small armed group, led by a lawyer who was barely 30 years old, could overthrow the established order in Cuba in less than six years, and later institute a socialist economy right in Washington's backyard at the height

PORTRAIT

of the Cold War, less than 200 kilometres from Florida, remains one of the great political and revolutionary feats of the 20th century, up there with Mao Zedong's Long March.

Fidel Castro was born on August 13, 1926, on an agricultural estate near Birán, in the Mayarí region of the former province of Oriente. His father, Ángel Castro y Argiz, was a Spanish emigrant from Galicia and was an orphan when he arrived in Cuba at age 13. Ángel Castro went into business in his early 20s in the Mayarí area, selling lemonade transported on muleback to workers in the sugar-cane fields. Around 1910, with the area under the economic control of big American corporations, he began renting small pieces of land from the United Fruit Company to grow sugar cane. He soon became an influential landowner in the area, managing nearly 10,400 hectares (more than 25,000 acres) of land.

Fidel was born of his father's second marriage, to Lina Ruz González, about 20 years her husband's junior. Fidel Castro's happiest childhood moments were when he swam in the Río Birán, rode on horseback and hunted freely. He showed his great physical strength from an early age. As an adolescent, he was sent to study in Santiago de Cuba, where he attended a school run by Marist priests and then a Jesuit college until beginning his law studies at the University of Havana in 1945. There he became involved in the student movement until Batista's coup d'état.

The political journey of this young *barbudo* (bearded one) is almost a miracle. In 1952, Fidel began organizing the resistance and the risky attack on the Cuartel Moncada, a military barracks in the city of Santiago. This manoeuvre proved disastrous. On July 26, 1953, the Generación del Centenario political group, under Fidel Castro's command,

attacked the barracks right at carnival time. At 5 o'clock in the morning, 120 armed men, all dressed in Cuban army uniforms, caused confusion among the guards at the barracks. But the army was not completely taken and reacted quickly. Six rebels were killed in the attack, and 55 others were tortured and then executed the same day. Fidel managed to flee to the east with several of his comrades-in-arms, but he would be captured several days later. Fidel thus made a very noisy entry onto the Cuban political scene.

Fidel prepared his own defence and presented his vibrant account, *La Historia Me Absolverá* (History Will Absolve Me) before the court that was to judge him. Held in the model prison on the Isle of Pines, now called Isla de la Juventud (Isle of Youth), Castro and members of his group took advantage of the good treatment they received to continue their education, turning the infirmary where they were prisoners into a school for future rebels. In 1954 Fidel was released under a general political amnesty granted by Batista, who had been re-elected to the presidency unopposed. He went into exile in Mexico to prepare for a landing in Cuba that would kick off the Revolution.

In Mexico he met one of the key figures in the Revolution, the Argentine doctor Ernesto Guevara. Born on June 14, 1928, in the Argentine city of Rosario, "Che" Guevara became the most celebrated *soldado de América* (soldier of America) thanks to his risky participation in the Cuban Revolution and in the armed struggle in Bolivia, where he lost his life in 1967 to Bolivian army bullets. The political and ideological journey of this intellectual, poet and soldier, the "purest" of Latin American Marxists, fascinated the entire world. Jean-Paul Sartre, for example, described him as "the most complete man of our times". In 1952, despite his chronic asthma,

Guevara undertook a seven-month motorcycle voyage across South America with a companion and then returned to Argentina to complete his medical studies. His future political commitment was affirmed on this trip, where he discovered the misery of the people he met. After resolving to become politically active, he left Argentina for Guatemala, where he played a minor role in the government of the anti-imperialist president, Colonel Jacobo Arbenz. Wherever the winds of revolution blew, Guevara found fresh air for his lungs. But the fun was not to last long. On June 18, 1954, the Guatemalan capital was bombed by U.S.-backed forces. A few days later, Arbenz laid down his arms, and Guevara left for Mexico, where he had the most fateful meeting of his life, with Fidel Castro.

In 1956, after carefully preparing a military landing and securing political support within Cuba through his *Movimiento 26 de Julio*, Fidel Castro and his men, including Che Guevara, left the port of Veracruz aboard the *Granma*, a small yacht barely big enough to hold the armed men aboard. The foiled landing led to a real catastrophe: the *Granma* ran aground in the marshes of Los Colorados, at the eastern end of the country, south of the Sierra Maestra, forcing the rebels to leave their supplies there. Moreover, the Cuban army had been alerted to the rebels' arrival, who faced a heavy attack. Only 12 men survived. Fidel, hidden in a sugar cane field with only two companions, claimed victory. Fidel Castro's unshakable optimism, even in defeat, would be one of the rebel group's key assets.

In his march to the Sierra Maestra, Castro was far from the end of his troubles. He quickly fell into an ambush and lost even more men. A small, hunger-stricken lot, with just a few rifles, would have to take on the entire Cuban army. Two years later, however, Fidel Castro would overthrow this army. Fulgencio Batista would flee to the Dominican Republic on the night of January 1, 1959, and the rebel army would make a triumphal entry into Havana.

Castro's success had as much to do with the Cuban people's unanimous wish to get rid of Batista as with Castro's political and military skill, the luck that accompanied him throughout his political career, the friendships he established with peasants in the mountains, the outside assistance, and an urban action network. The Batista dictatorship was one of the most corrupt and repressive in the history of the republic; it saw the country led by gangsters and a capital city, Havana, run by American mafiosi.

Stormy Relations with the Americans

Soon after Fidel Castro rose to power, relations between Cuba and the United States became tumultuous and tense. After more than 60 years of American domination over the island, with two-thirds of Cuban trade depending on the U.S. at the time of the Revolution, Fidel and his rebels would cause serious headaches for the various American governments that followed in the years to come.

During the conflict that pitted Batista against Fidel Castro from 1957 to 1959, the United States was not especially wary of Castro, although American fighter planes were sold to the Cuban military during the conflict. Though Batista's rule started to come under criticism, even by the Americans, all signs seemed to indicate that U.S. authorities, including the CIA with its active role in Cuba, preferred the option of a coup by the Cuban military as a way of cutting the ground out from under Castro. However, it is worth remembering that the Americans had little notion of what measures might emerge from the Revolution. During the struggle, written statements from the *Comandante en Jefe* called for democratic elections and never came down hard on the U.S. Government. History would remember things very differently, of course, and U.S. arrogance would speed the pace of radicalization in the measures adopted by Fidel Castro.

On May 17, 1959, tension between the two countries rose a notch as agrarian reform kicked in, which gave 250,000 peasant families ownership of their lands. In the following days, *The New York Times* sounded the alarm by stating that the more the new Cuban laws were studied, the more anxiety they created. An article in the *The Wall Street Journal* explained that the American aim in Cuba was to place Castro in quarantine. In the middle of 1960, new measures seemed to indicate an imminent blockade against Cuba. The big U.S. oil companies decided to halt fuel shipments to Cuba and to forbid the use of their Cuban refineries to process Soviet crude. In response to this policy, the Castro government expropriated the Esso, Shell and Texaco refineries. Things escalated when the U.S. Congress and the administration of President Dwight Eisenhower chose to reduce, and even to suspend, purchases of Cuban sugar. Seriously affected by this policy, Castro retaliated by nationalizing sugar companies on Cuban territory. The U.S. Government then expanded the blockade to other products and ended up prohibiting the sale of any merchandise to Cuba, including food and medicine. At the same time, the U.S. launched a vast diplomatic offensive culminating in the breaking of relations between the two countries and the botched invasion of Cuba in April 1961, when CIA-financed anti-Castro mercenaries landed in the Bay of Pigs.

The Bay of Pigs Conflict

With Cuba living under the threat of imminent invasion, the El Encanto department store in Havana was completely destroyed on April 13, 1961 by a fire resulting from an act of sabotage. Two days later, American B-26 fighters, bearing Cuban Air Force colours and piloted by Cuban exiles, bombed the Ciudad Libertad and San Antonio de los Baños air force bases as well as the civilian airport at Santiago de Cuba. Several Cuban civil aircraft were destroyed in the bombing, but Fidel Castro's air force remained intact. Right afterward Fidel announced, for the first time, the socialist character of the Cuban Revolution.

On the night of April 17, the landing of 1,500 Cuban mercenaries, backed by the U.S. Army and the CIA, began at Playa Larga and Playa Girón. They came from Miami, Puerto Rico and Nicaragua to take power in Cuba. The invasion plan was devised in Eisenhower's time, but it was carried out by the new U.S. president, John. F. Kennedy. The failure of the invasion was staggering.

Alerted by local militia members, Fidel Castro quickly mobilized his forces and established his command post at the Australia sugar plantation. In just 72 hours, the invaders got bogged down in the marshes. The result was the death of about 200 Americans and the capture and emprisonment of 1,197 others. They would be judged the following year in a court set up in a Havana school. Fidel Castro was surprised and dumbfounded by Kennedy's approach. He had expected the landing of a far more powerful force. "In the first

PORTRAIT

two days we expected the real invasion to begin," he said at the time. Following his victory, Castro asked the United States to send $60 million in farm equipment in exchange for the prisoners. An embarrassed Kennedy administration sent Cuba $50 million in medicine to obtain the prisoners' freedom.

In Cuba itself, the victory was followed by the rapid arrests of nearly 100,000 people identified as counter-revolutionaries. Judged and imprisoned, most of them would be freed, but thousands would remain incarcerated for a number of years. Wayne A. Smith, in his excellent book *A Portrait of Cuba*, wrote that the most conclusive result of the Bay of Pigs affair was the very destruction of a possible anti-Castro rebellion. Dissident elements never recovered from the blows they suffered on April 17 and 18, 1961. From that historical moment right up to 1989, Castro would lose no sleep over internal opposition. For all intents and purposes, there was no longer any opposition, Smith stated.

For the first time since the proclamation of the Monroe Doctrine in 1823, the United States had been repulsed from its "backyard". This symbolic Cuban victory was also the first defeat of U.S. imperialism in Latin America. The American response was not long in coming. Cuba was banished from the Organization of American States at the request of the U.S. emissaries. Every country in the Western Hemisphere, except Mexico and Canada, broke diplomatic relations with Cuba, and the American embargo was strengthened. Then in October 1962, the Cuban missile crisis broke out.

The Cuban Missile Crisis

The Cuban missile crisis was set into motion when American spy planes brought back photos showing the presence of Soviet missile launching pads on Cuban soil, some 200 km off the coast of Florida. The entire world held its breath at the brink of nuclear war. Negotiations intensified between Nikita Khruschev in Moscow and Kennedy in Washington. In a call for reconciliation, Kennedy made a proposal to Khruschev: if Moscow pulled back its nuclear warheads, Washington would promise not to invade Cuba. Moscow accepted the American proposal without consulting Castro, thus embittering relations between Cuba and the Soviet Union. On February 7, 1962, Kennedy imposed a total embargo against Cuba, forbidding, among other things, the importation of any product made in Cuba or transiting through Cuba. These drastic economic measures would have a serious impact on the country's economy, forcing Cuba to ally itself economically with the Soviets.

Cuba Embraces Socialism

Upon taking power in 1959, Castro designated a new president, Manuel Urrutia Leo, whom he promptly dismissed a few months later, accusing him of slowing reform. Fidel took hold of the reins of government definitively from that point on. His government gradually adopted measures indicating radical change in the political and economic system with the adoption of agrarian reforms, rent reductions and nationalization of American properties. The task facing the Fidelistas was enormous. Even if Cuba still had the highest per capita income in Latin America in the 1950s, this economic prosperity masked blatant social inequality, with nearly a quarter of the population living in extreme poverty. Out of two million people, nearly a half-million were jobless, and 650,000 held only seasonal work. The illiteracy rate was high, and health services reached only part of the population.

With financial and economic assistance from the Soviet giant, the Castro regime managed to change the country's face completely. In 1961 one person in six was unable to read or write; 30 years later, Fidel's regime could boast of a literacy rate of 97 per cent. As well, a complete reform of health services brought about a drastic reduction in the infant mortality rate. In 1959, the figure stood at about 40 infant deaths per 1,000 live births; in 1995 it fell below 10 per 1,000, the lowest rate among developing countries, scarcely higher than the U.S. rate of 8.3 per 1,000. Thanks to the Revolution, life expectancy reached levels comparable to those of industrialized countries, standing at 74.7 years for men and 79.2 years for women. In comparison, Americans have a life expectancy of 72.6 years for men and 79.4 years for women; in Canada it is 74.7 years for men and 81.7 year for women, in France 74.3 years for men and 82.3 years for women.

For the Cuban people, these changes represent the Revolution's greatest successes. But for others, even if Fidel's regime had freed the country from the American yoke, it appeared evident that Havana had simply traded its dependence on the U.S. for dependence on the Soviet Union. It seemed difficult to do otherwise for a country that had always depended upon a metropolitan power. After Madrid and Washington, Moscow took over. In 1986, 86 per cent of Cuba's trade occured with socialist countries.

Sugar exports, long the country's economic mainstay, went to Eastern Bloc countries after being banned from the U.S. market. In exchange, the Soviet Union gave Cuba 130 million barrels of oil per year, exceeding Cuba's needs

and leaving it free to sell the surplus on world markets. After 36 years of Fidelismo, the Cuban economy remained just as dependent on white gold. The regime had not managed to diversify the economy. Cuba depended heavily on the outside world for items of basic consumption. Toward 1980, Cuba imported 94 per cent of the edible oils, 80 per cent of the beans, 40 per cent of the rice and 24 per cent of the milk consumed in the country. Although access to food had become easier for much of the population, this remained one of the weaknesses of the regime and the main source of discontent toward the Castro government.

The Embargo Reinforced

With East European socialist regimes dropping like flies from 1989 onward, the Fidelista regime was given few chances of survival. On October 23, 1992, in Miami, U.S. President George Bush signed a bill promoted by Congressman Robert Torricelli aimed at driving the final nail into the coffin of Communism in Cuba which, in Bush's words, could not last another three months. Although this law was supposed to favour the advent of democracy in Cuba, many Cubans perceived it as a preamble to an eventual armed attack under the guise of meeting humanitarian ends.

The Torricelli act broadened the scope of the embargo considerably, forbidding subsidiaries of American companies in other countries from trading with Cuba and preventing boats from docking at American ports within six months of transporting goods or passengers to Cuba. The Torricelli act also provides for sanctions against countries that provide economic assistance to Havana. The extraterritorial aspect of this act has been condemned by the international community. Madame Lorangel, the Canadian Ambassador to Cuba, declared in 1992 that it was unacceptable that companies falling under Canadian law should suddenly have to meet the demands of another nation.

The Castro regime managed to resist the hazards of this new law, but then an even more stringent law was passed in the U.S. Senate: the Helms-Burton Act sought to suspend U.S. contributions to any international organization providing assistance to Cuba (as well as to Iran, Iraq and Libya), to oppose Cuban membership in any international financial organization, and to deny U.S. visas to foreigners who use formerly American-owned property nationalized by the Cuban Government.

Cuba Breaks Through International Isolation

To overcome its isolation caused by the American embargo and accentuated following the collapse of the Eastern Bloc, Cuba has sought and found allies all around the world, especially in Canada, Mexico and France. The international community is generally opposed to the American embargo and has vigorously denounced the Torricelli and Helms-Burton acts, which target countries other than Cuba. In a United Nations vote, only the U.S. and Israel defended the Cuban embargo. Other countries, including France, Spain and Canada, which are among Cuba's main trading partners, have preferred not to become involved in Cuban internal politics. They have chosen instead to cash in on the spectacular profits resulting from the absence of American competition and from the Eastern-bloc desertion of a Cuban economy in a state of rebuilding.

Canada and the countries of the European Community were long in the opposite camp from Cuba in matters of international relations, especially during the Cold War period. These differences centred on Cuba's involvement in Africa and Latin America and, more recently, on human rights questions. The European countries and Amnesty International have decided to pay particular attention to the *plantados* ("those who stay put"), some of them held as political prisoners since the 1960s. In 1982, the insistence of French President François Mittérand led to the liberation of Armando Valladares, one of the *plantados*. Relations between France and Cuba have improved since then; Fidel Castro made his first official visit to France in 1996.

Canada marked its 50th anniversary of uninterrupted diplomatic relations with Cuba in 1995. This is important to the Cuban Government, since Canada was the only Western Hemisphere country apart from Mexico to maintain relations with the Castro regime when Cuba was expelled from the Organization of American States in 1964. In one of its rare departures from the *diktats* of 20th-century American foreign policy, Canada has maintained friendly and broad relations with Cuba, even though the two countries were in opposing camps during the Cold War. This relationship rests on political dialogue, trade, scientific and academic cooperation, and tourism. Bilateral trade between the two countries exceeded $300 million (Canadian). Relations between the two countries go beyond trade and tourism: more than 15 Canadian universities cooperate with Cuban institutions in the areas of health, management, economics, and scientific research. The people of Canada, France and Spain have extended a helping hand to Cuba whenever they could.

What is the Future of U.S. Policy Toward Cuba?

Cuba had chances, especially during the 1970s, to normalize diplomatic relations with the United States, particularly under the administrations of Gerald Ford and Jimmy Carter, when immigration agreements were signed on friendly terms. But Cuba's role in the Cold War — whether the deployment of thousands of Cuban soldiers to Angola or arms shipments to Marxist groups in Nicaragua, El Salvador and Chile — gave Ronald Reagan a ready excuse to reinstate anti-Cuba policies with renewed fervour.

With the end of the Cold War, and with it the end of the Communist "threat", several observers wondered why the U.S. Government maintained its rigid policy toward Cuba. At first glance, nothing prevents the American government from maintaining economic and diplomatic relations with countries that have different systems. In the past, the U.S. has had close, even cordial, relations with Poland and Rumania, and nowadays with Vietnam and China, both of them Communist countries. Of course, the physical distance of these countries, compared to Cuba's position in the U.S. "backyard", along with the anti-American rhetoric of the Castro regime, are variables that Cuba does not share with China, for example.

American policy aims are clear: overthrow the Castro regime and promote a transition to American-style democracy. The failure of the embargo, whose main effect has been to aggravate the precarious living conditions of ordinary Cubans without toppling Castro, has led some liberal observers in the United States to suggest that a lifting of the embargo and a massive influx of American tourists and business people could destabilize the Castro regime in the long run. This proposal would also be welcomed by the Cuban people, enabling them to do away with the serious shortages of food and other essential items such as medicine.

Although international political conditions allow the U.S. Government to show a certain opening, the reality of the domestic political situation is rather different. Over the years a big and influential Cuban exiled community has developed in the United States, with the great majority opposed to dialogue with the Castro regime. This community constitutes the single biggest voting bloc in Florida, and is strongly represented in New Jersey, California and New York. It put pressure on Congress to adopt the Torricelli and Helms-Burton acts, tightening the trade embargo on Cuba.

Dissidence

Despite an apparent tendency toward liberalization, which reached its peak during the pope's visit, the regime continues to constantly and adamantly battle against all dissent, and new, more restrictive laws in this area were passed in February of 1999. In fact, even foreign journalists should worry about taking a too pro-American stance.

In March 1999, the Cuban government condemned four dissidents to heavy prison sentences for demanding greater democracy on the island in a document entitled "The Homeland Belongs to All". Following this event, Canada decided to review the entire scope of its relations with Cuba. "Cuba sends a distress signal to her friends in the international community when people are jailed for peaceful protest," declared the Canadian prime minister.

POLITICS

Building a socialist democracy in Cuba was not something that could be done overnight. The first 10 years of the Revolution were devoted largely to surviving U.S. economic aggression. During that period, Castro worked on uniting various political tendencies behind his revolutionary project. Creating the new Communist Party of Cuba (CPC) in 1965, the only legal political party in the country, was an arduous task and enabled him to rule in a highly centralized manner for better or for worse, often for worse.

The CPC governed the country single-handedly until the constitution was adopted in 1976, creating new political institutions. Since then, the National Assembly has become the supreme legislative power. Since 1993, its members have been elected by universal suffrage to five-year terms.

Besides the National Assembly, which meets twice a year, the State Council, composed of 31 members appointed by the National Assembly, has the power to adopt statutory orders. The Council of Ministers is the executive branch of government and its members are elected by the National Assembly.

Each of the 15 provinces established by the 1976 administrative changes has its own provincial assembly with 169 members elected by universal suffrage by Cuban citizens 16 years of age and older.

Populist movements also play an important role in Cuban political life. The Committees for the Defense of the Revolution (CDR) is probably the largest of these. Originally created to protect Cuba against foreign aggression, the CDR is made up of volunteer citizens who administrate municipal affairs. Almost half the population of Cuba belonged to the CDR until recently, when it lost some of its political power.

ECONOMY

Food Puts the Revolution at Stake

The future of the Revolution will be played out on people's plates. That, at least, is an observation made by Raúl Castro, Fidel's brother and heir apparent, in an interview at the height of the economic storm that followed the collapse of the Soviet Union. "Today, the country's political, military and ideological problem is to find food," Raúl commented. "This is the main task from every point of view." After the Communist bloc crumbled, Cuba found itself shorn overnight of its main trading partner, suddenly losing $4 billion to $5 billion in annual subsidies. The boats loaded with petroleum, food, spare parts for industrial equipment, cars, and buses no longer called on the ports of Havana and Santiago.

Between 1989 and 1993, the size of the Cuban economy was suddenly cut in half. To cure the country's economic headaches, the Castro regime launched a program of economic measures which it called the *periodo especial en tiempo de paz* (special period in peacetime). These measures included severe rationing of food supplies, consumer goods, fuel and electricity. The consequences had an immediate impact on a people who had lived more than three decades in a system of full employment and near-certain welfare. Hospitals faced dramatic shortages of medicine, and ration booklets provided food for only 20 days a month. Food became an obsession in Cuba, and the quest for food became the true national sport.

Hunger returned to the country after a 30-year absence. On the one hand, there is the *libreta*, the little green ration booklet with which Cubans can obtain essential items at reduced government-set prices based on a quota system; the personal ration includes one bun per day and monthly allocations of 2.5 kilograms of rice, 60 grams of beans and seven eggs, plus milk for children and pregnant women. On the other hand, for cheese or chicken, for instance, there are stores that accept only dollars, and then there is the black market, generally formed by groups of farmers who travel to the big cities and go door to door. There is food on the shelves, but prices are unaffordable for most people. In the farmer's markets that opened for business starting in November 1994, a half-kilogram of pork recently cost 45 pesos, equal to one-third of a technician's monthly salary. Ham sold for 200 pesos a kilogram, and turkey was 70 pesos a kilogram. The cost of food is a constant theme of conversation, anxiety and discontent for the entire Cuban population.

Cuba has no choice but to become integrated with the world economy, and that means giving up socialist economic principles for a market economy. The Castro regime has only one goal, and that is to save the essential accomplishments of the Revolution, namely education and universal health service. Even at the height of the budget cuts and economic reforms, not a single hospital or school was closed. But the entire country has been shaken, and the economy will never be the same. With each new day, Cuba applies the principles of market economics a little more.

Opening the Economy

The first measures aimed at opening the country's economy were introduced in 1993. Since then, Cubans have been legally permitted to hold foreign currency, creating two parallel economies, one working with Cuban pesos and the other with U.S. dollars. The quest for dollars began in earnest across the country, with shops and supermarkets that accept only dollars opening their doors for the first time in 30 years and offering all sorts of imported goods. Cubans have latched onto the so-called "D system" to get hold of dollars. With activities ranging from prostitution to the sale of stolen products and the offering of rides in unlicensed taxis, Cubans use every means available to them. Others obtain foreign currency through family members living in exile. Cuban exiles send up to $400 million a year to their friends and relatives living in Cuba.

In preparation for an end to official policies of full employment, finally announced in May 1995 when virtually the entire economy was officially in state hands, the government allowed Cubans without university diplomas to create independent family businesses. Thousands of plumbers, mechanics, cooks and taxi drivers opened their first small businesses. To overcome the underproduction of food on the island, a majority of state farms were reconverted into farming cooperatives, numbering some 2,600, which were added to the 3,000 existing cooperatives. They employ nearly 400,000 workers. To attract foreign investment, which was seriously lacking since the withdrawal of Soviet aid, foreign business can now hold majority shares in Cuban companies and invest in the great majority of economic sectors. In September 1994, the government authorized the opening of free peasant markets, where farmers can sell their goods according to the rules of supply and demand.

Despite these measures, the country's economy remains highly state-controlled, with an overwhelming proportion of economic mechanisms, as well as internal trade and distribution, subject to government regulation. In 1995 Cuba added to the structure of its nascent market economy with the adoption of a new law on foreign investment allowing foreigners to hold 100 per cent of the shares in a Cuban company.

Tourism

Since the fall of the Communist Bloc in 1989, tourism was the first industry to take off in Cuba thanks to foreign investments mainly from Canada, Spain, Mexico, Germany and Italy, among other countries. This kicked off a hotel boom with foreign-owned resorts springing up everywhere in the Cuban landscape. The number of hotel rooms in Cuba increased from 6,000 in 1984 to more than 22,000 ten years later; there are 30,000 hotel rooms in Varadero alone.

The number of visitors to Cuba is also on the rise. More than 600,000 people visited Cuba in 1993, over 1.2 million in 1997, and 2.5 million more are expected by the year 2000. Most of these visitors are Canadian tourists, followed by Latin-Americans, Italians, Spaniards, French and Germans.

Grossing over 2.5 million dollars, the tourist industry today is the mainstay of the Cuban economy. Fidel Castro even remarked: "Before, we thought tourism would be harmful to us, but the truth is, tourism is gold."

Harmful Results of the Market Economy

Carlos Lage, secretary of the Council of Ministers and the author of Cuba's economic reforms, was blunt in describing the perverse effects of moves toward a market economy. "In opening the windows of the economy, plenty of fresh air came in, but also spiders and vipers," Lage said in an interview in his Communist Party central committee office.

Following the legalization of private holdings in U.S. dollars, a true "dollar apartheid" sprang up, creating social equalities rarely seen since the triumph of the Revolution in 1959. With the dollar worth about 25 pesos on the parallel market in mid-1996, a new set of rules quickly set in. The average monthly salary in Cuba was about 250 pesos, equal to about $10 on the black market; a doctor's monthly earnings were about 400 pesos, or $16. This meant that a taxi driver or a cigar vendor could easily earn just as much with just a few days' work.

Workers in the tourism industry receive tips in dollars, and Cubans with family members abroad benefit from money transfers, but most people continue to receive their monthly salary in pesos (apart from a few jobs with bonuses paid in dollars). Along with the quest for food, the quest for dollars has become Cubans' main concern. While some use subterfuges that stretch the limits of morality, thousands of others go into prostitution. The tourism boom has thus created a return to sex tourism in Cuba, a phenomenon that the Revolution had nearly wiped out for more than three decades. For some, these perverse effects are the price to be paid for getting over the worst economic crisis to hit the country since 1959.

PORTRAIT

POPULATION

The Cuban population is now estimated at more than 11 million inhabitants, one third of whom are under the age of 30. The density of 99.1 people per square kilometre is exaggerated since 72 percent of the population is concentrated in urban areas. Havana alone is home to 2.2 million residents, one fifth of the total. The second city, in terms of population, is Miami, Florida, home to over a million Cubans.

The feature of the Cuban people that draws most attention is its blended cultural heritage. Mestizos, Morenos (black Africans), Criollos (European descendants), Chinos (Filipinos and Chinese) and Blancos (Europeans) live together on good terms and in relative harmony.

Cubans possess a tremendous sense of hospitality. They are warm, open and likeable. Always smiling and good-natured, Cubans laugh easily and have a great sense of humour. All of the bother of everyday life has comedic potential and nothing, and no one, is exempt. The Americans, Castro, the *periodo especial*, or "special period", even tourism, everything qualifies as material.

Cuban Emigration

In December 1994, thousands of Cubans fled the island on makeshift rafts, headed for Miami. Some of them never made it after falling prey to the sea or to U.S. authorities. In mid-August of 1994, the U.S. naval base at Guantánamo was sheltering more than 22,000 Cuban refugees following the decision of President Bill Clinton not to accept them in the United States and to send them to the camps. Many of those who risked their lives to leave their country for Florida under perilous conditions suddenly found themselves imprisoned in camps back on the island of Cuba.

Others decided to remain in Cuba, like seventy-five-year-old Gustavo, the oldest lifeguard in Guanabo, a little resort and fishing town located about 30 km east of Havana. From his beach, thousands of *balseros* (raftsmen) departed for Miami, leaving behind wives, children, friends, homes, cars and everything else. To escape the disastrous economic situation that followed the collapse of the Eastern Bloc, the only remaining hope for many was the not too distant horizon of the Florida coast. On Christmas Eve of 1994, some 36,000 of them escaped in spectacular fashion. Entire families, including dogs, would set themselves adrift on truck tires under the complicit eyes of the Cuban authorities, who had given the starting signal. Letting malcontents leave was one way of defusing the crisis.

Until a century ago, Cuba was a country of immigrants, with Europeans and Africans arriving in large numbers. Starting in the 1920s, there were more emigrants than immigrants, although only 60,000 left the island between the 1930s and 1959, when Fidel Castro took power. That was when Cubans began to emigrate *en masse*. Some 50,000 left in 1959, another 120,000 in 1965 from the port of Camarioca, and 260,000 from Varadero between 1966 and 1973. Then came the exodus from the port of Mariel in 1980. The world would have to wait until Christmas 1994 to see as massive a wave of Cuban emigration.

Gustavo, the dean of Cuban lifeguards, does not know these figures. But he does know that these exoduses have separated families in tragic ways. He knows that some of his friends were devoured by sharks. He knows that some luckier ones have a new life in the United States. His decision not to leave his beach has nothing to do with the slogan inscribed on the decrepit walls of Guanabo's Committee for the Defence of the Revolution saying *Yo me quedo!* (I shall remain!). Gustavo says he is in love, in love with his grandchildren and in love with the sea. On his beach, he has seen American smugglers leaving drugs, arms or alcohol before the Revolution. He has seen American yachts come at night to leave anti-Castro propaganda. On this beach, he has seen his friends leave.

The Status of Women

The status of women has improved in Cuban society since the Revolution, allowing easier access to education and to jobs in all spheres of work, although they are still under-represented in the area of political power. *Machismo* is still very much alive, and women are still considered responsible for looking after household chores. The creation of the Federation of Cuban Women soon after the Revolution has made it possible to hold many debates on the place of women in Cuban society, including recent debates touching on the delicate subject of prostitution.

Prostitution

Prostitution has grown enormously in Cuba with the rise in international tourism since the late 1980s. The big cities such as Havana and Santiago de Cuba, as well as the resort towns, especially Varadero, are having to cope with the growing problem of prostitution. The *jineteros* and *jineteras* (see p 51) accost tourists with impunity to seek money

and gifts from them in exchange for their company.

This phenomenon has caught the Castro regime unprepared, stuck in the belief that it had wiped out this phenomenon and that it had inculcated a strong socialist morality in its citizens. This practice is not highly institutionalized (there are no brothels in Cuba), but it operates on the street and on the beach. To try to wipe it out, the authorities carry out regular "cleaning" operations in the cities, sending young girls and boys back to their native villages; most of them come from other parts of the country, drawn by the chance to make money.

Hotels systematically refuse to allow Cubans to enter foreigners' rooms. Far from stopping prostitution, this measure has led instead to the opening of rooms for rent in private homes, as well as to corruption in some of the bigger hotels, with porters allowing Cubans to go up to a room. Fidel Castro, seemingly overtaken by events, once stated sarcastically in a speech that "at least Cuba offers the best educated prostitutes on the planet."

Gay Life in Cuba

The status of homosexuals in Cuba today seems neither better nor worse than in other Latin American countries. Gays have always been victims of certain forms of repression that find their source more from the weight of old family values and *machismo* than from political will. *Machismo*, based on the notion of male superiority, remains alive and kicking in Cuba. An obsession with categorizing people according to sexual stereotypes contributes more than anything else to the oppression of homosexuals and to keeping women in traditional roles.

However, the Cuban film *Fresa y Chocolate* (Strawberry and Chocolate) seems to have helped raise people's consciousness of the harm caused by repression toward gays and has probably led to a broader acceptance of homosexuals. The song *El Pecador Original* (The Original Sinner) by the popular Cuban singer Pablo Milanés, which was a hit with the Cuban public, can be cited in the same vein. The social situation of gays in Cuba, as in the U.S. or Canada, is very much better nowadays than it was in the 1960s.

With that said, there are fewer specifically gay spots in Cuba than in cities in North America or Europe, and that can probably be explained by the fact that the Latin American gay community is not as closely knit. Gays remain attached to their families and seek acceptance as homosexual individuals within a society that they wish could be more pluralistic. Parallel to this phenomenon, bisexuality seems to be more common.

All the same, across Cuba, even in the small towns, the gay social scene can often be found along the *malecón* (the seaside boulevard in the centre of town) or at the *fiestas de cinco pesos* or *fiestas de diez pesos* (five- or ten-peso parties) held in private homes, usually at the same address.

RELIGION

The triumph of the Cuban Revolution considerably diminished the influence of the Church and, thereby, the practice of religion. In fact, although freedom of worship is guaranteed by the Constitution of 1976, in reality religious activity has been disdained for a long time. Those who openly expressed their faith often found themselves excluded from social advancement.

However, since the mid-1980s, the State has been more lenient in this area. In 1988, it authorized the importation of bibles and allowed foreign religious figures to enter the country. In 1991, the Cuban Communist Party, for the first time in its history, permitted its members to practice their religions. In 1997, with the approval of government authorities, a high mass was celebrated by several thousand Cubans at Havana's cathedral. This permissive trend culminated in January 1998 with an official visit to Cuba by Pope John Paul II. Since that momentous event, religious practice has been experiencing a sort of revival. The celebration of Christmas in Cuba, long prohibited by government authorities, took place again in 1998.

Besides Catholicism, historically the dominant faith in Cuba, there is a significant Protestant minority and an even smaller Jewish community. However, Afro-Cuban religions remain by far the most popular and widespread. Three faiths that originated in Africa are practised in Cuba: the Rule of the Stick, Abakuá Secret Society and *Santería*, the last being most prevalent.

Santería, or the Rule of Ocha

Santería, or the Rule of Ocha (Ocha means god and saint) is one of three Afro-Cuban religions, referred to as such because they come from a syncretism between the religious observances brought by African slaves and the Catholic religion. Of the three religions of African origin practised in Cuba — the Rule of the Stick, the Abakuá secret society and *Santería* — it is *Santería* that is most widespread.

The Yoruba people, originally from Benin, brought with them the Rule of Ocha in the middle of the 17th century and created a liturgy in Cuba to preserve its 450 deities. *Santería* was practised then in the *cabildos*, places located outside the towns where black slaves from the same area or ethnic group could gather to practise their religion, their dances and their language. To become initiated to *Santería*, a whole series of animals has to be sacrificed — doves, hens, roosters, ducks and goats. On the first day of initiation the blood of these animals is used in special rituals to feed the gods. You can easily recognize followers of *Santería* by their distinctive garb, usually white, and by their multi-coloured necklaces representing the gods.

The Rule of the Stick

The Rule of the Stick comes from the Congo, Angola and Zaire. The slaves uprooted from these areas brought *engangas* with them. These are receptacles containing everything that resonates in nature — earth, water and metals. During initiation to the Rule of the Stick, incisions are made in several places on the body of the person being initiated so that he can commune with his *enganga*. The ritual goes as follows: it begins by etching the body of the initiate to see if an *enganga* matches him and if he can possess one; if so, new etches are made on the arms, the nape of the neck, the tongue, the thighs and the back. The initiate's blood is then drunk by the sorcerer and the initiate himself.

The Abakuá Secret Society

Only the Abakuá secret society has temples used for rituals and initiations. The society was created in the late 17th century by and for men from southeastern Nigeria. These very strong men were brought as slaves to work on the docks, and they gathered around the ports of Havana, Matanzas and Cárdenas. They came together to pool money and help those who were still slaves by buying their freedom. This secret society, which resembles the Freemasons in its structure, is still very much alive today. Members of the Abakuá secret society must follow a rigorous social ethic.

"If we have to go back to clandestinity, we will!"

Natalia Bolívar is one of the great specialists in Afro-Cuban religions and has published many books, available in bookshops across the country. Here she speaks about the tolerance of Afro-Cuban religions in Cuba.

"Although Afro-Cuban religions are generally identified with the black population, whites have historically opened up to the cults. Since the 16th century, whites have had black maids in their houses, who breast-fed the children of the whites. All Cubans thus have this culture in their blood, for it is also part of what a Cuban upbringing has been. Up to the end of the 19th century, there were always more black people than white people. There were social differences, certainly, but when the child of a white or even an adult fell ill or if there was no doctor or if he could not cure the illness, whom did they turn to for care? To the *santero*! Because it was he or she who had the power of the herbs, who knew, for example, how to cure fever with herbs.

"In Cuba, the Spanish were more tolerant toward this sort of thing, even if it was done clandestinely at times. Fundamentally, this type of religion is personal. Whoever practises it has direct contact with the divinities and thus doesn't need to make this belief public. It is a religion without temples, without churches. The temple is the home of the believer.

"During the Revolution, it was not forbidden. However, jobs were generally refused to people who indicated on their application forms that they were believers, whether in any of the western or African religions. Nowadays, and since 1989, religious practice is more widely permitted than in the past. However, if we have to go back to clandestinity we will, that's all. There's nothing new in this. It's called double morality. To survive, the black has always needed the Catholic religion on one side and his African divinities on the other side."

Celebrating a *Santería* Saint

*The following is by **Carlos Soldevila**, a Québécois journalist and one of the authors of this Cuba guide.*

I had to wait several weeks before a musician friend who practises *Santería* invited me to a ceremony. "It's the feast day of a saint. Bring a bottle of rum and a little money to give as an offering. You can record it, but no photos."

We met at dusk in a building in Old Havana. In the spot where the ceremony was to be held, it was already dark. The rhythm of drums could be heard from the street. We had to climb three floors in the dark hallways of a somewhat dilapidated building. As we climbed each floor, the music became louder, and its echo spread across the hallways. Each step seemed to carry me away from America and bring me closer to Africa.

In a small apartment, about 15 people were gathered around five percussionists. A tall black man led the ceremony and the chants to Afro-Cuban divinities. This was the *babalao*, the intermediary between gods and men. He invited me into another room to leave my offerings. The room was decorated entirely with little wooden statues, mirrors and mystical tables. In the middle was the statue of a Catholic virgin dressed in a long green and yellow dress and wearing a golden crown. At her feet were cakes, biscuits, wine, rum, and coconut shells filled with money. I was received by a woman dressed all in white. She explained to me that this was her anniversary as a "saint". In *santería*, followers mark the anniversary of the day of their religious initiation. Each year, she thus offers feast to Ochun, the saint who protects her and guides her.

Good humour is evident among the guests, and a festive spirit reigns. However, something I cannot quite grasp is floating in the air. I feel a sense of expectation, almost of bewitchment. The *babalao* strikes up a new chant, and the percussionists produce a sustained, deafening rhythm. After several minutes, something seemingly incredible occurs: a woman begins to writhe, to twist herself around, seized by a sort of trance. In a brief moment of lucidity, she tries to leave the room, to flee, but men stand in front of the door and prevent her from leaving. She is pushed back toward the centre of the room, in front of the musicians. She emits guttural sounds, shouting and dancing like a rooster, ever more quickly, twisting herself around, while the *babalao* utters prayers in Yoruba.

This spectacle is staggering in the eyes of the layman, but the other participants in this ceremony do not seem surprised by the turn of events. After several minutes, the *babalao* asks this young, saint-possessed woman and the other women there to go into the room with the temple. The music stops. The young woman comes out of the room dressed in the green and yellow colours of her saint, seemingly still in a trance. She comes near me, takes my hand between her own and kisses me on the cheek, fixing her eyes upon mine with an other-worldly look, a look that came from very far away.

Fascinated by this, I have since met many *babalaos*, who are generally quite open to foreigners. They foretold my future by pulling on coconut shells and observing the contours of cigar smoke. They are very popular in times of crisis, and I duly had to wait my turn in line. Now every time I hear the rhythm of drums in the dark Havana nights, I think of these thousands of followers who had read the advice of the worthy Marx and Engels, starting in elementary school.

THE ARTS

Music

Cuba is the birthplace of an extraordinary musical culture that has influenced the entire American continent in the 20th century. Starting from Afro-Cuban rhythms, numerous musical forms have developed in Cuba and have got the whole continent dancing. These include the *cha-cha-cha*, *danzón*, *mambo* and *rumba*. Nowhere else in Latin America have African-based rhythms been as preponderant. The adoption of *cabildos* in colonial times enabled slaves to preserve their languages and religions, as well as their complex, rhythmic musical styles. These were often closely linked to religious observance, with ceremonies taking place in harmony with the wild beating of the drums. Cuban music has inherited many musical instruments of African origin, including *batá* drums and the *shekere*, a small percussion instrument.

Rumba

Born in the black neighbourhoods of the town of Matanzas, *rumba* is one of the purest Afro-Cuban-inspired musical forms, combining ritual music with more contemporary rhythms. *Rumba* is divided into three traditional styles, *yambú*, *guaguancó* and *columbia*. *Rumba*'s rhythm is provided by *batá* drums or by *congas*, and by the *clave*, two short wooden sticks one of which goes into the hollow of the hand to create a resonance chamber. The *clave* also constitutes the rhythmic base for *salsa* and for Latin jazz.

Danzón

Danzón became popular in the 1920s. Its origins come from a syncretism between a form of quadrille that arrived from Haiti in the 18th century and Afro-Cuban rhythms that were gradually married with it, bringing new complexity to its rhythm. The French-style wooden flute and the violin are *danzón*'s favoured instruments, played by *charanga* bands, as opposed to the more typical bands that use brass instruments. True master flautists would grace Cuban music starting in the 1930s, among them Arcaño and his group, known as Arcaño y sus Maravillas, as well as Richard Egües and his Orquestra Aragón. *Danzón* is the base from which two other popular rhythms sprang, the *cha-cha-cha*, played by renowned flautists, and the mambo.

Son

The greatest legacy of Cuban music remains *son*, which stands out today as the most influential rhythm in Latin music and serves as the rhythmic base for a multitude of contemporary Latin musical forms, including salsa and Latin jazz. *Son* was born in the province of Oriente, in Santiago de Cuba, from the blending of Haitian, African and Spanish cultures in the 19th century. The originator of this rhythm is said to have been the musician and composer Miguel Matamoros. Using the *clave*, as in *rumba*, it also adds percussion instruments such as the *bongó*, the *maracas* and the *guiro*. This musical form was developed further in Havana in the 1940s, thanks especially to the Sexteto Habanero (known before that as the Trio Oriental), who added the piano and brass. Thanks to Félix Chapotín, the Sexteto Habanero became one of the most influential groups in the 1940s and 1950s. Later, the well known singer Beny Moré further popularized this rhythm.

Salsa

To this day, salsa is indisputably the most popular music in the country. Derived from African and popular rhythms, salsa has one of the most complex rhythmic bases in Latin music and reverberates throughout the continent. Cuban musicians will tell you salsa comes from Cuba. Even though salsa's rhythmic base is the typically Cuban *son*, salsa developed in its early days mostly in the smoky bars of New York thanks to a confluence of Cuban and Puerto Rican musicians. Today Havana swarms with popular *salsa* bands. The words of their songs often carry an ironic and sometimes subtly critical look at daily life in the country.

For instance, the theme song of Los Van Van is *La Habana No Aguanta Más!* (Havana Can't Take It Any More!), which deals with the housing shortage in Havana and the "funny" consequences this entails, such as promiscuity. Today *son* has become blended with salsa and with Latin jazz,

thanks in particular to innovative groups such as Irakere.

Jazz

Cuban musicians have long shared with their black Louisiana brothers a taste for jazz, adding typically Cuban rhythms such as *son*. Although jazz was prohibited in the early days of the Revolution, it made a dramatic return to the Havana musical scene with the founding of the Havana jazz festival by the musician Bobby Carcassés in the 1970s. It is held annually in February. In the last two decades, Irakere is the Latin jazz (or Cuban jazz) group that has led the way for an entire generation of great Cuban musicians. Under the direction today of the pianist Jesús "Chucho" Valdés, Irakere has brought a number of international giants of Latin jazz into the limelight, among them Paquito de Rivera and Arturo Sandoval.

The Blockade is Not Cultural

The young Roberto Carcassés, son of a well known Havana jazzman, comes across as a true musical explorer. Cuban rhythms, classical music, jazz and rock all form part of his compositions, creating an explosive mixture whose reputation has enabled him to travel around the world. He shared a few comments with us.

"Cuban musicians have always been able to draw inspiration from the music of all the countries in the world. Here, despite the conflicts between the Cuban and U.S. governments, we musicians have never denounced a certain cultural imperialism. American culture was already present when modern Cuban culture was just being born. Even if Cuba tried to distance itself from American culture with the triumph of the Revolution by presenting Russian films, by saying that jazz was the music of the enemy, and by forbidding the Beatles, it was impossible to avoid these influences. The Cuban people and artists have never had prejudices against the cultural creation that comes from the United States.

"When we travel outside Cuba, we live in fear of being cut off from the constant musical development going on in Havana. The rhythmic evolution of Cuban music is no doubt among the most dynamic and most sophisticated in the world. However, culture is not doing very well in Cuba because there is no money to subsidize artists, nor do we have the cultural infrastructure necessary for their development. Beyond politics, I love Havana. I love its people, and I love those who have left."

Trova

The *trobadores* (troubadours) who once criss-crossed the island of Cuba now set out across the entire world. The well known songs *La Bayamesa* and *Guantanamera* are among the *trovas* marking the beginnings of this movement, which was modernized in the 1970s by the *Nueva Trova* current, thanks especially to singer-composers Silvio Rodríguez and Pablo Milanés. Carlos Varela, who is not as well known abroad but very popular in Cuba, is more critical than his companions; he casts a caustic look at the political and economic problems that are rampant in Cuba.

Classical Music

Cuba is one of the few countries in the world where folk, popular and classical music complement one another so masterfully. A long tradition of learned music arose in the country starting in the 18th century with its first famous composer, Esteban de Salas (1725-1803). The most important musical contribution would come in the 20th century with Ernesto Lecuona, justly considered the country's greatest composer. He knew how to blend all of the country's musical forms with classical music; he leaned gradually to film music and founded a popular band called the Lecuona Cuban Boys.

An Island that Dances

*This section on Cuban dance was written by **Rakel Mayedo**, a Cuban television host, a professional ballerina and a dance critic. We thank* Topo Magazine *for its collaboration.*

If there is one thing Cubans are proud of, it is that they are very good dancers. Throughout their bodies, Cubans feel the need to dance. They express this each day in the way they walk, in the gestures they make, and in their everyday behaviour. The origin of this plasticity of movement may be found in the union of the African and Spanish cultures, a union which, to a large degree, has formed the cultural identity of the Cuban people.

The gradual assimilation of the strong African tradition helped create an impressive rhythmic quality among Cubans. This comes from Yoruba, Locumi, Congo and Bantu drumming. Other influences were added later, including Haitian rhythm and French dance. These came to Cuba in the 18th century, among them the quadrille, as it was called in Europe but which Cuban Creoles called "counterdance". In this dance one may perceive Cuban elements such as brief rhythmic combinations set in succession. This rhythmic element is found even more in *danzón*, in which rhythmic figures are superposed in two different senses.

With all these influences, Cuban music and dance develop along very precise rhythmic bases, expressed not only in the form of foot-tapping but also in the movement of the shoulders, arms, hips and head, as if the music were gradually carrying away the dancer. A foreigner seeking to learn how to dance like a Cuban will always get the same observation from his or her teacher: Cuban dance can be felt but not described.

It is essential to feel the music in every pore of one's skin. Everything has to dance, because this is the only way to exert full independence of movement. This is the basic formula for performing popular Cuban dance forms, several of which, including *danzón*, *mambo* and *cha-cha-cha*, have travelled across boundaries to become true successes in several countries in the Americas and Europe. Currently, *salsa* is the culmination of this whole process, with its very characteristic rhythm, its melody and its personal energy.

The link between a couple is important in Cuban dance. A very sensual relation is expressed not only in the closeness of the bodies but also by the movement of the man's pelvis and the undulation of the woman's hips. In all these forms and movements of Cuban dance, the man always woos the woman, protects her and idealizes her.

Film

*This section on film was written by **André Pâquet**, who represented Québec at the 1996 Havana International Film Festival. We thank* Topo Magazine *for its collaboration.*

It was not until the time of the Second World War that Cubans could see their own images, their own imaginations and their own stories begin to brighten the silver screen. Cuba experienced a period of development between 1939 and 1959, with a film industry and a studio structure employing nearly 8,000 people in Havana alone. Various waves of immigration from Europe brought a familiarity with European cinema; a number of business people, creative artists and technicians transplanted their activities and their knowledge to Cuba, as well as to Argentina, Mexico and Brazil. In Cuba, as elsewhere in Latin America, new facilities plus a cheap, abundant and well qualified work force were soon used to produce musical films and B-grade thrillers. Concurrently, some entrepreneurs filmed pornographic movies, whose production was then forbidden in the United States.

The real dawn of Cuban cinema would come after the 1959 Revolution, with the founding of the *Instituto Cubano de Arte y Indústria Cinematográfica*, under the direction of Alfredo Guevara. Inspired by the European School through a familiarity with "neo-realism" or the French "new wave" cinema, producers such as García Espinoza, Tomás Gutiérrez Alea and several documentary film-makers including José Massip and Jorge Fraga offered the first flamboyant images of the young Revolution. An innovative type of creative freedom came to the fore at that time, calling for a decolonization of the silver screen.

The establishment of a film archive and of the magazine *Cinecubano* spurred the momentum of Cuban cinema, which moved into the vanguard of Latin American film-making for decades to come. The cinema institute became a sort of beacon for this cultural and political decolonization, defended by film-makers from an entire continent. Havana became the hub of a cinematographic renaissance, forged in political struggle and aimed at breaking away from a film industry tradition mired in the production of melodramas and folksy musical films.

Today it goes without saying that Cuban cinema, along with its infrastructure and its leadership role in Latin American film production, have trouble hiding the consequences of the sudden and brutal collapse of the Soviet Empire. Power cuts, dilapidated movie theatres, and the unavailability of spare parts for Soviet-made equipment, together with a lack of resources for the purchase and screening of foreign films, are among the problems afflicting Cuban cinematographic reality.

The film decolonization conducted with such fervour 30 years ago soon after the triumph of the Revolution, which provided a varied program of Cuban and foreign films during those many years, is now threatened by a return of American productions. Since American films are not subject to the trade embargo, pirated copies are shown in movie theatres and on television. The recent success abroad of certain Cuban films provides revenues in U.S. dollars but forces Cubans to sell their films to the distributors.

Tomás Gutiérrez Alea

Tomás Gutiérrez Alea, one of Cuba's greatest film-makers, died on April 16, 1996. Born in 1928, Gutiérrez Alea produced the well known film *Fresa y Chocolate* (Strawberries and Chocolate) in the early 1990s. This film deals with themes that are controversial in Cuba, such as prostitution, homosexuality and personal spying. More than any other Cuban creative artist, Gutiérrez Alea achieved the prodigious triumph of

producing several works critical of Cuban revolutionary society while respecting the will of Fidel Castro, who told artists early on in the Revolution that he would accept criticism only if it contributed to a deepening of revolutionary spirit: *"Dentro de la Revolución, todo; fuera de la Revolución, nada."* (Within the Revolution, everything; outside the Revolution, nothing.) Gutiérrez Alea's greatest film is no doubt *Memorias del Subdesarrollo* (Memories of Underdevelopment), produced in 1968. He was one of the main figures of Cuban cinema and a founder of the Cuban Institute of Cinematographic Art and Industry.

Literature

Cuba produced several good writers in the 19th century whose works mostly conveyed a message critical of colonial society. José María de Heredia (1803-1839), the first great Cuban poet, would be banished for his revolutionary activity. The country's first novelist, Cirilo Villaverde (1812-1894), stood out as a precursor of realism with a novel titled *Cecilia Valdés* before this current even reached Spain, which not only was the colonial power but also greatly influenced Cuban literature during that period. It was José Martí's monumental body of work that really set the stage for modernism in Cuba. An orator, essayist, novelist and poet, Martí became the leading figure on his country's literary scene, even though only three of his books were published during his lifetime.

Cuba contributed to 20th-century world literature, thanks to three great writers: Nicolás Guillén, Alejo Carpentier and José Lezama Lima. Guillén, a *mulato* born of a slave mother, began the black consciousness movement in Cuban literature and quickly became the best known of Cuban poets, nominated several times for a Nobel Prize (which he never won). Born in Camagüey in 1902, he became famous with the publication of his first work, *Motivos de Son*, a collection inspired by the sonority of languages and of his country's African culture. A poet, journalist and Communist, he introduced the theme of blacks, misery and exploitation to Spanish literature. In his collection *West Indies Ltd.* and in a number of subsequent works, he denounced injustice 30 years before Castro's arrival, in a rotation of African rhythms that revolutionized the Castilian tongue. During the Revolution, he was named director of the Union of Cuban Writers and Artists, and he continued with politically committed literary work until his death. Here is an extract from *Tengo*, a poem dealing with the achievements of the Revolution:

I have, just wait and see,
the joy of walking a country that is mine,
master therein and I abide
with things so close that were denied
before in every way to me.
Harvest I can say,
fields I can say,
city I can say,
army I can say,
now mine and yours forever,
a brilliance ever ours,
a brilliance of stars,
lightning and flowers.

(Translated by Richard J. Carr)

Alejo Carpentier (1904-1980) is the greatest Cuban novelist of the century and one of the masters of Latin American literature. *The Century of Lights*, *The Kingdom of This World* and *Lost Steps* are universal works that speak of the hazards facing Caribbean societies. Inspired as much by African as by European cultures, Carpentier displays an exemplary degree of erudition in his novels, that only adds to the pleasure of reading them. More than anyone else, Carpentier managed to exhibit his social criticism with brio and to evoke Afro-Cuban beliefs without sinking into exoticism.

José Lezama Lima (1910-1976), a contemporary of Carpentier's, joined the tight circle of the greatest Latin American writers with his novel *Paradiso*, the chronicle of the romantic and poetic awakening of a young man in Havana. With its incursions into the violence, innocence and sexual deviations of early 20th-century Cuba, *Paradiso* is a colossal and difficult work that should be approached slowly but surely. Lezama Lima took an active part in the literary circles of his era and founded the magazine *Orígenes*.

Among contemporary Cuban writers living in exile, one that stands out is Guillermo Cabrera Infante.

Painting and Sculpture

The colonial period offers works portraying Cuban landscapes and drawings showing daily life. In the 18th century, José Nicolás de Escalera was regarded as the first Cuban painter, while Vicente Escobar became the best known artist of his period as official painter to the captains-general. According to legend, Escobar was Goya's protégé during his visit to Spain. The development of painting really got started early in the 20th century with the establishment of the Association of Painters and Sculptors in 1910. René Portocarrero and Wilfredo Lam are the most renowned of 20th-century Cuban painters. Lam was close to Pablo Picasso and was part of the surrealist movement along with André Breton and Paul Éluard. His master work, *Selva* (Jungle), is displayed at the Museum of

Modern Art in New York. His work as a whole explores Afro-Cuban culture and esthetics. During the 1970s, the canvases of Raúl Martínez, with a pop art style inspired by Andy Warhol, explored the Revolution's popular imagination, especially the famous portrait of Che Guevara.

Cigars

*The following is by **Carlos Soldevila**, a Québecois journalist and one of the authors of this Cuba guide.*

Smoking a cigar is a purely sensual experience. Enjoying and producing the best cigars in the world is a real art, as is letting a fortune go up in smoke!

One does not smoke a Havana cigar the way one would smoke a simple cigarette. Like *champagne* and *cognac*, *habano* is a special designation for a product from a particular region, in this case for Cuban cigars. If the language of wine is French, the language of cigars is Spanish, although of course the Anglicized term Havana is widely used.

To smoke an *habano* is an art. During a visit to Havana, I spoke with Adriano Martínez, a representative of Cubatabaco, the Cuban cigar-exporting firm. I asked him about the best way to smoke a Montecristo Churchill No. 2, which I had just selected from among the cigars of various brands and sizes that he offered me. Wearing a *guayabera*, the long, baggy white shirt that is traditional in Cuba, and with a malleable and slightly cracked face, almost like a tobacco leaf, Martínez responded in a totally serious tone. "I believe in human freedom. Everyone can smoke a cigar as he pleases. You can't dictate to people how to make love."

With the mildness of the smoke in the mouth and the tip of a moist cigar on the lips, smoking an *habano* is highly sensual. The curious old Cubatabaco representative explained several basic rules for increasing the pleasure of smoking an *habano*. Of course, you have to cut off the tip of the cigar to allow air to flow. To light a cigar, Martínez advises against using a gas lighter or wax-coated matches. He recommends traditional lighters or wooden matches. "On the other hand," he pointed out, "the ritual way to do it is to light it with a cedar splint, since *habanos* are packaged in cedar boxes. This wood and its characteristic aroma add to the flavour of good cigars."

Some smokers like to warm the cigar beforehand by passing the flame of a lighter or match over its entire length. To light the cigar, others like placing it at a 45-degree angle above the flame and, without puffing on it, turning the cigar slowly in one hand until it is lit.

"There is a great tradition in Cuba that involves dipping the tip of a cigar in strong, sweetened coffee or in cognac. These are all suggestive, sensory things." Captivated by Martínez's remarks, and engrossed in jotting them in my notebook, I forgot to smoke my cigar which, unfortunately, went out. The ever paternalistic Martínez decided to go a little further with the upbringing of a young, inexperienced smoker who was asking so many questions. "An *habano* should be treated like a woman. If you don't look after it, if you don't caress it regularly with your mouth, the flame goes out. The cigar of a good smoker does not go out." And you say Cubans are *macho*?

PORTRAIT

From Winston Churchill to John F. Kennedy

Forbidden early in the Spanish colonial period "because cigars were the work of the devil," they were adulated by figures as famous as Winston Churchill, whose name is used on the large-sized cigars he appreciated. The Onassis family made a fortune on cigars, while others saw their fortunes go up in smoke. Did you know that just a few days before announcing his decision to impose an economic blockade on Cuba, John. F. Kennedy ordered hundreds of boxes of Havana cigars? I have also been told that Arnold Schwarzenegger, during a 1994 visit to Havana, made quite an impression on the employees of the Partagas cigar factory and supposedly received several proposals of marriage from female workers.

Adulated by their *aficionados* but hated by many people because of their odour, cigars are a leisure tool for the wealthy. A box of 25 Cohiba Lanceros, the *nec plus ultra* of Havana cigars, sells for more than $400. Some people actually dare to order unique, made-to-measure cigars. With more than 30 brands and 600 selections once the size is factored in, there is certainly no lack of choice.

A gift of the gods or the work of the devil? No doubt a cigar is a little of each, aided by the sunshine and the skills of the growers and craftsmen who produce them by hand. Since my meeting with Martínez, I admire the perfection of an *habano* just as enthusiastically, with the outer leaf that gives it its beauty and the brown tones of the approximately 50 inner leaves. But I no longer smoke them as before. I treat an *habano* with the same regard that a woman deserves, and I make sure the flame never goes out.

PRACTICAL INFORMATION

ontrary to popular wisdom, it is easy to travel throughout Cuba, whether alone or with a group. It is best to be well prepared, however, to make the most of your stay; this chapter is intended to help travellers plan and organise their trip. You'll find general information as well as practical advice to help familiarize you with the Cuban way of doing things.

ENTRANCE FORMALITIES

Make sure you bring all the necessary papers to enter and exit the country. Though requirements are not very strict, certain documents are required to travel in Cuba, so keep these papers are in a safe place.

Passport

To travel in Cuba, visitors must have a passport in their possession at all times. The passport must be valid for the full length of the stay. American travellers are allowed to travel in Cuba and must have a valid passport to do so. See the section for American travellers below.

It is a good idea to keep a photocopy of the key pages of your passport, and to write down your passport number and its expiry date. This will make it much easier to replace your passport in the eventuality that it is lost or stolen. If this should occur, contact your country's consulate or embassy (see addresses below) to have a new one issued.

Tourist Card

In Canada, the tourist permit (*trajeta de turista*) is included in the price of vacation packages. If you pay only the airfare to Cuba, you must pay an additional $15 U.S. for a tourist permit. If you are arriving from another country, consult your travel agent about purchasing this permit.

Cuban regulations require you to have reserved a hotel room for at least two nights upon your arrival. If you do not do this, the immigration officers may delay your entry and even choose a hotel room for you, regardless of the price. If you have not already made a hotel reservation or if you are staying with a family, write the name of a well-known hotel on your tourist permit. This can save you a lot hassle.

American Travellers

American travellers are allowed to visit Cuba, and are usually treated well by authorities and the population in general. There are, however, no flights from the United States to Cuba; visitors must therefore purchase their tickets and make a stopover in Mexico or Canada. Americans who have been in Cuba may have difficulty returning to the United States. For this reason Cuban customs officers will not stamp your passport if you don't want them to. There is a disadvantage, however; U.S. consular authorities will not be able to help you while you're in Cuba. You will have to visit either the Canadian or Mexican embassy.

Departure Tax

Each person leaving Cuba must pay a departure tax of $15 US. The tax is collected at the airport when you check in for your return flight. Remember to keep this amount in cash, as credit cards are not accepted.

Customs

Visitors may enter the country with up to one litre of alcohol, 200 cigarettes and up to $100 US worth of goods (not counting personal belongings). Bringing in illegal drugs and firearms is of course prohibited.

EMBASSIES AND CONSULATES

Embassies and consulates can be an invaluable source of help to visitors who find themselves in trouble. For example, consulates can provide names of doctors or lawyers in the case of death or serious injury. However, only urgent cases are handled. It should also be noted that any cost resulting from these services is not absorbed by the consulates.

Diplomatic Missions in Cuba

Belgium
Avenida 5 no. 7408 at the corner of Calle 76, Miramar, ☎24-2410 or 24-2561.

Canada
Calle 30 no. 518 at the corner of Avenida 7, Miramar, ☎24-2517.

Germany
Calle B no. 652, Esq. A 13, Vedado, ☎33-2539 or 33-2569, ⊶33-1586

Great Britain
Calle 34 no. 708, between Calles 7 and 17, Miramar, ☎24-1771 or 24-1772.

Italy
Calle Paseo no. 606, between Calle 25 and 27, Vedado, ☎33-3334 or 33-3356.

Netherlands
Calle 8 no. 307, between Avenida 3 and 5, Miramar, ☎24-2511 or 24-2512.

Spain
Calle Cárcel no. 51, at the corner of Calle Zulueta, Habana Vieja, ☎33-8025 or 33-8026.

Switzerland
Avenida 5 no. 2005, Miramar, ☎24-2611 or 24-2729

Calzada between Calle L and M, Vedado, ☎30-0551 or 33-3550.

United States
There is a "US Interest Office" at the Swiss Embassy.

Cuban Embassies and Consulates Abroad

These offices emit the necessary visas, for business trips for example and also usually house a tourist office of sorts in order to assist travellers in the preparation of their trip to Cuba. Staff here answer questions and give out brochures.

Canada
Cuban Embassy, 388 Main St., Ottawa, Ontario, K1S 1E3, ☎(613) 563-0141, ≈(613) 563-0068

Cuban Consulate
1415 avenue des Pins Ouest, Montréal, Québec, H3B 1B2, ☎(514) 843-8897

Cuban Consulate
5353 Dundas W., Kipling Square, Suite 401, M9B 6H8, ☎(416) 234-8181, ≈(416) 234-2754

Cuban Tourist Office
440 boulevard Réné-Lévesque Ouest, Bureau 1402, Montéal, Québec, H2Z 1V7, ☎(514) 875-8004, ≈(514) 875-8006

Belgium
Cuban Embassy, 77 rue Robert-Jones, 1180 Bruxelles, ☎343-0020, ≈344-9691

Great Britain
Cuban Consulate, 15 Grape St., London, WC1V 6P4, ☎240-2488

Italy
Cuban Embassy, Via Licinia, 7, 00153 Roma, ☎396-575-5984, ≈396-574-5445

Spain
Cuban Embassy, Paseo de la Habana, 194, between Calle de la Mcarena and Rodrigues Binilla, Madrid, ☎341-359-2500, ≈341-359-6385

Switzerland
Cuban Embassy, Seminarstr 29, 3006 Berne, ☎4131-302-2115, ≈4131-302-2111

United States
Cuban Interest Section, 2630 16th Street NW, Washington, D.C., 20009 ☎(202) 797-8518 or 797-8609, ≈(202) 797-8521 or 986-7283

PRACTICAL INFORMATION

TOURIST OFFICES

Canada

Toronto: 55 Queen St. E. #705, Toronto, ON, M5C 1R6, ☎(416) 362-0700, ≈(416) 362-6799.

Montréal: 440 Boul. René Levesque Ouest, #1402, Montreal, QC, H2Z 1U7, ☎(514) 875-8004.

Italy

Via G. Fara, 30, 20124 Milano, ☎39 2 66981463, ⇌39 2 6690042.

ENTERING THE COUNTRY

Several companies offer packages including airfare on a charter flight, accommodation and dining. The advantage of these "all-inclusive" deals is that you have nothing to worry about once you arrive in Cuba. These packages generally place visitors in tourist villages like Varadero, Cayo Coco, Guardalavaca, Playa Girón, Playa Santa Lucia, Isla de la Juventud, Cayo Largo or Santiago de Cuba. Check with your travel agent to find out what packages are available.

It is also easy to head off with just an airline ticket and to find accommodation on your own in one of the numerous hotels all over the island once you arrive. The advantage of this type of travel is that you will see much more of the island and can choose where to stay each day. Except during peak travel times (Christmas vacation and Easter week), you should not have any trouble finding accommodation without reservations, either in out-of-the-way Cuban villages (if you don't require the utmost in comfort) or in the popular resort towns. Various airline companies offer flights to Cuba: Cubana de Aviación, Air Transat and Royal Airlines fly out of Montreal, Cubana de Aviación also offers flights from Paris. British Airways and Viasa offer flights to Cuba via Caracas. It is impossible to reach Cuba from the United States. U.S. travellers can however enter the country from Mexico, Central America, the Caribbean, South America or Canada.

The majority of flights land in Varadero or Havana; charter flights land in Santiago de Cuba, Ciego de Ávila and Holguín.

Independent travellers, who are becoming more and more numerous in Cuba, can save significant amounts of money by organizing their trip with a Cuban wholesaler before leaving. Your hotel and car rental will be much less expensive if you reserve ahead of time. Three wholesalers in Havana can make the necessary arrangements, no matter what your plans.

Cubatur: Calle 23, at the corner of Calle L. Vedado, ☎32-6507.

Cubamar: Calle 15 no. 752, at the corner of Avenida Paseo, ☎30-5536.

Havanatur: Calle 2 no. 17, Miramar, ☎24-2273.

By Plane

There are several international airports in Cuba, in Havana, Santiago de Cuba and Varadero. The other airports only receive small aircraft and charter flights.

Airports

The airports in Havana, Santiago de Cuba and Varadero are sizeable, full-service airports. They do not, however have a good selection of boutiques, and not surprisingly, the shopping is more expensive here than it is in the cities. All the big airports in the country have taxis that can bring travellers to the surrounding cities. The taxis are metered, so there is no price negotiation, even for long distances. Generally there are no buses at the airports,

Table of distances (in kilometres)

	Baracoa	Camagüey	Cienfuegos	Guantánamo	Holguín	Havana	Matanzas	Pinar del Río	Sancti Spíritus	Santa Clara
Camagüey	431									
Cienfuegos	873	327								
Guantánamo	115	431	758							
Holguín	224	207	534	224						
Havana	1080	534	251	965	741					
Matanzas	1018	272	200	903	679	102				
Pinar del Río	1240	694	411	1125	901	160	262			
Sancti Spíritus	728	182	145	613	389	352	290	512		
Santa Clara	808	262	65	693	469	272	210	432	80	
Varadero	1020	474	202	905	681	144	42	304	292	212

Example: the distance between Pinar del Río and Cienfuegos is 411 km except those chartered by wholesalers for travellers with reservations.

All of the car rental companies have small counters at the airports, so you can rent a car as soon as you arrive. They are all located one next to the other, so be sure to compare rates.

Aeropuerto Internacional José-Martí
Located 15 kilometres from Havana, ☎33-5177 to 79.

Aeropuerto Juan Gualberto Gómez
Located 26 kilometres southwest of Varadero, ☎53-616.

Aeropuerto Máximo Gómez
Located east of downtown Ciego de Ávila, ☎3-2525 or 4-3695.

Aeropuerto Internacional Antonio Maceo
Located five kilometres south of Santiago de Cuba, ☎9-1014 or 9-1865.

INSURANCE

Cancellation Insurance

Your travel agent will usually offer you cancellation insurance when you buy your airline ticket or vacation package. This insurance allows you to be reimbursed for the ticket or package deal if your trip must be cancelled due to serious illness or death. Healthy people are unlikely to need this protection, which is therefore only of relative use.

Theft Insurance

Most residential insurance policies protect some of your goods from theft, even if the theft occurs in a foreign country. To make a claim, you must fill out a police report. Usually the cover-

age for a theft abroad is 10% of your total coverage. It may not be necessary to take out further insurance, depending on the amount covered by your current policy. As policies vary considerably, you are advised to check with your insurance company. European visitors should take out baggage insurance.

Life Insurance

Several airline companies offer a life insurance plan included in the price of the airplane ticket. However, many travellers already have this type of insurance and do not require additional coverage.

Health Insurance

This is the most useful kind of insurance for travellers, and should be purchased before your departure. Your insurance plan should be as complete as possible because health care costs add up quickly, even in Cuba. When buying insurance, make sure it covers all types of medical costs, such as hospitalization, nursing services and doctor's fees. Make sure your limit is high enough, as these expenses can be costly. A repatriation clause is also vital in case the required care is not available on site. Furthermore, since you may have to pay immediately, check your policy to see what provisions it includes in such a situation. To avoid any problems during your vacation, always keep proof of your insurance policy on you.

HEALTH

Cuba is a wonderful place to explore, and you can do so without having to worry about tropical diseases since

Typical Cuban houses on Plaza de la Catedral, Havana. - *Jean Terroux*

Havana's Palacio Presidencial - *Tibor Bognar*

In search of sun
and relaxation at
Havana's Plaza
de la Catedral.
- Tibor Bognar

:rip to Cuba
wouldn't be
complete
hout a stroll
ng Havana's
malecón.
Denis Drolet

Havana's large cathedral square attracts visitors for its beautiful religious architecture. - *Tibor Bognar*

most of these illnesses, including malaria, typhoid, diphtheria, tetanus, polio and hepatitis A have been eradicated from the country. No vaccinations are required to enter the country. It is nevertheless a good idea to visit a traveller's clinic before leaving for advice on what precautions to take.

Illnesses

Diphtheria and Tetanus

Most people have been vaccinated against these potentially serious diseases as children. Before leaving home, however, make sure you were in fact inoculated; a booster shot may be needed. Diphtheria is a bacterial infection that is spread by secretions from the nose and throat or skin lesions of infected persons. Its symptoms include sore throat, high fever, lethargy and, on occasion, skin infections. Tetanus is also caused by a bacteria. Infection occurs when a cut in the skin comes in contact with contaminated matter (dirt or dust).

Ciguatera

This illness is caused by the ingestion of ciguatoxin, a toxin found in contaminated fish (infected by feeding on seaweed growing on coral reefs). Among the fish that become contaminated are the red snapper (*huachinango* in Spanish) and grouper. The toxin is tasteless and odourless and resists cooking. The only way to avoid it, therefore, is not to eat these fish. Symptoms can appear quickly, sometimes only minutes after ingesting the toxin, or up to 30 hours later. They include nausea, vomiting and diarrhoea, as well as neurological symptoms like muscular aches, fatigue and an inability to tell hot from cold.

There is no cure for this illness, but the symptoms can be treated.

Other Illnesses

Cases of Hepatitis B, AIDS and certain venereal diseases have been reported in Cuba, in particular in the touristy areas, it is therefore wise to take the necessary precautions.

Bodies of fresh water are frequently contaminated by the bacteria that causes schistosomiasis. This illness, caused by a worm-like parasite that enters the body and attacks the liver and nervous system, is difficult to treat. Swimming in fresh water should thus be avoided.

Remember that consuming too much alcohol, particularly when accompanied by prolonged exposure to the sun, can cause severe dehydration.

Despite a lack of financial resources, Cuban medical facilities are on a par with North American and European standards. Medical clinics outside the big cities may appear modest, but they usually have all the necessary equipment. Medical care is free for Cubans; foreigners, however, must pay for these services in U.S. dollars. In tourist areas, there is usually an English-speaking doctor. Before a blood transfusion, be sure (when possible) that quality control tests have been carried out on the blood.

The quality of Cuba's tap-water is generally quite good, and can be drunk throughout the country. However, to avoid possible upset stomach, drink bottled water. When buying bottled water, whether in a restaurant or store, always make sure that the bottle is properly sealed. Water is normally treated in the big hotels, but check with the staff first. Raw fruit and vegetables washed in tap water (those not peeled before eating) may cause the same symptoms.

If you do get diarrhoea, there are several ways to treat it. First, try to soothe your stomach by avoiding solids; instead, drink carbonated beverages, bottled water, or weak tea or coffee (avoid milk) until you recover. As the resulting dehydration can be dangerous, drinking sufficient quantities of liquid is crucial. To remedy severe dehydration, a solution containing a litre of water, two or three teaspoons of salt and one teaspoon of sugar will help re-establish the body's fluid balance. Pharmacies also sell ready-made preparations to help cure dehydration. Finally, gradually reintroduce solids to your system by eating easily digestible foods. Medication, such as Imodium or Pepto-Bismol, can help control intestinal discomfort. If more serious symptoms develop (high fever, intense diarrhoea), a visit to a doctor and antibiotics may be necessary.

Food and climate can also cause or aggravate various illnesses. Make sure that the food you eat is fresh (especially fish and meat) and that the food preparation area is clean. Proper hygiene, such as washing hands frequently, will help prevent you from catching something.

Walking around with bare feet is also to be avoided, as parasites and tiny insects can get into your skin and cause a variety of problems, including dermatitis and fungal infections.

Insects

Insects, which are numerous throughout the country, can be a real nuisance. They are particularly abundant during the rainy season. To avoid getting bitten or stung, cover up well, avoid bright-coloured clothing, do not wear perfume and use a good insect repellent, (minimum 35% DEET). Remember that insects are more active at sundown. When walking in the mountains or in wooded areas, wear socks and shoes that protect both feet and legs. It is also wise to bring some ointments to soothe the itching in case you do get bitten. Insect coils will allow you to enjoy more pleasant evenings on the terrace or in your room with the windows open.

The Sun

Despite its benefits, the sun causes several problems. Always bring a sunscreen (SPF 15 for adults and 25 for children) that protects against the sun's harmful rays, and apply it 20 to 30 minutes before exposure. Overexposure can cause sunstroke (fainting, vomiting, fever, etc.), especially the first few days, as your body is getting used to the change in temperature. It is important to cover up and avoid prolonged exposure while you get used to the sun. Sunglasses and a hat will also help protect against the harmful effects of the sun.

First-Aid Kit

A small first-aid kit can help you avoid many discomforts; prepare it carefully before leaving home. Ensure that you have enough of all your regular medications, as well as a valid prescription in case you lose this supply. It can be very difficult to find certain medications in smaller Cuban towns. Other medication, including anti-malaria pills and Imodium or Pepto-Bismol, should also be bought before leaving. In addition, bring adhesive bandages, scissors, aspirin, disinfectants, analgesics, antihistamines, an extra pair of glasses, contact lens solution, and pills for upset stomach.

CLIMATE

There are three seasons in Cuba: the cool season (from December to April), the rainy season (from May to August) and finally the hurricane season which affects the Gulf of Mexico coast from September to November. The cool season is the most pleasant, as the heat is less stifling, the rain less frequent and the humidity lower. Daytime temperatures hover between 21 and 25°C, with cooler nights. It is still feasible, however, to travel during the rainy season, when the showers are heavy but short. Rain is most frequent from May to mid-June. In the rainy season, the average temperature is 30°C. The number of hours of daylight remains fairly constant throughout the year.

Packing

The type of clothing required does not vary much from season to season. In general, loose-fitting, comfortable cotton or linen clothes are best. When exploring urban areas, wear closed shoes that cover the entire foot rather than sandals, as they will protect against cuts that could become infected. Bring a sweater or long-sleeved shirt for cool evenings, and rubber sandals (thongs or flip-flops) to wear at the beach and in the shower. During the rainy season, an umbrella is useful for staying dry during brief tropical showers. To visit certain attractions you must wear a skirt that covers the knees or long pants. For evenings out, you might need more formal clothes, as a number of places have dress codes. Finally, if you expect to go hiking in the mountains, bring along some good hiking boots and warmer clothes.

SAFETY AND SECURITY

Cuba is not a dangerous country, in fact it is one of the safest countries in the Caribbean. It has its share of thieves, however, particularly in the resort towns. Keep in mind that to the majority of people in the country, some of your possessions (things like cameras, leather suitcases, video cameras, and jewellery) represent a great deal of money, especially when you consider that the minimum monthly salary is 250 pesos ($20 US). A degree of caution will help you avoid problems. For example, do not wear too much jewellery, keep your electronic equipment in a nondescript shoulder bag slung across your chest, and avoid revealing the contents of your wallet when paying for something. Be doubly careful at night, and stay away from dark streets, especially if there are strangers lurking about.

A money belt can be used to conceal cash, traveller's cheques and your passport. If your bags should happen to be stolen, you will at least have the money and documents necessary to get by. Remember that the less attention you draw to yourself, the less chance you have of being robbed.

If you bring valuables to the beach, it is strongly recommended to keep a constant eye on them. It is best to keep your valuables in the small safes available at most hotels.

Prostitution

Prostitution, which is increasing as fast as tourism, has taken on new meaning in Cuba. Subtlety is the key

PRACTICAL INFORMATION

here — these men and women don't consider themselves prostitutes. In Cuba, prostitution is known as *"jineterismo"* and applies to young men and women who offer up their admiration to unsuspecting tourists in exchange for as much money and as many gifts as they can get. These very subtle characters act as gallant hosts to fool you. Unlike a prostitute, the ultimate goal of a *jinetero* or *jinetera* is to marry his or her conquest in order to leave the country. These people are generally not dangerous, though theft is common as soon as any personal objects belonging to an unsuspecting tourist are left unattended. *Jineteros* are easy to spot by their clothes: the women wear risque and chic clothing, while the men wear expensive sunglasses, jeans and baseball caps. They usually approach tourists and ask them the time (*que hora es?*) or their nationality.

Male prostitution has also risen considerably in Cuba. This is not regular male prostitution, but rather a means of extracting whatever they can from foreigners. A bit of innocent conversation, and you feel almost obliged to invite them out for the evening with you, pay their way into a bar and buy them a few drinks. Then comes the story of the poor family in need (a sick mother or father...), fabricated 90% of the time. Cubans have a strong sense of dignity, and true friends will rarely ask you to pay their admission fees to a nightclub, and certainly will not ask you to give them money to help their family.

TRANSPORTATION

Distances can be long in Cuba, especially since the roads, though generally in good condition, often go through small villages where drivers must slow down. Furthermore, very few roads have passing lanes. It is therefore important to plan your itinerary carefully.

By Plane

Flying is definitely the most efficient way of travelling long distances across the country; prices, which are in American dollars, are generally very affordable. Tickets can be purchased a few days in advance or even the day before in travel agencies or at the offices of **Cubana de Aviación**.

Aerotaxi charter company (*Calle 27 no. 102 between Calle M and N, Vedado, Havana, ☎33-4063*) also offers various daily flights to the major tourist destinations in the country. Aerotaxi's fleet consists of great biplanes. You can reserve single or double seats, or even rent a whole 12-seater for about $500 a day.

By Train

The train network serves most of the towns in the country. The train is a good way to get around Cuba, though it is slower than the bus. Delays are frequent, and sometimes the trains even leave early! Nevertheless, travelling by train can be a unique experience. Train tickets are easier to purchase than bus tickets since the sale of tickets in big cities is managed by a private company called Grupo Ladis. Prices are listed in American dollars and can usually be bought the day before your departure. Certain smaller towns, however, still sell tickets in pesos, which means they are much less expensive. Throughout the country, but particularly in Santiago de Cuba, there is a black market for train tickets. It is often the station masters themselves who sell these tickets, in U.S. dollars, for half the regular price, but still more than the price in pesos, which is generally reserved for Cubans.

There are several train categories in Cuba, but only tickets for the *trenes especiales* and *primera especial* are sold by the **Grupo Ladis** *(Calle Arsenal, at the corner of Calle Cienfuegos, Havana, ☎61-1770)* to foreign travellers. To get tickets on the *segunda* (second-class) train, you'll have to rely on shrewdness and luck, and hope that a Cuban friend will by your tickets for you. *Primera especial* and *especial* train cars are usually air conditioned.

Public Buses (*guagua*)

Public buses, called *guagua*s by the Cubans (pronounced "oua-oua"), travel along every type of road in Cuba and are an efficient way of getting around the island since fares are always in pesos. Purchasing tickets can however be a complex process, since in the big cities you must go through a reservation agency. But as the Cuban saying goes, *"todo se resuelve"* (there is a solution to everything)! The black market for bus tickets is often run by the administrators of the bus stations, and you only have to show some American money to get a spot on the bus fast. These buses stop frequently, and are often jam-packed and somewhat uncomfortable. On the positive side, this is the cheapest way to get around the island.

By Car

Renting a car is the most efficient way of seeing Cuba. Rental cars, mostly Japanese models, are generally in good condition. Rental rates vary between $40 and $70 per day, plus insurance ($15). You must be at least 25 years old to rent a car and carry a valid driver's license from your country. Choose a vehicle that is in good condition, preferably a new one. Most rental companies charge about the same rates. When you rent, it is a good idea to take out sufficient automobile insurance to cover all costs in case of an accident. Before signing any rental contract, make sure the methods of payment are clearly indicated; the limit on your credit card will have to be high enough to cover both the rental fees and the deductible in case of an accident. While some credit cards insure you automatically, still check if the coverage is complete.

Getting gas is no longer the headache it once was for tourists. **Cupet** service stations are now located throughout the country. Cupets are modern and sell gas in dollars for about 90¢ a litre. The catch is that most big cities have only one Cupet station. Be sure to find out where these stations are located before heading out. Havana does, however, have several Cupets, so filling up is easy. Gas is also available on the black market, but take note that this gas is often mixed with oil and can cause problems with the motor.

Driving and the Highway Code

In general, the main roads and highways are in good condition, though the odd pothole does crop up here and there. Furthermore, even though there are no shoulders, traffic still moves pretty fast; a small minority of Cubans actually own cars. Driving on the secondary roads is a whole other story, as several are littered with potholes of all sizes and traffic moves quite slowly. Drivers must be particularly careful when passing through villages where there are many pedestrians and cyclists. Road signs are rare in many places. If you get lost, therefore, the sole means of finding your way might be to ask local villagers, who are usually more than happy to help out.

Heavy traffic is rare on Cuban roads, except in Havana, where driving can get tricky, especially at peak hours when drivers and cyclists compete for space on the road. Elsewhere in the country, bicycles, carriages, tractors and pedestrians weave their way dangerously between the cars. The basic rules of the road sometimes seem to be ignored, though traffic generally moves quite slowly since what few cars there are usually date from the 1950s.

Due to the lack of signs and street lights on Cuban roads, driving at night is strongly discouraged. If your car breaks down you will be stranded.

Hitchhiking is a common practice in Cuba, since drivers of State-owned cars are obliged to car-pool. It is therefore safe to pick up hitchhikers.

Accidents

In the event of a road accident, the police will be called to the scene to assess the situation. If there are injuries or damages, witnesses automatically become "primary witnesses". It can take up to 48 hours before the case is resolved. This rarely happens, but should you find yourself in such a situation, stay calm and be patient.

Car Watchers

Throughout Cuba, youths will offer to wash or keep an eye on your car – for a small fee, of course. Sometimes they will even perform these services without being asked, and still expect to get paid. When it comes to car watchers, it is often best to pay a small sum even if you don't want their services. Expect to pay between 10 and 15 pesos (50¢

to 75¢) for an evening of car surveillance or a car wash. Of course, you'll have to pay up front.

The Police

Police officers are posted all along Cuban highways. In addition to stopping drivers who break traffic laws, they are authorized to pull over any car they wish and ask to see the identification papers of the driver. The police have been told not to harass tourists. Don't be alarmed if the police pull you over to check your papers. In general, they are approachable and ready to help if you have problems on the road.

Motorcycles and Scooters

In most resort areas it is possible to rent a motorcycle for $3 to $8 an hour. You will need to leave a deposit, such as your passport (or another valid piece of identification) and may need to show your driver's license. Drive carefully, since car drivers do not always watch for motorcycles. Always determine the price and payment conditions before leaving with your rental.

By Taxi

Taxi services are offered in every resort area and moderate-sized city. The cars are often in very good condition. In all cases, rates, which are in dollars only, are determined by a meter.

Collective Taxis

In a collective taxi, the cost of the trip is shared between all the passengers, even if their destinations vary. These taxis operate in the big cities only and can be identified by the sign reading

"Taxi" in the windshield. They are often in pretty bad condition, since most are old American vehicles from before 1959, they are nevertheless a picturesque way of getting about town. Much less expensive than taxis, the fare is paid in pesos not dollars. The cars do not have meters, so fares are at the discretion of the driver. Do not pay more than 20 pesos ($1) per person for a long trip in the city.

Particulares

Cuba's economic crisis has lead to an explosion of the black market in the transportation business. Several car-owners, many of them underpaid professionals, will offer city and intercity taxi service. More expensive than the bus, hiring one of these taxis is nevertheless cheaper than renting a car. Suggested prices, as well as where to find these cars (drivers will often approach you before you even have a chance to search them out), are indicated throughout this guide. Don't be afraid to bargin and keep in mind that drivers often try to charge tourists double or more than they would charge Cubans. Also be sure to compare this cost with renting a car.

In general, these cars are in poor condition, and you run the risk of spending your afternoon stranded by the side of the road instead of on the beach! Also be careful before putting luggage in the trunk. Because of the difficulty of getting gas, Cubans often carry some extra black-market gasoline in the trunk. To avoid soiling your personal belongings, always check the trunk before putting anything there.

Using *particulares*, the majority of which do not have permits, is illegal, though you are not in any danger. It is

the drivers who risk the heavy fine (1,500 pesos).

Hitchhiking

Cuba is a veritable paradise for *botella* (hitchhiking). Hitchhiking is virtually a mode of public transportation, and a large majority of Cubans do it every day to get to work. To solve transportation problems, carpooling has become indispensable and obligatory for drivers of State-owned cars, whose license plates read *"Estado"*. These drivers must stop for hitchhikers and ask which way they are going. The best way to stop these vehicles is to wait at intersections where there is an official in a yellow uniform. Commonly called *"amarillos"*, the officers will flag down State cars with empty seats.

Cars whose license plates read *particular* are privately owned. Drivers of these vehicles do occasionally stop for hitchhikers; tourists, however, will be asked for a couple of dollars for the trip. Negotiate a price before getting in.

Women hitchhike as much as men in Cuba.

MONEY AND BANKING

Money

Three types of currency are legal tender in Cuba: the peso, the convertible peso and the American dollar. The peso is the country's official currency. You will not need to exchange any of your money for pesos unless you are travelling for several weeks in the country's interior or are travelling alone, since the peso allows you to buy small amounts of anything, except produce at the *mercados agropecuarios* (non-existant

Exchange Rates					
$1 US	=	$1.46 CAN	$1 CAN	=	$0.68 US
$1 US	=	$1.51 AUS	$1 AUS	=	$0.66 US
$1 US	=	£0.61	£ 1	=	$1.61 US
$1 US	=	$0.93 EURO	1 EURO	=	$1.06 US
$1 US	=	1.83 DM	1 DM	=	$0.54 US
$1 US	=	1.50 SF	1 SF	=	$0.66 US
$1 US	=	37.82 BF	10 BF	=	$0.26 US
$1 US	=	155.98 PTA	100 PTA	=	$0.64 US
$1 US	=	1,815.20 ITL	1000 ITL	=	$0.55 US

in resort areas), public bus tickets for long and short journeys and trips in collective taxis. The American dollar has been legal tender since 1994 and it makes it much easier to buy anything. Hotels, restaurants, boutiques, as well as taxis, car rental companies, and airline and train companies only accept American dollars. Finally, distinct from the Cuban peso is the convertible peso, which has the same value as the American dollar, but only in Cuba. Before your departure, be sure to exchange your convertible pesos for American dollars, either at your hotel or at the airport.

Banks

Banks of the Banco Financiero Internacional network are open Monday to Friday, from 8:30am to 3pm. They can be found in all large and medium-sized cities. They all exchange U.S. dollars and other foreign currencies, usually at better rates than in the hotels. It is nevertheless a good idea to have some cash with you at all times.

Exchanging Money

Cadeca foreign-exchange offices are found in tourist areas. Their rates are usually the same as those of the banks, and they also cash traveller's cheques. You must present your passport for either transaction.

We recommend bringing a good many U.S. one-dollar bills to use as tips and even to get things moving in a difficult situation without it costing too much. All American money is green, so offer the smallest denomination!

Avoid bringing money in dominations larger than $50, because they can be difficult to use.

Traveller's Cheques

It is always best to keep most of your money in traveller's cheques, which are accepted in some restaurants, hotels and shops (only if they are in U.S. dollars). They are also easy to cash in banks and exchange offices as long as they were not issued by a U.S.-based bank. American Express cheques will be refused. Always keep a copy of the serial numbers of your cheques in a separate place; this way, if the cheques are lost, the company can replace them quickly and easily. Nevertheless, always carry some cash.

Credit Cards

Credit cards are accepted in some stores and restaurants, and in all hotels. Only Visa and MasterCard are accepted; American Express cards and all other cards issued by U.S. banks are systematically refused. The following cards are accepted at the Banco Financiero Internacional and in several hotels in the country, as long as they were not issued by a U.S. bank: Access, Banamex, Bancomer, Diners Club International, Eurocard, MasterCard, Carnet, Jcb, Visa.

MAIL AND TELECOMMUNICATIONS

Mail

There are post offices in every city, and some hotels offer postal services and sell stamps. Regardless of where you send your letter from, do not expect it to reach its destination quickly; the postal service in Cuba is not known for its efficiency. If you have something important to send, you are better off using a fax machine, available in most hotels. Stamps are sold in post offices and in some shops.

Telephone and Fax

International telephone calls can be made from the larger hotels or from the few large international telecommunication centres. It is impossible to make collect calls from hotels and telecommunications centres. The only way to make a collect call is from a private residence. Pre-paid phone cards are available throughout the country for $10 and $20, these can only be used in public phones adapted for this purpose.

Before buying one of these cards, ensure that one of these phones is located nearby.

The rates for calling overseas are quite high. To avoid any unpleasant surprises, take the time to ask the rate per minute before making your call.

The staff at the telecommunications centres will explain how to make overseas calls in Spanish, or if you are lucky, in broken English.

Internet

The spider is far from having spun its web on Cuban soil. Only the State has access to the Internet and other users must find clandestine networks if they really want to get on line.

At the **Capitolio** *(at Paseo Martí and Calle Brasil)* in Havana you can use the Internet for a monthly fee, but this option is strictly limited to those staying in the country for a long period of time for business purposes.

To date, travellers who wish to send and/or receive E-mail can only do so at a major hotel offering this service, for a considerable fee. Moreover, you will have to use the hotel's E-mail address and server, which means you cannot access your own E-mail address at home. Despite this, you can still use the hotel's E-mail to send and receive messages. Remember to bring the addresses of those to whom you wish to send sunny holiday greetings. To give you an idea of prices, this service costs $2 to send a message and $1 to receive a message at the **Hotel Nacional** (see p 103) *(at the Malecón and Calle 23, 6th floor, Oficina Ejecutiva, Havana).*

ACCOMMODATIONS

Hotels

There are three categories of hotels. The low-budget places, near the downtown areas, offer only the basics in comfort. The prices are usually listed in pesos, and the rooms are usually reserved for Cubans. It is not impossible for a foreigner to stay here, though many establishments will simply refuse to rent you a room. These rooms generally have a small bathroom and an overhead fan, and you are advised to bring your own sleeping bag or sheets, as cleanliness is not guaranteed. Medium-budget hotels typically offer simple air-conditioned rooms that are reasonably comfortable. These can usually be found in resort areas, and each large town has at least one of these establishments whose architecture varies little, as they were all constructed according to the same model after the Revolution. Rates are in U.S. dollars. Finally, there are the luxury hotels, found in resort towns, in Havana and in Santiago de Cuba, on exceptional properties. They all try to surpass each other in comfort and luxury. Several hotels in this last category belong to European and Canadian international hotel chains and offer packages where the price of the room includes two or three meals per day, all locally produced drinks and service charges.

Casas Particulares

Casas Particulares are legal throughout the country except in Varadero and on the islands of Cayo Largo or Cayo Coco. However, inhabitants who take in visitors must pay $100 a month to the government. Some Cubans choose to rent rooms illegally and specifically ask not to be mentioned in travel guides, thus avoiding problems with the government. When we last visited, all the *Casas Particulares* mentioned in this guide were paying for their monthly permits.

To find other places, especially those not listed because of their unauthorized situation, you have only to ask "*¿Conoce alguien que alquila cuartos?*" (Do you know someone who rents out rooms?) in shops or restaurants.

Youth Hostels

There are no youth hostels in Cuba. Those who are looking for inexpensive accommodations should look for a small hotel whose rates are in pesos or for a Bed and Breakfast.

Camping

Cuba has a little-known yet excellent network of campsites across the country. Created just a few months after the Revolution, the *bases de campsimo* are managed by the Communist Youth Movement and are available in pesos essentially to Cuban citizens. These campsites are rudimentary. **Cubamar** *(Calle 15 no. 752 at the corner of Avenida Paseo, Havana, ☎30-5536)*, a camping and tourism organization run by the Communist Youth Movement, offers its services to international tourists. However, even though Cubamar can arrange your transportation on the island as well as reserve *cabañas* on a campsite, remember that tourists will have to pay in U.S. dollars.

RESTAURANTS

Cuban Cuisine is often the object of most tourists' complaints about the country. Surprisingly for a Caribbean country, the cuisine is quite bland and lacks spice; so much so that some travellers even bring their own spices. Large establishments, however, have begun hiring European and Canadian chefs to prepare dishes that are more in keeping with foreigners' tastes, and the situation has improved considerably in recent years. There are a few restaurants specializing in Cuban or international cuisines, usually French or Italian, near the resort centres. Restaurants outside the touristy areas serve only local cuisine.

Service is usually friendly and attentive in both small and large restaurants.

Paladares

Paladares are little family-run restaurants, and are often the best places to eat in Cuba. These small enterprises have been legal for years, and their tasty fare rarely disappoints. Unlike larger dining establishments, *paladares* pride themselves in serving up delicious home-style cooking. Do not pay more than $10 per person. Usually, Creole cuisine is served.

Cuban Cuisine

Cuban cuisine is actually quite succulent. Pork is the meat of choice, and it is prepared in many different ways (baked, grilled and fried) and is often basted with *mojo*, a sauce with a base of oil, lemon and garlic. Rice, plantain and manioc accompany the meat. *Arroz moro* or *congrí* is a dish that is available in all good Creole restaurants; it consists of rice cooked with black and red beans, onions and spices. Surprisingly, Cubans do not eat much fish. Seafood, including rock lobster, is available in many restaurants.

Food Glossary

Agua	water
Ajo	garlic
Arroz	rice
Batido	beverage made of fruit, ice and milk
Camarone	shrimp
Carne	meat
Carne de res	beef
Cerveza	beer
Chichárron	marinated and cooked meat or chicken
Chivo	goat
Chuleta	cutlet
Conejo	rabbit
Empanadas	small turnovers stuffed with meat or vegetables
Filete	steak
Granadilla	grenadine
Huevo	egg
Jamón	ham
Jugo	juice
Langosta	crayfish
Leche	milk
Limón	lemon
Mariscos	seafood
Mermelada	jam
Naranja	orange
Pan	bread
Papas fritas	fried potatoes (French fries)
Pescado	fish
Piña	pineapple
Plátanos fritos	fried bananas
Pollo	chicken
Pollo frito	fried chicken
Postre	dessert
Queso	cheese
Sopa	soup
Tamarindo	tamarind
Tortilla	omelette
Tostada	toast
Vino	wine
Zanahoria	carrot

PRACTICAL INFORMATION

SHOPPING

It isn't for the shopping that people come to Cuba. There are few boutiques outside the touristy areas. However, each town does have a branch of the Fondo de Bienes Culturales, which offers a good selection of arts and crafts. These are referred to throughout the guide.

Opening Hours

Most stores are open from 9am to 5pm. Stores rarely close at lunchtime, especially in resort areas.

"Shoppings"

Called "shoppings" by the locals, these small grocery stores sell food, cosmetics, alcohol, cigarettes, rum and bottled water.

Mercados Agropecuarios

These farmers' markets sell fruits andvegetables as well as meats. Everything is sold in pesos.

Alcohol

Alcohol, most often rum and beer, is sold in all little grocery stores.

What to Bring Back

Rum is a must; it is both good (the best is definitely *Habana Club Añejo 7 años*) and inexpensive. Cigars are the other souvenir of choice. Different types and brands are available throughout the country, consider either Montecristo or Cohiba brand cigars. The black market for cigars is everywhere, and you will surely be approached by merchants in the street. Take note that these cigars are often not the real thing, even though they come in the right boxes and are sealed with an official label. Amateur smokers will not detect any difference and will save a few dollars. Aficianadoes, on the other hand, are better off sticking to the boutiques specializing in cigars, where they know they are buying real cigars that have been stored under the proper conditions. Local crafts are also interesting; you can find pretty wood sculptures and ceramic pots.

Duty-free Shops

There are duty-free shops in the airports. Most of the products sold are foreign. All purchases must be paid for in U.S. dollars.

TOUR GUIDES

You will likely be approached in tourist areas by Cubans speaking broken English, offering their services as tour guides. Some of them are quite capable and trustworthy, but many have little valuable information to share. Be careful. If you want to hire a guide, ask for proof of his or her qualifications. These guides not only do not work for free, but often charge a substantial fee. Before starting off on a guided tour, establish precisely what services you will be getting at what price, and pay only when the tour is over.

TIPPING

Good service is generally rewarded with a tip. In addition to the 10% service charge automatically added to the bill, a 10% to 15% tip should be left depending on the quality of the service.

HOLIDAYS

All banks and many businesses close on official holidays. Plan ahead by cashing traveller's cheques and doing last-minute souvenir shopping the day before. Things generally slow down during holidays.

January 1	New Year's Day
May 6	Labour Day
July 26	anniversary of the attack on the Cuartel Moncada
October 8	anniversary of the death of Che Guevara
October 10	anniversary of the beginning of the wars of independence of 1868

MISCELLANEOUS

Electricity

Like in North America, wall sockets take plugs with two flat pins and work on an alternating current of 110 volts (60 cycles). European visitors with electric appliances will therefore need both an adaptor and a converter.

Women Travellers

Women travelling alone should not encounter any problems. For the most part, people are friendly and not aggressive. Generally, men are respectful toward women, and harassment is uncommon, although Cuban males do have a tendency to flirt. Of course, a certain level of caution should be exer-

cised; for example, avoid walking around alone in poorly-lit areas at night.

Smokers

There are no restrictions with respect to smokers, Cuba being the cigar capital of the world. Some restaurants in big hotels have no-smoking sections.

Time Zone

Cuba is on Eastern Standard Time and therefore six hours behind continental Europe and five hours behind Great Britain.

Weights and Measures

Cuba uses the metric system.

Weights
1 pound (lb) = 454 grams (g)
1 kilogram (kg) = 2.2 pounds (lbs)

Linear Measure
1 inch = 2.54 centimetres (cm)
1 foot (ft) = 30 centimetres (cm)
1 mile = 1.6 kilometres (km)
1 kilometre (km) = 0.63 miles
1 metre (m) = 39.37 inches

Land Measure
1 acre = 0.4047 hectare
1 hectare = 2.471 acres

Volume Measure
1 U.S. gallon (gal) = 3.79 litres
1 U.S. gallon (gal) = 0.83 imperial gallon

Temperature
To convert °F into °C: subtract 32, divide by 9, multiply by 5
To convert °C into °F: multiply by 9, divide by 5, add 32.

PRACTICAL INFORMATION

OUTDOORS

Cuba's beaches and mountains are fast making the country a hot destination for outdoor tourism. Each year the 289 beaches attract an increasing number of visitors. Whether they border the waters of the Caribbean to the south, the Gulf of Mexico to the north or the Atlantic Ocean to the northeast, these white sand beaches are perfect for a wide range of outdoor activities. The vibrant variety of plant and animal life that gravitates around the stunning coral reefs delights scuba divers and snorkellers who flock to the country's many dive sites. Less well known, but still full of natural beauty and breathtaking scenery, is the country's interior. Mountain chains, covered by lush forest, or sparse vegetation, are protected in national parks which are ideal for hiking and horseback riding.

PARKS

Much of Cuba's natural beauty is protected by the island's national parks and UNESCO biosphere reserves. These parks, found in every corner of the country, protect distinct natural environments. More and more efforts are being made to allow visitors to discover these settings, but not all parks are easily accessible; Baconao park in the Sierra Maestra is only starting to welcome visitors and companies now organize excursions. Those parks located close to the resort areas are easy to reach, especially those in the province of Pinar del Río and in the Topes de Collantes region. These last parks have a few marked trails; nevertheless, visitors who head off to conquer these wild spaces should still be very careful.

OUTDOOR ACTIVITIES

 Swimming

Swimming is a favourite sport of Cubans in the summer and of visitors year-round, and what better place to take a dip than the biggest island in the Caribbean? The currents can be strong, though, so be careful. You are better off staying close to shore when the waves get high. Furthermore, never swim alone.

Those beaches frequented by tourists are well-maintained. Please respect these natural areas by not leaving any garbage behind.

A completely deserted beach is a rarity in Cuba. The good beaches are usually overrun with visitors, though they remain relatively quiet as there are few vendors, unlike other Caribbean destinations.

 Scuba Diving

Several diving centres provide visitors with the opportunity to explore the underwater world. Reefs are numerous, and there are diving centres on both the northern and southern coasts.

Certified divers can explore the secrets of the Cuban coastline to their heart's content. Others can still experience the underwater world, but must be accompanied by a qualified guide who will supervise their descent (to a depth of 5 m). There is little danger; however, be sure that the supervision is adequate. Some guides take more than one first-time diver down at once, although safety regulations stipulate that the guide accompany only one student at a time. Equipment can easily be rented

from the different centres along the coasts.

Scuba diving makes it possible to discover fascinating sights like coral reefs, schools of multi-coloured fish and amazing underwater plants. Don't forget that this ecosystem is fragile and special rules apply. All divers must respect a few basic **guidelines** in order to protect these natural sites: do not touch anything (especially sea urchins, as their long spikes can cause injury); do not take pieces of coral (it is much prettier in the water than out, where it becomes discoloured); do not disturb any living creatures; do not hunt; do not feed the fish; be careful not to disturb anything with your flippers and, of course, do not litter. If you want a souvenir of your underwater experience, disposable underwater cameras are available.

 Snorkelling

It doesn't take much to snorkel: a mask, a snorkel and some flippers. Anyone can enjoy this activity, which is a great way to develop an appreciation for the richness of the underwater world. Not far from several beaches, you can go snorkelling around coral reefs inhabited by various underwater species. Some companies organize snorkelling trips. Remember that the basic rules for protecting the underwater environment (see scuba diving section) must also be respected when snorkelling.

  Surfing and windsurfing

Some beaches in Cuba, especially those on the northern coast, are known for their great waves, though the majority are washed by much calmer waters. If you would like to try surfing or windsurfing, you can rent equipment at most of the hotels on the beaches of Varadero, Playa Santa Maria, Cayo Coco, Guardalavaca, Playa Santa Lucia and Santiago de Cuba. Some hotels also offer courses.

If you have never tried these sports, a few safety pointers should be followed before hitting the waves: choose a beach where the surf is not too rough; steer clear of swimmers; don't head too far out (don't hesitate to make a distress signal by waving your arms in the air if you need to) and wear shoes to avoid cutting your feet on the rocks.

 Sailing

Excursions aboard sailboats and yachts offer another enchanting way to explore the sea's sparkling waves. Some centres organize trips, while others rent sailboats to experienced sailors. You'll find a few addresses throughout the guide.

 Jet Skiing

These high-speed contraptions that fly across the water provide thrills for many travellers. Learning to drive them takes little time, but reasonable caution should be exercised in order to avoid accidents. If you are careening about, always give the right of way to slower, less easily manoeuvrable boats (windsurfers, pedal-boats), and watch out for swimmers and divers. These are often hard to spot, so keep your eyes peeled and stay away from the shore.

 Fishing

Deep-sea Fishing

Deep-sea fishing enthusiasts will be pleased to note that several places offer fishing excursions, including trips out of Havana and Varadero. Whether you are interested in big fish (like marlin, for example) or smaller ones will determine how far from the island you go. These trips usually last about 3 hours and are quite expensive. Whether or not you come home with the big one or not, it is pleasant simply to be out on the water.

Freshwater Fishing

Cuba has many lakes where fishing is possible. Less expensive than deep-sea fishing, this type of angling is much more popular with beginners, especially Europeans.

 Hunting

Small game abounds in the few *cotos de caza* (hunting lands) established throughout the country, particularly in the area extending from the centre to the east. The necessary equipment and permits are quite expensive, however.

 Hiking

Hiking and walking are undoubtedly the most accessible activities. However, parks with well-marked trails are hard to find, so anyone heading off to explore must be well prepared. A few trails near the resort towns are worth a quick visit; just be sure to bring along everything you might need during your outing.

OUTDOORS

There are a few things to keep in mind when hiking. Before heading off on any trail, try to find out its length and level of difficulty. Remember that there are no maps available at the parks, and that if you should get lost, there are no rescue teams.

You will have to be well prepared and bring along anything you might need during your hike. The longer the hike, the better prepared you must be. First of all, bring a lot of water (you won't find any along the way) and sufficient food. Remember that the sun sets between 6pm and 7pm, and you can't do much hiking after dark, so plan to be back before then. Ideally, you should start out early in the morning; that way you can avoid hiking when the sun is at its hottest, and get back before the day is done.

Sunstroke

Some trails include long sections in the open, with no shade. The risk of sunstroke, which threatens anyone hiking in the tropics, is thus even higher. Cramps, goose bumps, nausea and loss of balance are the first signs of sunstroke. If these symptoms arise, the affected person needs immediate shade, water and ventilation.

To avoid this problem, always wear a hat and a good sunscreen. By getting an early start, you'll have time to hike in cooler temperatures.

Clothing

Appropriate clothing is one of the best ways to avoid the little inconveniences of the outdoors. Thus, remember to wear lightweight and light-coloured clothing; long pants to protect your legs from underbrush, thorny bushes and bug bites and thick-soled hiking

boots that are lightweight but solid, with good traction. Bring water- resistant clothing, as downpours are frequent, and don't forget your bathing suit if you plan on cooling off in one of the many waterfalls in the mountains.

What to Bring

To be prepared for any eventuality, it is a good idea to bring along a few necessities, including a pocketknife, antiseptic, bandages (both adhesive and non-adhesive), scissors, aspirin, sunscreen, insect repellent, food and above all enough water for the trip.

 ## Bicycling

The road system in Cuba is made up mostly of one-lane highways with no shoulders and secondary roads strewn with potholes. Not exactly a cyclist's dream. In addition, it gets very hot during the day, and the roads are not always shady. This said, cycling can still be a very pleasant way to see the countryside outside the large cities. Caution is advised, however, as people drive fast. Bicycles can be rented in most of the larger cities for a few dollars. If you plan on travelling long distances, bring along a few tools, since bike repair shops are few and far between.

 ## Horseback Riding

Horseback riding is another interesting way to see the country. In some parts of the island, the inhabitants use horses as their main form of transportation on the often narrow dirt roads. Many of the large hotels organize excursions in the interior on horseback.

HAVANA

Havana is the lively, dynamic capital of a country whose political and economic systems are unique in the Americas. With just over two million inhabitants, Havana is the very heart of Cuba where government buildings stand alongside the headquarters of major Cuban and foreign companies on the city's wide, palm-lined avenues. While it shares these traits with other big cities around the world, Havana has a rhythm all its own, halfway between the easy tempo of a sleepy tropical resort and the feverish pace of a metropolis like New York.

When we arrived in Cuba, the capital was mysteriously enveloped in darkness. Energy-saving measures had left certain neighbourhoods without electricity, and the city slowly revealed itself in countless shades of blue. Havana passed before our eyes like a movie set: decaying colonial buildings, couples lounging beneath palm trees and others simply hanging about, waiting for who knows what. Up ahead, the taxi's glaring headlights revealed the silhouettes of hundreds of cyclists zigzagging their way down the middle of the road. It suddenly struck us that we were in a different place, and there, huddled deep in our seats, we knew that we would be swept away by the sensual and subtly decadent offhandedness of Havana. I guess you could call it love at first sight. . .

Havana is no ordinary tropical city, one of those places that make you feel like you're looking at a postcard. It has depth and character (don't expect to learn all its ins and outs overnight), emanates mystery from every nook and cranny and is a past master in the art of seduction.

Havana is a victim of all the clichés spawned by our image of socialist countries, and many people still think of it as a closed city where people can't move about freely, a sort of tropical Moscow, a grey metropolis in the sun. Well, for the record, Havana is the complete opposite of Siberia! Cubans did indeed share the same political and economic systems as their Soviet counterparts, but with completely different results. Cubans never stopped dancing the rumba, the mambo and the salsa. And you can roam about Havana as freely as any other city in the world; what's more, you can do so to a lively pace.

Right next to a dilapidated sign vaunting the merits of socialism, *Cuba si, Imperialismo Yankee no* (Yes to Cuba, No to Yankee Imperialism), there are now brand-new advertisements for Benetton and Labatt Black ICE beer. Havana is changing; the U.S. dollar dictates the laws, and Habaneros have returned to commercialism as if 37 years of socialism were simply a minor historical digression. With *divisas* (currency), an ingenious euphemism for *dolares americanos* (some people jokingly say *dolores*, meaning "pains"), you can purchase anything you want in Havana; some underpaid professionals abandon their jobs to sell crafts, open *paladars* (family restaurants) or work under the table as taxi drivers. Lured by the dollar, more and more women casually offer their charms to tourists under the not-so-watchful eye of obsolete authorities. These *jineteras* (escorts) gallantly offer to escort foreigners, then, with that subtle and langorous Cuban joie de vivre, proceed to wheedle every last dollar out of them. Broken hearts are a dime a dozen in Havana.

The Old World Meets the New

Whatever may be happening in Havana now, the city is first and foremost a living museum of nearly four centuries of Spanish domination. Founded in 1514 by Panfilio de Narváez by the orders of Diego Velázquez, it has been declared a UNESCO World Heritage Site, for Old Havana boasts a rich architectural legacy. This international recognition says a lot about this historic city, which was the jewel of the Spanish colonies. In those days, it was a mandatory stop for all Spanish galleons transporting silver and gold from all the country's colonies to Europe, and it was from here that the Spanish set off to conquer America.

A seaport and commercial centre, Havana was also an important market for African slaves, who were sold off to merchants from Central America. The city's growing wealth attracted pirates, who attacked the capital on numerous occasions. The most famous assaults were launched by the French pirate Jacques de Sores in 1555 and English navigator Francis Drake in 1589, although the latter was unsuccessful. To thwart these undesirables, the Spanish built the Castillo de la Fuerza and the Castillo de los Tres Reyes del Morro, one on either side of the Bahía de La Habana. These fortresses gave the port an air of invulnerability, further promoting the city's economic growth.

Ever since, the Cuban capital has been at the centre of all major developments in the country's turbulent history, from the wars of independence in the previous century to the Revolution of 1959. As a first-hand witness to these events, it has a unique cultural and historical legacy. It is here, in the shadow of the thousands of columns that characterize Havana, earning it the nickname "City of Columns", that politicians have determined the history of the country.

From 1898 to 1902, Havana was ruled with a firm hand by the United States following the signing of the Treaty of

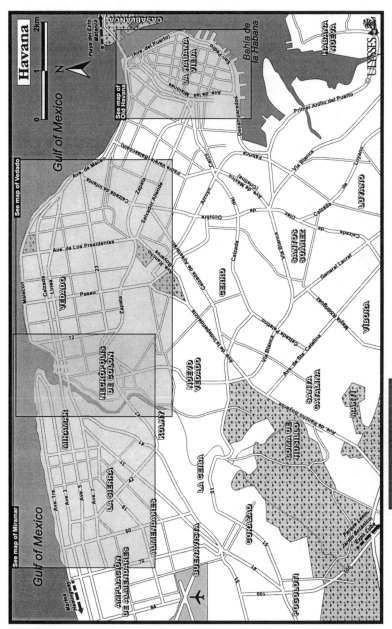

Paris by the Americans and the Spanish. The Republic, indirectly governed by Washington, saw its capital city change radically under the Americans' influence, which affected everything from local residents' lifestyle to the city's architecture. Habaneros still love pizza and Coca-Cola and gladly don the colours of professional sports teams from the United States. Some buildings serve as reminders of the 1940s and 1950s, when the capital was dominated by casinos, cabarets and nightclubs. In those years, it was known as the "Pearl" or "Monte Carlo" of the Caribbean; rum flowed like water in plush lounges, and American gangsters and mafiosi flocked here to gamble. Their favourite haunts — the Hilton (now the Habana Libre), the Hotel Riviera and its famous nightclub, the Hotel Capri and the Hotel Nacional — have lost none of their splendour and take visitors back to that controversial era in the city's history. American writer Ernest Hemingway and English author Graham Greene both drew inspiration from Havana during those years.

Of course, Havana is no longer what it was; Fidel Castro's ascension to power in 1959 and the establishment of a socialist system altered the habits of local residents. Smiling schoolchildren in red and white uniforms storm the city's many parks after class; the streets are filled with Ladas and Chinese-made bicycles; roosters socialize day and night, comfortably ensconced on the balconies of the numerous public housing units built by groups of volunteers; the lines are long at government food warehouses, and more and more communal gardens are springing up right in the middle of the city; a big mural of Che Guevara watches over the Plaza de la Revolución, and the Cuban Communist Party headquarters are decorated with the colours of the Revolution. All these things reflect the changes brought about by the only socialist system in the West and make this city unique in the Americas — though how much longer it will remain that way is anyone's guess.

For a city of its size, Havana is is surprisingly quiet. The 1989 collapse of the Soviet Union, which Cuba depended upon for 80% of its foreign trade, led to a local gas shortage, and automobiles have thus given way to bicycles. There is an irresistible charm about the sight of thousands of cyclists winding their way through the streets; one, two, three or even four people can be seen perched on the handles, seat and baggage rack of a single Chinese-made bike.

There is no question that Havana has everything a traveller could ask for: a rich architectural heritage, an intense cultural scene, friendly residents and all the inherent advantages of a tropical destination. You could easily spend anywhere from two to ten days in this city and still feel that you haven't uncovered all of its mysteries. Exploring Havana by bike or on foot is a sheer delight, and the more you get to know the city, the more unique it will seem to you.

 FINDING YOUR WAY AROUND

By Plane

Entrance Formalities

Foreign visitors to Cuba only need their passport and the tourist permit (*trajeta de turista*). In Canada, the tourist permit is included in the price of vacation packages. If you pay only the airfare to Cuba, you must pay an additional $15 U.S. for a tourist permit. If you are arriving from another country, consult your travel agent about purchasing this permit.

Cuban regulations require you to have reserved a hotel room for at least two nights upon your arrival. If you do not do this, the immigration officers may delay your entry and even choose a hotel room for you, regardless of the price. If you have not already made a hotel reservation or if you are staying with a family, write the name of a well-known hotel on your tourist permit. This can save you a lot hassle.

Transportation to the City

Taxis wait outside the various exits of the Aeropuerto José-Martí, located 15 kilometres from the city on Avenida Rancho Boyeros (☎45-3133). It will cost you between $15 and $20 to get downtown or to Old Havana. If you're on a tight budget, opt for the **Panataxi** company, whose rates are by far the lowest. Otherwise, you can wait for one of the public buses on Avenida Boyeros or simply stick out your thumb; hitchhiking is very common in Cuba. With a little luck, you'll get to ride in an old American car from the 1950s and you'll immediately find yourself immersed in the picturesque world of Havana.

International Flights

You will be charged a $20 departure tax when you check in at the airport for your return flight. This tax must be paid in cash.

Terminals: The Aeropuerto José-Martí has three terminals. The first two are located side by side in the same building. The third is used for Aerocaribbean and Aerotaxi flights to various tourist destinations, including Cayo Largo and Isla de la Juventud.

Domestic Flights

Flying is definitely the most efficient means of covering long distances in Cuba, and the fares are relatively affordable. There are a number of daily flights from Havana to other major towns. You can purchase your tickets several days in advance or even the day before at one of the travel agencies in the big hotels or at the **Cubana de Aviación** offices.

There are daily flights to **Santiago de Cuba** *($90-100 one way)*; one flight per day to **Holguín** *($82-88 one way)*; one flight per day and two on Wednesday to **Camagüey** *($72-76)*; one flight Monday, Thursday and on weekends to **Bayamo** *($82-88)*; one flight Monday and every other Sunday to **Manzanillo** *($82-88)*; one flight per day to **Guantánamo** *($100)*; one flight Monday, Friday and Sunday to **Baracoa** *($108-116)*; one flight Monday, Tuesday, Thursday and Friday to **Las Tunas** *($80-84)*; one flight Tuesday, Thursday, Saturday and Sunday to **Ciego de Avila** *($60-64)*; one flight Tuesday and Saturday to **Moa** *($100)* and two flights per day to **Gerona** *($22)*.

If you like adventure and prefer to do things your own way, a flight with **Aerotaxi** *(Calle 27 No. 102 between Calles M and N, Vedado, ☎33-4063)* should be right up your alley. Not only does this airline offer customized flights, operate charter planes on the surrounding islands and arrange skydiving trips, but a ride aboard one of their biplanes is an air adventure worthy of Humphrey Bogart!

Airlines

Aerocaribbean: Calle 23, at the corner of Calle P, Vedado, ☎33-4543, ☞33-5016.

Aerotaxi: Calle 27 No.102, at the corner of Calle N, Vedado, ☎32-8127, ✆32-8121.

Aeroflot: Mon to Fri 8:30am to 4pm; Sat 8am to noon; Calle 23 No. 64, ☎33-3200 or 33-3759, ✆33-3288.

Cubana de Aviación: Calle 2 No. 64, ☎33-4949, ✆33-4950.

Iberia: Mon to Fri 9am to 4pm, Sat 9am to noon; Calle 23 No. 74, ☎33-5041 or 33-5042, ✆33-2751.

KLM-Royal Dutch Airlines: Calle 23 No. 64, ☎33-3730, ✆33-3729.

LTU: Calle 23 No. 64, ☎33-3254 and 33-3525, ✆33-2789.

Mexicana: Calle 23 No. 74, ☎33-3531, 33-3532 or 33-3533, ✆33-3077.

TAAG: Calle 23 No. 64, at the corner of Infanta, ☎33-2527, ✆33-3049.

Viasa: Calle L, at the corner of Calle 23, Hotel Habana Libre Tryp, ☎33-3130, ✆33-3611.

By Train

There are daily departures from Havana to all the major towns in the country. Foreign tourists must purchase tickets in U.S. dollars from the company **Grupo Ladis** *(Estación de Trenes, Calle Arsenal and Cienfuegos)*, whose small offices are located not in the big central building of the train station, but about 100 metres away, near the railway tracks. You can usually purchase your tickets a day in advance and sometimes even the same day if you arrive a few hours before the train leaves. Credit cards are not accepted.

Havana-Matanzas: the trains running east sometimes take the Matanzas line. The most picturesque route, however, is with the old electric train (the only one in the country) that links the two cities along the Hershey line, which slowly winds its way through the north-coast countryside. Departures for the four-hour train ride are at 4am, 9am, 4pm and 9pm *($2)*. The train station is on the other side of the bay; it can be reached by taking the ferry from Old Havana to Casablanca.

Havana-Ciego de Avila-Camagüey-Las Tunas: the train to Las Tunas leaves at 1:25pm and costs $27. The train stops in Ciego de Avila *($18)* and Camagüey *($22)* along the way.

Havana-Cienfuegos: Departure: 10:40am. Travel time: seven hours. Fare: $10.

Havana-Sancti Spíritus: Departure: 9:20am. Travel time: eight hours. Fare: $14.

Havana-Manzanillo: Departure: 10:30pm. Travel time: 16 hours. Fare: $28.

Havana-Bayamo: Departure: 11:20pm. Travel time: 14 hours. Fare: $33.

Havana-Pinar del Rio: Departures: 2:43pm and 9:40pm. Travel time: seven hours. Fare: $5.

The **Havana-Guantánamo *Tren Especial No. 1*** leaves every day at 4:25pm. This train, the one most commonly used by foreign tourists, stops in the following towns: **Matanzas** *($4)*; **Santa Clara** *($12)*; **Guayos** *($15)*; **Ciego de Ávila** *($18)*; **Camagüey** *($22)*; **Las Tunas** *($27)*; **Holguín** *($31)*; **Santiago de Cuba** *($35)*, **Guantánamo** *($38)*.

By Bus

The **Estación de Omnibus Nacionales** (bus station) is located on Avenida Boyeros, near the Plaza de la Revolución. Services have recently been substantially reorganized and obtaining a ticket is not as tiresome as it was a few years ago. Moreover, the information counter is conveniently located right at the entrance, saving you time, and the knowledgeable staff there can give you good advice. Timetables are not clearly displayed though, so you will have to go to the companies' offices, along the corridor to the right of the entrance, and check departure times before purchasing your ticket. Be sure to buy your ticket a day in advance. Though there are sometimes seats available on the same day, going last-minute is risky. Regardless of whether or not you have a ticket, you will have to arrive at the station one hour prior to departure.

The **Víazul** *(Avenida 26 y Zoológico,* ☎*81-1413, 81-5652 or 81-1108,* ⌐*66-6092)* company has the most comfortable (air-conditioned) and regular buses in the country. It is necessary to reserve a day in advance and arrive an hour prior to departure. All departures leave from the **Estación de Omnibus Nacionales** on Avenida Boyeros, near the Plaza de la Revolución.

Havana-Varadero: departures for the three-hour trip are at 8am, 8:30am and 4pm. A one-way ticket costs $10.

Havana-Cienfuegos-Trinidad: one departure only, at 7:30am. Travel time is about six hours, with a stopover in Cienfuegos. The trip to Cienfuegos costs $20, and $25 to Trinidad.

Havana-Playa Girón: departure at 7:45am and arrival in Playa Girón at 4pm. The fare is $15.

Havana-Santiago de Cuba: reaching the nation's second biggest city involves enduring a 25-hour bus trip as well as numerous stops in the following cities: **Santa Clara** ($18), **Sancti Spíritus** ($23), **Ciego de Avila** ($27), **Camagüey** ($33), **Las Tunas** ($39), **Holguín** ($44), **Bayamo** ($44) and, finally, **Santiago de Cuba** ($51). Departures every day at 3pm.

Guantánamo: one departure only, at 3:15pm. A one-way ticket costs $46.

Baracoa: the bus that serves this city (closer to Port-au-Prince than Havana) leaves every second day at 10:45am. The fare is $53.

You can buy black market bus tickets by offering a few dollars to a station employee. These tickets are sold by station managers or through receptionists or parking attendants. It is best to go to the station on the eve of your departure. These illegal dealings are common practice, but if you decide to use this particular option, you do so at your own risk, of course.

The **Oficina de Reservaciones** *(Calle 21, at Calle 4, Vedado)* is still open. It is thus possible to obtain bus tickets here, though doing so is not recommended: the lines are endless and the place is badly organized. However, this office can be useful for those wishing to purchase tickets between inland cities and thus organize their trip in advance.

The little street beside the bus station is packed with independent taxi *(particulares)* drivers offering their services for long trips. The most common destinations are Trinidad or Pinar del Río. Never pay more than $25 for a trip to either place. Most drivers will ask for

HAVANA

$60 to $80, so be prepared to bargain if you don't want be had!

By Car

Driving

Driving in Havana is no more complicated than in any other big city in the world. You do, however, have to get used to sharing the streets with thousands of cyclists and remember that bicycles always have the right of way over cars. For example, if you are at an intersection and you have to turn right, wait until all the cyclists have passed; they will rarely stop to let you go by. Cyclists are unpredictable: they generally pay little heed to the rules of the road, so be careful, especially at night. They will often take up an entire lane of a large avenue, and even ride right in the middle of the road as if they had every right to be there. Always pay attention to what's happening around you and be prepared to react to any situation that might arise.

Parking

Parking spots are not hard to come by in Havana. In many places, self-appointed "parking attendants" wait by the side of the road. They will offer to wash your car and keep an eye on it during your absence. It is customary to give them some change when you return. Another option is to leave your car in the parking lot of a nearby hotel.

Car Rentals

A number of companies rent out cars at rates ranging from $50 to $70 per day. **Havanautos** *(Calle 36 No. 505, between Avenidas 5 and 5A, Miramar, ☎24-0647)* has branches in many ho-

tels in Havana, as well as at the Aeropuerto José-Martí *(☎42-2175)*. The company **Transautos** also has branches in many of the city's hotels and in terminals 1 and 2 at the airport *(☎33-5177 to 79)*.

Taking into account the growth of tourism and the rigidity of the Cuban economic system, there is frequently a shortage of cars to rent. To avoid inconveniences, it is often easier and more economical to rent a car when you buy your plane ticket.

Another interesting option, particularly if you do not go far from Havana, is to hire a car with a driver for the day *(about $20 to $30, see the "taxis particulares" section further below)*.

Public Transportation

By Bus

The Cuban tour operator Rumbos now runs a tour bus for visitors, the Vaivén. It makes a long circuit from the Palacio de las Convenciones to the Morro Cabaña, passing the Plaza de la Revolución and the Malecón.

For $4 you can buy a day pass and use the bus as much as you wish. It runs every day from morning until nine in the evening.

This bus aside, Havana's public bus service is a real nightmare.

There are no printed schedules or maps of bus routes. The best way to take the bus is to go to one of the numerous stops and tell someone waiting there where you're trying to go. Travelling during rush hour requires a lot of patience, and the long lines are sure to discourage even the most determined tourists from using this means of transportation. The bus is very cheap (one to three pesos), however, and if you spend a few days in Havana, you should try to take it at least once; it's a colourful experience. Known as *camellos* (camels), the long, overcrowded trailer trucks are a prefect example of the city's public transportation crisis. If you're game for rubbing shoulders with the local populace, go ahead and hop on!

By Taxi

There are many taxi companies to help you get around. **Panataxi** *(☎81-4444)* has a large fleet of Ladas and offers the best rates in town. Their taxis are rarely parked in front of hotels or other places frequented by tourists, however, so you'll have to telephone for one.

Turistaxi *(☎33-5539)* has the best cars, and its drivers usually park at hotel entrances. All tourist taxis have meters, and the rates are not negotiable, even for long trips. For example, there is no fixed rate for a trip from the airport to downtown Havana (usually about $15), or from Havana to Varadero.

Local Taxis

Since January 1996, scores of taxi permits have been issued in Havana, following the recent easing of restrictions on private and family enterprises. These cars roam the streets of Havana with a cardboard sign reading "taxi" in their windshield. The rates are determined by the driver, but you should never pay more than $1 for a trip within the city, or $5 per hour.

Particulares

Many underpaid Cuban professionals have abandoned their jobs to become black-market taxi drivers. They park in front of the most touristy places in town. You can use their services for just one trip or hire a driver for an entire day. These "taxis" are very useful, and are in great demand for trips outside of the city, since they can make an excursion to the beach much more affordable. To get to the Playas del Este (eastern beaches), for example, you can go to the Estación de Trenes (train station), where you'll find drivers ready to chauffeur you about. Cubans are usually charged between one and two dollars per person for a trip to the beach in Santa Maria. Ten dollars for a full car is the minimum a foreigner can hope to pay, however. If you are planning to spend the afternoon at the beach and would like the driver to wait for you, $15 is sufficient ($20 to $30 for the day). If you want to make an inexpensive trip outside the city, this is definitely your best option.

By Bicycle

The bicycle is the most pleasant and most common means of getting about Havana. You will feel the urge to hop on a bike the whole time you're here. The fastest way to rent a bicycle is to call **Panataxi** *(☎81-0153 or 81-4142)*, which will deliver one to you anywhere in Havana for $1. It will cost you $1 an hour, plus $1 more to have someone pick up the bike wherever you wish.

There are scores of bicycle parking lots, or *parqueos*, in Havana, and you'll have no trouble finding one near any place you visit. The rates vary between one and two pesos per bicycle, and you usually have to pay when you leave. Make sure to lock your bike when you leave it in a *parqueo*. As all the bikes look pretty much the same, the attendant will have a hard time knowing which one is yours. For identification purposes, you will likely be given two little numbered plates; attach one to your bike and keep the other one with

HAVANA

you. To pick up your bike, you need only show the two matching plates. These *parqueos* are a much safer alternative to leaving your bicycle on the street, even if it is locked. An unattended bicycle may well end up stripped of its wheels, pedals, handlebars and seat, since all of these parts are highly coveted in Havana.

Hitchhiking

Foreign visitors might be surprised to discover how common a practice hitchhiking is in Havana. In response to the city's transportation problems, car pooling has become popular and sometimes even mandatory. On some license plates, you'll see the word *Estado*. The drivers of these cars, which belong to State-owned companies, are required to stop for hitchhikers and ask them which way they're going—provided, of course, that there is room for them. If the driver is going in the same direction you are, hop in! The best way to stop these cars is to stand at an intersection monitored by an official in a yellow uniform. Commonly known as *amarillos*, these law enforcers flag down State-owned cars with empty seats.

Cars with the word *particular* on their license plates are privately owned. Some drivers will stop for hitchhikers, but will usually charge tourists a few dollars. Make sure to negotiate a fixed rate before getting in the car. A word of advice: offer the driver at least half what he asks for and never pay more than $5 for a trip inside city limits or more than $10 to go to the suburbs.

All in all, hitchhiking is an excellent way to get around Havana, and you're likely to make some interesting acquaintances at the same time. It is as common to see women hitchhiking as men.

PRACTICAL INFORMATION

Tourist Information

Infotur, the Havana tourist bureau, has an office at the airport, as well as in the old quarter of Havana *(Obispo 358)* and in Miramar *(5ta. Ave. Esq.A112)*. In addition to getting tourist information, you can also make reservations for excursions and buy bus tickets here.

Cubatur *(Calle F No.157, between Calle 9 and Calzada, Vedado, ☎33-4155, ≈33-3529)*. This agency specializes in group and private tours. **Havanatur** *(Calle 2 No. 17, between 1 and 2, Miramar; ☎33-2273, ≈33-2877)* offers more or less the same services.

Casa de la Amistad *(Paseo No. 646, between Calles 17 and 19, ☎33-3544, ≈33-3515)*. This old colonial residence houses a competitively priced hotel-reservation service for the whole country. You can also sign up for interesting cultural excursions here.

Tour Operators and Travel Agencies

Caribe Sol: Calle 2 No. 17, between Miramar No. 1 and 2, ☎24-2161.

Havanatur: Calle 2 No. 17, between Miramar between No. 1 and No. 3, ☎24-22161, ≈24-2877.

Hola Sun: Calle 2 No. 17, between Miramar No. 1 and No. 2, ☎24-2273, ≈24-2877.

Currency Exchange

Most hotels have a **Cadeca** currency exchange office. The rates are generally the same as at local banks. These places will also cash traveller's cheques. To carry out either of these transactions, you must show your passport.

Another option is to go to the **Banco Financiero Internacional** *(Mon to Fri 8:30am to 3pm; Linea No. 1, Vedado, ☎33-3423)*, although it's usually crowded so you'll have a wait. The Banco Financiero can also help you with any banking transactions you might need to take care of. You can also go to the **Banco Nacional de Cuba-Sucursal Internacional** *(Mon to Fri 8:30am to 1pm; Calle M, at the corner of Linea, Vedado, ☎33-4241).*

Post Offices

The most reliable way to send mail from Havana is to use the postal services in the big hotels; the one in the Habana Libre is open 24 hours a day. A few private companies provide efficient national and international service for priority mail: **DHL Mensajeria Mundial** *(Mon to Fri 9am to 6pm, Sat 9am to noon; Avenida 1, at the corner of 42, Miramar, ☎29-3318)*, **CUBAPOST** *(Mon to Fri 8am to 4pm, Sat 8am to 2pm; Avenida 5 No. 8210, at the corner of Calle 112, ☎33-0483)* and **CUBAPACKS** *(Mon to Fri 8:30am to noon and 1:30pm to 5:30pm; Calle 22 No. 4115, Kohly, ☎24-2134).*

The **Tele Correos** company provides telephone, fax and mail services. It is located at the airport and in certain tourist areas.

Internet

The spider is far from having spun its web on Cuban soil. Only the State has access to the Internet and other users must find clandestine networks if they really want to get on line.

At the **Capitolio** *(at Paseo Martí and Calle Brasil)*, it is possible to use the Internet for a monthly fee, but this option is strictly limited to those staying in the country for a long period of time for business purposes.

To date, travellers who wish to send and/or receive E-mail can only do so at a major hotel offering this service, for a considerable fee. Moreover, you will have to use the hotel's E-mail address and server, which means you cannot access your own E-mail account at home. Nevertheless, you can still use the hotel's E-mail to send and receive messages. Remember to bring the addresses of those to whom you wish to send sunny holiday greetings. To give you an idea of prices, this service costs $2 to send a message and $1 to receive a message at the **Hotel Nacional** (see p 103) *(at the Malecón and Calle 23, 6th floor, Oficina Ejecutiva).*

Medical Care

If you have the misfortune of falling ill during your stay in Havana, you need not worry, as the local hospitals generally provide fast, excellent care. The best hospitals and clinics are open to tourists. Payments are made in U.S. dollars; the medical centres have agreements with the major international insurance companies.

The biggest hospital in **Havana** is the **Hospital Hermanos Ameijeiras** *(Calle San Lázaro No. 701, between*

HAVANA

Calle Marqués González and Calle Belascoaín, Centro Habana, ☎70-7721 to 29 or 79-8531 to 39, ⌐33-5036).

In **Vedado: Hospital Comandante Manuel Fajardo** (Calle Zapata, at the corner of Calle D, Vedado, ☎33-8022 or 32-2477, ⌐33-3120).

In **Miramar: Clínica Central Cira García** (Calle 20 No. 4101, at the corner of 43, Miramar, ☎24-2811 to 144, ⌐24-1633).

Pharmacies

All the hospitals and clinics mentioned above offer pharmaceutical services. Although there is sometimes a shortage of drugs due to the American embargo and the country's economic problems, medical centres and large hotels can provide tourists with medication. You can also go to the **Farmacia Internacional** (Avenida 41, at the corner of Calle 20, Miramar, ☎24-2051).

Optician

Optica Miramar (Calle 4, corner of Calle 24, Miramar, ☎24-2990, ⌐24-2893) is an excellent optician's shop with a prime location in Miramar.

Safety

Havana is a relatively safe city. However, the increase in tourism and the economic crisis have led to a rise in crime. It is best to keep your personal belongings with you at all times and to be doubly careful in areas where tourists don't usually go. Pickpocketers have reportedly been targeting people on the Malecón and in the busiest parts of Old Havana. Fortunately, the police have started monitoring these areas much more carefully.

You will constantly be approached by people trying to sell you various products, exchange your dollars for pesos, or accompany you. Most of those in the tourist areas are "professionals", whose sole aim is to extract as much money from you as possible. At best, they'll try to get you to buy them a beer or two. These *jineteros* and *jineteras* (escorts) seem friendly at first, and are not usually dangerous. However, if you choose to trust them with your personal belongings unattended, even if only for a few moments, you can easily get robbed. The more stylish the person is (jeans, walkman, gold chains, brand-name sunglasses, etc.), the more likely it is you're dealing with a true "professional".

There is no magic solution for escaping quickly when someone like this approaches you. You can, however, try saying immediately: *No tengo guaniquiqui, amigo!* (I don't have any money, my friend). *Guaniquiqui* is a term made popular by a salsa, so you'll make the person smile while at the same time stating your position clearly. In any case, it is best not to give anything at all to people who come up to you; otherwise, you might end up surrounded by a whole mob. At most, carry a supply of candies or pens to give to children.

 EXPLORING

Havana is a sprawling city, and although each part of town has its own attractions, your explorations are likely to lead you to four main areas. The first is Old Havana, where people come to stroll, snap photos and delve into Cuban history and culture. Plaza de La Catedral, Plaza de Armas and Parque

Central are all extremely beautiful showcases of colonial architecture. Strongly influenced by Arabic culture, many visitors find this cluster of squares, turrets and narrow streets more reminiscent of Seville than a Caribbean city. The accent is on culture in Old Havana, and the streets are lined with museums and art galleries.

However, some of the colonial buildings are in an appalling state of abandon – the result of 37 years of socialism and, more importantly, the economic crisis in which Cuba has been mired since the collapse of the Soviet Union in 1989. For the past few years, the Cuban government, having rediscovered Havana's potential as a tourist draw, has made efforts to restore the city's historic centre. Certain parts of Old Havana have thus regained their former splendour; restoration aside, however, the entire area is full of life and bustling with artisans and second-hand booksellers who lend colour to its winding little streets, much to the pleasure of strolling passers-by.

You can enjoy the gentle ocean breeze by taking a leisurely stroll along the Malecón, the thick wall that runs along the edge of the city for nearly eight kilometres, separating Havana from the mighty sea. The Malecón is a popular meeting place for lovebirds, while little children, kites in hand, add life to the coastal landscape. Local residents come out in droves to watch the sun set over the ocean and savour the double pleasure of the beautiful twilight scene and the fresh evening breeze. It is, however, best to avoid coming here after dark, as a number of tourists have reportedly been hassled and robbed here of late. The Malecón was built in several stages. It was begun in 1898, when the Americans first occupied Havana. Walking along it today, you can admire several of the architectural styles that characterize the Cuban

capital. The Malecón provides access to all four areas covered in these pages. From Old Havana, it runs past the Vedado and Avenida Paseo, which will lead you straight to the Plaza de la Revolución. The west end of the Malecón ends at the edge of Miramar, at the Río Almendares.

The Vedado is a good place to explore by bicycle. This is where you'll find La Rampa, the avenue where most airline companies have their offices. Parque Coppelia, whose ice cream and terraces attract big crowds, is located at the corner of La Rampa and Calle L. A visit to the Universidad de La Habana is worth the climb up the long flight of stairs at its main entrance. Heading toward the Malecón, you'll discover some irresistibly charming turn-of-the-century houses, each one prettier than the last. The loveliest of these are now occupied by various cultural organizations, ministries and foreign companies, but the vast majority are still private homes.

Stepping onto the Plaza de la Revolución is like plunging headlong into the world of Cuban-style socialism. Shaped like a star, it has a tower in its centre, which rises up like an obelisk behind an enormous statue of José Martí. Facing onto the plaza are the headquarters of the Central Committee of the Cuban Communist Party, the Parliament and various ministries. Built under the rule of former dictator Fulgencio Batista, these big government buildings are now decorated with the colours of the Cuban Revolution and with a large fresco of Che Guevara facing that of José Martí. It is here that Fidel Castro delivers his lengthy speeches and that large-scale government celebrations are held.

Separated from the rest of the city by the Río Almendares, Miramar is the chicest neighbourhood in Havana. It

HAVANA

was once the domain of the Cuban upper class, and is graced with truly magnificent colonial-style houses. Avenidas 5 and 7, which run through Miramar, are lined with palm trees, and your gaze will naturally be drawn to its turn-of-the-century homes. The scores of little boats along the Río Almendares make the setting that much more picturesque.

There are a number of places to visit on the outskirts of Havana. The Hemingway Tour will take you to the writer's home in San Francisco de Paula, while the tour of the South includes the little village of Bejucal, the Jardín Botanico, EXPOCUBA and Parque Lenin, all of which are located in pleasant surroundings, almost in the countryside. The tour of the West leads to the drab port town of Mariel, then to one of the loveliest natural sites in the province of La Habana, on the border of the province of Pinar del Río. To the east, on the other end of the tunnel that runs under the Bahía de La Habana, the Guanabacoa area and the Playas del Este are perfect for daytrips.

Old Havana

Old Havana is a walker's paradise, and there really is no better way to explore it than on foot. The numerous outdoor cafés, bars and restaurants tucked away in the inner courtyards of old colonial houses make this the perfect place to escape the "rigours" of the tropical heat. Restored under the auspices of UNESCO, some of the streets and houses of Old Havana have regained their former beauty and colour. All sorts of little museums are tucked away here, mainly around Plaza de la Catedral, Plaza de Armas and Parque Central.

Catedral de La Havana

Plaza de la Catedral ★★★

Plaza de la Catedral, an attractive square usually overrun with tourists and vendors selling handicrafts, is a good place to start off a tour of Old Havana. It was the last square laid out inside the city walls in 1587, and wasn't given its present name until the 18th century, when the church facing onto it was designated a cathedral. This church, the **Catedral de La Havana ★★★** *(Calle Empedrado No.158)*, has one of the most beautiful baroque façades in all of Latin America. Begun by the Jesuits in 1748, it was completed in 1777, although this religious order was expelled in 1767.

Facing onto Plaza de la Catedral is a colonial house that now serves as the **Museo de Arte Colonial ★** *($2; Wed to Mon 10:15am to 5:45pm, Sun 9:15am to 12:45pm; Calle San Ignacio No.61, ☎62-6440)*. Built in 1720 for the governor of Cuba, Luis Chacón, the building is characteristic of houses of that era, with a central courtyard surrounded by galleries, arches and roofs made of carved wood. Founded in 1969, the museum contains a small collection of colonial-style furniture and decorative objects and a room devoted to means of transportation from this period.

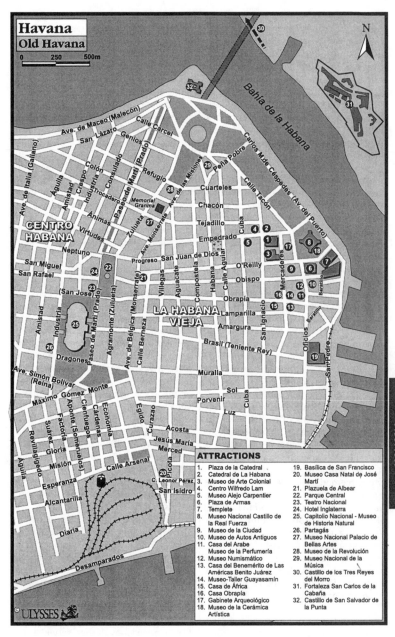

Havana
Old Havana

0   250   500m

Bahía de la Habana

N

ATTRACTIONS

1. Plaza de la Catedral
2. Catedral de La Habana
3. Museo de Arte Colonial
4. Centro Wilfredo Lam
5. Museo Alejo Carpentier
6. Plaza de Armas
7. Templete
8. Museo Nacional Castillo de la Real Fuerza
9. Museo de la Ciudad
10. Museo de Autos Antiguos
11. Casa del Arabe
    Museo de la Perfumería
12. Museo Numismático
13. Casa del Benemérito de Las Américas Benito Juárez
14. Museo-Taller Guayasamín
15. Casa de África
16. Casa Obrapía
17. Gabinete Arqueológico
18. Museo de la Cerámica Artística
19. Basílica de San Francisco
20. Museo Casa Natal de José Martí
21. Plazuela de Albear
22. Parque Central
23. Teatro Nacional
24. Hotel Inglaterra
25. Capitolio Nacional - Museo de Historia Natural
26. Partagás
27. Museo Nacional Palacio de Bellas Artes
28. Museo de la Revolución
29. Museo Nacional de la Música
30. Castillo de los Tres Reyes del Morro
31. Fortaleza San Carlos de la Cabaña
32. Castillo de San Salvador de la Punta

© ULYSSES

HAVANA

A magnificent colonial house dating from 1760 and formerly known as the Casa de los Condes de San Fernando de Peñalver, the **Centro Wilfredo Lam** ★★ *($1; Calle San Ignacio, at the corner of Calle Empedrado)* displays works by contemporary artists from Cuba and various Latin American countries. Of course, it also exhibits pieces by the internationally renowned Cuban painter and sculptor Wilfredo Lam (1902-1982).

Literature buffs should make sure to visit the house that helped inspire Cuban author Alejo Carpentier to write one of his major works, *Siglo de los Luces*. The **Museo Alejo Carpentier** *(free admission; 8:30am to 3:30pm; Calle Empedrado No. 215)* is very peaceful and sure to catch your fancy. Numerous original manuscripts by the author are on display, and there is a guide to accompany you on your tour. The museum also has a research centre and a library, where many Carpentier experts come to work.

Plaza de Armas ★★★

Second-hand booksellers vie to outdo each other in terms of enthusiasm and originality on **Plaza de Armas**, Havana's most attractive square, and surely the one with the richest history. First, there is the **Templete** ★ (Little Temple), which memorializes the official founding of the city in 1519 by Panfilio de Narváez, who was acting on the orders of Spanish conquistador Diego Velázquez. On November 16 each year, the first mass ever to have been celebrated in Havana is commemorated here. This historic moment is depicted inside in a fresco by French artist Jean-Baptiste Vermany.

Access to the Plaza de Armas from the Bahía de La Habana was once guarded by the oldest colonial fortress in the Americas, which is now the **Museo Nacional Castillo de la Real Fuerza** ★★ *($1; Thu to Mon 9:30am to 4:45pm; Calle O'Reilly, between Avenida del Puerto and Calle Tacón)*. Erected in 1577 to defend the city from repeated pirate attacks, it houses a large collection of ceramics, including lovely pieces by renowned Cuban sculptors Wilfredo Lam (1902-1982) and René Porto Carrero (1912-1985). Two galleries are used for exhibitions of contemporary art. The castle is very well preserved, and contains pieces of period armour, including a magnificent helmet made for a horse. The pleasant rooftop terrace offers a unique view of the Christ of Havana, on the other side of the bay, and of Old Havana in general. Furthermore, if you look at the northwest tower of the castle, you'll see *La Giraldilla*, the symbol of the city and the most famous Cuban sculpture, whose image is featured on the label of Havana Club rum. According to legend, the woman who inspired the sculpture, created by Geronimo Martínez Pinzón, was the wife of a captain who was often away at sea. Awaiting her husband's return, *La Giraldilla* gazes down at the ships entering the port of Havana.

The **Museo de la Ciudad** ★★★ *($3; Tue to Sat 10:30am to 5pm, Sun 9am to 1pm; Calle Tacón, between Calle Obispo and Calle O'Reilly, ☎61-2876)*, also on the Plaza de Armas, is devoted to the city of Havana, and is a must for all visitors to the Cuban capital. The building is the former Palacio de los Capitanes Generales of the Spanish army, which was the administrative centre of Cuba under the monarchy. It was here that the Treaty of Paris, which placed Cuba under American control, was signed in 1898. During the U.S. occupation (1898-1902), and until 1920, the palace was the seat of the Cuban presidency. It then served as the city hall until 1958. The palace's baroque architecture makes it one of the finest in Havana. Reigning over the inner courtyard is a statue of Christopher Columbus in Italian marble, which dates from 1862. It is surrounded by medicinal and aromatic herbs and stands in the shadow of two royal palms, the official emblem of Cuba. A historical and architectural treasure, this museum contains numerous works of art and colonial objects, all attractively displayed. No other museum of history on the island has a richer collection of objects from the 19th century wars of independence, so a guided tour is well worth your while. The Museo de la Ciudad also houses the offices of the official historian of Havana, Eusebio Leal.

Take **Calle Oficios**, which lies to the west of the Plaza de Armas and is presently being restored under the auspices of UNESCO. A number of little museums and other places of interest are located along it. The **Museo de Autos Antiguos** *($1; Tue to Sun 9am to 7pm; Calle Oficios, between Calle Obispo and Calle Obrapía)* displays a collection of vintage cars of considerable historical interest, including the first car to have arrived in Havana (a 1905 Cadillac) and Che Guevara's Chevrolet. You must purchase your ticket in the house across the street, at the **Casa del Arabe** *($1; Tue to Sun 9am to 6pm; Calle Officios No.12, between Calle Obispo and Calle Obrapía)*. Built in 1688 and perfectly maintained in its original state, the Casa del Arabe presents ethnological and cultural exhibitions on Arab and Muslim societies. Perfume lovers will want to stop in at the little **Museo de la Perfumería** *($1; Tue to Sun 9am to 6pm)*, located at the same address; it was undergoing renovations when I was there. The nearby **Museo Numismático** *(free admission; Tue to Sat 10am to 5pm; Sun 9am to 1pm; Calle Oficios No. 8, between Calle*

Obispo and Calle Obrapía, ☎61-5857) has a large collection of Cuban coins.

From Calle Oficios, turn right on **Calle Obrapía**, which is lined with charming houses. Most of these are now cultural centres for various Latin American nations and other countries around the world. Dedicated to Mexican culture and history, the **Casa del Benemérito de Las Américas Benito Juarez** *(free admission; Tue to Sun 9:30am to 5pm; Calle Obrapía No. 116, at the corner of Calle Mercaderes, ☎61-8166)* presents exhibitions on the popular crafts of Mexico.

The **Museo-Taller Guayasamín ★** *($1; Tue to Sat 10:30am to 5pm; Sun 9am to 1pm; Calle Obrapía No. 111, between Mercaderes and Oficios, ☎61-3843)*, across the street, is the Havana studio of celebrated Ecuadorian painter and sculptor Guayasamín (1919-). When the artist is absent, his workrooms and bedroom are open to the public. In addition to displaying a large number of Guayasamín's paintings, the museum hosts temporary exhibits of modern art.

Right nearby, the **Casa de Africa** *($2; Tue to Sat 10:30am to 12:30pm and 2pm to 4pm, Sun 10am to noon; Calle Obrapía No. 15, between Mercaderes and San Ignacio, ☎61-5798)* houses two large collections of objects related to the various Afro-Cuban religions. A number of its galleries are devoted exclusively to African culture. While you're in the neighbourhood, you can also stop by the historic **Casa de la Obrapía** *(free admission; Tue to Sat 10:30am to 4pm, Sun 9am to 1pm; Calle Obrapía No. 158, at the corner of Mercaderes, ☎61-3097)*, the former residence of Spanish captain Martín Calvo de la Puerta.

East of the Plaza de Armas is the **Gabinete Arqueológico** *($1; Tue to Sat 10am to 5pm, Sun 9am to noon; Calle*

HAVANA

Tacón No. 12, between Calle O'Reilly and Calle Empedrado, ☎61-4469), which displays a small collection of colonial artifacts. The **Museo de la Cerámica Artística** ($1; Thu to Mon 10am to 5pm; Calle O'Reilly, between Avenida del Puerto and Calle Tacón, ☎61-6130) is located right nearby.

If you head towards the port, where the tourist industry has been growing rapidly since a cruise ship dock was built in 1995, make sure to stop in at the **Basílica de San Francisco ★** ($2; 9:30am to 6:30pm). The concert hall has fantastic acoustics, and its museum displays some 18th-century silver coins found during recent archaeological excavations.

A little farther out of the way, near the train station, the birthplace of the greatest ideologist and hero of Cuban independence, José Martí, has been converted into the **Museo Casa Natal de José Martí** ($2; Tue to Sat 9am to 5pm, Sun 9am to 1pm; Calle Leonor No. 314 Pérez, between Calle Picota and Calle Egido, ☎61-3778). The various personal belongings on display bear witness to Martí's intense political and literary career.

From Calle Obispo to Parque Central

Calle Obispo ★★, one of the main pedestrian and commercial streets in Old Havana, links the Plaza de Armas to Parque Central. It is lined with shops, terraces and art galleries, as well as many solares, and is thus crowded with both tourists and locals. Typical of Havana, solares are big, rundown houses shared by several families. Feel free to venture into their yards for a glimpse of the daily goings-on of thousands of Habaneros.

If you follow Calle Obispo all the way west, you will end up at the charming **Plazuela de Albear**, which is surrounded by craft shops and opens onto Avenida de Belgica (or Monserrate), home of the **El Floridita** restaurant, one of Hemingway's favourite restaurants and the birthplace of the daiquiri which was Ernesto's favorite cocktail. **La Zaragozana**, another excellent restaurant (see p 110) is also located on Avenida de Belgica. The Plazuela de Albear is the last square in Old Havana and marks the entrance to Parque Central.

Parque Central ★★★ lies like a buffer zone between the tranquillity of the walls of Old Havana and the hustle and bustle of the modern city outside. Many locals come here to discuss pelota (baseball) or politics, and you're likely to encounter some of the most eccentric characters in town here. The park is lined with palm trees, and the first statue of José Martí to be erected in Cuba (1905) stands at its centre.

Parque Central is surrounded by the city's loveliest late 19th-century buildings. It stretches along the Paseo del Prado, also known as Avenida Martí, a wide avenue dating from the 18th century, with a centre lane for pedestrians. In the shade of the jagüeys you'll find a series of sculptures made with metal from the cannons that protected the city during the colonial era. It is worth stopping in at the **Teatro Nacional ★**, which faces the park and is commonly known as the **Teatro Garcia Lorca**, after the name of its main theatre. Also noteworthy is the **Hotel Inglaterra**, Havana's oldest hotel, built in 1875. Its history and neoclassical façade have earned it official status as a national monument.

Erected prior to the Revolution (1929) as the Senate and House of Representatives, the **Capitolio Nacional** is a colossal building recognizable by its dome. Inside stands the largest indoor bronze statue in the world. The building now houses the Academy of Science and the **Museo Nacional de Historia Natural** *($1; Fri to Wed 9:15am to 3:45pm; Thu 9:15am to 1:45pm; Calle Paseo del Prado, between Calle Dragones and Calle San José, ☎62-0353)*, which has the largest natural history collection in the country. Behind the Capitolio Nacional is the **Partagás cigar factory** ★★ *(Calle Industria No. 520)*, built in the late 19th century. Cigars are still hand-rolled here, and a tour of the facility is well worth your while.

The Museum District ★★★

Havana's major museums all lie within a quadrant bordered by Calle Montserrate and Avenida de Las Misiones. From the Plazuela de Albear, head along Calle Montserrate toward the bay to reach the **Museo Nacional de Bellas Artes** ★★★ *($3; Thu to Mon 10am to 5pm; Calle Trocadero, between Zulueta and Montserrate, ☎62-1643)*, the country's main museum of fine arts and an absolute must-see. It exhibits a large number of works by local artists, and houses the most extensive collection of Greek and Roman ceramics in Latin America. The colonial gallery is essentially devoted to 19th-century Cuban landscapes, and prints from the same era offer a glimpse of what the city looked like and how its inhabitants lived. A number of works from the 16th century are also on display. Make sure to take a look at the 18th-century prints by José Nicolas de Escalera, considered the first Cuban painter, and even more importantly, those by Vicente Escobar. The latter was the most celebrated artist of his time, for he was the official painter of the Captains-General, and painted local notables. According to legend, Vicente Escobar was Goya's protégé during his stay in Spain, although there are no documents to support that theory. The contemporary Cuban gallery is not to be missed. If you are interested in paintings produced since the *vanguardia* in 1920, your attention will surely be drawn to the works of Raúl Martinez. Adopting the pop art style inspired by Andy Warhol, Martinez searched the popular imagination of the Revolution for his images. The painting of Che and the principal figures of the Revolution (Castro, Maceo, Martí, Cienfuegos) is superb.

The museum is unfortunately closed for renovations. If all goes according to plan, it should reopen in early 2001.

If you walk down Avenida de Las Misiones, you can't miss the **Museo de la Revolución** ★★★ *($3; Tue to Sun 10am to 5pm; Calle Refugio No. 1, between Avenida de Las Misiones and Calle Zulueta, ☎62-4092)*. This museum was founded in honour of the civil war that brought Fidel Castro to power and displays various objects relevant to that period. Anyone with the slightest interest in the Cuban Revolution will find this place fascinating. There are all sorts of pictures and documents retracing the steps of the small group of revolutionaries who changed the course of Cuban history. The Museo de la Revolución occupies the former **Palacio Presidencial**, which was erected in 1917 and became the seat of the Cuban presidency in 1920. The building itself is extraordinary, and visitors with little interest in the Revolution might spend an hour or two simply admiring the architecture. The **Memorial Granma**, adjacent to the museum, displays the boat that carried the revolutionaries from the coast of Mexico to Cuba in 1956. Constructed in Mexico in 1943, the yacht has been classified as a national monument. The Granma Memorial is surrounded by warplanes and

HAVANA

Castillo de los Tres Reyes del Morro

trucks that were used during the Revolution and the Bay of Pigs invasion.

Musicians and music lovers can stop in at the **Museo Nacional de la Música** *($1; Tue to Sat 9am to 4:30pm, Sun 8am to noon; Calle Carce No. 1, between Calle Habana and Calle Aguiar, ☎61-9846)*, a museum dedicated to traditional Cuban musical instruments and the history of Cuban music from the 16th century to modern times. Unfortunately, the collection is not representative of the importance of music in Cuban culture.

Castillo del Morro ★★★

The largest Spanish military construction in the Americas stands on the east coast of the Bahía de La Habana. Seven hundred metres long and set on 10 hectares of land, the **Complejo Militar-historica Morro-Cabaña** *($3; every day, 10am to 8pm; ☎62-0353)* consists of three fortifications, two of which are open to the public. The most important one is the **Castillo de los Tres Reyes del Morro** *($2; every day, 9am to 6pm; ☎62-0353)*, erected in 1589 to protect the city from an invasion, although an engineer at the time asserted that whoever controlled the hill of La Cabaña, to the west of the Castillo de los Tres Reyes del Morro, would control the city. History proved him right, for it was from that hill, which had been left unfortified, that the English launched an attack on Havana in the 18th century and took possession of the city. In 1762, the **Fortaleza San Carlos de la Cabaña** was built on this strategic site at the entrance to the city. Political prisoners were incarcerated here under the Republic. On January 3, 1959, Che Guevara took over the fortress. He encountered no opposition, and remained here for three months, but had to leave because the damp air aggravated his asthma. Today, you can see his office in what is now the **Museo de la Comandancia del Che**. It is worth touring the entire military complex, for it contains several historical and military exhibitions, including a museum on the Cuban missile crisis, where you can examine a Soviet nuclear missile. These fortifications were used as a political prison both before and after the Revolution. Make sure to go to the castle in the evening to hear the 9pm cannon shot, which, in keeping with tradition, is fired by men dressed in the colours of the Spanish colonial army. On the other hand, the fortifications command an excellent view of Havana, and the best time to take pictures is early in the day.

The Vedado ★★

From the Malecón, turn onto **La Rampa**, the most dynamic street in Havana. At the bottom, you'll find the offices of various airline companies, the *Centro de prensa internacional*, a gathering place for journalists, and the offices of various news agencies, including *Prensa Latina*. If you turn right on Calle P, you'll come to the entrance of Havana's most beautiful hotel, the **Hotel Nacional ★★**. If you're looking for a peaceful atmosphere, the surrounding gardens are the perfect place to relax a bit.

Since 1994, an artisans' and second-hand booksellers' market has occupied a prime location halfway up the hill on La Rampa. Along with the numerous restaurants and nightclubs on this avenue, the **Hotel Habana Libre**, formerly the Hilton, is a vestige of the days when the Americans ruled the roost in Havana. Also at the intersection of La Rampa and Calle L, the Yara cinema shows all sorts of films at ridiculously low prices, and a small art gallery

serves as the lobby. On the other side of the street, Parque Coppelia is where *Habaneros* go to satisfy their sweet tooth. The ice cream here is so popular that line-ups are often hundreds of people long. A special entrance was recently set up for tourists, but you have to pay in U.S. currency. If you decide to continue along La Rampa, you'll find a whole series second-hand bookstores that run all the way to pleasant, palm-lined Avenida G.

Another option is to take Calle L, at the intersection of La Rampa, in front of the Hotel Habana Libre. This leads to the **Universidad de La Habana ★**, a cluster of neoclassical buildings erected at the beginning of the century on Plaza Ignacio Agramonte. There are two museums on campus. The **Museo Antropológico Montané** *($1; Mon to Fri 9am to noon and 1pm to 4pm; Edificio Felipe Poey, Plaza Ignacio Agramonte, Universidad de La Habana, ☎79-3488)*, one of the oldest museums in Cuba, is located behind some lovely indoor gardens. It houses the most extensive assortment of pre-Columbian artifacts in the country, including a collection of Taino art featuring coral sculptures and the Idol of Bayamo, the first piece of 17th-century indigenous art discovered. The Tobacco Idol, a wooden sculpture with shells for eyes, is definitely the most popular piece in this little museum. Natural history lovers can stop in at the **Museo de Historia Natural Felipe Poey** *($1; Mon to Fri 9am to noon and 1pm to 4pm)*, located in the courtyard of the same building.

The **Museo Napoleónico ★** *($1; Tue to Sat 10am to 5:30pm; Sun 9am to 12:30pm; Calle San Miguel No. 1159, at the corner of Ronda, ☎79-1460)*, housed in a Florentine-style palace, displays articles that once belonged to Napoleon Bonaparte. It is considered one of the most important museums of its kind in the world. What is the larg-

HAVANA

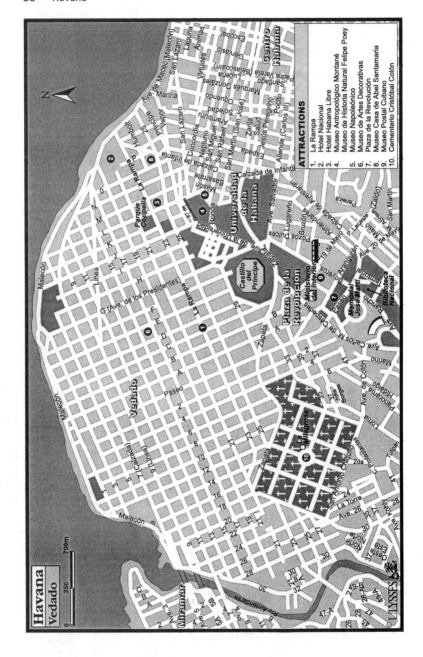

Havana
Vedado

0   350   700m

ATTRACTIONS

1. La Rampa
2. Hotel Nacional
3. Hotel Habana Libre
4. Museo Antropológico Montané
5. Museo de Historia Natural Felipe Poey
6. Museo Napoleónico
7. Museo de Artes Decorativas
8. Plaza de la Revolución
9. Museo Casa de Abel Santamaría
10. Museo Postal Cubano
    Cementerio Cristóbal Colón

© ULYSSES

est collection of Napoleon's belongings in the Americas doing in Havana? Multimillionaire Julio Lobo, the richest man in Cuba before the Revolution and a great admirer of Napoleon, purchased these pieces in Europe, mainly in France. They include a lamp Napoleon gave to Josephine, several pieces of furniture, porcelain figurines, bronzes, pistols, telescopes and various other objects used by the former Emperor of France. The multimillionaire's sumptuous home is worth a visit in itself, especially the fourth floor, with its lavish library containing over 4,000 books on Napoleon. Unfortunately, you cannot handle the books without obtaining special permission beforehand.

The country's most extensive collection of decorative arts is displayed at the **Museo de Artes Decorativas** *($1; Wed to Sun 9am to 4:45pm; Calle 17 No. 507, at the corner of Calle E, ☎30-9848)*, which occupies an early 20th-century house in the heart of the Vedado.

Plaza de la Revolución ★

Plaza de la Revolución (formerly known as Plaza Cívica) was laid out when Fulgencio Batista first came in power in the 1930s. The seat of power in Cuba now resides in this group of government buildings. Massive gatherings are held on this gigantic square, which can hold nearly a million people. The concerts and political events don't draw the same crowds as they used to, however, except at New Year's and when young and not so young gather for popular music concerts. The enormous statue of José Martí is 142 metres high; an exhibit is scheduled to open in the base soon, and plans are in the works to once again allow visitors to the top of the monument. The square is flanked to the east by the National

Plaza de la Revolución

Library, the Ministry of Defense and the head offices of *Granma*, the official newspaper of the Communist Party of Cuba; to the south by the austere Party headquarters, and to the north by the Ministry of the Interior, whose façade features an enormous portrait of Che Guevara.

The building where the young revolutionaries who attacked the Moncada Garrisons used to hold their meetings now houses the **Museo Casa de Abel Santamaría** *(Calle 25, at the corner of Calle O)*.

Opposite the bus station stands the uninviting Ministry of Communications. Inside, the **Museo Postal Cubano** *($1; Mon to Fri 9am to 4pm; Avenida Independencia and 19 de Mayo, ☎57-4021)* displays a large collection of old stamps and recounts the history of the Cuban mail service.

Cementerio Cristóbal Colón ★★★

Undoubtedly the loveliest cemetery in Cuba and one of the most famous in all of Latin America, the immense **Cementerio Cristóbal Colón** *(Calle 12, at the corner of Avenida 23)* was laid out in 1876. It contains over 800,000 graves, and many of the tombstones

are veritable works of art by such famous sculptors as Saavedra and Ramos Blancos. Take a bike ride or a walk through the cemetery to discover how truly magnificent it is. Don't be surprised to find little handcrafted dolls scattered on the ground near some of the tombstones; many locals carry out Afro-Cuban religious rituals here. The dolls and scraps of colourful cloth are *trabajos*, offerings made to various deities so that they will grant the supplicant's wishes.

Ask for directions to the grave of **La Milagrosa** (the Miraculous Woman), where many Catholics go to leave offerings or ask for blessings. According to legend, the woman in question died while she was pregnant and was buried while the fetus was still alive. The tomb was apparently opened, and the baby was found in its mother's arms.

Miramar ★★

Miramar is Havana's chicest neighbourhood. Many of the area's beautiful colonial-style houses were abandoned by Cubans who fled the country when Fidel Castro came to power in 1959. They have since become the homes of prominent members of the regime, or have been converted into embassies, local offices of foreign companies and some of the finest restaurants in Havana.

Parque Emilio Zapata, named after the famous Mexican revolutionary, lies on Avenida 5, at the corner of Calle 26, right at the end of the Malecón. It is graced with majestic *jagüeys*, distinguished by their aerial roots, which hang down like branches.

Avenida 1, which runs along the waterfront, is lined with dilapidated old houses. Both young and old gather by

the sea, and it is common to see Habaneros swimming or simply catching a few rays here. The area has not, however, been equipped with any facilities for swimmers. The surroundings are in ruins, for the loveliest houses and private pools were abandoned by wealthy homeowners after the triumphant success of the Revolution. This is a magical place with a certain air of decadence and freedom about it. The local youths show off their motorcycles and their American baseball caps, and you can't help wondering if they are enjoying the sunset or dreaming about the Florida coast, which lies only about 200 kilometres away...

Dotted with little fishing boats, the **Río Almendares** is truly picturesque. Its shores are liveliest around the **Puente de Hierro**. Cars are not allowed on this little steel drawbridge, which is used by thousands of cyclists to cross the Almandares. Vendors walk around selling meals, cakes and all sorts of items. There are a few small cafeterias in front of the Chinese restaurant El Mandarín (see p 112), on the Miramar side.

A large model of the city of Havana is displayed at **Rumbos** *($3; Tue to Sun; Avenida 3 between Calle 26 and Calle 28, ☎24-2661)*. Guides from the *Grupo de desarollo integral de la ciudad de La Habana* provide information on the scaled-down replica, which will be of particular interest to those interested in urban planning.

The Hemingway Tour ★★

A revolutionary by nature, the celebrated American writer and journalist Ernest Hemingway was never let down by this city, where he began vacationing in the 1930s and then set up residence in 1939. Hemingway left an

HAVANA

Deep-Sea Fishing

For many years, all the most seasoned travellers believed that venturing out onto the turquoise waters for a deep-sea fishing trip was an integral part of any visit to the Cuban capital. This tradition is still very much alive today. Cruising around the warm, transparent sea off the coast of Havana you might just come across a marlin, a tuna, a barracuda or even a shark.

Borobo, our skipper, and Guillermo, his assistant, invited us aboard their fast, lightweight boat at the **Marina Tarará**, near Cojimar, in the Playas del Este region. We had everything we needed: long fishing rods, sardines for bait and, of course, a bottle of rum. When it came time to do a little fishing, Borobo kept the boat at a steady speed and we let our lines out about ten metres, tracing a delicate trail on the turquoise waters behind us.

"This month [October], we've caught about 30 marlin – and it isn't even the right season!" His spirits bolstered by the rum, Borobo was enthusiastic, even though the best time to fish is early in the morning or late in the afternoon, and we had set out at midday. What's more, the best season for deep-sea fishing is from mid-June to September. You must think that we're already making excuses for ourselves, and you're right. We didn't manage to catch any marlin, which can weigh up to 200 kilos. We did, however, come home full of stories.

"I know a few secrets of the sea," our skipper said humbly. "The full moon has a powerful influence on the marlin and the swordfish. They eat more when the moon is full. Also, fish bite harder when the current is strong. Marlin and swordfish swim crossways, zigzagging. Every two or three hundred metres, they turn into the current so that the water won't go into their gills."

Deep-sea fishing is a battle between man and nature. It is not surprising, therefore, that Hemingway, a bullfighting fanatic, took up this sport of endurance. The struggle between man and fish can last anywhere from 25 minutes to an hour and a half. "The battle is not won by force," Borobo remarked wisely; "The strain should be on the rod, and when the fish pulls harder, you have to give it some slack. Then, as soon as it eases up a bit on the line, you have to pull it towards you."

Not everyone can afford to go deep-sea fishing. At the Marina Tarará, a day at sea costs between $185 to $350. Fishing tournaments are held here regularly, some of the more noteworthy being the Torneo de la Hispanidad (October 10-14), which commemorates Christohpher Columbus's arrival in Cuba, the Torneo Cuba-Canaria (mid-February) and the Torneo El Viejo y el Mar (July).

Deep-sea fishing trips can also be arranged at the **Marina Hemingway**.

indelible stamp on Havana, and many local bars, restaurants and hotels claim him as a former patron. Following in his footsteps requires a stop at **La Bodeguita del Medio** (see p 109) for a *mojito*, a cocktail made of rum, lime juice, sugar and freshly crushed mint leaves. Next, head over to **El Floridita** (see p 110) for a second drink, but this time make it a daiquiri, the house specialty, supposedly invented right on the premises. The *papa especial* is Hemingway's personal mix, made with a double shot of three-year-old rum, lemon and crushed ice. Ask for the menu; this is one of the best restaurants in town! At the end of the evening, take a walk into the heart of Havana, to the **Hostal Valencia**, and ask for room No. 21, Hemingway's favourite, here you can collapse on the bed and sleep off your cocktails, just like Hemingway used to do!

Die-hard Hemingway fans will want to head out to the Nobel Prize winner's sumptuous former residence, the **Finca la Vigia**, located about 15 kilometres from town. Built in 1887, it is now the **Museo Ernest Hemingway ★★** *($2; Mon and Wed to Sat 9am to 4:30pm, Sun 9am to 1pm, closed on rainy days; San Francisco de Paula, ☎91-0809)*, though little has been altered since the author died in the United States. It contains a large number of tastefully furnished, rustic rooms, a library with over 9,000 volumes, including original editions of a few of his novels and an assortment of his hunting trophies. Hemingway purchased this immense villa in 1940 after renting it for several months. Unfortunately, you can't actually go inside the house. However, the doors and windows are left wide open, so that visitors can peek in at the bar and look at various photographs, and retrace the life of one of America's most famous storytellers. A guided tour is essential to hear all sorts of anecdotes about Hemingway's fourth wife,

Mary Welch, who lived here with him and had a tower built where he could write (he never used it though; his typewriter is on a high table on the ground floor; a leg wound forced him to work standing up). The Hemingways had 57 cats, which are buried in their own cemetery on the grounds. The animals lived on the second floor of the tower, which commands a panoramic view of the San Francisco de Paula valleys and of Havana, outlined in the distance.

Right near the big swimming pool (no swimming permitted), you'll find *El Pilar*, Hemingway's fishing boat, made famous by his numerous fishing chronicles and the novel *The Old Man and the Sea*. Surrounded by luxuriant tropical vegetation made up of no fewer than 18 different species, Hemingway's home is perched on a magnificent hill in the suburb of **San Francisco de Paula**, 10 kilometres outside of Havana.

No Hemingway tour would be complete without a stop at the little port of **Cojimar ★**, where the famous author usually moored the *El Pilar*. Cojimar is located in the eastern beach area, about 10 kilometres from Havana. It is easily accessible by car via the tunnel under the Bahía de La Habana, then follow the signs right after the stadium built for the Pan-American Games, which will be on your left. It is worth visiting Cojimar, if only to stroll along its winding streets. There are pretty little houses all along the coast. The village fishermen erected a monument to Hemingway on the Malecón, in front of a small fortified tower. Follow the promenade to the excellent seafood restaurant **Las Terrazas**, one of Hemingway's favourite places to eat—a fact underscored by the many photographs on the walls. A few show Hemingway awarding Fidel Castro first prize in a fishing tournament. Unlike other places

HAVANA

in Havana with connections to Hemingway, at Las Terrazas, you will find someone who actually knew him. Gregorio Fuentes, the hero of *The Old Man and the Sea* and captain of *El Pilar*, is almost part of the furniture at this restaurant. He has been eating lunch and dinner here like clockwork for years. Although he is 98 years old, if you're lucky (and understand Spanish), he just might tell you a few anecdotes about Hemingway and in so doing will take the opportunity to denounce the American embargo. During our visit to Las Terrazas, Gregorio Fuentes wasn't there, but we did get to enjoy a succulent seafood paella while gazing out at the bay. After our meal, we walked past the old man's modest home *(Calle Pesuela No. 209, between Buena Vista and Carmen)*; and found him sitting on a chair in the street. Gregorio has a face that is reminiscent of the sea bed, a gritty complexion, pearly eyes and tousled hair. "Hemingway was a great man, a generous man with a big heart," he said to us by way of introduction. "In Cuba, Hemingway was happy." To flatter him, we told him jokingly that Hemingway might never have won the Nobel Prize in Literature without him, since he was the inspiration behind the novel *The Old Man and the Sea*. "He was a great writer, and I was just a skipper. *The Old Man and the Sea* is a true story."

Hemingway described meeting Gregorio in an article that appeared in *Holiday* in 1949. At the time, Gregorio Fuentes had been the captain aboard the *El Pilar* since 1938. He was 50 years old and had been sailing since the age of four. He got his start in Lanzarote, one of the tiny Canary Islands. Hemingway met Gregorio at Dry Tortuga in 1928, when the latter was the captain of a fishing boat. They both found themselves stranded on shore when a strong northeasterly wind blew up. Hemingway and his group boarded Gregorio's boat to get some onions. But when they tried to pay for them, Gregorio wouldn't let him, and offered them some rum to boot. Hemingway recalls thinking that Gregorio ran a very tight ship, the tightest he'd ever seen. Hemingway went on in the 1949 article to say that he was sure Gregorio would rather have had a freshly painted and freshly varnished boat than go fishing. But Hemingway was also sure that Gregorio would rather fish than eat and sleep anyday!

Gregorio doesn't appear to have changed since then. When we left, he told us he needed paint for his house. We promised to bring him some on our next trip. If you plan on paying him a visit, bring him a little gift; he'll appreciate it.

The **Marina Hemingway**, near Miramar, is a sailing harbour presently undergoing massive development to cater to the needs of tourists. There is already an assortment of shops and restaurants, and several hotels are being built. This is a good place to get away from the hubbub of the city; you can stroll along canals stretching nearly 15 kilometres, rent a small sailboat or a catamaran or relax on a pleasant terrace.

Touring the Province of La Habana

Aside from the capital itself, Cuba's smallest province has few attractions. There are only a few towns, most of which are industrial, although some of those to the south have a certain charm about them. If your goal is to visit picturesque areas, opt for the provinces of Pinar del Río and Matanzas instead of La Habana. Those planning a daytrip to Pinar del Río might want to take the short tour of the West described below. If you do, Playa Baracoa is a good place

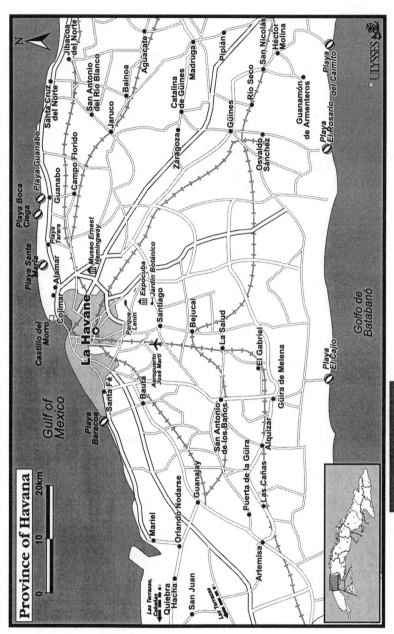

Province of Havana

to stop, and the small, little-travelled road to the province of Pinar del Río and the Soroa region is a real treat. The tour of the South will take you from the little town of Bejucal to Parque Lenin, the Jardín Botanico and EXPOCUBA.

The West

You can pick up the highway that leads to the town of Mariel by taking Avenida 5, in Miramar, then heading west on Avenida 7. This is not the fastest route to the province of Pinar del Río, but it does lead through some interesting landscape, and also allows you to make a loop rather than taking the same road there and back. This short highway leads past the small seaside resort of **Playa Baracoa** (not to be confused with the extraordinary town of Baracoa, in western Cuba). Although the place is somewhat shabby, the beach is nonetheless inviting and is not overrun with tourists, making it a good spot to soak up some peace and quiet, cool off a bit beneath the palm trees and enjoy the sea. The highway then leads west to **Mariel**, a dusty, grey industrial town that unexpectedly earned a place in Cuban history when thousands of Cuban refugees set out for Miami from its port in 1980. Washington and Cuba had reached an agreement sanctioning this massive exodus to Florida. At the same time, Cuban authorities shipped off a large number of convicted criminals to the United States. Unless you have a particular interest in this episode in history, there is no reason to stop in Mariel.

You do, however, have to pass through the town to get to the little road that leads to the village of **Cabañas**, where you will slowly start heading out of the industrial zone on your way to one of the loveliest parts of the province of

La Habana. From Cabañas, head left on the road to **Las Terrazas ★★**, located about 60 kilometres west of Havana. This is a strange-looking, relatively modern community whose Soviet-style concrete architecture thumbs its nose rather spectacularly at the mountainous terrain (see p 124). The little road winds through luxuriant vegetation. A profound lack of road signs means you'll surely have to ask for directions along the way. Going through **Soroa ★★**, you'll reach Highway A-4, which leads to the town of Pinar del Río or back to Havana.

The South

This daytrip south of Havana is a good way to visit some typical little Cuban towns and tour a couple of the country's parks. The trip is fairly long, and you might want pick out a few places to visit rather than spending the whole day on the road. If you like picturesque villages and prefer to relax in the shade of a tree and let your mind wander rather than hurrying about from one museum to the next amidst the hustle and bustle of a big town, make sure to stop at the sleepy hamlet of **Bejucal ★**, whose central square is an oasis of tranquility at noontime. Bejucal has no attractions per se, and resembles many other villages in Cuba. Nevertheless, the colonial buildings surrounding the square have a unique charm about them, especially the irresistible José-Martí cinema. The ambiance and friendly service, perhaps more than the food itself, make the **El Gallo** restaurant a necessary stop for lunch or drinks.

The next part of the tour covers two parks, the Jardín Botanico and Parque Lenin (see below). In front of the Jardín Botanico lies one of Fidel Castro's proudest achievements, **EXPOCUBA**

Havana's Gran Teatro is better known as the Teatro García Lorca because of the many statues of the hero that adorn its exterior. - *Tibor Bognar*

The lovely Art Deco-style Edificio Bacardi factory in Havana produces countless barrels of rum each year. - *Tibor Bognar*

Havana's old Castillo de la Real Fuerza slightly resembles a lighthouse.
- *Tibor Bognar*

The Castillo de los Tres Reyes del Morro keeps watch over Havana - *Tibor Bognar*

(Wed to Sun 9am to 6pm; Km 3 of the Carretera del Rocio, Calabazar), which hosts several exhibitions on the glories of the Cuban Revolution. You might also want to take this opportunity to visit Finca la Vigia, Hemingway's former home, which has been converted into a museum (see p 93). It is located two kilometres from the Jardín Botanico.

  PARKS AND BEACHES

La Habana is the smallest province in Cuba in terms of area, but it is also the most densely populated. As a result, it has no vast expanses of undeveloped land. For "natural" excursions, you are much better off going to the province of Pinar del Río, a veritable paradise for eco-tourism. La Habana does, however, have two parks where you can enjoy some recreational activities. **Parque Lenin** *($2; Tue to Sun 10am to 6pm; Calle 100 and Cortina de la Presa)*, located 25 kilometres outside the city, is a gigantic leisure centre. Built in 1972, it covers 750 hectares and includes a riding club, an amusement park, a sports complex, art galleries and an aquarium. Nothing has been left out at this giant playground, which used to be very popular with local residents. While you're in the area, you might want to stop for a meal at one of the province's finest restaurants, **Las Ruinas**.

The nearby **Jardín Botanico** ★★ *($3; every day 8am to 4:30pm; km 3.5 of the Carretera del Rosario)*, also about 25 kilometres from the city, is sure to be a hit with plant-lovers and those who enjoy wide open spaces. Covering an area of 600 hectares, the numerous gardens are linked by 35 kilometres of roads and are so vast that you'll want to use your car or climb aboard the little tractor-pulled train. The gardens contain a large collection of tropical and subtropical plants from all five continents. The Jardín Botanico is divided into three large sections, one for the various plant species and soils of Cuba, another for tropical and subtropical vegetation from Central America, the Antilles, Asia and the South Pacific and finally a series of greenhouses in three pavilions. The meticulously reproduced Japanese garden is one of the loveliest, graced with fountains and a waterfall, in front of which stands the Restaurante Ecológico (see p 113). Another restaurant, the Restaurante El Ranchón (see p 113), lies hidden in a forest of pine trees. A large research centre and the botany department of the Universidad de La Habana are also located on the grounds of the Jardín Botanico.

The Playas del Este (Eastern Beaches)

The most popular place to go day-tripping is the Playas del Este region located about 15 kilometres from the city. The roads linking the various beaches are in excellent condition and are fairly well marked on the whole. The simplest route is to take the road that leads from Old Havana through the Bahía de La Habana tunnel and then past the stadium built for the Pan-American Games. If you go this way, you'll be on the white sandy beaches of Santa Maria in less than 20 minutes.

You can also take a quieter and more picturesque road that runs past a number of villages and farmer's fields. To do so, take Avenida Máximo Gomez to Via Blanca. If you are only staying in Cuba for a week, this is the perfect chance to venture inland. This route takes half an hour to an hour longer than the one mentioned above, due to the traffic on the little country road. On the way through the outskirts of Ha-

HAVANA

vana, you might want to stop at the **Museo Municipal de Guanaboca** *($1; Mon and Wed through Sat, 10:30am to 6pm, Sun 9am to 1pm, Calle Martí No. 108, between Versalles and San Antonio, ☎90-9117)*, which displays all sorts of objects accumulated since the English took over Havana in 1762. The signs from Guanaboca are not very clear; take Avenida Independencia (also known as the **Carretera de Campo Florido**) to Campo Florido. When you reach the village of Campo Florido, head north (to the left) toward Guanabo on the Carretera de Justiz, and get ready to hit the beach.

There are some excellent beaches just a few kilometres from Havana. The most inviting one is definitely the **Santa Maria Beach ★**, an expanse of white sand that is every bit as lovely as the beaches of Varadero. The village itself is devoted essentially to tourism, and has many hotels. Also very beautiful, the beaches of **Boca Ciega ★**, the neighbouring village to the east, are overlooked by many tourists. Boca Ciega is a charming village of small vacation homes owned by *Habaneros*. Farther east is the village of **Guanabo ★**, which doesn't have the most attractive beaches in the area, but offers the widest range of waterfront activities. If you are staying in Havana, these beaches are worth a daytrip; in fact, they are so close that you can even come here for half a day.

 OUTDOOR ACTIVITIES

 Hiking

There aren't many places to go hiking in the province of La Habana, and the best two are located on the borders of the neighbouring provinces. In the West, you can go to **Las Terrazas** (see p 124), at the edge of the province of Pinar del Río, where a large number of trails have been cleared through the luxuriant vegetation. Some trails run past waterfalls, rivers and small lakes. For further information, stop by the Hotel La Moka in Las Terrazas (see p 130).

About 60 kilometres east of Havana, the **El Abra campground** has several mountain trails. Nestled between the sea and the mountains, El Agra is a perfect place to discover some of the region's plant and animal life. The local beach is superb, mainly because of its unspoiled setting. El Abra (see p 105) is also the starting point for excursions on the Río Canimar.

 ACCOMMODATIONS

Generally speaking, the hotels in Havana offer quality accommodations. The vast majority have rooms with air conditioning, hot water, private bath, colour television and a radio. The dining services usually leave something to be desired, however. Few hotels have menus that make eating all your meals there an inviting proposition.

Old Havana

The hotels in Old Havana have a colonial charm unique to this part of the city, and are well-suited to those who prefer walking to taking taxis.

Hotel New York *($15; sb, ⊛; Calle Dragones 156, ☎62-5260)*, a large building in the middle of downtown, right near the train station, is mainly frequented by Cubans passing through the capital. The decor is modest and the noise may disturb a fair share of guests. The rooms themselves could not be simpler, but at least each one of them has a fan. Moreover, the price is unbeatable. You may be refused access under the pretext that the hotel is reserved exclusively for Cubans. Bargain hunters will thus have the opportunity to test their powers of persuasion.

The **Hostal Valencia** *($46-50; ≈, ℜ, pb, ⊗; Calle Oficios No. 53, ☎62-3801, ≈33-5628)* lies 200 metres from the Plaza de Armas, in one of the loveliest sections of Old Havana. This small, 12-room hotel is extremely charming and authentic, and is sure to appeal to visitors with a romantic bent. Nowhere else is *el sabor cubano* more tangible! This 18th-century palace is built around an inner court, a pleasant place to relax, read, get your bearings or simply to meet some Cubans. The rooms are rustic and very clean, and the service is extremely friendly. The place is very popular, though, so try to reserve a room as far in advance as possible. Some rooms do not have air conditioning. If you're lucky, you might land in room No. 21, where Hemingway used to stay when he came to Havana. The breakfasts served in the restaurant La Paella (see p 109) are very generous, and at dinnertime you won't regret abandoning Cuban cuisine for the night and sampling an authentic Valencian *paella*.

Near Parque Central, the **Hotel Plaza** *($69-122; ≈, ℜ, pb, ctv; Calle Ignacio Agramonte No. 167, at the corner of Calle Neptuno, ☎33-8583-90 or 57-1075, ≈33-8591)* has a unique charm about it. Its fountains and high-ceilinged entryway create a wonderful ambiance. The rooms are clean and all have air conditioning (which can, however, be a bit loud).

Located in front of Parque Central and right near the Capitolio, the **Hotel Inglaterra** *($70-90; ≈, ℜ, pb, ctv; Avenida Paseo del Prado No. 416, ☎33-8593, ≈33-8254)* is very popular

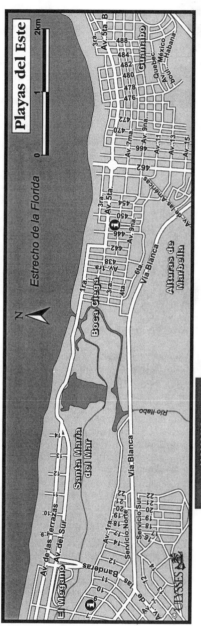

Playas del Este

HAVANA

with all different kinds. Local artists and intellectuals used to gather here once upon a time. This hotel, built in 1875, has a distinctive character and looks slightly outdated, but still reflects the splendour of the turn of the century. It is the oldest hotel in Cuba, and its architecture and historical importance have earned it official status as a national monument. The decor is perfectly suited to the majestic neoclassical façade. The relaxing bar/restaurant at the entrance is patronized by travellers with an adventurous air about them—a fairly colourful crowd on the whole. The rooftop bar offers one of the best views in town. The rooms, soberly decorated with antique furniture, are very beautiful. Keep in mind that those with a balcony face onto Parque Central, a noisy area with a lot of traffic.

Made famous by Ernest Hemingway, who lived here in the 1930s, at a time when this part of the city was an artistic and intellectual centre, the **Ambos Mundos** *($90-$100; ≡, pb, ☎, tv, ℜ; Calle Obispo No. 153, at Mercedes, ☎66-9529, ⊷66-9532)* is a luxury hotel located a stone's throw from the many cafés frequented by the eminent writer. You can even visit his old room, No. 511, which has been kept intact. The view of old Habana from the hotel's top floors is magnificent. The turn-of-the-century ambiance is still palpable in of the vintage Otis elevator and the lobby made entirely of wood, in the middle of which stands an equally old grand piaNo.

The architecture and decor of the lobby of the **Hotel Sevilla** *($102-150, ≡, ≈, ℜ, pb, ctv; Calle Trocadero No. 55, ☎33-8560, ⊷33-8582)* will transport you to Andalusia. This lovely turn-of-the-century hotel has been entirely renovated, and the mood here falls somewhere between relaxed elegance and a certain Mediterranean offhandedness. Located between the Paseo del Prado and the Museo de la Revolución, the Sevilla is just a few steps from Old Havana. Come nightfall, however, the streets around the hotel are rather dark and empty. If you plan on walking about at night, you're better off staying at the Inglaterra or the Plaza in this part of Havana. The Sevilla's rooms are a bit outmoded for the price, and the wall-coverings and furnishings show signs of wear in places. Nevertheless, if you can afford this place, you'll certainly be enchanted. The Sevilla's clientele consists mainly of European tourists. It has three restaurants, and offers a package rate that includes morning and evening meals. The buffet-style breakfast served on the ground floor features a well-balanced assortment of fruit, meat and pastries. The fresh rolls, occasionally topped with pineapple, are among the best in Havana. In the shopping arcade on the lower floor is a restaurant that serves traditional Andalusian cuisine; the Roof Garden on the ninth floor is one of the finest and most beautiful restaurants in the capital.

Caressed by the gentle breeze from the Bahia de La Habana, the colonial building of the **Santa Isabel** *($150-$170; ≡, pb, ☎, tv, ℜ; Calle Baratoillo No. 9, at Calle Obispo, ☎33-8201, ⊷33-8391)* is sure to give you the impression of having stepped back more than a century in time. Leading out onto a pleasant square where second-hand booksellers peddle their revolutionary literature, it is undeniably charming. Enormous doors link the various rooms, decorated in colonial Cuban style and offering flawless comfort. As a matter of fact, the pope stayed here during his famous January 1998 visit, just steps from the cathedral.

Centro Habana (Central Havana)

The **Hotel Lido** *($16-35; ℛ, pb, ◎, cold water only; Calle Consulado No. 210, ☎62-0653)*, with its pleasant terrace that stays open late into the night, attracts independent travellers. I found the service to be extremely friendly. Although this place is not unappealing, it has no air conditioning, which can make for long nights when the weather is hot. Those who prefer sleeping with the window open won't have any problem, however, as most of the rooms open onto balconies overlooking a quiet street.

Very popular with visitors on a shoestring budget, the **Hotel Caribbean** *($30-48; ≡, ℛ, pb, cold water only; Avenida Paseo del Prado No. 164, ☎33-8233)* has a friendly atmosphere. Its excellent location, right on the Paseo del Prado, is its main attraction. It lies within walking distance of Old Havana, the Malecón and even the Vedado. There are a number of inexpensive restaurants in the area as well. The place is a little outdated, but clean; the watchword here is simplicity. A few of the rooms have air conditioning, making them a real bargain for the price. Last but not least, guests are allowed to use the swimming pool at the Hotel Sevilla.

🦐 The **Casa del Cientifico** *($31-$55; ≡, ℛ, pb, ☎, ctv; Prado 212, at the corner of Trocadero, ☎62-4511 or 63-8103, ⇒63-8103)* is in another old colonial building in the very heart of La Habana. It welcomes passing scientists, but others can find accommodation here now and again, when the place has vacancies. The establishment offers the best quality for the price. Indeed, you will have the impression of staying in a 19th-century mansion — especially since the nation's president lived here at the turn of the century. With its neoclassical interior courtyard and balcony overlooking the Prado, this hotel is a real gem.

The **Hotel Lincoln** *($34-42; ≡, ℛ, pb, tv; Calle Galiano between Calle Virtudes and Calle Anima, ☎33-8209)*, at the edge of Old Havana, has an essentially Cuban clientele. It is a bit old-fashioned, but its rooftop bar/restaurant affords a unique view of the city.

The **Hotel Deauville** *($44-70; ≡, ℛ, pb, tv; Calle Galiano, at the corner of the Malecón, ☎62-8051 to 59)* has the advantage of being centrally located right on the Malecón, not far from Old Havana. The place is a little noisy, so it's best to request a room on the upper floors facing the sea.

The **Hotel Parque Central** *($180; ≡, ℛ, pb, ☎, ctv, ≈; Neptuno, between the Prado and Zulueta, ☎66-6627 to 29, ⇒66-6630)* is the newest addition to the capital's central district. The hotel offers exquisite luxury. Not only does it boast impeccably comfortable rooms, a rooftop pool and a conference room, but it is also remarkably well situated, near the park, the Capitolio and Vieja Habana.

The Vedado

The Vedado district inarguably has the most *casas particulares* (see p 58), private homes that rent out rooms for $15 to $30 a night, depending on the level of comfort. The problem is that most do not have the required government permit, so listing them here might cause them trouble. To find such establishments, ask around in restaurants and shops: *"¿Conoce alguien que aquila cuartos?"* (Do you know anyone who rents out rooms?)

HAVANA

If you're on a tight budget, your best option is the **Hotel Bruzón** *($17; ≡, sb, ⊛, cold water only; Calle Bruzón No. 217, ☎70-3531 to 33)*, located near the Plaza de la Revolución's Estación de Omnibus Nacionales. With its friendly, almost homey atmosphere, this little hotel is very popular with locals and is often full. You can walk to Old Havana in 25 minutes or rent a bicycle. The rooms do not come with a private bath, but some are air-conditioned. The hotel also has a danceclub and a cabaret.

The **Hotel Isla de Cuba** *($18; ≡, cold water only; Calle Monte No. 169, between Calle Cienfuegos and Calle Aponte, ☎62-1031 to 34)*, next to the Capitolio, is run-down and noisy, and you might find some small insects in your room. On the other hand, this is one of the cheapest places in Havana. Ask for a room with air conditioning.

Among the *casas particulares*, **Hospedaje Eddy Gutiérrez Bouza** *($30; ≡, pb, ☎, K; Calle 21 No. 408, between Avenidas F and G, ☎32-5207, permit number 091-1997)* is a superb colonial estate which offers suites as comfortable as those of hotels. The place is tasteful, with its private kitchen, separate side entrance and a garage where you can leave your car in all safety. There are also numerous *paladares* worth checking out across the street. Should the house have no vacancies, Eddy can refer you elsewhere.

Hotel Morro *($28-$32; ≡, ℝ, pb, ctv; Calle 3, between Calles C and D, ☎33-3908, ⁓33-3907)* will be undergoing major renovations soon, so it might be closed during your stay. If not, this is one of the least expensive hotels around, well situated near the Malecón, but with rooms so small that they make guests want to go out and explore the city.

The **Hotel St. John's** *($36-58; ≡, ℛ, pb, tv; Calle O, No. 206, ☎33-3740, ⁓33-3561)*, located in the heart of the Vedado commercial area, near La Rampa, is a real bargain for the money. The service is pleasant, the atmosphere is relaxed and the rooms are well kept. Many visiting Latin Americans stay here.

The very hospitable **Hotel Universitario** *($40; ≡, ℛ, pb, ☎, ctv; at Calle K and Calle L, opposite the gas station)* is perfectly located to avoid the expense of taking taxis, but is also in pleasant surroundings. The lobby's elegant and well-arranged furniture equals the comfort of the rooms.

Right next to the university, the **Colima** *($50 bkfst incl.; ≡, ℛ, pb, ☎, ctv; Calle L between Calles 27 and Jovelar, ☎33-4103, ⁓33-4104)* is not very inviting. Indeed, the hotel lacks light, plants and that certain something that gives a place appeal. Fans of Cuban literature, however, will want to attend literary events held here at night (see p 113).

Two other hotels were under renovation at press time: the **Presidente** *($60; Calle Calzada 110, at Avenida G, ☎33-4394, ⁓33-3753)* and the **Vedado** *($60 bkfst incl.; 244 Calle O, between Avenidas 25 and 27, ☎33-4072, ⁓33-4186)*.

The **Hotel Capri** *($65-104; ≡, ≈, ℛ, pb, ctv; Calle 21, at the corner of Calle N, ☎33-3747, ⁓33-3750)* is a good deal. A legacy of the American mafia, it has an attractive lobby, and the pool, located on the roof of the tall building, offers an extraordinary panoramic view. The restaurants, unfortunately, are in the basement.

The immense **Hotel Habana Libre** *($80-120; ≡, ≈, ℝ, ℛ, pb, ctv; Calle L, at the corner of Calle 23, ☎33-4011, ⁓33-3141)*, formerly the Hilton, looks a bit like a factory. The ambiance, however, is unparalleled. The Habana Libre lies at the centre of La Rampa, and is surrounded by all sorts of little shops.

The **Hotel Victoria** *($100-120; ≡, ℝ, ℛ, pb, ctv; Calle 19, at the corner of Calle M, ☎33-3510, ⇝33-3109, reserva@victo.gca.cma.net)* caters to travelling businesspeople and vaunts itself as the chicest five-star hotel in Havana. Combining luxury and tradition, it offers personalized service and an elegant ambiance. This small hotel also has a pool at the back.

Habana Riviera *($120; ≡, ℛ, pb, ☎, ctv; Calle Paseo, at the Malecón, ☎33-4051, ⇝33-3739)* is pleasantly situated by the sea. This former Mafioso haunt gives you a taste of Cuba in the 1950s, before the Miramar region became a tourist mecca. It is characterized by old-fashioned luxury and somewhat bizarre taste, that can even be called kitsch. As for the rest, the hotel is very comfortable and offers most services.

The **Hotel Nacional** *($120-240; ≡, ≈, ℝ, ℛ, pb, ctv; Calle O, at the corner of Calle 21, ☎33-3564, ⇝33-5054)* is without question the most beautiful hotel in Havana, and is remarkably charming for a place of its size. Its five stars are well deserved. The entrance, built in 1930, the vast gardens and the magnificent swimming pool will soon make you forget you're in the middle of the city. The rooms have ultramodern furnishings; those with a view of the sea are especially desirable. Visitors looking for a good restaurant to enhance their stay will be thrilled by the buffet. The ambiance is particularly interesting, with journalists, film directors and businesspeople rubbing shoulders in the gardens and the lobby. The Nacional also hosts the prestigious Latin-American Film Festival in December.

The brand new **Hotel Melia Cohiba** *($140-325; ≡, ≈, ℝ, ℛ, pb, ctv; Calle Paseo, at the corner of Calle 1, ☎33-3636, ⇝33-4555)* is the most modern five-star hotel in Cuba. A symbol of the phenomenal expansion of the tourist industry, it is not the place to go if you're looking for authentic Cuban charm.

Miramar

This region has been experiencing a hotel boom over the last few years. Complexes are being built farther and farther west along the coast. The hotels in Miramar are generally quieter than those in the Vedado and Old Havana. They offer the dual advantage of a seaside atmosphere and a location relatively convenient to downtown Havana. On the other hand, you won't find any cheap hotels or restaurants in Miramar, and the taxi ride to Old Havana costs between 10 and 15 dollars.

A fair distance from the city, the **Mariposa** *($27-$50; ≡, ℛ, pb, ☎, tv; Autopista del Mediodia, Km 6.5, La Lisa, ☎24-9137 to 39, ⇝24-6131)* is fairly luxurious but considerably less expensive than hotels of the same calibre. This is probably because it is so far away from both the city and the seashore. The rooms are comfortable, though rather drab and without any particular charm. Anyone staying here should rent a car or have an ample budget for getting around by taxi.

The **Residencia Universitaria Ispaje** *($44; ≡, pb, ☎, ctv, ≈; at Avenida 1 and 22, ☎23-5370 or 23-6633)* is located by the sea, next to the large complexes. This small 12-room hotel mainly welcomes university professors, but anyone else can stay here provided there are vacancies. The rooms are clean and well-appointed, and the outdoor swimming pools, when they are actually filled with water, are a pleasure.

A little outside the hotel zone, **Hostal Icemar** *($48; ≡, pb, ☎, ctv; 104 Calle 16, between Avenidas 1 and 3, ☎29-5471, ⇥23-6130)* has an ambiance that is much less stuffy than that of Miramar's huge complexes. The rooms are simple and comfortable and there is a terrace in the interior courtyard adjacent to a small cafeteria. Also close to the sea.

🦐 With a dozen rooms, the charming seaside **Villa Costa** *($54; pb, ☎, ctv, ≡, ≈; Avenida 1, between Calles 34 and 36, ☎29-2250 or 29-0558, ⇥24-4104)* is hard to find. Though modern, it has successfully preserved its colonial charm, and mostly welcomes young tourists. The staff here is very affable.

The **Bosque Gaviota** *($58 bkfst incl.; ≡, ℜ, pb, ☎, ctv, ≈; Avenida 28A, between Calles 49A and 49C, ☎24-9232, ⇥24-5637)* is also set back from the coast. The expanse that stretches beyond the outdoor terrace leads to a river. The palce is breathtaking. The hotel, which opened in 1998, has undeniable charm and delightful rooms. Request a room with a view of the backyard overflowing with greenery. The Gaviota's restaurant offers nightly salsa shows (see p 113).

Still at somewhat of a distance from the coast, the **Bellocaribe** *($61-$77; ≡, ℜ, pb, ☎, ctv; Calle158 at Calle 31, ☎33-9906 to 09, ⇥33-6839)* is located next to the capital's biotechnology research centre, and thus mainly receives scientists. It offers no real advantage to passing tourists, however, save perhaps for its buffet-restaurant (see p 112) which serves one of the most commendable cuisines in the capital. A superb miniature jungle makes up part of the interior.

Hotel Kohly *($66; ≡, ℜ, pb, ☎, ctv, ≈; at Calle 49 and Avenida 36A, opposite the Nuevo Vedado, ☎24-0240, ⇥24-1733)* is a mid-class establishment ideal for families wishing to spend a pleasant holiday while exploring the city, as the hotel is not too far from Old Havana. The hotel's other strong point is its activities, not to mention the always-smiling staff. A pleasant oasis in the heart of the city.

The **Hotel El Comodoro** *($67-90; ≡, ≈, ℝ, ℜ, pb, ctv; Avenida 3, at the corner of Calle 84, ☎24-5551, ⇥24-2028)* has a number of rooms with ocean views. It stands next to a small artificial beach separated from the water by a sea wall, against which the waves crash spectacularly. The place rents out both rooms and bungalows.

The **Hotel Copacabana** *($75-108; ≡, ≈, ℜ, pb, ctv; Avenida 1, at the corner of Calle 44, ☎24-1037, ⇥24-2846)* has a pretty friendly, relaxed atmosphere for such a big place. All the rooms offer a partial view of the sea. The hotel nightclub is packed almost every night.

The **Hotel Neptuno** *($80-110; ≡, ≈, ℜ, pb, ctv; Avenida 3, at the corner of Calle 70, ☎24-1606, ⇥24-0042)*, located in one of the two big towers near the imposing Russian embassy, is decidedly lacking in charm. It is almost entirely made of concrete, the orange upholstered furniture is outdated, and the big dining room looks more like a school cafeteria than a restaurant. On the other hand, the balconies of some of the rooms offer panoramic views of the sea, and the swimming pool, flanked by gardens, is extremely attractive. The other tower houses the **Triton** hotel, managed by the same chain and virtually identical to its twin. Indeed, there is no difference between the two as far as comfort and quality are concerned.

Although it offers the same basic services as superior-grade hotels, the **Palco** *($94; ≡, ℜ, pb, ☎, ctv; Calle 146 between Avenidas 11 and 1, ☎33-7235, ⊷33-7236)* is a little out of the way, near the convention centre. The luxury complex's 180 rooms are generally occupied by people attending conventions and seminars.

One of Miramar's newest luxury hotels, the **Chateau Miramar** *($130; ≡, ℜ, pb, ☎, ⊷, ctv, ≈; Avenida 1, between Calles 60 and 62, ☎24-1952, ⊷24-0224, reservas@chateau.cha.cyt.cu)* is fully equipped to receive businesspeople and the most demanding of clients. Since the hotel has only 50 rooms, it offers more personalized services.

The **Melia-Habana** *($140-$175; ≡, ℜ, pb, ☎, ctv, ≈; Avenida 3, between Calles 76 and 80, ☎24-8500, ⊷24-8505, depres@habana.solmelia.c ma.net)* is Miramar's newest hotel. It offers the utmost in luxury, with all the perks imaginable. Indeed, the rooms can't get more comfortable than this. The hotel looks out onto the sea, but the beach (like others in the Miramar region) is not well groomed. The swimming pools here are more pleasant thanks to their enormous size and the many promenades surrounding them. The hotel is located halfway between Old Havana and the airport.

The **El Viejo y El Mar** *($150; ≡, ≈, ℝ, ℜ, pb, ctv; Marina Hemingway, ☎24-6336, ⊷24-6823)*, named after Ernest Hemingway's famous novel (*The Old Man and the Sea*), is located at the Marina Hemingway. It has been completely renovated and is run by Delta, a Canadian hotel chain. This place is far from the hubbub of the city and has a swimming pool and a gym.

Some people come to the **Marina Hemingway** by boat and rent out a cottage here. Inside the marina, food counters, restaurants and nightclubs await crews fresh off the boat. The marina resembles a little village in the interior of the region.

The Playas del Este (Eastern Beaches)

The shoreline between Havana and Matanzas and Varadero is studded with hotels. There is something for every taste and budget. You can easily rent a bedroom or even an entire house in any of the little coastal villages along the way. This is definitely the cheapest option, and often one of the most pleasant. All you have to do is ask a Cuban in one of the local restaurants, hotels or shops if he or she happens to know of a safe, comfortable and friendly place to stay (*Conoce alguien que alquila cuartos?*), and you're set! Although this practice is very common, especially in this region, it is still technically illegal. For the cheapest hotels and rooms, go to Boca Ciega or Guanabo.

About 65 kilometres from Havana, along the road that leads past the Playas del Este to Varadero and the province of Matanzas, there are two campgrounds open year-round. Nestled between the sea and two hills, **El Abra** *($18 per cabin; ℜ, ≈, ⊛)* is a campground that also rents out modest little cabins. It has good facilities and its beach is superb, mainly because of its unspoiled natural setting. Introductory scuba courses are offered at the swimming pool, and packages for excursions from the Canimar marina are sold on the premises. El Abra is also the starting point for outings on the Río Canimar. The underwater scenery in front of the campground is superb, as are the trails in the surrounding mountains. A few of the latter have been designed for nature lovers, making it easy to observe the local flora and fauna. The meals served in the restaurant are excellent, especially if you order à la carte. The house specialty is pork. If you decide to rent a *cabaña*, make sure it's clean first. Also, don't leave food there, as squirrels and rodents apparently go scavenging when no one's home.

Hotel Gran Via *($21-$25; ≡, ℜ, pb, ☎, ctv; at Avenida 5 and Calle 462, Guanabo, ☎2271)* is less luxurious than its neighbours, but has the same excellent level of comfort. The rooms are inviting, albeit tiny. The building also houses the coziest of restaurants and bars. Inexpensive accommodations right on the beach.

At the foot of the hill, right near the sea, the **Villa Playa Hermosa** *($22-30; Avenida 7, between Calle 472 and Calle 474, ☎2-774)* is a series of small, fully-equipped cottages. The place is unfortunately a bit noisy, since buses and trucks travel along nearby Avenida 5 during the day.

The white, sandy beach at the seaside resort of Santa Maria stretches several kilometres and is lined with hotels. The **Aparthotel Horizontes Atlántico** *($40-60; ≡, K, ℜ, ≈, ℜ, pb, tv; Avenida de las Terrazas No. 21, ☎97-1636, ┅97-1494)* is the least expensive choice in this area. The rooms are decorated with simple furnishings and all have a balcony and a refrigerator. Some have a kitchen and a dining room as well. All you have to do is cross one street, and you're at the beach.

The **Hotel Tropicoco** *($40-60; ≡, ≈, ℜ, pb, ctv; Avenida de las Terrazas, ☎97-1371, ┅97-1389)* is hands-down the most popular hotel is Santa Maria, due to its all-inclusive packages, which include lodging, meals, drinks and non-motorized sports activities (cycling,

windsurfing, catamaran sailing). The hotel has 188 rooms, some of which offer a view of the sea. Its nightclub is also very popular after dark.

A stone's throw from the turquoise sea, the **Aparthotel Las Terrazas** *($43-$53; ≡, K, ℜ, ℜ, pb, ☎, ctv, ≈; Avenida Las Terrazas, near Calle 10, Playa Santa Maria del Mar, ☎97-1344, ┅97-1316)* offers fully equipped, simple and comfortable apartments. The beach is very pleasant, but often crowded on weekends. Though the interior of the buildings is particularly charming, the same cannot be said for the hospital-like exterior, whose light-green colour tries in vain to recall the sea. Better to go straight to the beach!

The **Hotel Atlántico** *($50; ≡, ≈, ℜ, pb, ctv; Avenida de las Terrazas No. 21, ☎97-1085 to 98, ┅80-3911)*, located opposite, is a relatively modern, well-kept place with good service. The building faces right onto a section of the beach monitored by a lifeguard. A sports complex (tennis, archery, etc.), several restaurants and a discotheque are also located on the premises.

The **Hotel Miramar** *($50; ℜ, ℜ, pb, tv, ⊗; Calle 9, between Calle 476 and Calle 478, ☎2-507 to 09)*, in Guanabo, is perched on a hill overlooking the sea. This tranquil, inviting place is much less touristy than the hotels in Santa Maria. The rooms are small but pleasant, and some offer a view of the sea. Poolside festivities and barbecues are organized regularly, so if you're looking for peace and quiet, don't take a room facing the pool.

The **Panamericano Resort** *($56-$68; ≡, ℜ, pb, ☎, tv, ≈; at Calle A and Avenida Central, Cojimar, ☎33-8545 or 33-8811, ┅33-8580)* is the first hotel in the Playas del Este (Eastern Beaches) region when coming from the capital, but is nowhere near the beach! To compensate, the hotel offers its guests a daily mini-bus service to Havana. Built to welcome dignitaries and other representatives of the 1991 Pan-American Games, the hotel is lacklustre in style and is already a bit worn. On the other hand, a bar, several restaurants, a pool and a nightclub make the place more appealing and compensate for the small rooms.

Prior to the Revolution, wealthy Americans would spend their holidays at the **Marina Puerto Sol Tarará** *($57-$79; ≈, ☉, ℛ, pb, ☎, ctv, ≈; Via Blanca, Km 19, Tarará, ☎97-1462, ⇒97-4499)*. Today the Marina attracts travellers from other countries with its well-appointed cottages and many services, including a fitness centre offering massage and acupuncture as well as introductory scuba-diving lessons. The beach is certainly one of the most pleasant, as it is more private and thus less frequented.

Hotel Megano *($85-$90; ≈, ℛ, pb, ☎, ctv, ≈; Via Blanca, Km 22, ☎97-1610, ⇒97-1624)* is 500 metres from the beach and seems only to cater to tourists going through certain agencies. During our visit, for instance, the great majority of guests were Italian. The place is luxurious and has many attractions, including an inviting bar and a restaurant with their open-air concept allowing for abundant natural light. The rooms all have a view of the sea and provide decent comfort. The hotel also offers a half-board package for an extra charge.

At the gateway to Boca Ciega and by the Río Itabo, the **Hotel Club Arenal** *($130-$160; ≈, ℛ, pb, ☎, ctv, ≈; Avenida de Las Terrazas, Laguna de Boca Ciega, ☎97-1272, ⇒97-1287, srosso@pantravel.ch)* stands on a small peninsula surrounded by tropical vegetation. Entirely rebuilt in 1998, the enormous all-inclusive-style 156-room complex has replaced the small Hotel Itabo that once stood here. Very opulent and managed by Italians, the hotel will satisfy even the most discerning guests, with its welcoming staff, spacious rooms, tennis courts, peace and quiet, cleanliness, bars, restaurants and numerous activities.

You can also rent a house at the **Villa Los Pinos** *($93-97; ≈, ℝ, K, pb, ctv; Avenida las Terrazas, ☎97-1361, ⇒80-2144)*, at the edge of Santa Maria. These fully renovated, two-bedroom houses are located in a peaceful setting near the sea.

If you are travelling in a group or with your family, you can rent a house at the **Marina Tarará** *(Via Blanca, Km 19, ☎97-9015)*, about 15 kilometres east of Havana. This marina rents out comfortable houses that are ideal for visitors looking to enjoy both the peaceful atmosphere of a seaside resort and the cultural advantages of the nearby capital.

 RESTAURANTS

Old Havana

Cuban families were recently given permission to operate their own restaurants, and you'll come across countless of these *paladares* in Havana. You won't be disappointed if you decide to eat in one. You'll usually be served a Creole dish; never pay more than $10 per person. Unfortunately, a few of the best restaurants illegally serve fresh lobster, which the government only permits according to a strict law. Legal or not, young children will lead you to particular restaurateurs who give them a $5 commission for every client they bring in. Inquire about prices beforehand and feel free to change ven-

HAVANA

ues if a particular one is not to your liking.

The most popular *paladar* in Old Havana is definitely **Doña Eutimia** *($; 62 Callejón del Chorro, ☎61-9489)*, a small, inviting colonial house owned by a sculptor and located at the end of a little dead-end street that branches off the Plaza de la Catedral. The Creole cuisine is succulent, especially the *cerdo asado* (oven-baked pork). Parties of several people are advised to reserve a table, as the place is usually packed. If there's no room, you can try one of the six other *paladares* on the same charming dead-end street.

A large number of restaurants and terrace cafés have set up business in Old Havana over the past few years. Most serve good food, but the menus vary little from one place to the next, and the prices are generally rather high. Aside from cafeteria-style restaurants, which are becoming more and more common, the least expensive places are located near the port and outside the historic section of Old Havana.

Also located in the old part of the city, **Café Paris** *($; open 24 hours a day; Calle San Ignacio 202, at Calle Obispo, ☎62-0466)* serves simple, affordable meals (chicken, pizza, ...) and boasts a side counter open around the clock. The place also sometimes features live music, but most of the time it plays recorded Latin music.

For Cantonese food, head to **Torre de Marfil** *($; Tue to Sun noon to 10pm; Calle Mercadares, between Calles Obispo and Obrapía, ☎62-3466)*, where the variety of dishes is rather amazing. Try the delicious Cantonese-style chicken.

With its long, seemingly endless counter, **La lluvia de Oro** *($; open 24 hours a day; Calle Obispo 316, at Habana)* is

a wonderful place open 'round the clock. Its menu offers a variety of snack food such as chicken, pizza, sandwiches and pasta.

Next to the Casa de Mexico, the **Cafetería Torre La Vega** *($; Mon to Sat 9am to 7pm; Calle Obrapía 114)* is the perfect low-budget alternative. Spaghetti is served in generous portions and costs barely $1. But get there early, because the place closes as early as 7pm, and customers wishing to take advantage of the establishment's low prices must sometimes push their way through to the counter.

Despite its name, **Restaurante Hanoi** *($; every day noon to 11pm; Calle Teniente Rey 507, at Calle Brazil, ☎63-1681)* offers fare that is more Cuban than Vietnamese, since Vietnamese ingredients are often in short supply here. The restaurant therefore offers its patrons a menu of chicken-, pork- or meat-based dishes served with rice and beans. The place is usually fairly quiet.

Beautiful period furnishings create a pleasant colonial ambiance at **El Mesón** *($$; Avenida del Puerto, at the corner of Calle O'Reilly, Plaza de Armas)*, perched on the roof of the Castillo de la Real Fuerza. The menu features traditional Cuban cuisine, as well as cafeteria-style food. The view of Old Havana and the bay is superb, and there are cabaret shows on Friday, Saturday and Sunday.

If you've got a big appetite, head to the **Bar Restaurant Cabaña** *($$; Calle Cuba No. 12, at the corner of Calle Peña Pobre)* for some Creole cuisine. This is a new place whose all-you-can-eat policy has made it an instant hit. It is located on the outskirts of Havana, near the old castle that now serves as a police station. Although the atmosphere is friendly, the service can be a bit rushed.

In Old Havana, the **Castillo de Farnés** *($$; open 24 hours a day; Calle Monserrate 361, at Calle Obrapia, ☎63-1260)* is decorated in the style of an old English pub, and attracts many clients because of its reputation. The international cuisine is of good quality and the atmosphere is relaxed, even bohemian.

The **Restaurante Almedina** *($$; Calle Oficio No. 12, west of Plaza de Armas, between Calle Obispo and Calle Obra Pia, ☎63-0862)* is tucked away inside the Casa del Arabe, which presents ethnological and cultural exhibitions. Built in 1688 and now completely restored to its original state, this house is an example of Mozarab architecture. The restaurant is located on the second floor. Decorated with pouffes and cushions in the Arabic tradition, it is flanked by a refreshingly cool mezzanine with vine-covered walls. A veritable oasis, this is the perfect place to escape the rigours of the tropical heat and the hubbub of the city. The Almedina's menu and cuisine are unparalleled in Havana, and the grilled meat dishes are sure to please even the most demanding palate.

Don Giovanni's *($$; Calle Tacón, between Calle Empedrado and Calle O'Reilly, ☎63-3560)* is – surprise, surprise – where lovers of Italian food go to get their fix. The place is friendly and comfortable, and the cuisine, rarely disappoints.

La Paella *($$; Calle Oficios No. 53, ☎62-3801)* specializes in the Valencian dish for which it is named. Located in the charming Hostal Valencia, this little restaurant has a relaxed atmosphere. The portions are generous, and guests are always given special treatment. You might enjoy having your aperitif or

coffee at one of the ⸙ inner courtyard of the

La Bodeguita del Me(*Empedrado No. 207, 57-1374)* is a veritable ⸱⸱ιοn of Cuban cuisine, and it is worth coming here just to see the place. In typical Cuban fashion, it is usually packed with tourists inside, with throngs of Cubans posted out front. *Jineteros* hang out on little Calle Empedrado, and you can't walk by without someone asking you for a dollar or a pen, or trying to sell you a box of cigars. There is an extremely festive atmosphere in the restaurant, whose walls are covered with graffiti, signatures, poems and thoughts handwritten by every Tom, Dick and Harry over the years, as well as a few contributions by such famous figures as Ernest Hemingway and Fidel Castro. Hemingway used to come here regularly for a *mojito*, a cocktail made with rum, sugar and mint, so it would be flouting tradition not to try one while you're here. The menu consists of Creole dishes made with pork, rice, black beans and manioc and served with a garlic and oil sauce known as *mojo*. Although the place has a good reputation, its tremendous popularity has had a somewhat negative impact on the quality of the food. Nevertheless, you will rarely be disappointed by a meal at La Bodeguita, and it remains a must in Havana. Don't be shy about clearing your way through the crowd that is perpetually gathered out front, if only to stop by for a *mojito* at the bar.

Located on Plaza de la Catedral, **El Patio** *($$$; ☎57-1034)* is always busy and has a convivial atmosphere. Its roofless courtyard, with its pretty fountain and profusion of tropical plants, will transport you back to colonial times and also offers some shelter from the sun. Musicians liven up the atmosphere both inside the courtyard and out on the terrace on the Plaza de

.a Catedral. The food is excellent, especially the Creole dishes. If you want to take in the scene on the plaza, you can order from the cafeteria menu on the terrace; the fried chicken makes a great lunch. The terrace is also one of the best places in Old Havana to enjoy an afternoon cocktail, as long as the crowds of tourists don't bother you.

A unique gastronomical and historical experience awaits you at **La Floridita** *($$$; at the corner of Calle Obispo and Calle Montserrate; ☎33-8856 or 57-1300)*, by far the most famous restaurant in Havana. Hemingway's very favourite place to eat, La Floridita celebrates all the delicious subtleties of seafood. Its history dates back over 178 years, and it is considered the birthplace of the daiquiri. Ask for the *papa especial*, made with a double shot of rum, the way the great man liked it.

La Zaragozana *($$$; Calle Montserrate, near Calle Obispo, ☎57-1033)*, in the house adjacent to La Floridita, is an excellent Creole and Spanish restaurant. The fish dishes are particularly succulent. The decor, adorned with precious hardwood, is magnificent, and the cordial service does justice to the quality of the cuisine.

Centro Habana

The **Oasis** *($; Avenida Paseo del Prado No. 258, ☎62-6858)* serves inexpensive cafeteria-style Arabic food and has a pleasant interior courtyard. The bakery's cookies and cakes are very popular with local residents.

The cheapest places to eat in all Havana are in **Chinatown**. Many vendors in the little market here prepare complete Creole and Chinese meals. Served in small cardboard boxes for less than a dollar, these dishes are surprisingly good. You do, however, have to eat standing up. These Cuban-style fast food joints are very common in Havana, and you'll find others like them in the various farmer's markets known as *agros*.

The Vedado

There are many restaurants in the Vedado, some of which have unfortunately been hard-hit by the country's current economic crisis. It doesn't help that this area is not very popular with tourists. Nevertheless, a few restaurants, several of which have become veritable insititutions of Cuban cuisine over the years, have recovered their former prestige. A number of new places have also opened up, including several charming, quality *paladares*.

One of these is the **Restaurante Los Amigos** *($; Calle 19, at the corner of Calle M)*. Located kitty-corner to the Hotel Victoria, this family restaurant lies tucked away at the end of a little lane leading to the back of the house. It is usually crowded with locals, so you might have to wait a few minutes for a table. The Creole cuisine is succulent and served in generous portions, and the prices are unbeatable. This is an excellent place to escape the throngs of tourists and mingle with the locals.

Right in the middle of the Vedado, **La Carreta** *($; every day 5pm to 11pm; at Calle 21 and Avenida K)* is a small, unpretentious restaurant where musicians liven up the evenings. The food is typically Cuban, the usual mix of rice, beans, chicken and salad. For those on a tight budget, there is a **cafeteria** next door that offers a limited menu including delicious ham and cheese sandwiches for only a dollar each (for some reason, sandwiches are payable in pesos and drinks in dollars). Watch out for the sub-arctic air conditioning that can sometimes freeze you in your tracks.

One of the traditional restaurants in this area, **El Conejito** *($$; Calle M, at the corner of Calle 17, ☎32-4671)*, is modelled after a 16th-century English tavern. As its name suggests, it serves rabbit dishes.

La Torre *($$; Calle 17 No. 155, at the corner of Calle M, ☎32-4630)*, located on the 35th floor of the FOCSA building, offers a stunning panoramic view of the city. The food is not on par with the view, however, so stop by for drinks or coffee instead.

To enjoy a meal in a unique setting, head across the street to **Don Agamemnon** *($$; Calle 17 No. 60, between Calle M and Calle N, ☎33-4529)*. This extremely pleasant little restaurant has an unusual decor: all the chairs are different. The menu lists traditional Cuban dishes, but if the *table d'hote* is out of your price range, you can always have a pizza or a sandwich on the terrace.

The **Castillo de Jagüa** *($$; 3pm to 2am, closed Mondays; Calle 23, at Avenida G)* is a charming little bar-restaurant that features both Cuban and international cuisine. A young university crowd gathers here in an unpretentious setting. You can pay in either pesos or dollars, depending on how glaringly obvious a gringo you are.

Located at the mouth of the Río Almendares, at the west end of the Malecón, **1830** *($$; Calzada No. 1252, ☎34-504)* boasts an enchanting oceanside setting. Its extravagant stone architecture is complemented by Japanese-style landscaping, complete with terraces, fountains and foot bridges, making you feel as if you've stepped into a fairytale. The highlight here is the 17th-century castle, the Chorrera. The Creole cuisine is decent, and the seafood dishes are especially recommended. What you'll remember most is the extraordinary ambiance and magical setting.

The restaurant of the Habana Libre hotel, **El Barracón** *($$; every day 5pm to 11pm; at Calle 23 and Avenida L, ☎33-4011)* features good, typical Cuban *Criolla* cuisine. Make sure to go up to the top floors which have a magical view of the city. A bar is sometimes open here, as well.

Located closer to Miramar's hotels than to the old city, **El Ranchón** *($$; noon to 11:30pm; at Avenida 19 and Calle 140, ☎23-5828)* is just the place for those seeking a typically Cuban ambiance in which to enjoy marvellous grilled meats or other classic Cuban culinary delights.

Opposite the Hotel Nacional is the **Monseigneur** *($$-$$$; every day noon to 2am; Calle 21, at Avenida O, ☎32-9884)*, a state-owned restaurant specializing in international cuisine but also offering a good variety of seafood dishes (try the freshly caught shrimp, yum!). Prices are reasonable.

Miramar

Rumbos *($; Avenida 3, between Calle 26 and Calle 28)*, an attractive cafeteria with a terrace, is open around the clock. Although the menu is limited, the place is very popular with the local youth, since the music is always terrific, and live bands perform here from time to time. There is no dance floor, but couples often kick up their heels between the tables. The restaurant also houses a small shop, a tourist office and a scale-model of the city *($3)*. There is a similar restaurant in Havana.

For Chinese food, head to **El Mandarín** *($$; Calle 23, at the corner of Calle M, ☎32-0677)*.

El Aljibe *($$; Avenida 7, at the corner of Calle 26, ☎24-1584)*, an excellent choice in Miramar, serves nothing but Cuban chicken dishes. The portions are very generous. This family restaurant existed before the Revolution and has remainted very popular with *Habaneros*. It has a pretty, traditional terrace.

La Cova-Pizza Nova *($$; Marina Hemingway, ☎24-1150)* has a laid-back atmosphere and serves excellent pizza. Guests have a choice of dining inside or outside, on a pleasant terrace looking out onto a canal. The place also delivers.

The restaurant of the Hotel Bellocaribe (see p 104), **La Estancia** *($$; Hotel Bellocaribe)*, has a shining reputation, made even shinier after it was awarded first prize during the 1997 *Feria internacional de La Habana*. The restaurant offers two options: a traditional menu or the buffet. We highly recommend the latter. The chefs here constantly outdo themselves. The grilled chicken dishes are particularly outstanding.

El Aljibe *($$; every day noon to midnight; Calle 7, between Avenidas 24 and 26, ☎24-1583)* also offers a *Criollo* menu. Tourists and Cuban high society gather here beneath thatched roofs to savour chicken-based specialties. The service is flawless and the quality of the food leaves no one indifferent.

El Tocororo *($$$; Calle 18, at the corner of Avenida 3, ☎24-2209 or 24-4530)* is original on all scores. Named after the national bird of Cuba, it has an extravagant decor featuring a blend of tropical ambiance, graffiti and fake *tocororos*. The menu is just as creative, and the food is lovingly prepared. Very chic and expensive.

La Casa de 5ta y 16 *($$$; Mon to Sat 5pm to midnight; at Calle 16 and Avenida 5, ☎24-1185)* is an upscale restaurant featuring Cuban cuisine. Since the place is closed on Sundays, you should be sure to go during the week to dine in its magnificent gardens. Portions are generous and you can order a chicken breast combo with fillet of fresh fish and rice and beans accompanied by a salad.

La Ferminia *($$$; Avenida 5 No. 8807, between Calle 182 and Calle 184, ☎24-6555)* is not only one of the best restaurants in Cuba, but also one of the loveliest. Once a private home, it has numerous individual rooms, each able to accommodate from 10 to 30 people. These rooms are decorated with Louis XV furniture and furniture made of *caoba*, a precious Cuban wood. Three outdoor terraces enable diners to feast in the ambiance of their choice. The restaurant also offers courses in gourmet cooking and hotel management, so naturally the service is excellent and courteous. The mixed grill, meat dishes and seafood are house specialties. The maitre d' will be happy to give you a tour of the premises.

La Cecilia *($$$; Avenida 5 No. 11010, between Calle 110 and Calle 11, ☎24-1562)*, considered one of the finest restaurants in Havana, is named after a novel by Cuban author Cirilo Villaverde. Luxuriant tropical plants adorn the entrance and the dining room at the back lies under two marquees made of African wood, creating a peaceful, inviting atmosphere. Seafood and *criollos* dishes are the house specialties. The restaurant has an excellent wine cellar and a very competent staff, and has recently started hosting a cabaret show on a large stage surrounded by tropical trees *($3; Wed to Mon; outdoor shows starting at 10pm)*.

The Hemingway Tour

The port town of Cojimar has an excellent seafood restaurant, **Las Terrazas** *($$$; Calle Real No. 161, between Calle Río and Calle Montaña, ☎65-3471)*, a favourite with Hemingway and his skipper, Gregorio Fuentes. The latter, the hero of *The Old Man and the Sea*, is still alive, and you can find him here at lunchtime. Although he is now 98 years old, he can still tell you all sorts of anecdotes about Hemingway. As far as the seafood is concerned, I recommend the baked *paella*.

The South

The **Restaurante Ecológico** *($$; everything included)* lies in front of the falls in the Japanese garden at the Jardín Botanico. Most of the dishes served on this attractive terrace, where you can cool off a bit when the weather is hot, are vegetarian. The quality of the food is somewhat uneven, considering the prices. You might opt instead for the **Restaurante El Ranchón** *($$)*, which serves a Creole buffet in a lovely rustic house – the same kind that is used for drying tobacco leaves – topped with a roof made of palm fronds. This restaurant is set in a forest of pine trees, a species commonly found in Cuba, but rare in the Caribbean as a whole.

The Playas del Este (Eastern Beaches)

Set on the hilltop in Guanabo, the **Guanabo Club** *($; Calle 468, between Calle 3 and Calle 15, ☎0-87-2884)* boasts a gorgeous view of the little town and the sea. The clientele consists mainly of vacationing Cuban sol-

diers, as there is a military leisure camp nearby. The atmosphere is relaxed early in the evening, but gets very lively later, when the danceclub opens and the crowds of foreign tourists arrive.

  ENTERTAINMENT

Bars and Nightclubs

There are all sorts of cultural activities and other forms of entertainment to be enjoyed in Havana after dark. You'll find all the information you need to make an informed choice in *Cartelera*, a free, bilingual weekly (Spanish-English) available in all the big hotels.

At press time, several bars and nightclubs were closed by Castro's direct orders. It is difficult to foretell which will remain shut and for how long, and which will reopen under a different name, etc. Thus, some of the information listed below may not be accurate.

Old Havana

There are no discotheques in Old Havana, nor are there any live music venues for popular bands. On the other hand, you can sometimes catch a cabaret show or some live folk music in one of the area's many restaurants.

The Vedado

At **Colima** *(Calle L, between Calles 27 and Jovelar, ☎33-4103, ↝33-4104)*, literary evenings are held regularly, as are concerts featuring local bands.

Bosque Gaviota *(every day 8pm to 2am; Avenida 28A, between Calles 49A and 49C, ☎24-9232, ↝24-5637)* has a restaurant-amphitheatre where

Cuban music shows are presented every night. Set on the riverbank, its enchanting decor imparts a very special flavour to the music.

The **Copa Rum** *($10 cover charge, $5 per drink; at Calle Paseo and the Malecón, Vedado,* ☎*33-4051)*, formerly known as the Palacio de la Salsa, is a must for salsa lovers. Variety shows are featured here on a regular basis. Call to inquire about the program.

Right next door, the **Habana Café** *(in the Hotel Melia Cohiba)* is a very popular spot and a venue for musical performances you are sure to enjoy. The energetic musicians get you off your feet and moving on the dance floor! A memorable evening for Cuban music lovers.

The **Hotel Habana Libre** hosts live salsa and Latin jazz bands once a month in **El Salón de los Embajadores**.

One of the hottest salsa places in town is the **Café Cantante** *($20; at Paseo and Calle 39, near the bus station,* ☎*33-5713)* in the Teatro Nacional de Cuba. Not to be missed if you enjoy salsa.

Jazz aficionados should come to Cuba the week before Christmas. Cuba's very own **Jazz Festival** hosts both local and international stars (Chucho Valdéz is a regular!) who perform in the capital's theatres and clubs, spoiling fans with a variety of events. Show tickets cost as much or even more than they do back home.

If you won't be in Cuba in December but want to savour the incredible Latin-jazz experience, you still have the opportunity to do so. **La Zorra y El Cuervo** *($20; every day 9pm to 3am; 155 Calle 23, between Avenidas N and O,* ☎*66-2407)* presents established musicians and new talents every night

of the week. Simply go down the small stairway that serves as an entrance and you will fall right into the intimate universe of Latin jazz. Though shows start at 9pm, it's a good two hours before things really get cooking.

Miramar

If you're a bit of a romantic soul, you'll love **Dos Gardenias** *(Avenida 7, at the corner of Calle 26)*, where live musicians play the languorous boleros that were all the rage in Latin America back in the 1940s and 1950s. The place is pretty kitschy, and in between the romantic songs, you'll probably have a hard time smothering a smile. The Dos Gardenias has a tiny, intimate room known as **El Salón del Bolero**, which is perfect for incurable romantics. Love lost and rekindled, jealousy, hidden passions... *toda la noche cabe en un bolero* (the whole night is contained in a bolero). At midnight, the *descarga* begins, and various singers and musicians join the featured group.

The Hotel Commodoro has the only trendy mega-discotheque in Havana. The atmosphere at the **Havana Club** *($10; Mar and Calle 84, Miramar,* ☎*22-5511)* is electrifying night after night, and even if you only hit the town once during your stay, this is the best place to go. Crowds of *Habaneros*, men and women alike, wait at the door to be invited inside, and large numbers of gays turn out on Monday nights.

The **Ipanema** *($10; Avenida 1, corner of Calle 44)* danceclub is located in the Hotel Copacabana. It is a rather sophisticated place with a huge capacity and ocean views. For a $10 cover charge, you're likely to have a terrific evening. The place occasionally features live salsa music.

Gay Life in Havana

Sadly, the persecution of the gay community is nothing new, particularly in Cuba. However, it seems that one of the meeting places most tolerated by the authorities (for the moment) is **Fiat** *(every day 24 hours a day; on the Malecón, slightly west of Calle 23)*, which takes its name from the car dealership next door. People come here to drink rum on the terrace, to meet tourists and fellow Cubans, or simply to people-watch. For a few dollars, you can enjoy the music of the venerable Cubans guitarists who play here.

The following is a list of some of the top gay hangouts in Havana:

The favourite haunt of the characters of the film *Fresa y Chocolate*, the **Copelia** *(near the Habana Libre hotel, El Vedado)* café is a mecca of sorts;

The **Malcón**, near the Rampa;

In Miramar, west of the river, gays have taken to gathering on **Playita de 16** *(opposite Calle 16)* and on **Playa Tritón**, which is otherwise not a very nice beach;

The **Boca Ciega** beach in the Playas del Este;

Like elsewhere in the country, *fiestas de diez pesos* are organized in private homes, and in Havana also on the *azoteas*, the roofs of certain buildings.

Finally, as astonishing as it may seem, gays have gotten into the habit of attending midnight mass at Christmas, to the point where this has become the homosexual community's most important event of the year.

Glossary

ambiante	the homosexual milieu
cheo	heterosexual
civilizado	a heterosexual that accepts gays and occasionally frequent the same places
entendido	gay
loca	a dandy (very effeminate homosexual)
maricón	effeminate homosexual
pepillo	handsome young man
redada	police raid

Festivals

Havana has a full schedule of festivals devoted to the various performing arts.

Festival de la Guaracha (traditional music): November

Latin-American Film Festival: December

International Jazz Festival: First week of February

International Folk Festival: May

Carnaval: Last two weeks of July

The **Tropicana** *($50; Calle 72 and Avenida 45)*, located in the Marianao area, presents the most spectacular and celebrated cabaret show in all of Cuba. Although the entrance charge is prohibitive, you won't be disappointed by the colourful, red-hot performance. On an outdoor stage, thousands of dancers will sweep you up in a whirlwind of feathers and exoticism.

Another Miramar establishment renowned for its salsa nights is **La Cecilia** *($20; Wed to Sun; Avenida 5, between Calles 110 and 112, ☎24-1562)*. The music here is loud, sometimes a bit too much so.

The Playas del Este (Eastern Beaches)

The beach area does not have many nightclubs. We suggest the **Guanimar** *($20; Thu to Sun 9pm to 2am; Avenida 5, between Calles 466 and 468, Guanabo, ☎2947)*, a good place that often puts on salsa shows.

Cultural Activities

Havana is the cultural centre of Cuba, and probably the cultural capital of the Caribbean. Aside from museums, the city has all sorts of cultural institutions, theatres and art galleries. If you spend a few days in Havana, let the local performers lure you into the inner recesses of the city. You'll find these artists not only in official venues, but in parks all over town, with a trumpet or some other instrument in hand.

Performing Arts

The magnificent **Gran Teatro de La Habana** *(Avenida Paseo del Prado, at the corner of Calle San Rafael, ☎61-3078)*, located in front of Parque Central, attests to Havana's rich tradition of theatre and ballet. It is popularly known as the Teatro García Lorca, since its main theatre is named after the celebrated Spanish poet.

Theatre lovers interested in discovering contemporary Cuban plays should head to **El Sótano** *(Calle K, between Calle 25 and Calle 27, ☎32-0632)*.

The kids will enjoy a trip to the **Guiñol** *(Calle M, between Calles 19 and 21, ☎32-6262 or 32-8292)*, which puts on marionette shows.

The **Mella** *(Avenida 1, between Calles 8 and 10, ☎3-8696 or 3-5651)* pres ents performances of modern and folk dance, as well as variety shows.

The decidedly modern **Teatro Nacional** *(Calle Paseo, at the corner of Calle 39, on the Plaza de la Revolución, ☎79-6011)* presents classical music concerts, plays and national and international variety shows. This is where the city's symphony orchestra performs.

The **Sala-Teatro Hubert de Blanck** *(Calle Calzada, between Calles A and B, Vedado, ☎30-1011)* hosts many excellent concerts of both classical and contemporary music.

In Miramar, the **Teatro Karl Marx** *(Avenida 1, between Calles 8 and 10, ☎30-0720 or 30-5521)* is a very large, modern theatre where national and international variety shows are presented.

 SHOPPING

The well-known market that used to be held on Calle G has moved to the Malécon, between Calles F and E and on Calle 21. You can browse through a vast array of local crafts here from Tuesday to Sunday until sunset. You'll also pass by the crafts market on the **Plaza de la Catedral**, which is supposed to be held every other day, although the schedule tends to change. Numerous vendors sell a wide range of crafts and books on the square and along the adjacent streets.

The **Palacio de l'Artesania** *(Calle Cuba No. 64, Old Havana)* has an excellent selection of crafts and an entire section devoted to music (tapes and CDs) aa well as many instruments traditionally used by Cuban musicians. In general, the crafts are priced slightly higher than at the local markets. However, if you have a little time and money to spare, this is a great place to find top-quality pieces.

More and more shops are opening in Havana, and shopaholics, who were often disappointed by the city in the past, are beginning to find things more to their liking. What should you buy? Well, the brand-name Cuban cigars sold in specialty shops are always a good deal, since they are twice as expensive outside of Cuba. People in the street will probably try to sell you black-market cigars. Eighty percent of the time, these products are not authentic. Although many cigar smokers won't notice the difference, true aficionados are sure to be disappointed. The prices may be higher in specialty shops, but are guaranteed to be quality cigars that have been stored in ideal conditions. **La Casa Partagás** *(Calle Industria No. 520, behind the Capitolio)* has an excellent selection of cigars, and offers tours of the factory. Cigars are also sold in most big hotels in Havana.

In terms of clothing, Havana (and Cuba in general) is not the best place to buy a new wardrobe. There are, however, a few exclusive boutiques along the central hallway of the **Hotel Sevilla** *(Calle Trocadero No. 55)*, near the Paseo del Prado in Old Havana.

El Quitrin *(Calle Obispo and Calle San Juan, Old Havana)* is a workshop where lace is hand-made. It is worth coming here just to see the people at work, not to mention the flawless and unique finished products.

La Maison *(Calle 16, at the corner of Avenida 7, in Miramar)* in Miramar specializes in women's fashions and has the best selection of handbags, accessories and exclusive clothing by Cuban fashion designers. Fashion shows are held here regularly. A few shops at the **Marina Hemingway** also have an interesting selection of casual sportswear and eveningwear.

Art Galleries

Since the government has forbidden the export of its cultural property, make sure to obtain a certificate from the Fondo de Bienes Culturales if you buy a major work, such as a large painting, to make sure it won't be seized at the border when you leave. In Havana, the Fondo is located in the La Casona art gallery (see below).

The **Galería La Casona** *(Mon to Fri 10am to 4pm; Calle Muralla No. 107, at the corner of Calle San Ignacio, ☎62-2633 or 61-2875)* in Old Havana is also the parent institution of the Cuban Cultural Heritage Fund. Located in a large colonial house, it sells sculptures, paintings and ceramics by Cuban artists.

Galería Forma *(Calle Obispo No. 255, between Calle Cuba and Calle Aguiar, Old Havana, ☎62-2103)*.

The **Galería La Acacia** *(Mon to Sat 10am to 4pm; Calle Sain José No. 114, between Calle Industria and Calle Consulado, Centro Habana, ☎63-9364)* sells works by the greatest Cuban artists of all time.

Fans of contemporary Latin American art will enjoy visiting the **Casa de las Américas**, a large cultural organization which houses the **Galería de Arte Haydée Santamaria** *($2; Mon to Fri 10am to 4:30pm; Calle G, at the corner of Avenida 3, Vedado, ☎32-3587, ☎32-7272, casa@tinored.cu)*.

Shopping Centres

Summer clothing, shoes, food, electronic merchandise, household appliances – you'll find it all at the **Centro Comercial 5ta y 42** *(Avenida 5, at the corner of Calle 42)* in Miramar. This is the largest shopping centre in Havana, but is still small by North American standards. It is an excellent place to run errands, or to buy fresh French bread and other specialties. There are cafeterias where you can grab a Coke or a slice of pizza to fortify yourself before hitting the stores again.

Supermarkets

Supermarkets have been popping up here and there in Havana since American currency was legalized. They are usually open Monday to Saturday from 9am to 5pm and Sunday from 9am to noon. Here are a few:

Old Havana

Mercado Bellamar *(Calle Prado and Calle Dragones, ☎33-8328)*.

Centro Habana

Supermercado Amistad *(Calle San-Lazaro and Calle Infanta, ☎33-5832)*.

The Vedado

Mercado Carimar *(4 Calle D, ☎33-3879)*.

Miramar

Supermercado 3ra y 70 *(Avenida 3 and Calle 70, ☎33-2890)*.

Farmer's Markets

As a result of one of the government's recent economic reforms, farmer's markets have sprung up all over the country. Havana has a large number of these *mercados agropecuarios*, commonly known as *agros*, where all transactions are made in Cuban currency. Although the choice is not always very wide, these are the best places to buy fruits and vegetables at ridiculously low prices. It is worth visiting the local *agros*, if only to immerse yourself in the everyday life of the city's residents, far from the touristy areas.

You'll find a typical *agromercado* in the Barrio Chino (Chinatown), which is located in Centro Habana. This market has the largest selection of spices in all Havana. The *agromercado* in Nuevo Vedado *(Calle Tulipán, near the Estación de Trenes 19 de Noviembre)* offers an uneven selection of fruit and vegetables, which varies from season to season. Nevertheless, it is usually crowded, making it a great place to take some photos.

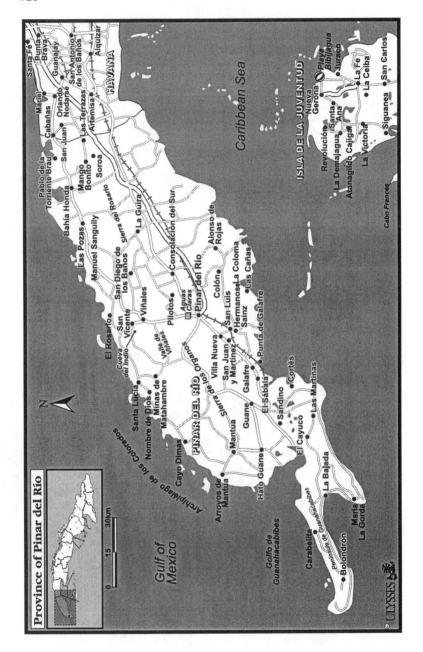

Province of Pinar del Río

ULYSSES

0 15 30km

N

Gulf of
Mexico

Caribbean Sea

HAVANA

PINAR DEL RÍO

ISLA DE LA JUVENTUD

Santa Fé
Punta Brava
Guanajay
Alquízar
San Antonio de los Baños
Orlando Nodarse
Mariel
Cabañas
San Juan
Las Terrazas
Artemisa
Soroa
Pablo de la Torriente Brau
Mango Bonito
Bahía Honda
Las Pozas
Manuel Sanguily
San Diego de los Baños
Sierra del Rosario
La Güira
Consolación del Sur
Alonso de Rojas
El Rosario
San Vicente
Viñales
Pilotos
Aguas Claras
Pinar del Río
Colón
San Luis
Hermanos Sainz
La Coloma
Las Cañas
Punta de Galafre
Cueva del Indio
Valle de Viñales
Sierra de los órganos
Santa Lucía
Nombre de Dios
Minas de Matahambre
Villa Nueva
San Juan y Martínez
Guane
Galafre
El Sábalo
Cortés
Sandino
Cayo Dimas
Mantua
Hato Guane
El Cayuco
Las Martinas
Arroyos de Mantua
Archipiélago de los Colorados
Carabelita
La Bajada
Bolondrón
María La Gorda
Península de Guanahacabibes
Golfo de Guanahacabibes

Nueva Gerona
Revolución
La Demajagua
Atanagildo Cajigal
La Victoria
Santa Ana
Playa Bibijagua
Juraco
La Fe
La Ceiba
Siguanea
San Carlos
Cabo Francés

PROVINCE OF PINAR DEL RÍO

T he province of Pinar del Río, which has long lagged behind the rest of the country economically, is now becoming a mecca for eco-tourism. Natural wonders lie hidden away in the hills and vales of this province, which is sculpted by the Guaniguanico mountain range. To hell with Cuba's famous beaches! Hikers and nature lovers come here, to the country's westernmost province.

This region has some of the best farmlands in Cuba, and for many years its only source of wealth was its tobacco plantations. The province's agribusinesses began to thrive during the Revolution, before the present economic crisis hit. Today, the tourist industry is booming.

The province is perhaps best symbolized, however, by the tobacco drying huts tucked away in its extraordinary landscapes. A large portion of the rural population still grows tobacco using

traditional methods, and while ultramodern greenhouses are becoming more and more common in amongst these huts, with their roofs made of palm fronds, tractors are still rare and oxen are legion on these red lands.

The national highway runs west from Havana to Pinar del Río, the capital of the province of the same name, covering a distance of 147 kilometres. On the way, you'll cross the Sierra del Rosario (on the right), which is home to some positively spectacular vegetation, partly because of this microclimate's heavy rainfall. It is not uncommon to see trees nearly 30 metres high in this region, the first in Cuba to be designated a Biosphere Reserve by UNESCO (1985). The special community of Las Terrazas and its superb hotel, La Moka, are only a few kilometres from Soroa and its marvelous orchid garden.

Founded in 1774, the sleepy town of **Pinar del Río** was originally named

Nueva Filipina, after the then Captain General, Felipe Fondes Viela. The capital of the province of the same name, the town was very slow to develop and thus given all sorts of derogatory epithets. Habaneros often make wisecracks about residents of this region. Of course, these jokes are unjustified; the people of Pinar del Río are friendly, unpretentious and eager to be of help.

The Valle de Viñales, in the Sierra de los Organos, contains the most unusual and spectacular geological formations in the country. It is hard to describe the overwhelming feeling of discovery and disorientation that comes over one while contemplating the *mogotes*, a series of steep, detached mountains resembling a giant field of mushrooms. You will be continually amazed on your way through this legendary valley. The artist who first painted this landscape back in the 19th century was accused of trying to pull one over on his compatriots: there was no way that such a landscape could exist, people claimed, it was simply his wild imagination! This valley also contains the largest grouping of caves in the Americas, including the Caverna de Santo Tomás, which has about thirty kilometres of superimposed subterranean tunnels.

The Sierra de los Organos, where the Valle de Viñales is located, has an extremely varied landscape, and plant and animal life peculiar to this region. Some sixty winged species inhabit the area, making it an excellent place for bird-watching. The highest point in the region, the Pan de Guajaibón (692 metres above sea-level) is located at the west end of the Sierra de los Organos, in a group of mountains known as the Mil Cumbres (Thousand Summits).

The westernmost part of Cuba is somewhat hard to get to, but more adventurous travellers won't want to miss the Península de Guanahacabibes, which stretches out into the Gulf of Mexico and has been designated a Biosphere Reserve.

The Los Colorados archipelago, off the northern coast of the province, is virtually undeveloped and harbors a number of unspoiled beaches.

 FINDING YOUR WAY AROUND

The province of Pinar del Río is linked to Havana by the national highway. The roads are particularly good in this region, and driving is the best means of reaching and exploring the province.

By Plane

There are few flights from other parts of the country to the town of Pinar del Río, but the company **Aerotaxi** *(Aeropuerto Alvaro Barba, ☎6-3088 or 6-3196)* offers individual flights and all sorts of expeditions aboard its biplanes.

By Train

The **Estación de Trenes** *(Calle Ferrocarril and Comandante Pinares, ☎2-106)* is located at the south end of Calle Comandante Pinares, not far from downtown Pinar del Río. Because buses (save for the new service offered by Víazul) are often too jam-packed and not always very comfortable, the train proves to be a wise – though much slower – choice. The train schedule varies, but there are always two or three trains leaving Pinar del Rio for Havana each day. Passengers are advised to purchase their tickets a day in advance and to arrive at the station an hour prior to departure. Tickets cost $5 each and the trip takes about five and a half hours.

By Bus

The **Estación de Omnibus** *(Calle Delicia, at the corner of Colón, ☎2-878)* is not only the local bus station, but also where you will find private taxis for trips to the Valle de Viñales or elsewhere in the province. It is usually packed. There are four daily buses to Havana, at 5am, 7:30am, 11am and 2pm. Tickets cost 10 pesos apiece, but you might have to negotiate a fare in dollars. If so, don't pay more than $7 per ticket.

Renting a Car

Havanautos *(Hotel Pinar del Río, ☎5-071 to 79)* is the only car rental company in **Pinar del Río**.

Outside of Pinar del Río, you'll have to go to **Viñales**; **Havanautos** has a branch at the Hotel La Hermita *(☎9-3204 or 9-3207)* and **Transautos** has one at the Hotel Los Jazmines *(☎9-3205)* and another at the Hotel Rancho San Vicente *(☎9-3200)* in the **Valle San Vicente**.

Taxis

For a taxi, call **Turistaxi** *(☎92-2040)*, located in the Hotel Los Jasmines.

Black-market taxis, called *particulares* are available at the local bus station. You can choose from among a number of excursions in the region. The least expensive fares are $15 for a car and driver for a full day in the Valle de Viñales; $5-10 for a one-way trip to Viñales and $50 per car to Maria La Gorda, on the Península de Guanahacabibes (160 km of poorly maintained roads).

As usual when opting for this illegal but routinely used means of transportation, you should take a few precautions, such as making sure that there are no containers full of gas in the trunk if you want to put your belongings there. Furthermore, the cars are in such pitiful condition that you might end up spending the afternoon by the side of the road rather than at the desired destination. All things considered, though, this is an inexpensive and colourful means of transportation.

 PRACTICAL INFORMATION

Tourist Information

Most hotels in this region have tourist information offices where you can reserve rooms in the province and elsewhere in Cuba. Also, especially in the Valle de Viñales, these offices organize and sell all sorts of excursion packages. The rates and itineraries vary little from one place to the next.

On the other hand, if you're an adventurous soul, are on a tight budget and are fleeing the hordes of tourists, you can take part in another kind of excursion by stopping in at one of the region's family restaurants, such as the **Restaurante Don Miguel** *(108 Calle Geraldo Medina, between Calle Virtudes and Calle Medina)*, in Pinar del Río. Your best option hands-down, however, is to contact **Ricardo Alvarez** *(Calle Ceferino Fernandez 2, next to the park)*, Viñales's unofficial historian. He knows the region like the back of his hand, and can act as your guide or simply answer any questions you might have. Ask for him at the **Paladar Valle-Var** *(100 Calle Salvador Cisneros, Valle de Viñales)*. Ricardo Alvarez is a pleasant, serious man who not only knows the best places to go trekking or

PROVINCE OF PINAR DEL RÍO

spelunking, meet local farmers and fighting cock breeders, but is also interested in the region's flora and fauna, and can tell you all kinds of legends. Of course, if you know a little Spanish, you'll learn even more!

Currency Exchange

As elsewhere in Cuba, the local hotels are the best places to change your money into U.S. dollars.

Post Offices

Once again, the most (and perhaps only!) reliable way to send mail out of the country is to use the postal services at one of the local hotels. Your mail is likely to reach its destination faster if you send it from Havana, however.

 EXPLORING

The Sierra del Rosario ★★

Las Terrazas ★, located about 60 kilometres west of Havana, is a relatively modern community whose Soviet-style concrete architecture thumbs its nose rather spectacularly at the mountainous terrain. Located in front of a small lake, Las Terrazas was founded in 1971 in a region that was declared a Biosphere Reserve by UNESCO in 1985. This reserve, which covers an area of 25,000 hectares, contains six million trees that have been planted in an extensive reforestation program. Numerous trails have been cleared, some leading to the ruins of coffee plantations dating back to the 19th century, when large numbers of French immigrants from Haiti settled in the area.

Hidden away in the forest, the **Hotel La Moka** fits in perfectly with the natural setting. Trees tower over the roof, and the different stories of the hotel follow the shape of the mountainous terrain. The location is absolutely beautiful, and the hotel is just the place to take a breather between two outings. For that matter, hiking excursions on area trails can be organized from here. To reach the hotel, you have to take the little country road that runs under the arch of the buildings in Las Terrazas.

Soroa ★★

You can take either the national highway or the small country road from Las Terrazas to Soroa, about 15 kilometres to the west. The latter is by far the more scenic route, winding through the Biosphere Reserve and the Sierra del Rosario. Although the road is not well marked, the soldiers at the guard posts will be able to show you the way. Soroa is a small seaside resort nestled against a mountain.

The **Orchideario Soroa ★★** *($2; every day 8am to 4pm; Carretera Soroa, km 8, ☎2558)* is a botanical garden containing over 900 species of orchids and some 11,000 ornamental plants. Perched on a mountainside 206 metres above sea-level, it was once the estate of Tomás Camacho, a wealthy Spanish lawyer from the Canary Islands. He laid out the garden, which covers 3.5 hectares, in memory of his daughter. It now belongs to the Universidad de Pinar del Río. Not only are the trails magnificent, but the belvedere at the top commands a magnificent panoramic view of the valley and has an outdoor cafe where you can sample a wide variety of natural juices.

Pinar del Río

0   200   400m

N

ATTRACTIONS

1. Museo de Ciencias Naturales
2. Teatro Milanes
3. Museo Provincial
4. Fábrica de Guayabita del Pinar «Ceferino Fernández»
5. Parque de la Independencia
6. Centro Provincial de Artes Plásticas
7. Centro de Producción y de Desarollo de la Literatura
8. Fábrica de Tabacos Francisco Donatién

© ULYSSES

North of the Sierra del Rosario are the thermal, mineral and medicinal baths of **San Diego de los Baños** *(Calle 23, ☎3-7812)*. On the way there, you'll pass the **Parque Nacional la Guira** set near an old mansion where woods and lakes are teeming with rich animal and plant life.

Pinar del Río

Avenida Martí

The **Museo de Ciencias Naturales** *($1; Tue to Sat 2pm to 6pm, Sun 9am to 1pm; Avenida Martí no. 202, at the corner of Comandante Pinares)* occupies an old family residence built at the turn of the century. Formerly known as the **Palacio Guasch**, the building has a somewhat extravagant design, definitely the most unusual in town. Sup-

posedly, its original owner ruined himself building the place. The museum, devoted to natural science, will appeal mainly to children; the tyrannosaurus on the patio is sure to thrill the littlest ones.

The **Teatro Milanes**, also on Avenida Martí, is worth a quick look. Erected in 1880, it is made entirely of wood and can seat over 520 people. Right nearby, the **Museo Provincial** *($1; Tue to Sat 2pm to 6pm, Sun 9am to 1pm; Avenida Martí no. 58, between Calle Recreo and Calle Colón, ☎4-300)* traces the history of the province of Pinar del Río from the days when it was inhabited by natives to the Revolution of 1959. This museum merits a short visit, if only to take a look at its colonial architecture and the handful of objects bearing witness to the region's past, including an old fire engine.

The **Fábrica de Guayabita del Pinar "Ceferino Fernández"** *(free admission; every day 8am to 4:30pm; Calle Isabel Rubio no. 189, between Calle Ceferino Fernández and Calle Sol, ☎2900)* produces *guayabita*, a kind of liquor typical of this region.

Parque de la Independencia ★

Located all the way at the west end of Avenida Martí, across from the Hotel Pinar del Río, Parque de la Independencia is surrounded by houses with neoclassical façades. Among these, two places are sure to appeal to visitors interested in cultural pursuits. The **Centro Provincial de Artes Plásticas** *(free admission; Parque de la Independencia, between Avenida Maceo and Avenida Martí)* displays works by contemporary artists from the province of Pinar del Río. Make sure to stop in and take a look at the paintings, sculptures and other pieces included in the temporary exhibitions.

Literature buffs won't want to miss the **Centro de Producción y de Desarollo de la Literatura** *(free admission; at the corner of Avenida Maceo and Avenida Martí)*, located in the upper section of the park. Here, behind a superb neoclassical façade with yellow-coloured walls, local writers get together in offices and sitting rooms for coffee and literary discussions. The house used to belong to a family of prolific artists by the name of Loynaz. The Loynaz family poets and musicians were well known locally, and Dulce María Loynaz earned international recognition for her literary achievements. Spain awarded her the Cervantes prize, the Hispanic equivalent of the Nobel Prize.

When you leave Parque de la Independencia, take Avenida Maceo east toward the centre of town. The **Fábrica de Tabacos Francisco Donatier** ★ *($2; Mon to Fri 7:30am to 4:30pm, Sat 7:30am to 11:30am; Avenida Maceo no. 157, between Calle Galiano and Calle Antonia Tarafa, ☎3-424)* is easy to spot at the first intersection. Erected in 1868, this imposing blue-coloured colonial house was used as a prison until the Revolution of 1959. Hundreds of sick people were also quarantined here during a cholera epidemic that wiped out part of the town during the colonial era.

The house was converted into a cigar factory in 1961. Given that the province's primary agricultural resource is tobacco, the importance of this factory is obvious. Visitors can observe the various stages involved in making cigars and admire the workers' remarkable manual dexterity. A tour of the premises is a feast for the senses: the distinctive fragrance of tobacco leaves blends with the smoke from the craftsmen's cigars; the matte colours of the tobacco leaves and the workers' faces contrast with the bright blue walls; and whether you smoke or not, why not take the opportunity to sample one of the cigars made exclusively at this factory? Dip the tip into a small cup of coffee or a glass of cognac and let the smoke dance across your palate.

Aguas Claras ★

Located on the road to the Valle de Viñales, 7.5 kilometres from Pinar del Río, Aguas Claras is the former estate of a wealthy local doctor, who bequeathed his land to the Communist Youth Movement. For many years, young Cubans came here to go camping and explore the area. Since adapted to attract foreign tourists, the estate now boasts a number of superb bungalows and a charming restaurant. Even if you don't want to stay at Aguas

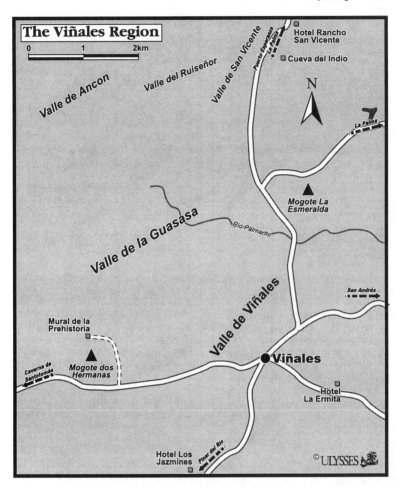

The Viñales Region

0   1   2km

Hotel Rancho San Vicente
Cueva del Indio
Valle de San Vicente
Puerto Esperanza / La Palma
Valle del Ruiseñor
Valle de Ancon
N
La Palma
Mogote La Esmeralda
Valle de la Guasasa
Río Palmarito
Valle de Viñales
San Andrés
Mural de la Prehistoria
Caverna de Santotomás
Mogote dos Hermanas
●Viñales
Hotel La Ermita
Hotel Los Jazmines
Pinar del Río
©ULYSSES

Claras, it is worth stopping by for a look.

The entrance to the estate is lined with magnificent, lush vegetation. There is also a wooden bridge spanning a little pond, where, if you're lucky, you'll see hundreds of water lilies showing off their lovely colours. The numerous gardens on the estate are adorned with fountains and tropical plants. More unusually, there are specimens of all the fruit trees found in the country, complete with signs to identify them.

Valle de Viñales ★★★

The little village of Viñales is probably one of the most charming communities in Cuba. Calle Salvador Cisnero is the only major road that crosses Viñales and its little Parque Martí. The modest old houses dating from the colonial era and the turn of the century make it seem as if time had stopped, leaving the village the way it was back when the first daring colonists arrived here. For that matter, the details about Viñales's founders remain somewhat vague.

According to legend, the credit goes to two Spanish brothers by the name of Viñas, who settled here during the colonial era, in the 1680s, although the town wasn't officially founded until 1879. There were no roads linking the Valle de Viñales to the town of Pinar del Río; instead, it was linked to the little town of La Esperanza, located to the north, in the Los Colorado archipelago. The little village of Viñales, inhabited by tobacco and *malanga* (a kind of potato typical of this region) farmers, remained virtually unknown until the 1930s. It was discovered in a manner of speaking, around this time by a group of American photographers who organized an expedition to the Valle de Viñales after Domingo Ramos, a painter from Havana, exhibited his works in New York. One piece was particularly noteworthy: a mural about 10 metres long showing the Valle de Viñales. The "experts" in New York declared that such a landscape could not exist, and that it was a product of the painter's imagination. From that moment on, the curiosity of people around the world was piqued. The photographs, for their part, would reveal the truth.

The Valle de Viñales has the oldest geological formation in Cuba, and thus contains numerous fossils dating from the Jurassic period, as well as petrified shells. Believe it or not, the area's cork palms (*mycrocyca calocoma*) are actually living fossils.

What will really grab your attention, however, are the *mogotes*, a series of limestone mountains that sprang up abruptly in this valley, which spans

nearly 25 kilometres. The celebrated Spanish poet Garcia Lorca supposedly said that "at dawn, the *mogotes* are like elephants in single file". These hills result from the erosion of a plateau that was located here 160 million years ago. Local villagers simply explain them as a freak of nature. Each *mogote* has its own unique features. Apparently, the fossilized shells they contain account for their different colours.

A stroll along Calle Salvador Cisneros will take you to Parque Martí, a charming little public square where the **Casa de Cultura** organizes cultural activities for the community. The schedule of events is posted at the entrance. Right nearby, in a small house with two columns, the **Galeria de Arte** *(Tue and Wed 8am to 5pm, Thu to Sat 1pm to 9pm, Sun 8am to noon)* regularly presents exhibitions of contemporary Cuban painting. The **Museo Municipal de Viñales Adela Azcuy** *(Calle Salvador Cisneros)* displays a small collection of articles related to the history of the village.

Two or three streets north of Calle Salvador Cisneros, you can say goodbye to the asphalt and hello to a small dirt road that leads directly to the spectacular mountains of the Valle de Viñales. To set off on this little jaunt, just head left on Calle Adela Azcuy. There is also a road leading to the Mural de la Prehistoris (see below).

North of Viñales

The road heads out of Viñales and comes to an end at the region's most traditional tourist attractions. Unfortunately, due to the booming tourist industry, a number of the sites mentioned below are overrun with so many buses and tour groups that their beauty has been somewhat marred. On your way, you can skip the **Cuevas de Viñales** *($1)*, a group of little caves that have been converted into a bar and a nightclub. The place might be of interest to you, however, if you feel the need for some refreshments. The more spectacular **Cueva del Indio ★** *($3)* consists of four kilometres of subterranean galleries. You can take a 15-minute ride aboard a motorized rowboat, which runs along an underground river known as **El Abra del Ancón**, carrying passengers a distance of about 700 metres. Since 1920, a number of archaeological excavations have uncovered sculptures dating back three to four millenia. Furthermore, Guanahatabey Indians supposedly took refuge in these caves after the Spanish conquered the territory. During our visit, tourists seriously outnumbered the Aboriginals, with their flashes bombarding the impressive walls of the cave.

The next stop on the traditional tourist itinerary is the Dos Hermanas *mogote*, whose slopes are adorned with a mural depicting the evolution of man. Entitled **Mural de la Prehistoria ★**, this painting is of impressive size, truly larger than life. It was commissioned by Fidel Castro and executed by Cuban artist Leovigildo González, a student of the celebrated Mexican muralist Diego Rivera. Many tour buses stop here at noontime during the high season, so if you want to fully appreciate the tranquility of the site, it is best to come here early in the morning.

Península de Guanahacabibes ★★

The seaside resort of **Maria La Gorda** *(☎3-121)*, located on the Península de Guanahacabibes, features white sandy beaches and scores of coconut trees, among other things. The untouched forests farther inland lend themselves

well to outings for those interested in discovering the region's plant and animal life. This area is somewhat difficult to get to, but its isolation creates a peaceful, relaxed atmosphere.

 OUTDOOR ACTIVITIES

 Hiking

The **Valle de Viñales** lies in the Sierra de los Organos, and this entire region is a veritable hiking paradise. Visitors can organize all sorts of expeditions in one of the valleys in this mountain range; in addition to the Valle de Viñales, the best-known by far, there are no fewer than five other valleys that you can explore: the Valle del Silencio, the Valle del Reuiseñor, the Valle de San Vicente, the Valle de Ancón and the Valle de Dos Hermanas.

It is best to hire a guide for these expeditions. To do so, inquire at the **El Hermita** or **Los Jazmines** hotel, or contact **Ricardo Alvarez** *(Calle Ceferino Fernandez 2, next to the park Valle de Viñales, no 111)*, who offers excellent tours of the region.

Running through the Valle de Viñales is a trail about four kilometres long, which leads past groups of trees growing right out of the limestone of the *mogotes*. In addition to orchids, you'll see cork palms, living fossils peculiar to this region. The trip takes about four hours (return).

The region's most fascinating sight is **Los Acuaticos**, perched atop the **Sierra de los Infiernos**. The patriarch of this isolated, water-worshipping community is named Félix. The trail leading there runs through local farmlands for about six kilometres, and includes a few moderately difficult uphill sections. Along the way, you can visit a number of huts used for drying tobacco. Altogether, the trip takes between five and six hours.

Ricardo Alvarez's favourite excursion leads along a trail he cleared himself. It runs from the **Valle de San Vicente**, near the **Cueva del Indio**, and climbs up a *mogote* to the magnificent little **Valle del Ruiseñor**. It then passes through a 200-metre natural tunnel formed by a river, which opens onto the Valle de Ancón. The hike covers a total of five kilometres.

The **Caverno de Santo Tomas** is the largest cave in Latin America, with 45 kilometres of superimposed subterranean tunnels. Its scientific value is tremendous, and it naturally attracts spelunkers from all over the world. The Caverno de Santo Tomas is located in the Valle de Quemado, and visitors looking for a truly extraordinary adventure can take part in an underground expedition of a day or more. To do so, you must be properly outfitted to deal with the difficult conditions of subterranean life. Don't even consider exploring the cave without a guide! The El Ermita and Los Jazmines hotels in Viñales both organize spelunking expeditions.

All sorts of excursions in the Biosphere Reserve on the Península de Guanahacabibes can be arranged at the seaside resort of Maria La Gorda. This region is harder to get to than the Valle de Viñales, however.

 Scuba Diving

One of the best places to go diving in Cuba is off the western tip of the province of Pinar del Río. There are 35 scuba diving sites at the **International Diving Centre of Maria La Gorda** *(Cabo Corrientes y Cabo de San Anto-*

nio, ☎3-121). The seabed abounds with marine animal life (barracudas, rays, rock lobsters, etc.), red and black coral and sponges.

 Horseback Riding

Horseback riding is an excellent way to explore the expansive farmlands surrounding **Aguas Claras** *(Carretera de Viñales, Km 7.5, ☎2-722)*. Accompanied by Multi, who runs the estate singlehandedly, we set off on horseback at dawn. Our first stop was the home of a farmer named Machito. After sampling some coffee made with beans grown on his land, we helped milk the cows, then visited one of those strawroofed huts, innumerable in this region, which are used for drying tobacco. Finally, we explored stretches of farmland planted with tobacco, manioc and fruit trees. Along the way, we passed through a number of tiny farming villages and came across far more oxen than tractors.

 ACCOMMODATIONS

Las Terrazas

The finest hotel in the Sierra del Rosario region lies hidden away in the mountains, behind the extravagant buildings of Las Terrazas. The **Hotel La Moka** *($50-75; ≡, pb, ≈, ℛ, tv, ☎; highway km 51, ☎80-5516, ≈33-5516)* was built in 1994, and staying here is one of the most gratifying experiences imaginable. The place fits in perfectly with the natural surroundings. Trees tower over the roof, and the building is completely engulfed by vegetation — putting guests in perfect harmony with nature. Although the restaurant and bars are very pleasant, nothing surpasses the comfort and exotic charm of the rooms, with their brick arches, wooden furnishings and decorative ceramics. The terrace faces right onto the woods, and it is doubtful that you have ever slept so close to the wilderness in such great comfort. To top it all off, the bathroom is as romantic as can be, with a big tub at the base of an enormous window looking out at the woods, making you feel as if you are bathing in a stream. The Hotel La Moka is an ideal place for a honeymoon, and will appeal to all romantics.

Soroa

The accommodations in Soroa are inexpensive. The **Villa Soroa** *($30; ≈, pb, ≈, ℛ; Carretera de Soroa, Km 8, ☎85-2122 or 85-2041)* is a series of pleasant little bungalows (*cabañas*). Three-bedroom houses complete with a kitchen and private pool are also available for $84. Reservations for the latter are made at the Villa Soroa, though the houses are a short distance away, on the Carretera del Castillo de las Nubes.

Pinar del Río

There are few quality hotels in the town of Pinar del Río, as the tourist industry in this region is centred around Viñales rather than the capital. Your best option is the **Hotel Pinar del Río** *($24; ≈, ≈, ℛ, pb; Avenida Martí, ☎5-070 to 5-074)*, which has just about all the standard facilities of good hotels. If you're looking for someplace a little more comfortable, however, ask for one of the *cabañas ($45)*, which are equipped with a television and a refrigerator. There are about a dozen hotels just like this on the island. Its entryway is fairly large and attractively surrounded by tropical plants, which adds a delicate touch to the concrete forms of the big building. The rooms, decorated with simple, functional 1970s-style furnishings, open onto an outdoor passageway in the front and a small private terrace at the back. Those facing onto Avenida Martí can be noisier than the others, especially if you like to sleep with the windows open. The hotel is well located, at the edge of town, right near the highway exit. It faces the student residences of the Universidad de Pinar del Río. It is a five minute walk along Avenida Martí to the downtown area and local points of interest.

The **Hotel Globo** *($25; ⊛, ℛ, pb, cold water only; Avenida Martí no. 50, ☎4-268)* is the most centrally located hotel in town. If price is your main concern, you won't be disappointed. The turn-of-the-century architecture of the lobby lends the place an air of bygone luxury that is sure to appeal to nostalgic types. Guests receive a warm welcome, and there is a common TV room on the second floor. The maid service (cleaning, sheets, etc.) is barely adequate. In any case, it is always best to bring a pair of clean sheets or a sleeping bag with you when you stay in this type of place in Cuba.

Aguas Claras

The perfect compromise between the Viñales area and the town of Pinar del Río, the superb *cabañas* at **Aguas Claras** *($30-50; ℛ, ≈, ≈, pb; Carretera de Viñales, km 7.5, ☎30-0662)* offer both comfort and an outstanding natural setting. Built on the estate of a wealthy local doctor who left his land to the Communist Youth Movement, these bungalows look out over the swimming pool. The restaurant is extremely charming and serves excellent food, and the staff is as friendly as can be, as if the serenity of the surroundings had rubbed off on them. A tradi-

PROVINCE OF
PINAR DEL RÍO

tional Cuban house located next to the ranch is also available for rent. A ranch wouldn't be a ranch without horses, of course, and mounts can be rented by the hour. A man named Multi runs Aguas Claras singlehandedly, so if you want to head out on horseback be sure to tell him a few hours ahead of time to give him ample time to get the horses ready.

Valle de Viñales

The hotels in Viñales are of superior quality. Each has its own unique charm, and whichever you choose, you're sure to have a pleasant stay in the area. If you're on a tight budget, however, you can try renting a room in a private home. There are many *casas particulares* in Viñales, most of which are on the main street leaving the village toward the caves area. Your best option is a lovely two-story house belonging to **Inecita Nuñez** *($10-15; at the north end of Calle Salvador Cisnero)*. The elderly couple who live here will give you a warm, friendly welcome. Turning on *Ceferino Fernandez*, right across from the park, leads to the house of **Juana La Gorda**. This kind lady rents out simple and comfortable rooms *($10)* in a thoroughly Cuban ambiance. She also serves dishes as delicious as they are typical upon request, and will regale those interested with tales of how the revolutionaries set up their radio stations in the surrounding hills more than 40 years ago. For further information, stop by the **Paladar Valle-Bar** *(Calle Salvador Cisnero no. 100)*.

About five kilometres north of Viñales, the **Rancho San Vicente** *($30; ≡, ≈, ℛ, pb, ☺; Carretera Puerto Esperanza, Km 8, Valle San Vicente, ☎9-3200, ☛33-5020)* is not as charming as its local competitors. It does, however,

offer medicinal and mineral baths and it is located near the caves where you can get a good breath of fresh air.

The **Hotel La Ermita** *($34-52; ≡, ≈, ℛ, pb; Carretera La Ermita, Km 1, ☎9-3204, ☛93-6091)* is located about 20 minutes on foot from the village of Viñales. Peaceful and secluded, it is the perfect place to relax and drink in the lovely landscape. Each room has a balcony with wooden chaises longues, providing a little haven of comfort where you can relax with a book or write a few notes in your travel diary. The rooms are decorated in a simple fashion, and the wooden furniture creates a suitably rustic atmosphere. In the evening, the restaurant has a pleasant ambiance and serves excellent Creole cuisine. Nothing, however, compares to the breakfast served on the restaurant's terrace, as the view of the Valle de Viñales is positively breathtaking. If you are an early riser, don't miss the spectacular sight of the sun rising up from behind the *mogotes*. And don't forget your camera! This hotel is one of the best bargains in the Valle de Viñales. While you're here, you can go horseback riding, enjoy an excursion in the valley or explore the local caves.

The **Hotel Los Jazmines** *($48; ℛ, ≈, ≡, pb; Carretera de Viñales, Km 25, ☎9-3205, ☛33-5042)* is located on a mountainside by the road to Pinar del Río, a few metres from Viñales. Built in 1964, it has colonial-style architecture and is adorned with stained-glass windows, precious wood and gardens. Every effort has been made to create a setting that is both luxurious and picturesque. The terraces and belvedere command a spectacular view of the Valle de Viñales, and the mountainside swimming pool is a true delight. The hotel tourist office organizes excursions in the Valle de Viñales. This place is busier than La Hermita, and many motorists stop by during the day to take in the view from the belvedere, so there is less peace and quiet.

 RESTAURANTS

Pinar del Río

As elsewhere in Cuba, a number of family-run restaurants, or *paladares*, have recently opened in Pinar del Río. Cyclists and pedestrians will probably come up to you and recommend various places; these people are hired by the *paladares* and get a commission and free meals for bringing in customers. This practice is common in Pinar del Río, but you'll probably prefer to find a place on your own.

The most typical *paladar* in town is definitely the **Restaurante Don Miguel** *($; Calle Geraldo Medina no. 108, between Calle Virtudes and Calle Medina)*. Decorated with graffiti, a bit like the Bodeguita del Medio in Havana, this little restaurant serves what just might be the most delicious Creole cuisine in Pinar del Río. A convivial atmosphere is guaranteed, thanks to the owner, Miguel, who, if you're lucky, will pick up his guitar and play you a few tunes. Tourists from all over, many of them backpackers, gather here, so if you want to savour the flavours of Cuban cuisine and round up a group of people for an excursion in the area, Don Miguel's is the place to go.

Another local *paladar*, the **Restaurante Nuestra Casa** *($; Calle Colón no. 161, between Calle Virtudes and Calle Vendama)* serves Creole cuisine at affordable prices. Guests can sit on the rooftop terrace or inside the little house. The only drawback is the loud, rather unpleasant pop music coming out of the loudspeakers on the terrace (the young Cubans love it, however).

Fortunately, the management doesn't seem to mind lowering the volume or changing the music at their customers' request.

The **Palacio de la Artesanía** *($; 8am to 1am; Calle Sol, at the corner of Calle Cotoma, ☎2-706)* serves the best breakfasts in town. Slightly removed from the downtown area, but very close to the train station, this is a pleasant, comfortable place. It is set up inside a colonial house built in 1876, which once belonged to a Spanish journalist named Angel Ruiz Haya, credited with founding the first local newspaper. As indicated by its name, the Palacio de la Artesanía is also a sales outlet for Cuban handicrafts (second floor). The fare consists mainly of fried chicken and pizza, but the management is considering offering a Creole menu as well. If you'd like to sample some *guayabita*, a kind of liquor typical of this province, you can sip a glass before dinner in the restaurant's attractive entrance hall.

At the intersection of the road that leads out of Pinar del Río toward the Viñales region, the **Rumayor** *($$; noon to 2pm; Carretera a Viñales, km 1, ☎6-3007)* serves good food in a very unusual setting. The architecture is an oversized, modern version of the building techniques used by natives in this region. The immense dining room is decorated with an original (to say the least) assortment of Afro-Cuban and indigenous crafts. The overall effect is so spectacular that at first glance you might think you've landed on a tourist trap. Never fear; the place was built long before Pinar del Río began attracting tourists, and apparently used to be the local residents' favourite hangout. Unfortunately, the crowds aren't what they used to be, as most of the Cuban clientele was driven off when the place started listing its prices in U.S. dollars. Consequently, the enormous dining room is likely to be somewhat empty when you stop by. Thanks to its decor, however, it is still inviting. The menu is limited, and unfortunately as the evening progresses many of your requests may be greeted with the response *no hay* ("there isn't any more").

There are a few, easy-to-spot restaurants downtown on Avenida Martí. Although they have not yet succumbed to the economic crisis, these places are somewhat lifeless and decrepit in comparison to the *paladares* mentioned above. For traditional cuisine, the **Restaurante La Casona** *($; Avenida Martí, at the corner of Calle Colón)* seems a bit more inviting than the **El Marino** *($; Avenida Martí, at the corner of Calle Recreo)*, a rather gloomy-looking seafood restaurant. The prices at both places are listed in pesos.

Valle de Viñales

The **Paladar Valle-Bar** *($; Calle Salvador Cisnero no. 100)* is the least expensive and most picturesque place in Viñales. This family-run restaurant serves full Creole meals for $5 and $7 per person, including coffee and dessert. Lobster is also available for $8. The place is charming and friendly, and the colourful personality of the owner, Dagobert Rico Millo, adds to the atmosphere. There is also a fairly good selection of wine and spirits.

The restaurant in the **Hotel La Ermita** *($$; Carretera la Ermita, Km 1, ☎93-6071)*, located about twenty minutes by foot from the village of Viñales, serves succulent Creole cuisine in an enchanting setting at the foot of the *mogotes*. Come for breakfast on the terrace, which commands a magnificent panoramic view of the Valle de Viñales.

The bar-restaurant **Casa Don Tomás** *($$$; Calle Salvador Cisneros, Viñales, ☎9-3114)* occupies the most luxurious house in Viñales. Supposedly the finest restaurant in town, it serves excellent Creole cuisine, and boasts attentive and courteous service.

 ENTERTAINMENT

Pinar del Río

The **Rumayor** *(noon to 2pm; Carretera a Viñales, Km 1, ☎6-3007)* has the largest nightlife facilities in the region. Its outdoor stage is hidden beneath lush tropical vegetation and surrounded by bars and restaurants. Although the crowds have thinned down since the economic crisis set in, it's still a great place to take in an evening show or concert.

 SHOPPING

Pinar del Río

An excellent selection of handicrafts from this region and other parts of Cuba can be found on the second floor of the **Palacio de la Artesanía** *(9am to 5pm; Calle Sol, at the corner of Calle Cotoma, ☎2-706)*, near the train station.

THE VARADERO RÉGION

Hundreds of thousands of tourists come to Varadero each year, lured mainly by the white sandy beaches, which span a total length of over 18 kilometres. Since the collapse of the Soviet Union in 1990, the development of the local tourist industry has transformed the urban landscape, though a few old wooden houses and streets have survived unchanged.

Located on the Península de Hicacos, in the province of Matanzas, Varadero is a long, thin strip of land that juts into the sea. The beaches are magnificent, and Cubans rightly claim that they are the loveliest in the country. The calm, clear waters range in colour from turquoise to deep blue, with a million and one shades in between. The average temperature in Varadero is 25° C, and the ocean, warm year-round, is perfect for swimming and water sports.

Varadero is a seaside resort which has nothing in common with the rest of the country. Here, you are more likely to meet a European or a Canadian than a Cuban. The few residents you'll encounter are likely to be hotel or restaurant employees or, sadly, *jineteros* and prostitutes, who come here by the thousands to try to reap some of the benefits of the booming tourist industry. Customs certainly do change with the times; the peaceful, untouched paradise of the not so distant past now exists only in the minds of those who knew Varadero before 1990.

The vast majority of tourists come here on package trips of one or two weeks, and few abandon this carefree environment to explore the rest of Cuba. The real Cuba, however, is only a few kilometres away, so, by all means, go take a look!

Located 42 kilometres west of Varadero, the town of Matanzas, capital of the province of the same name, is nicknamed the "Athens of Cuba". One of the most important towns in the country in the 19th century, it later succumbed to an unstoppable economic decline. Since known as the "sleepy town", it still boasts majestic neoclassical buildings, which look out onto the wide Bahía de San Juan. A sizeable town (pop. 120,000), Matanzas is a pleasant place to wander about at random, although it seems like most people simply pass through here on their way from Havana to Varadero, as the streets are usually clogged with traffic. Matanzas, city of music, is the birthplace of the *danzón*, a musical style that has been popular for several decades now. You're sure to enjoy spending a day or two here.

Cárdenas, located about 15 kilometres south of Varadero, is a typical Cuban town, which owes its existence to sugar production. It was founded in the last century, when many French colonists fleeing the Haitian independence movement took refuge here. A sort of buffer between the modernity of Varadero and the country's colonial past, Cárdenas, a forgotten town, never realized its glorious expectations. Today, a number of neoclassical houses can be found here, along with one of the most amazing museums in the country and hundreds of cyclists zig-zagging along traditional avenues. All in all, a visit to Cárdenas will give you a foretaste of what the Cuban interior looks like. Anyone who spends half a day here is sure to return to Varadero happy about what they have discovered and surprised that their travel agent never mentioned this town to them.

Finally, San Miguel de Los Baños, south of Cárdenas on the road to the Bay of Pigs (see p 174), was a sea-water spa at the beginning of the century. Since abandoned, its stately structures try their best to brave the passage of the years, reminders of a more lavish era. The rolling landscape and cool breeze makes it easy to understand why this place was so popular. You can spend anywhere from half a day to two days in this area, and enjoy all sorts of hiking excursions while you're here.

FINDING YOUR WAY AROUND

Varadero

By Plane

The **Aeropuerto Juan Gualberto Gómez**, 26 kilometres southwest of Varadero, is well-equipped to meet travellers' needs and handle all the air traffic here in the country's most popular tourist spot. Bus transportation from the airport is included in most vacation packages. If this is not the case for you, there is unfortunately no other inexpensive means of getting into town. The taxis parked in front of the airport will charge you about $30 for the trip. You can try to take the workers' bus, which stops at the airport twice a day, at 4:10pm and at 8pm. Whether or not you'll be allowed on board depends on the driver's good will, though. Remember to give the driver a dollar once aboard. This is the expected fare for tourists who take the buses reserved for Varadero workers.

When you leave, be careful not to forget your jacket, coat or handbag on the tables or chairs in the cafeteria on the second floor; many people have reported being pickpocketed at the airport.

Airline Offices

Aerocaribean: ☎53-616
Aerotraviota: ☎6-3016

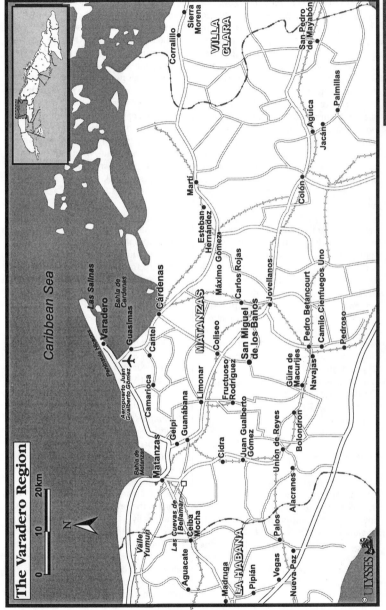

The Varadero Region

0   10   20km

Caribbean Sea

Villa Clara

Matanzas

La Habana

Aerotaxi *(Avenida Primera no. 2303, at the corner of Calle 24, ☎61-2929, ⊨66-7540)* offers a whole range of flights to Cayo Largo, the Isla de la Juventud, Trinidad and Cayo Coco. You can purchase your tickets right at their offices, although most hotels in Varadero also sell Aerotaxi packages. The flight to Cayo Largo is the most popular by far *($100 per person, including transportation to and from the airport, the 50-min flight, a boating trip off Cayo Largo and a meal)*. A bus will pick you up at your hotel around 6:30am, and the plane leaves at 7:30am. The return flight is scheduled for 4:30pm.

Groups of 10 to 12 people should seriously consider renting an entire airplane, and thus enjoy substantial savings. It is best to reserve two or three days ahead of time. The following rates are for a return flight aboard a 12-seat airplane, with the trip there and back on the same day (add $150 per plane if you plan on spending the night at your destination), excursions not included.

Cayo Largo: $473
Isla de la Juventud: $600
Trinidad: $550
Pinar del Río: $580
Cayo Coco: $770

By Bus

This is the most economical means of taking trips outside of Varadero and travelling to the major towns in the country. The **Estación de Omnibus Nacionales** *(Calle 36, at the corne of Auropista, ☎6-2626)* is located on the south shore of Varadero. Arrive at least an hour or two before the bus leaves to make sure you'll have a seat.

The least expensive way to get to **Matanzas** or **Cárdenas** from Varadero is, of course, to take one of the buses for the peninsula's hotel employees. Every night, several old German or French buses take these workers back to their home towns. The ride will only cost you a dollar, but this trick only works for those travelling in small groups or alone. At day's end, employees line up along Avenida Primera, where the bus stops. Remember to ask the driver or the people waiting in line where the bus is heading. If you are staying in one of the two aforementioned cities and wish to return to Varadero the same way, note that these buses make the return trip between 7am and 8am.

A brand-new luxury, air-conditioned bus service has just started up in Cuba. The Víazul company offers a reliable schedule for tourists. Their buses leave Varadero for Havana *($10)* at 8am and 4pm, and for **Cienfuegos** *($20)* and **Trinidad** *($25 and more than five hours' travelling)* at 8:15am.

Particulares

Illegal taxis are disappearing from the streets of Varadero. Police surveillance has been stepped up over the years, and in order to favour the big State companies, few licenses have been issued for private taxis. For long trips, however, you will find a number of *particulares* in front of the entrance of the Estación de Omnibus Nacionales. Although the drivers don't have a license for Varadero, all they have to do is cross the bridge to transport passengers legally. A driver might ask you to walk across the bridge so that he can pick you up on the other side of the canal. If this is the agreement, don't leave any personal belongings in the car. Taking *particulares* is a good way to add a touch of the picturesque to your trip.

Make sure, however, to haggle over the fare when you're dealing with unlicensed drivers. Their rates are usually two or three times higher for tourists, sometimes even more.

The following is a list of suggested *particular* fares from the Estación de Omnibus (per person, one way):

To Matanzas: $3.
To Cárdenas: $5.
To Havana: $10.
To Santa Clara: $10.

These are the same fares paid by Cubans. Your offer will generally be refused, but take the time to talk to a few drivers, and give them time to change their mind! If there are fewer than three people in your party, you can ask a reluctant driver to wait for other passengers, or suggest that he pick others up along the way.

Hitchhiking

The best place to thumb a ride is at the edge of Varadero, on the other side of the bridge, on the Vía Blanca, in the direction of Havana. There, you'll find an *amarillo*, a Cuban official wearing a yellow uniform. His job is to encourage carpooling, and he stops all State-owned cars and trucks with empty seats. If you want to head inland, go to the road that leads to Cárdenas.

By Car

Roads into Varadero are generally in good condition and well indicated. The Vía Blanca is particularly efficient. The 144-km-stretch of pavement between Varadero and Havana are presently being redone.

Two toll booths *($2 per car)* were set up on this tourist highway in 1996.

One is located at the exit of the Havana tunnel, the other at the intersection of Vía Blanca and the road to the airport outside Varadero.

Car Rental

The vast majority of hotels in Varadero have car rental counters, and the rates vary little from one company to the next. Take note that these rates are significantly higher than those in North America and sometimes even Europe. Three agencies have branches at the airport; the choice is up to you.

By Taxi

Varadero has scores of taxis, whose drivers cruise the streets or park outside the local hotels. All these vehicles are equipped with metres.

By Scooter

Popular and practical, scooters *($7.50 per hour; $24 per day)* are the perfect means of transportation for exploring Varadero and its surrounding area. They can be rented in many places; you'll need to show your driver's license. Check the condition of the scooter before accepting it.

Horse-drawn Carriages

The carriages in Varadero are light years from the cars found all over Cuba, and the rates are a clear indication of the target clientele: foreign tourists. There is no fixed rate for a ride in Varadero, and the drivers will gauge how much to charge you by your appearance. Try not to pay more than $8 per person for a two-and-a-half-hour ride.

By Bicycle

For as little as $15 a day or $5 an hour, cycling is a pleasant way to explore the peninsula, especially for anyone staying in the northern part of the peninsula and wanting to visit the village of Varadero in the centre. Always keep an eye on your wheels, for theft is frequent. Request a padlock and a chain from the person renting you the bike and above all, take it for a little spin just to check the brakes and gears. Many people rent out bicycles along Avenida Primera. If you wish to rent one for more than a day, do not hesitate to bargain the price down to a maximum of $10 per day.

Matanzas

By Train

The new station is far to the south, in the Miret area on Calle 181. The **Tren Especial No. 1 Havane-Guantánamo** leaves for **Matanzas** at around 6:25pm every day. This train stops in the following towns: **Santa Clara** *($12)*, **Guayos** *($15)*, **Ciego de Ávila** *($18)*, **Camagüey** *($22)*, **Las Tunas** *($27)*, **Holguín** *($31)*, **Santiago de Cuba** *($35)*, **Guantánamo** *($38)*. Trains returning to Havana leave early in the morning and late in the afternoon.

By Bus

Buses for distant destinations leave from the old **Estación de trenes de Matanzas** *(Calle 131 and Calle 272)*, the oldest station in the country. It was built in the 19th century to help develop the sugar industry. Departures for Havana are frequent but irregular. To travel east in the country, try to reserve your seat a day in advance or arrive a few hours before the departure time.

Buses for closer destinations (Varadero, Cardenas, etc.) use the bus station situated at the intersection of calles 127 and 298.

By Car

Vía Blanca, Cuba's main tourist highway, runs through Matanzas, which lies 102 kilometres from Havana and 42 kilometres from Varadero.

PRACTICAL INFORMATION

Varadero

Practical Information

The tourist information counters in the major hotels in Varadero offer numerous excursions, and are therefore more like travel agencies. For helpful information about this region and the rest of the country, you are better off heading to the **Centro de Información Turística** *(every day 8am to 8pm; Avenida Primera and Calle 23;* ☎*66-6666,* ⬝*66-7060)*. Here, you can learn everything you need to know about cultural activities (exhibitions, concerts, etc.) and cruises, and also reserve a table at any of the local restaurants.

If you're interested in taking a tour of the town or some other part of the country, stop by **Cubatur** *(Calle 38, between Avenidas Primera and Playa,* ☎*6-4143)* or **Havanatur Varadero** *(Avenida Playa no. 3606, between Calles 36 and 37)*.

Currency Exchange

The **Banco Financiero Internacional** *(Mon to Fri 8:30am to 7pm; Avenida Primera, at the corner of Calle 32; Sat* and Sun 8:30am to 7pm, at the back, Avenida Playa, ☎6-3144) offers the best exchange rates for U.S. currency. You can also make cash withdrawals on your credit card and exchange traveller's cheques here.

Post Offices

The **Agencia Postal Principal** *(Mon to Sat 8am to 6pm; Avenida Playa, between Calles 39 and 40, ☎6-2727 or 6-3324)* handles mail and telegrams and sells stamps.

The local mail service is generally erratic and very slow. An alternative is **DHL Mensajeria Mundial** *(Mon to Fri 8am to 5:30pm; Sat 8am to noon; Casa 318, Calle 10, at the corner of Camino del Mar, ☎and ☎66-7330)*, a private courier service.

Telecommunications

Centro Internacional de Communicaciones *(Calle 64 and Avenida Primera, ☎6-2103)*.

Most hotels in Varadero will send and receive faxes.

Medical Care

The **Farmacia** *(every day 8am to 10pm; Avenida Playa, at the corner of Calle 44, ☎6-2636)* sells natural medicines. There is one other pharmacy in town *(Avenida Primera and Calle 28, ☎6-2772)*.

The **Policlínico Internacional** *(24 hours a day, 7 days a week; at the corner of Avenida Primera and Calle 61, ☎66-7710)* offers emergency services and quality outpatient care. Certain skin diseases, such as vitiligo and psoriasis, are treated here with ointments made

with human placentas, a treatment developed by the Cuban pharmaceutical community.

The **Meliá Varadero** and the **Sol Palmeras** each have a bungalow infirmary to provide their guests with round-the-clock medical services.

Safety

Pickpocketing is more and more common on the beaches of Varadero. Make sure to take the necessary precautions, and try not to make a display of your personal belongings. To avoid unpleasant surprises, leave any valuable objects in a safe at your hotel. Here, as elsewhere in the country, you should be wary of Cubans who seem overly friendly.

Police

If you are robbed, go to the **Estación de Policía** *(Calle 39 and Avenida Primera)*.

Matanzas

Medical Care

Pharmacy: Calle 85 no. 123.

 EXPLORING

Varadero ★★

Before the Spanish arrived, the Siboney Indians lived on the Península de Hicacos, where Varadero is now located. Hunters and gatherers, they used shells, stones and wood to make tools. They belonged to the Cubanacán and Yucayo nations, two very similar indigenous cultures. Today, visitors can

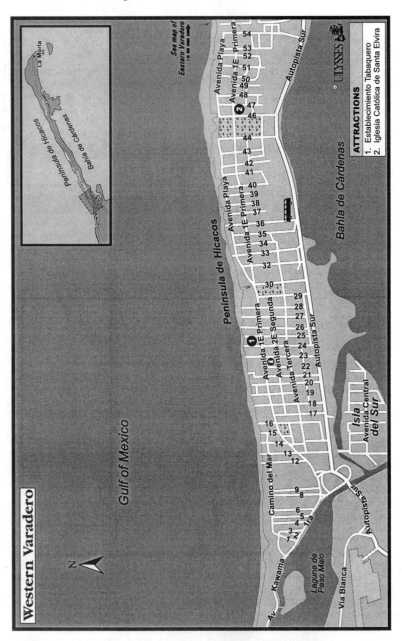

Western Varadero

Gulf of Mexico

Peninsula de Hicacos

Bahía de Cárdenas

Peninsula de Hicacos

Bahía de Cárdenas

La Moría

See map of Eastern Varadero

Avenida Playa
Avenida 1E Primera
Avenida Playa
Avenida 1E Primera
Avenida 1E Primera
Autopista Sur

Avenida 1E Primera
Avenida 2E Segunda
Avenida Tercera
Autopista Sur

Camino del Mar

Kawama
Laguna de Paso Malo
Vía Blanca
Autopista Sur

Isla
Avenida Central del Sur

ULYSSES

ATTRACTIONS

1. Establecimiento Tabaquero
2. Iglesia Católica de Santa Elvira

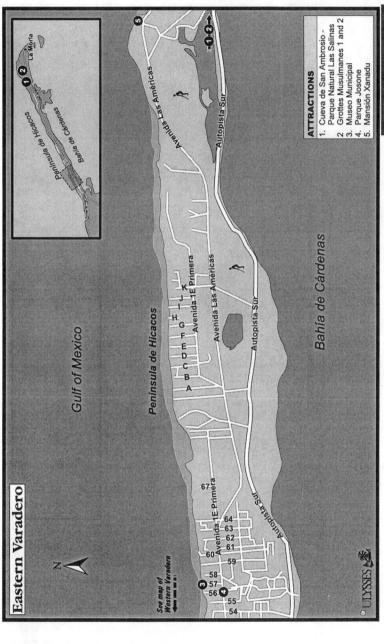

Eastern Varadero

N

Gulf of Mexico

Península de Hicacos

Bahía de Cárdenas

See map of
Western Varadero

ATTRACTIONS
1. Cueva de San Ambrosio -
   Parque Natural Las Salinas
2 Grottes Musulmanes 1 and 2
3. Museo Municipal
4. Parque Josone
5. Mansión Xanadu

© ULYSSES

The Wooden Houses of Varadero

During the first few decades of this century, the wooden buildings in Varadero reached a level of beauty and harmony unmatched anywhere else in the country. The vast majority, which exist to this day, were inspired by an American architectural style characterized by wooden porches and roofs that let the water run off away from the house. The influence of Cuban trends in construction is also evident in these houses, thus evoking a centuries-old architectural tradition. By the 16th and 17th centuries, wood was already being used for doors, windows and porches.

The primary reason wood came into use was its sheer abundance; in those years, the entire country was covered with trees. It wasn't until the 19th century, however, that the number of wooden houses increased significantly, with Cuba becoming the largest market for Louisiana's lumber industry. Along with the materials, the Cubans imported the American method of balloon framing, thus marking the area's first steps toward industrialization. Next, the growth of the country's sugar industry led to the massive felling of trees and the use of Cuban wood, as well as a return to more traditional methods of construction. Today, Varadero's architectural heritage bears witness both to American influence and the spirit and talent of the region's craftsmen.

admire the walls of the Cueva de San Ambrosio (see p 151), which are covered with about fifty Siboney drawings.

By 1555, the name Hicacos already appeared on Spanish maps. In 1587, the Spanish began working the salt mines in Las Salinas, which can still be visited (see p 151), and a small number of their slaves began living on the peninsula. It wasn't until much later, between 1872 and 1878, that the area's first landowners took up stockbreeding. At the same time, *Habaneros* began vacationing in Varadero, which was part of Cárdenas in those days. Sailboats and then steamers carried passengers from Cárdenas to Varadero, an area surrounded by uninviting swampland. The "historians" of Cárdenas are proud to point out that Varadero was the first place where lightweight bathing suits were worn. Music and cultural activities have added to the holiday atmosphere.

In 1929, the wealthy French-born American industrialist Pierre Samuel DuPont purchased 512 hectare of land in Varadero. His presence here would forever mark the area. Between 1928 and 1929, for over a million dollars, he built himself a superb residence known as the **Mansión Xanadu** ★★★, now Varadero's main tourist attraction. This majestic, Spanish colonial-style mansion, with its carved wooden balconies and windows, is reminiscent of an Andalusian palace. It stands on the San Bernardino butte, the highest point on the north coast of Varadero.

The Mansión Xanadu, as it was named by its owner, is a veritable jewel. Many Hollywood stars stayed here in the 1950s; Cary Grant, Esther Williams and Ava Gardner all visited Varadero regularly when it was still a little-known paradise with long, unspoiled beaches. Golf, deep-sea fishing, regattas... DuPont set the whole peninsula astir. He sold off pieces of his land to wealthy Americans and made numerous

Mansión Xanadu

donations to fund the construction of a church and the upkeep of a parochial school. He had to abandon his domain at the age of 85, when Cuba nationalized his property and transformed it into the Las Américas restaurant.

There are few places of cultural or historical interest in Varadero. A walk along Avenida Primera is the best way to tour the town; go early in the morning, in the late afternoon or on a cloudy day, when the sun isn't that strong. On your way back, take Avenida Playa, which runs along the north shore of Varadero. Typically Cuban places that are not geared to tourism are rare indeed in Varadero. The **Establecimiento Taba-quero** *(free admission; Mon to Sat 7am to 7pm; Avenida Primera no. 2701)* is one of the few. About twenty tobacco craftsmen from Havana live and work in this rundown house, hand-rolling the cigars sold in the hotels of Varadero. Feel free to step inside the tiny "factory", where you can watch some of the best cigar rollers in the country in action. If you speak a little Spanish, this brief sally off the beaten

tourist track will be that much more interesting. Ask for a tour of the premises!

The **Iglesia Católica de Santa Elvira** *(Avenida Primera no. 4604, at the corner of Calle 47)* is a simple yet beautiful little church, whose ceiling is made of *caoba* (mahogany). The sandy stones used to build the church are so soft that nails can easily be driven into them. The place has quite an incredible history. A chapel was built here in 1880, only to be destroyed by a hurricane eight years later. Disaster struck again in 1916, when the chapel was ravaged by fire; apparently, a drunkard had fallen asleep while smoking. As if that weren't enough, another hurricane destroyed the place again in 1933. The wealthy DuPont family, who already subsidized the parish school (the first in the country to provide free education), decided to help pay for a new church, on the condition that the local population would match each dollar with a peso. In those years, Varadero was a fishing village, and the parish priest declined the offer, not wanting to place such a heavy burden on the shoulders of a poor community. Finally, the wife of a local politician, Encarnación Sanchez, paid out the required sum and the church was rebuilt in 1938. That's the story as told by Father Yvon Bastarache, a Canadian who has been living in Varadero for years.

The **Museo Municipal** *(free admission; Mon to Sat 9am to 6pm; at the corner of Calle 57 and the waterfront, ☎61-3189)* occupies one of the most beautiful wooden houses in Varadero. Built in 1921, it proudly displays its wooden windows and porches, which were completely restored in 1996. The museum presents an exhibition on the short history of Varadero.

Parque Josone ★ *(Calle 56 and Avenida Primera)*, located north of the museum on Avenida Primera, is a pleasant park with little ponds, tropical plants and trees offering shelter from the hot midday sun. This is a good place to take a short rest. Seated on one of the public benches, you can watch ducks, flamingoes and other birds wander where they will. Although the restaurants, bowling alley, miniature golf course and craft vendors attract lots of tourists, the place is still quite peaceful.

Matanzas ★★

Matanzas means "slaughters" in Spanish, and the origins of the name are vague. According to one legend, in the year 1609 a group of Spaniards asked the Yucayos Indians, who lived in this region, to help them cross the bay. Once they were in the canoes and defenseless, the Spaniards were supposedly thrown into the sea, and only one woman survived to tell the tale. The historians of Matanzas offer a more plausible explanation, however. They assert that the Spanish general Panfilio Narváez ordered the massacre of local natives. In 1629, the Bahía de San Juan was the scene of a naval battle still talked about to this day. Dutch pirate Pieter Hayn, known as "Peg Leg", attacked four Spanish galleons loaded with gold and silver. He managed to loot two of them, but the two others sank. To this day, treasure hunters scour the bottom of the bay in hopes of finding them.

Founded in 1693, Matanzas was known as the *Athenas de Cuba* during the second half of the 19th century, when it was bustling with literary activity. The local art and literary scene reached its peak and the town thrived economically. The massive importation of African slaves and a boom in the sugar industry enabled the province of Matanzas, which in those days was responsible for 55% of the country's sugar production, to enjoy a few moments of glory. However, the wars of independence soon brought about the town's downfall, along with that of Cárdenas, another bastion of Spanish power. The nationalists chose to sacrifice the economic centre of the country by setting fire to the cane fields, a strategy initiated by General Máximo Gómez in 1898.

Once all the crops had been destroyed, the *Athenas de Cuba* became the *ciucad dormida* (sleepy town). The echo of Matanza's golden days still resounds in the streets leading into the surrounding hills and around the Yumurí and San Juan rivers, which run through the town. Matanzas is also known as the "city of bridges", and you'll cross many during your stay here.

Start off your tour of Matanzas at the **Plaza de la Vigia ★★**, home of the town's major cultural institutions, some of its oldest houses and what is surely the handsomest fire station in Cuba. In

THE VARADERO REGION

Bahía de Matanzas

Las Cuevas de Bellamar Varadero

Matanzas

600m
300

Casablanca

Río Yumurí

(San Juan) Calle 49
(Versalles) (Vera) Calle 51
(Santa) Calle 53
(Santa Alejandro) Calle 55
Calle 57
Calle 61
(San Isidro) Calle 260
(Santa Christina) Calle 270
(San Blas) Calle 6
(Versalles)

Puente Calixto García

Pueblo Nuevo

Gral. Betancourt

Vía Blanca

Calzada de Estabán
Calle 71
(Abalii) Calle 131
Calle 123
Calle 125
Calle 127
Calle 131

(Cienfuegos) Calle 272
(San Carlos) Calle 274
(San Vicente) Calle 276
(San Ambrosio) Calle 280

(Matanzas) Calle 280
(Jovellanos) Calle 282
(Ayuntamiento) Calle 288
(Santa Teresa) Calle 290
(Zaragoza) Calle 292
(Manzanedo) Calle 294
(2 de Mayo) Calle 298
(América) Calle 300
(Compostela) Calle 302
(San Carlos) Calle 304
(Domingo Mujica) Calle 306
(San Gabriel) Calle 308
(Capricho) Calle 310
(Buena Vista) Calle 312

(San Andrés) Calle 109
(San Sebastián) Calle 115
(San Juan Bautista) Calle 117
(San Francisco) Calle 119
(La Merced) Calle 121
(San Juan de Dios) Calle
(Santa Rita)
(San Rafael)
(Espíritu Santo)
(San Fernando) Calle 135
(Buen Viaje) Calle 139
(Tenaza) Calle 145

San Juan

Puente Sánchez Figueras

(San Luis) Calle 298

New Station

Río

AV. Martín Dihigo

Maceo) Calle 77
Bonifacio Byrne) (Milanés) Calle 79
(Independencia) Calle 83
(Tella-Lamar) Calle 85
(Cuba) Calle 91
Calle 95

(Daoiz) Calle 75
(Fortuna) Calle 61
(Jesús María) Calle 63
(Jáuregui) Calle 65
(Santa Isabel) Calle 69
(Salamanca) Calle 71
(Velarde) Calle 73

(Álvarez) Calle 97
(Embarcadero Blanco) Calle 99
(Zaragozo) Calle 101

Matanzas

Parque "René Fraga"

Contrera

(San Fabián) Calle 318
(Navarro) Calle 320
(Jimeno) Calle 322

N

© ULYSSES

ATTRACTIONS

1. Plaza de la Vigía
2. Museo Provincial de Matanzas - Palacio de Junco
3. Teatro Sauto
4. Catedral de San Carlos
5. Parque Central
6. Museo Farmacéutico

the centre is a monument to the unknown *mambi*, a tribute to all the unidentified freedom fighters who lost their lives in the 19th-century wars of independence. Unfortunately, the square is not designed for pedestrians, and is swarming with cars. It is usually noisy, and there are only a few benches scattered about.

Stop in at the **Museo Provincial de Matanzas** ★★ *($1; Tue to Sat 10am to noon and 1pm to 5pm, Sun 8:30am to 12:30pm; Calle Milanés, at the corner of Calle Magdalena, ☎23-195)* to check out its collections of historical objects, as well as the building itself, the **Palacio de Junco**. Erected in 1840 on Plaza de la Vigia, this colonial mansion was destroyed by a hurricane in 1845, and then immediately reconstructed. One of the oldest buildings in Matanzas, it was long used as a carriage-house for horse-drawn fire engines like those now on display. The building's most prominent features are its superb bright blue façade and its pretty colonial patio. Founded in 1959, the Museo Provincial describes itself as the first museum to have opened under the Castro regime. Originally housed in the basement of the Teatro Sauto, it was moved to its present location in 1980. The permanent exhibition, distributed throughout twelve little galleries, covers the history of Matanzas from the pre-Columbian era to the first years of the Castro regime. Articles on display include several sculptures, pieces of colonial furniture and the *barreta*, the staff that enabled Justo Wong to discover the Cuevas de Bellamar (see p 151). The museum also has a large collection of objects from the era of slavery.

Also on Plaza de la Vigia, the **Teatro Sauto** is the pride of the local residents. It bears witness to the cultural and economic wealth enjoyed by Matanzas in the previous century. Built in 1863, it has been listed as an historical monument.

Take Calle 83 east to Calle 282, where you'll see the **Catedral de San Carlos** ★, completed in 1840. This cathedral, erected on the ruins of a chapel that was destroyed by a hurricane in 1740, has unfortunately been neglected. The interior is like a disaster area; entire sections of the walls and ceiling have fallen away, and there is paint missing all over. Under these conditions, it is not really possible to appreciate this building's true worth.

Parque Central, also known as Plaza Libertad, is quieter than Plaza de la Vigia and boasts all sorts of attractions. It is home to the unusual **Museo Farmaceutico** ★★ *($1; Mon to Sat 10am to 6pm, Sun 9am to 6pm; Calle Milanés No. 4951, between Calle Santa Teresa and Calle Ayuntamiento, ☎3-179)*. Founded in 1882, this old French pharmacy, which belonged to Ernest Triolet and Juan Fermín Figueroa, has been preserved in its original state. Closed in 1964 in order to be turned into a museum, this pharmacy contains porcelain vases imported from France and 55 books detailing how to prepare nearly 1.5 million plant-based medicines. The laboratory is also original, and the various instruments found within are made of bronze, copper and glass, among other materials.

Cárdenas ★

Located only 15 kilometres south of Varadero, Cárdenas is a town that everyone staying in Varadero should visit. It has traditional (albeit sadly neglected) neoclassical architecture and a fascinating history. Exploring its streets, which are filled with cyclists

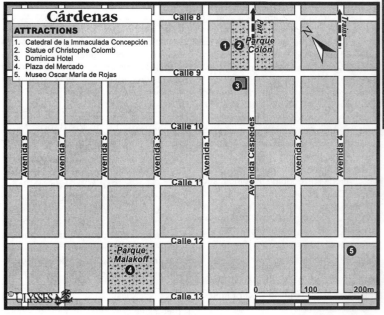

Cárdenas

ATTRACTIONS

1. Catedral de la Immaculada Concepción
2. Statue of Christophe Colomb
3. Dominica Hotel
4. Plaza del Mercado
5. Museo Oscar María de Rojas

©ULYSSES

and pedestrians, will give you an excellent idea of what Cuba is like outside the tourist resorts. Varadero was once an underdeveloped section of this then prosperous town. Who would have believed that the long beach would one day supplant Cárdenas and become one of the country's economic mainsprings?

Before Cárdenas had even been founded, the Haitian independence movement prompted large numbers of French men and women to flee, and dozens of families took up residence here in the late 18th century. They contributed greatly to the region's development, introducing more advanced technology for sugar production. They were also the first to grow coffee in this region. Cárdenas is a relatively young town for Cuba. Founded in 1828 by settlers from North America, France and England, it had a cosmopolitan flavour right from the start. By putting in a lot of hard work,

these families managed to build the town on a swampy piece of land, creating a sort of "Holland of the Americas". Cárdenas' economic and cultural development occurred at an astonishing speed. Barely 12 years after its founding, in 1840, it became the second town in the country to be served by the railroad. Cárdenas, which did not have a good port for exporting its sugar, thus gained access to what was then a revolutionary means of transport. On September 9, 1889, it became the first town in the country to have electric lighting. After that, however, it was all downhill. Cárdenas declined slowly but steadily with the onset of the wars of independence, which drove away the rich families. The ports of Matanzas and Havana prospered more than Cárdenas, and the second war of independence (1895-1898) ushered in the worst economic crisis the town had ever faced: the plantations were burnt by the nationalists, and the railway was destroyed. Cárdenas never recovered. In 1974, Varadero separated and became a town in its own right. Unfortunately, the profits of tourism have not reached Cárdenas, whose architectural heritage is thus endangered.

Cárdenas' main street is Avenida Céspedes, which runs through the historic quarter to the port. Here, you'll find **Parque Colón**, which marks the spot where the town was founded and boasts the first monument to Christopher Columbus erected in the Americas. All the surrounding buildings, such as the Casa de Gobierno and the Hotel la Dominica, south of the park, evoke the neoclassical style. Calle Princesa, formerly known as "Calle de los Franceses" (Street of the French), is definitely worth exploring.

One of the most eclectic museums in the country, the **Museo Oscar Maria de Rojas** ★★★ *($1; Tue to Sat 1pm to 6pm, Sun 9am to 1pm; Calle Calzada No. 4, between Calle Vives and Calle Jenes, ☎52-2417)* displays an extraordinary assortment of articles found during archaeological excavations, as well as various objects related to natural science. Highlights include fine collections of shells, snails, weapons and coins. Visitors will also learn about the history of the town through written documents and photographs. The museum's centrepiece is a 19th-century wooden funeral coach. There are also two rather strange items. One in particular is not to be missed: the preserved and shrunken head of a native from Ecuador, which is only a few centimetres in size. The second, modelled after a wedding cake, displays two newlywed... fleas! You will need a magnifying glass to see them! Founded in 1900, this is the oldest museum in the country, along with the Museo Bacardí in Santiago de Cuba. It is inside a neoclassical house built in 1862.

Fortunately, a few restoration projects have been launched in Cárdenas, the best example of which is the reconstruction of the **Plaza del Mercado**, a superb farmers' market covered by a metallic dome imported from the United States in 1859. The work should be finished by early 1997.

San Miguel de los Baños ★

Accessible from the little village of Coliseo, on the Carretera Central south of Cárdenas, San Miguel de los Baños is a former spa with sulphurous waters. It lies hidden in a mountainous area, which contrasts with the generally flat landscape of this agricultural region. After covering seven kilometres on the little road, you will see the main building of this seaside resort on your left: affluent Cubans used to come to this large palace to relax and take care of themselves, in keeping with the European spa trend of the second half of the 19th century. A few years after the Revolution of 1959, the palace began to fall into decline. Che Guevara is said to have sought relief from his chronic asthma here on one of his trips. Today, the palace is in a state of neglect, and the baths no longer function, but that simply adds to the charm of the village, a veritable haven of peace that has yet to be discovered by tourists. All around, little streets head off into the mountains, one leading to the village church, another to a swimming pool that is only open during summer.

The neoclassical **Hotel San Miguel** (see p 159), which stands in front of the abandoned palace, will transport you back to the prosperous days at the turn of the century. It would be the perfect setting for a movie, perhaps some day...

From here, you can set off on an excursion in the mountains. The walk to the Loma Jacan is a favourite since the trail leads to an old wooden cross.

 PARKS AND BEACHES

Varadero

The beaches of Varadero need no introduction, but the same can't be said of a little-known park also found on the peninsula. Accessible by scooter, it is an excellent place to spend half a day off the beaten track. Located on the northeast tip of Varadero, between the Casa DuPont (7 km to the east) and La Morla (4 km to the west), this uncrowded, unspoiled natural setting is also one of the few places in Varadero where you don't have to pay to get in. Fourteen archaeological sites lie hidden within its boundaries. The **Cueva de San Ambrosio** ★★ *($2; Tue-Sat 10am to 4pm)* is a cave adorned with about fifty drawings dating from the pre-Columbian era. In order to protect this cultural legacy, access to the caves is now limited. They were discovered in 1961 by two Cuban archaeologists, Rivero de la Calle and Orlando Pariente, who thought they had stumbled upon something unseen by human eyes for over five centuries. Superimposed African-style drawings would seem to indicate, however, that local slaves held rituals in these caves at one time. One of the drawings is red, with an oval shape and a number of geometrical figures in the middle.

Archaeologists have also discovered the remains of a *megalognus rodens*, a mammal from the Jurassic period, in the caves known as **Musulmanes-1** and **Musulmanes-2**, located in the same region. The remains of natives (probably Siboney Indians) were also found on

an inner terrace between the two caves, an area probably used as a burial and ceremonial site.

Finally, visit **Las Salinas** ★, an abandoned salt mine that was once the driving force behind the peninsula's economy. On the way, keep an eye out for "El Patriarca" by the side of the road. Carbon dating has shown that this tree was starting to grow when Christopher Columbus first voyaged to the New World!

Matanzas

Valle Yumurí ★

About 20 kilometres west of Matanzas, the Vía Blanca spans the magnificent Valle Yumurí below, across the highest bridge (110 m) in the country, the Puente Bacunayagua. Letting themselves be carried by the winds, birds of prey swoop over this valley, whose name refers to a legend that the Siboney Indians who lived here would throw themselves off the mountains to escape slavery. The word *yumurí* supposedly comes from the words *yo morir*, meaning "I to die" in Spanish.

The **Mirador de Bacunayagua** *(free admission; every day 8:30am to 6pm; Vía Blanca, km 18, Puente Bacunayagua)*, a lookout on the west side of the bridge, commands a good view of the valley and the Río Bacunayagua. It also has a cafeteria and a few souvenir shops.

Las Cuevas de Bellamar ★★

Las Cuevas de Bellamar ★★ *($3; every day 9am to 5am; Finca la Alcancia, ☎6-1683)*, five kilometres southeast of Matanzas, are amazing and easy to get to. A 520-metre tunnel plunges into a series of caves, where stalagmites and stalactites have been developing for nearly 26 million years. This geological formation is made of white and yellow limestone, which is rich in marine fossils. A Chinese slave named Justo Wong accidentally discovered the subterranean caves on the estate of the affluent Don Manuel Santos Pargas in 1861. While moving a stone, he dropped his staff into a hole and unsuspectingly went in to find it. Before he knew it, he had made the discovery of his life and thus made his way humbly into the history books. By the following year, the caves had been opened to the public. In 1940, Hershey, the American chocolate maker, built a house surrounded by palm trees over the entrance to the caves.

 OUTDOOR ACTIVITIES

 Boating

Cubanaútica *(Casa 12, Calle 3, Kawama, ☎66-7403)* and the **Marina Chapelin** *(Carretera Las Morlas, Km 12.5, ☎66-7550 or 66-7565, ▬66-7093)* both offer "seafaris" *($75)* on the coral reefs off the shores of Varadero.

The Cuban-American company **Jolly Rogers** *(☎66-7743 or 66-7565)*, at the Marina Chapelin, offers the most complete "seafari" in the region. Their ultramodern catamarans sail past Cayo Diana, Cayo Romero and Cayo Piedra del Norte and its lighthouse. The excursion costs $60 per person and includes a rock-lobster lunch and an open bar on board. Passengers can also go deep-sea fishing and scuba diving. At the end of the trip, you'll receive complementary tickets for a sunset cruise.

 Parasailing

If you like the idea of floating in the air with a parachute while being towed by a motor boat, **Cubanaútica** *($60; 9am to 5pm, Casa 12, Calle 3, Kawama, ☎66-7403)* offers parasailing packages that include transportation between your hotel and the marina.

 Deep-sea Fishing

As far as deep-sea fishing is concerned, the terms are identical from one marina to the next: a four-hour trip; $200 per boat; a maximum of four passengers; two fishing rods.

 Scuba Diving

Club Baracuda *(Calle 59 and Avenida Primera, ☎61-3481, ▬66-7072).*

Aqua Diving Club *(Casa 201 Avenida Kawama No. 201, between Calles 2 and 3, ☎66-8060, ▬66-7456)* is the cheapest place in Varadero for divers to practise their favourite pastime. The boat leaves every Thursday at 9am for a wreck that lies 10 metres underwater, and is inhabited by an enormous ray familiar to the instructors, who feed it out of their hands. Passengers can watch this spectacle, as the animal is safe to approach. The package, which includes two oxygen tanks, costs $55 per person. During the rest of the week, the boat travels to another enchanting spot, this time without a ray or a wreck, at a cost of $50 for two dives. On cloudy or rainy days, the crew travels to the south coast and Playa Girón; this excursion costs $60, including transportation and two oxygen tanks.

The **Club Tropical** *(Avenida Primera, between Calles 21 and 22, Varadero, ☎6-3915)* offers diving excursions at Playa Girón, in the Bay of Pigs, where you can take in some of the loveliest underwater scenery off Cuba. The $75 per person charge includes transportation to Playa Girón, a two-hour introductory course, two dives and all necessary equipment.

 Horseback Riding

Matanzas

The **Casa del Valle** *(Valle Yumurí, ☎4-584)* arranges horseback riding trips in the Valle Yumurí.

 ACCOMMODATIONS

Varadero

Casas particulares, legal throughout the country, are not so in Varadero. The reason is simple: the state receives a tax of $100 per month for every room a *casa particular* rents out. But because the state is in a bilateral partnership with hotel complexes, it collects approximately half the profits. Therefore, it is more profitable for the state if tourists go to hotels. There are nevertheless a great many *casas particulares* with rooms to rent. Be vigilant, however, because if your hosts get caught, they will not only be forcibly exiled from Varadero, but will also have to pay a hefty fine. Do not pay more than $30 for a room. For obvious reasons, the addresses of these places are not listed here.

The best **beaches** are located east of Calle 50. Avoid the hotels west of the canal.

The **Villa La Mar** *($28-46; ≈, pb, ≈, ctv; Avenida 3, at the corner of Calle 30, ☎61-2415)* stands on the north shore of Varadero, a few hundred metres from the beach. The rooms are clean and simple, and the service is friendly. Ask for a room with a balcony. You can also rent an apartment with a kitchenette, a very practical option for families.

Built a few years prior to the Revolution, **Villa Caribe** *($40-$47; ≈, ℜ, pb, ☎, ctv, ≈; at Avenida Playa and Calle 30, ☎61-6310, ⚏66-7488)* lost out on international tourism from 1959 to 1990. Since then, foreign tourists have returned and now mingle with the Cuban clientele. The place is simple and warm, in addition to being one of the most affordable establishments in the area. Most of the rooms are located too close together, but are suitable nonetheless. The decor is unpretentious and the villa is right on the beach.

The **Hotel Horizontes Caribe** *($40-47; ≈, ≈, ℜ; Avenida Playa, between Calles 30 and 31, ☎61-3310, ⚏66-7488)* has shared bathrooms, but if the place isn't very full, you can ask for a private bath. The entrance is a bit dark, and the rooms are merely adequate; some offer a partial view of the sea. The neighbourhood is one of the liveliest in Varadero come nightfall.

The **Hotel Pullman** *($40-50; ≈, pb, ℜ, ≈; Avenida Primera, between Calles 49 and 50, ☎61-7161)* is one of the cheapest places in Varadero, and also one of those with the most character. It is located in the middle of the old quarter and is surrounded by typical old wooden houses. The architecture is inspired by the 19th-century château style. On the down side, the rooms and the restaurant are dark, and the place is reputed to be abuzz with mosquitoes.

The **Hotel Dos Mares** *($43-52; ≡, pb, ℜ; Calle 53, at the corner of Avenida Primera, ☎61-2702, ☞66-7499)* is a good choice for the price. Small and inviting, it is located inside an old house with a Mediterranean-style tile roof, located in the heart of Varadero. The service is adequately provided by students from the hotel management school.

Hotel Bellamar *($45-$54; ≈, ℜ, pb, ☎, ctv, ≈; Calle 17, between Avenidas 1 and 2, ☎66-7490, ☞66-7733)* is one of the oldest buildings in Varadero. The best thing about the place is the price, because half the hotel is being renovated, so it is quite noisy. The building is in a sorry state and the rooms are utterly lacking in charm. But this should change soon, thanks to German investments; however, this means that the hotel must close its doors until 2001. Another drawback: the hotel is not right on the beach, but two blocks away.

🏖 Villa Punta Blanca *($46-$75; ℜ, pb, ☎, ctv, ≈; Avenida Kawama, ☎66-8050 to 53, ☞66-7004)* rents out stylish villas and rooms. The pre-Revolution villas were fully renovated about fifteen years ago. Not only is the hotel aesthetically pleasing, but it is also very intimate. Indeed, the buildings have been well spaced out along the beach, so it is not too crowded. Each villa has up to ten rooms with private entrances. The hotel shuttle runs all day long and takes vacationers back and forth between the restaurant, the performance hall and the swimming pool, which are all grouped together. We highly recommend this place for its intimate and original style as well as its welcoming staff.

The **Villa Herradura** *($53-64 bkfst incl.; ≡, pb, ≈, tv; Avenida de la Playa, between Calles 35 and 36, ☎61-3725, ☞66-7496)* stands out from the others due to its excellent beach-front location. Its outdoor restaurant serves meals prepared on the grill (ask for the lunchtime *table d'hôte*). This place was recently renovated, and the rooms are clean and generally well-kept.

Villa Caleta *($54-$60; ≡, pb, ☎, ctv; at Calle 20 and Avenida 1, ☎66-7080, ☞61-3291)* is a superb beachfront establishment. Magnificent trees surround a pool — which, granted, could have been bigger — visible as you enter the interior courtyard behind the lobby. The Villa has just recently abandoned its all-inclusive formula, so guests will have to make do with the beach and swimming. The same goes for night-time activities: there are no shows featured at night. In short, the place will suit those who go on vacation for peace and quiet and not for umpteen activities.

The 364 small apartments of the **Aparthotel Mar del Sur** *($56-$64; ≡, ℜ, pb, ☎, ctv, ≈; with K $180; Avenida 3, at Calle 30, ☎61-2246, ☞66-7482)* is affordable for families who do not wish to pay the high prices of luxury complexes. The Mar del Sur is charming, except for its pinkish pastel exterior. Though the establishment is not situated by the sea (hence its reasonable price), the deep is never very far in Varadero.

The **Aparthotel Verazul** *($60-$70 bkfst incl.; ≡, ℜ, pb, ☎, ctv, ≈; Avenida 1, between Calles 14 and 15, ☎66-7132, ☞66-7229)* is next door to and managed by the **Acuazul** *($70-$80; same address and services as above)*. The buildings are in the same style but the Verazul is better set up because it has a lobby and a swimming pool and offers several activities. Moreover, the place has some of the most appealing rooms on the peninsula for the price. Both spacious and pleasantly decorated, they are also graced with a huge balcony with a view of the sea. These two hotels are not as large as the mammoth complexes, but do boast the same activities and services. What is more, the staff is most gracious.

You'll also find houses for rent at the **Hotel & Villa Kawama** *($65-85; ≡, ≈, pb, ctv, ℜ; Punta Blanca houses $57-72; Carretera de Kawama, at the corner of Calle O, ☎66-7156, ≈66-7254)*, located by the sea and the canal that runs across the peninsula. Unfortunately, this part of the beach is not particularly attractive. You'll have to drive or take the bus across the canal to reach the best beaches, unless the hotel's Olympic-sized pool appeals to you.

Built in the 1950s, the **Hotel Varadero Internacional** *($75-100; ≡, ≈, ℜ, ctv; Carretera Las Americas, ☎66-7038 to 9, ≈66-7246)* touts itself as Varadero's first grand hotel. Set in front of one of the prettiest stretches of beach on the peninsula, it boasts excellent facilities right near the sea. Guests have access to equipment for a variety of water sports. The rooms are clean and extremely comfortable, and the place is looking quite good despite its age.

The **Villas Sotavento** *($70-$86 bkfst incl.; ≡, ℜ, pb, ☎, ctv, ≈; Calle 13, between Avenida 1 and Camino del Mar, ☎66-7132 to 34, ≈66-7229)* are well situated, right in the middle of the village and seconds from a variety of restaurants and nightclubs. The rooms are large, well decorated and quiet, since they are not on the main road, Avenida Primera, but on Calle 13 which is perpendicular to it and runs all the way to the seashore. Request a room as close as possible to the sea. The Sotavento is also managed by the Acuazul, just around the corner on Avenida Primera.

Hotel Arenas Doradas *($80-$110; ≡, ℜ, pb, ☎, ctv, ≈; Carretera Punta Hicacos, ☎66-8150 to 56, ≈66-8159, sistema@arenas.gca.cma.net)* is located next to the Brisas del Caribe and is very Andalusian in style, with its earth tone dwellings. Unlike the other big complexes on the peninsula, space and intimacy are given priority here, and the gardens make up an important part of the property. The hotel is one of the best in Varadero in terms of quality for the price as guests have more space and will feel less like they are in a shopping centre. Also, because the hotel is slightly set back from the beach, guests heading there will enjoy a pleasant walk amid the breezy palm trees. Moreover, the swimming pool will keep a fair share of guests within its gentle confines.

Villa Los Delphines *($86 bkfst incl.; ≡, ℜ, pb, ☎, ctv, ≈; at Avenida Playa and Calle 39, ☎66-7720, ≈66-7727)* is also located right on the beach, and mainly frequented by Italian holiday-makers. Many activities (sports, dancing, ...) are included in the price, which compensates somewhat for the rather small rooms. Suites with direct access to the beach are also available.

The best thing about the **Hotel Oasis** *($93-104 all inclusive; Vía Blanca, Km 130, ☎66-7380 to 82, ≈66-7489)* is its price, although the rooms are very comfortable as well. On the down side, it is located far from Varadero and the loveliest beaches on the peninsula, so you'll have to use the hotel bus service if you don't have a car.

Resembling bunkers and painted a hospital green, the **Copey Resort Hotel** and the **Siboney Resort Hotel** *($100-$110; ≡, ℜ, pb, ☎, tv, ≈; at Calle 64 and Autopista, ☎66-7505, ≈66-7509)* are not for those concerned with appearances. Looks aside, the rooms are very comfortable and much in demand due to their rates, which are lower than those of more upscale hotels. The complex is undergoing renovations, a process that will take several years, but the work has been planned so as not to compromise the quality of the stay.

⚓ Among the large complexes on the loveliest stretch of the Varadero beach, the **Cabañas del Sol** *($100-$120 all inclusive; ≡, ℜ, pb, ☎, ctv, ≈; Carretera Las Americas, ☎66-7038, ≈66-7246)* stand out for their originality. Each of the 149 dwellings is self-contained and, with its stone walls, looks straight out of another era, when people took the time to do things well. This establishment has also recently adopted the all-inclusive formula, including an impersonal character sometimes found in hotels of this grade. A central path winds its way through the hotel's gardens right to to the beach, 250 metres away.

Hotel Las Morlas *($110-$132 all inclusive; ≡, ℜ, pb, ☎, ctv, ≈; at Carretera Las Americas and Calle A, ☎66-7231 to 34, ≈66-7007)* is another complex that recently converted to the "all-inclusive" formula. The beige-painted exterior blends in perfectly with the beach, and the 143 rooms are as attractive as they are spacious and face a pool surrounded by palm trees.

The two hotel complexes run by Meliá, a Spanish chain, are in a category all their own, due both to their high rates and the overall excellence of their facilities. The **Sol Palmeras** *($110-240; ≡, ≈, ℜ, ctv; Carretera Las Morlas, Km 8, ☎66-7009, ≈66-7008)* is, simply put, the best hotel in Varadero, offering every imaginable amenity you might hope to find at a grand hotel. The swimming pool, bars, rooms and restaurant are all outstanding. The standards are equally high at the neighbouring **Hotel Meliá-Varadero** *($125-255; ≡, ≈, ℜ, ctv; ☎66-7013, ≈66-7012, melia.varadero@melia.solmelia.cma.net)*.

Well located by the sea, near the centre of Varadero, the **Club Tropical** *($113-130 all inclusive; ≡, ℜ, ≈, pb; Avenida Primera, between Calle 21 and Calle 22, ☎61-3915, ≈66-7227)* will appeal to travellers looking for reasonably priced all-inclusive packages. The atmosphere is pleasant and relaxed, and activities are organized by a Cuban and Québecois team. Guests have a choice between two kinds of rooms, with or without a private bath.

Unlike most of its neighbours, **Hotel y Villas Bella Costa** *($120-$140; ≡, ℜ, pb, ☎, ctv, ≈; Carretera Las Americas, Km 4.5, ☎66-7210, ≈66-7205)* does not only function according to the all-inclusive model, which gives guests the freedom to go out and see something other than the hotel. The services and activities offered are standard (day and night activities, aerobics in the pool, introduction to salsa, volleyball, etc. ...). And should you have a change of heart, you can turn your stay into an all-inclusive one for an additional $60 per day.

The most modern hotel on the peninsula is the **Cuatro Palmas Resort** *($120-160; bungalows $106-146; pb, ≡, ≈, ℜ; Avenida Primera, between Calles 60 and 62, ☎66-7040, ≈66-7583)*, located in the heart of Varadero, a few metres from Parque Josone. It faces a shopping centre to the north and an idyllic beach to the south. The bungalows are comfortable, and the overall layout of the place is conducive to kicking back and relaxing. This is the ideal spot for a carefree vacation. All sorts of water sports can be enjoyed right from the hotel beach.

The **Eldorador Villa Tortuga** *($136-146 all inclusive; ≡, pb, tv, ≈, ℜ, bar,*

☎61-4747, ◄66-7485) just added 180 rooms and 10 villas to Varadero's already impressive hotel park. Completely renovated and with a club formula, this vacation village is set amidst a 50-hectare garden that follows the beach. It is now managed by the French travel wholesaler, Jet Tours. The air-conditioned rooms, spread throughout several small two-story buildings, have either a balcony or a terrace. Windsurfing, sailing on a catamaran, tennis, archery, beach volleyball, ping-pong, petanque and bicycling are some of the activities you can try. There is always something going on at the small outdoor amphitheatre. There are also games and activities for children four years of age and up.

The largest hotel in the Gaviota chain is the **Hotel Coral** *($155-$310 all inclusive; Carretera Las Americas, between Calles H and K, Reparto La Torre,* ☎66-7240, ◄66-7194, *reserva@resort.gav.cma.net)*, with 230 rooms. The hotel has one of the most beautiful locations on the Varadero beach. It also has one of the longest pools on the peninsula: it twists and turns in every direction. Moreover, a well-kept landscape teeming with greenery makes for wonderful walks. And if you get a room on one of the upper floors, odds are that you will want to stay forever...

A stone's throw from the bridge spanning the peninsula, the **Hotel y Villa Barlovento** *($160-$180; Avenida 1, between Calles 10 and 12,* ☎66-7140, ◄66-7218, jfinan@ibero.gca.cma.net) is another all-inclusive establishment. What sets it apart from its neighbours is the height of its buildings, which do not exceed three storeys. The Barlovento boasts every sports activity and pastime for every taste, from tennis to massotherapy. The buildings housing the rooms are decorated in warm hues, though they are a little too

close together. The buffet is fresh and delicious. Cigar afficionados should meet Raúl at the reception desk, on the left as you enter. He is the hotel's master cigar roller, and is thus a foremost authority on the subject.

Right next to the Club Varadero is the **Hotel LTI-Tuxpán** *($170-$230 all inclusive; ≡, ℜ, pb, ☎, ctv, ≈; Carretera Las Americas, Km 4,* ☎66-7560, ◄66-7561), which offers the same kind of all-inclusive stay as its famous neighbour. The building is massive and unattractive but boasts comfortable, stylish rooms with elegant furnishings. The staff is delightful and the pleasant pool compensates for the place's lack of charm.

Hotel Meliá Las Americas *($170-$300 all inclusive; ≡, ℜ, pb, ☎, ctv, ≈; Autopista, Km 7,* ☎66-7600, ◄66-7625) is the newest link in the Meliá chain, already established on the peninsula. Like its counterparts, it offers top-notch luxury and comfort, with an enormous lobby furnished with leather sofas and a grand piano. Moreover, it is located right next to Varadero's only golf course. To top it all off, the huge pool, bordered by magnificent gardens, is only a stone's throw from the sea.

Sol Club Las Sirenas *($185-$340 all inclusive; ≡, ⊙, ℜ, pb, ☎, ctv, ≈; Calle K, Reparto La Torre,* ☎66-8070, ◄66-8075, sec_com_div@melia.solmelia.cma.net) bought the Caracol hotel in 1999, increasing its capacity to about 400 rooms. The focus of the hotel are its activities (Mini Club for children) and sports (sailing, scuba diving, two tennis courts, etc.). The restaurants, the bar and the evening shows are all of excellent quality and count for a lot in the general appreciation of the place. The hotel, slightly far from the beach, has a few lovely paths winding through the palm trees, making for pleasant walks.

The rooms are clean and of decent size. On the other hand, the balconies of the first-floor rooms don't get enough sun sun. Despite this, the buildings' interior courtyards are an oasis of greenery where guests can relax before they dive into the sea to wash away the last of their cares.

The lovely and convenient houses at the **Villa Cuba** *($188-216 all inclusive; ≡, pb, ≈, ℜ, ctv; Carretera de Las Américas, Rpto. La Torre, ☎66-8280, ⇔66-7207)* are located one kilometre east of the Hotel Cuatro Palmas, near the Casa DuPont, and look out onto one of the most beautiful stretches of beach in Varadero. Renting a two- or three-bedroom house is an excellent option for small groups of travellers, who will reap the benefits of the relaxed tropical atmosphere at this extremely popular spot.

Club Med *($194-$370 all inclusive; Autopista, Km 11, ☎66-8288, ⇔66-8340)* finally opened here in 1996. The name of the place says it all: the premises are as spectacular as one would expect. Once again, Club Med proves that paradise on earth is possible two weeks out of the year. Among the activities on the program are a circus workshop and salsa lessons. The yellow-coloured building is enchanting, as is its private beach.

The last big hotel on the peninsula before it disappears beneath the waves is the **Gran Hotel** *($226 all inclusive; ≡, ⊙, ℜ, pb, ctv, ≈; Carretera Las Morlas, ☎66-8242, ⇔66-8202)*. Not content with its 331-room capacity, it will add 200 units by the year 2000. A village in itself, as it were! The hotel offers all the services of a luxury hotel, from water aerobics to professional massages, as well as nighttime activities. The place is absolutely irreproachable, but might be a little too sterile for certain tastes...

Hotel Brisas del Caribe *($228 all inclusive; Carretera Las Morlas, Km 12, ☎66-8030, ⇔66-8005)*, with its 268 units, ranks among the biggest hotels in Varadero. And like the Gran Hotel (see above) it will be adding 174 new units by the year 2000. The hotel, of course, offers all services imaginable for this type of establishment. Unfortunately, nothing makes it stand out, except for the organized expeditions on the Canimar River, included in the package, and its nighttime activities. Indeed, a different show is presented here every night, so even if you stay for two weeks you won't see the same show twice. Returning guests receive dinner invitations and show tickets.

Club Varadero *($250-$300 all inclusive; ≡, ℜ, pb, ☎, ctv, ≈; Carretera Las Americas, Km 3, ☎66-7030 and 31, ⇔66-7008)* is part of the Superclubs chain. Every effort has been made to keep guests happy (though perhaps not delightfully surprised!). Restaurants, sports activities and a huge swimming pool, among other things, will delight vacationers who fill this resort's enchanting site to capacity year round.

Several hotel complexes were still under construction at press time. Among these, the **Villa Sol y Mar**, an enormous 444-unit all-inclusive hotel located right next to the International hotel, is slated to open in 2001. As well, the future **Tainos** luxury hotel is being built between the Brisas del Caribe and the Gran Hotel. This last project will add 272 new rooms to the peninsula by the spring of 2000. These two new hotel complexes will join a long list of upscale hotels north of the village, on the loveliest stretch of the long Varadero beach.

Matanzas

High-quality accommodations are rare in Matanzas. However, the hotels are inexpensive and are set in old colonial houses. The **Hotel Velasco** *($25; ≈, pb, ℜ; Calle Contrera, Plaza Libertad, ☎4443)* is a lovely, well-preserved place still haunted by memories of the colonial era. Guests can drink in the sumptuousness of the previous century at their own pace. The rooms haven't been renovated for ages, but are generally spacious and comfortable for the price. Pick one with a balcony on the Plaza de la Libertad.

Built in 1894, the **Hotel Louvres** *($30-45; ≈, pb, ℜ; 28820 Calle Milanés, ☎4074)* is a converted colonial house. It is a pleasant and inviting place, especially the colonial patio with its palm trees; this is the perfect spot to read or simply relax. The rooms are clean and quite elegant on the whole.

The **Casa del Valle** *($30-45; Carretera de Chirino, Km 2, Valle Yumurí, ☎4584, ≈63-118)* lies nestled in a rural setting. The clientele, mainly senior citizens, come here to take advantage of the wide range of clinical services, including an anti-stress treatment. The building itself is a pretty turn-of-the-century house, and is very well set up to accommodate travellers. During your stay, you can go horseback riding in the Valle Yumurí.

The **Hotel Canimao** *($35; ≈, pb, ≈, ℜ; Vía Blanca, km 5.5, ☎6-1014)*, located 5 km east of Matanzas, is the most modern hotel in the area. Isolated from the rest of the town, it has a peaceful atmosphere. The rooms are extremely comfortable, and the service is good. If you have a rental car, this is a safe bet.

San Miguel de los Baños

The picturesque but dilapidated **Hotel San Miguel** *(6 pesos; pb, ⊛; Calle 10, between Calles 7 and 9, ☎89-6126)* was built in 1929. Although somewhat neglected, the balconies are worth a visit, so that you can admire the surrounding landscape. The rooms are poorly kept, and you will definitely want to bring your sleeping bag with you.

Your other option is to rent out one of the four rustic cabins near the municipal pool *($8; ☎89-6168)*. Ask the bartender at the swimming pool to show them to you.

 RESTAURANTS

Varadero

For many years, the poor quality of the meals served in the restaurants and hotels of Varadero was foreign tourists' chief complaint. Fortunately, those in charge managed to improve the situation during the 1995-1996 tourist season by hiring Canadian and European chefs to train a new generation of Cuban chefs. Of course, the restaurateurs' goal is to offer food that will appeal to foreigners' palates. It should not be forgotten, however, that part of the pleasure of travelling is broadening one's culinary horizons.

Finding a good, inexpensive restaurant in Varadero is no easy task. The prices are much higher than in the rest of the country. For a reasonably priced meal, you'll have to make do with fast-food, since *paladares*, restaurants set up in private homes, have been strictly prohibited in Varadero, much to travellers' disadvantage. One of the least expensive places in town is a small **fast-food counter** one block west of Parque Josones *(Avenida Primera, between Calles 55 and 54)*. Try the fried chicken. The place has a terrace that is quite pleasant, albeit noisy at times.

A large cafeteria belonging to the Cuban fast-food chain **El Rapido** *($; Avenida Primera, at the corner of Calle 47)* has a huge outdoor terrace with tables set up under tents. The hot-dogs, hamburgers and pizzas are a big hit with local residents, who can afford to sample this typically American fare. All the ads surrounding the place create an exotic setting for Cubans, as advertising was banned here in 1959, and has only recently made a reappearance. The United States aren't so far away, after all!

A section of Calle 43 known as "El Bulevar" *(between Avenida Primera and Avenida Playa)* has been set aside for pedestrians. You'll find a good bakery here named **Doñaneli** *(Avenida Primera, at the corner of Calle 43)*, which sells French bread (a rare commodity in Cuba), cakes and a variety of pastries at reasonable prices.

Pizza Nova *($)*, facing Parque Josone, serves the best pizza in Varadero. The place is functional, with relatively speedy service.

The most affordable Italian restaurant in Varadero is the **Altro Castel Nuovo** *($; Avenida Primera, at the corner of Calle 11, ☎61-2428 or 66-7786)*, which offers a good selection of pasta dishes, as well as a few meat dishes, including breaded veal with cheese and tomato sauce.

Warm and pleasant, with its wooden furniture and huge straw parasols, the centrally located **Restaurante La Vicaría** *($; at Avenida 1 and Calle 38, ☎61-4721)* offers a Creole menu con-

sisting of chicken, pork and fillets of fish. The place is popular with both tourists and Cubans, who take advantage of its low prices. A stone's throw away, **El Caney** *(at Calle 40)* offers almost the same menu and ambiance.

A watered-down version of the famous Bodeguita del Medio in Havana, **El Bodegón Criollo** *($; Avenida Playa, at the corner of Calle 40, ☎66-7784)* is sure to please travellers unfamiliar with the real thing. The walls are covered with graffiti, but don't go looking for a contribution from Hemingway or Castro... Creole cuisine gets top billing, especially pork dishes, served with rice or *arroz morro* (rice and beans) and manioc. This might not be the best Creole restaurant around, but at least it's relatively affordable.

Though the **Pizzeria Capri** *($; at Avenida Playa and Calle 43, ☎61-2117)* does not always serve the best Italian food, its prices are unbeatable. This unpretentious eatery with minimalist decor attracts more Cubans than foreigners. The pasta is much better than the pizza, which sometimes tastes rather bland.

If you like Asian food, make a date at **Halong** *($; 3pm to 11pm; at Camino del Mar and Calle 12, ☎61-3787)*, a Chinese restaurant that serves up good portions of a variety of dishes, ranging from chicken to seafood. The lobster chop suey is particularly delicious, though one of the most expensive dishes on the menu.

A small restaurant with an intimate, charming, almost homey decor, **Mi Casita** *($$; Bulevar Camino del Mar, between Calles 11 and 12, ☎6-3787)* is a perfect spot for those staying west of the Varadero bridge, in the Kawama area. The menu consists of Cuban-style seafood and meat dishes, all served with a smile.

Another Chinese restaurant, **Lai-Lai** *($$; every day 6pm to midnight; at Avenida 1 and Calle 18, ☎66-7793)*, is a little pricier, but the difference is in the elegant presentation of the dishes, much better prepared than elsewhere. The imperial rolls are surprisingly delectable and not too greasy.

The **Barbacoa** *($$; at Avenida 1 and Calle 64, ☎61-3435)* serves typical Cuban fare and scrumptious grilled meats. A veritable little Cuban oasis among the posher restaurants around. The decor is not as dazzling, but tasteful nonetheless. This place is also open late at night.

La Casa del Queso *($$; Avenida Primera, at the corner of Calle 61, ☎6-360)* is one of your best options if you want a change from hotel food. The house specialty is a selection of succulent fondues, including chocolate fondue for dessert, of course. You can reserve a private room and thus enjoy a unique and very posh atmosphere.

A Creole menu complemented by pasta and pizza is offered at **Kiki's** *($$; every day noon to midnight; at Avenida Kawama and Calle 5, ☎61-4115)*, another restaurant that stays open until the witching hour. A great place to eat on the terrace in a quiet ambiance and breathe in the Varadero sea air.

Diners at the beachfront **El Arrecife** *($$; at Camino del Mar and Calle 13)* are not only treated to the caressing sea breeze, but also to seafood dishes such as the particularly delicious crayfish and well-presented grilled-fish dishes, which further complement the setting. If you happen to be strolling along the adjacent beach, you will likely encounter one of the restaurant's "PR reps", who will try to draw you to the restaurant.

West of the canal, **La Marisqueria** *($$; Avenida Primera, Kawama)* has a good selection of seafood, including calamari, octopus, lobster and shrimp. This is a new restaurant, and it should appeal to fans of this kind of cuisine. The atmosphere is pleasant, although the air conditioning could cool even the most fiery passion.

Parque Josone is home to a number of specialized restaurants, set about quiet, little ponds, around which you can enjoy a pleasant stroll after your meal. The best and most traditional place by far is **La Casa de Antiguedades** *($$$; Parque Josone, ☎6-67329)*, which serves the finest cuisine in Varadero in a setting reminiscent of the splendid lifestyle led by well-heeled Cubans in the 19th century. The meat, fish and seafood dishes are all grilled. Impeccable service.

For the most succulent Creole cuisine in Varadero, go to **El Mesón y Parillada la Campana** *($$$; Parque Josone, ☎6-67224)*, also in Parque Josone. This restaurant recreates a colonial atmosphere appropriate to the menu. Pork gets top billing, and is served in all different ways. Try it grilled on the *parillada.*

If you are craving "real" Italian cuisine, head to **El Dante** *($$$; closed Sun, Calles 1 and 56, ☎66-7738)*, also in Parque Josone. It serves a good selection of Italian dishes in an atmosphere that is relaxed and somewhat homey, thanks to the charming, almost Mediterranean decor.

More expensive, the Franco-Swiss cuisine of **La Fondue** *($$$; at Avenida 1 and Calle 61, ☎66-7747)*, near the Cuatro Palmas hotel, is sure to please discriminating gourmets. A wider selection of cheeses is offered here compared to anywhere else, and the best wines are served with the various fondues. This most stylish establishment boasts a refined ambiance enhanced by a chamber-music orchestra.

The most expensive restaurant in Varadero is unfortunately not the best. **Las Américas** *($$$; Casa DuPont, ☎66-7750)* is an exclusive place with a remarkable five-course meal. It also boasts one of the best wine cellars in the region. You won't be disappointed if you let yourself be swept away by the armosphere in the magnificent DuPont mansion. Go at sunset and have a drink on the second floor before dinner.

The best brunch in Varadero is served every morning at the **Vega de la Reina**, in the Hotel Melia Las Américas. The buffet costs $12 per person, and features an excellent selection of fruit, cold cuts, egg dishes and all sorts of breads and pastries. If you're tired of the same old breakfast, this is the place to go.

Matanzas

The family-run **Restaurante El Guajiro** *($; Calle San Isidro no. 4915, opposite the Hospital Provincial, west of Matanzas)* serves traditional Creole cuisine prepared over a charcoal fire. The pork dishes are succulent, especially the *mazas* (fried pork). With his colourful personality, owner Rolando Espino manages to create a friendly atmosphere. A meal including main dish and dessert will cost you around $4.

  ENTERTAINMENT

Varadero

As far as nightclubs are concerned, Varadero is definitely one of the best

places in Cuba. These places, all catering to tourists, offer a wide variety of music and atmospheres. For Latin music, try the **Rincón Latino** *($5; weekends)* in the Hotel Bella Costa, where live salsa and merengue are presented during the high season. Although you're likely to hear some standard dance music as well, the accent is on Latin rhythms.

The most popular bands in Cuba play at the **Amfiteatro de Varadero** *($5; at the corner of Vía Blanca and Carretera Cárdenas)*, near the Varadero bridge. It is best to call for information on upcoming shows.

Aspiring crooners won't fail to swing by **Karaoke 440** *($; every day 10pm to 5am; at Camino del Mar and Calle 15)*, an enjoyable place where the DJ gears the music toward the crowd. Depending on your mood, you can take part in a singing contest alternating with dance music. Interesting bands sometimes play here, as well.

When it comes to cabaret, **Jardines Mediterráneo** *($50; every day 9pm to 3am; at Avenida 1 and Calle 54, ☎61-2460)* wins the prize for its very colourful floor show only rivalled by those in the capital. For $50, you will be treated to the magic of an extravagant, typically Cuban cabaret.

Latin music rules at **La Cueva del Pirata** *(Mon to Sat 8pm to 2:45am; Autopista Sur, Km 11, ☎61-3829)*, another good place to see popular Cuban bands. Cabaret shows are also presented here occasionally.

The little **Disco Azucar** *($2; Calle 25 and Avenida Primera, ☎61-3915)*, in the Hotel Club Tropical, is sure to be a hit with those who prefer a more intimate atmosphere over a big discotheque, although unfortunately it is located in a semi-basement. You'll mostly hear dance music, with a few Latin tunes mixed in. Some of the shows are organized by a Québecois expatriate.

The **Havana Club** *(☎66-7500)* is located between the Hotel Siboney and the Cuatro Palmas. It is one of Varadero's best nightclubs, although the light show isn't very dramatic—something certain travellers consider a plus.

In an altogether different category, the **Casa DuPont** *(☎6-6162)* has a bar on its top-floor belvedere. With its woodwork, grand piano and magnificent view of the sea, this place couldn't be more charming. A band livens things up during happy hour (5 to 7pm), when a small buffet is served up by the house and you can enjoy the splendid sunset.

The trendy nightclub on the peninsula these days is **La Bamba** *($20; Hotel LTI-Tuxpán, ☎66-8210)*, which draws crowds upon crowds of people. The place, whose size is fairly exaggerated (it seems to have been built to accommodate several herds of elephants!), is considered the best danceclub in town.

The **Casa de la Cultura de Varadero Los Corales** *(Avenida Primera, between Calle 34 and Calle 35)* offers free classes in traditional Cuban music, and occasionally hosts concerts by amateur musicians on Thursdays. *El Sabado de la Rumba*, every Saturday night, is a show featuring boisterous, rhythmic Afro-Cuban music inspired by religious rites. You can't miss it, as it's presented outside. The Casa de la Cultura Los Corales also houses the **Galeria Sol y Mar** *(Mon to Sat 9am to 5pm)*, a small art gallery which presents exhibitions of contemporary art and hand-crafted objects; a selection of art magazines are also available.

While you're in Varadero, why not hop on over to the **Ciné Varadero** *(Avenida Playa, between Calles 42 and 43)*? The

movies shown here are usually in Spanish and are all made in Cuba. Admission is $2.50.

Matanzas

The **Museo Provincial de Matanzas** *(Calle Milanés, at the corner of Calle Magdalena, ☎3195 or 3464)* hosts all sorts of cultural activities on its charming patio. The band El Rincón Lírico *(free admission; Sat 4pm)* puts on traditional Cuban music concerts. The place also organizes children's activities *(10am; 3rd Sat of the month)*.

 SHOPPING

Varadero

The **Taller y Galeria de Cerámica Artística** *(Mon to Sat 9am to 7pm; at the corner of Avenida Primera and Calle 60, ☎6-2703, ⌐66-7554)*, the largest contemporary art gallery in Varadero, exhibits sculptures and ceramics by renowned Cuban artists. The adjoining shop sells many quality pieces. Ask for an export permit so that you won't have any problems leaving the country with your purchases.

The little **Libreria Hanoi** *(at the corner of Avenida Primera and Calle 44)* has a good selection of books in Spanish, as well as a few in English and French.

A sure sign that the winds of change are blowing in Cuba, **Benetton** *(Avenida Primera, at the corner of Calle 42)* now has a store in a prime location in Varadero. You'll find all the bathing suits and sportswear you could want here.

If you need to purchase some batteries or have your camera repaired or your film developed, head to **Photo Service** *(Avenida Primera, at the corner of Calle 42).*

Lost or broken glasses or contact lenses? There is an optician on duty at **Optica Varadero** *(Avenida Primera, between Calles 42 and 43).*

Cigar aficionads will want to stop in at the **Casa del Habano** *(9am to 7pm, Calle 63 and Avenida Primera, ☎66-7186),* whose owners make it their duty to store all sorts of cigars in the best possible conditions.

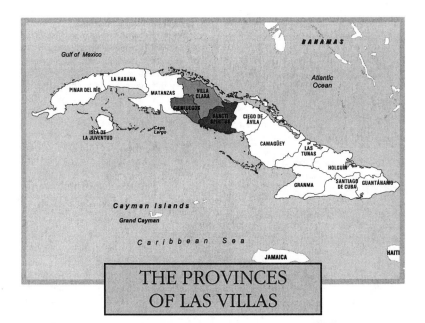

THE PROVINCES
OF LAS VILLAS

A tour of this region is popular with travellers because it covers one of Cuba's most varied regions, including the historic towns of Trinidad, Sancti Spíritus, Remedios and Santa Clara, as well as the beaches of the Bay of Pigs and the Ancón peninsula south of Trinidad, the marshes of Ciénaga de Zapata national park, and the Escambray mountains. If you have a week or two to travel, this tour will provide a good knowledge of the country as you enjoy mountains, beaches and charming colonial towns.

You can embark on this tour from Havana by train or from Varadero by rental car or bus. Travellers departing from Varadero will want to stop along the way to explore the charms of the almost abandoned turn-of-the-century resort village of San Miguel de los Baños in the province of Matanzas (see p 150).

Nature takes an unexpected turn at Ciénaga de Zapata, with immense marshes hugging the Caribbean coast. Stretching along the south of the province of Matanzas, these 3,300 square kilometres (1,270 mi²) of marshland are home to a rich variety of flora and fauna that will thrill nature lovers. Though only part of this area lies in the Parque Nacional Ciénaga de Zapata, the entire peninsula has an extraordinary variety of exotic animals and birds. There are an estimated 50,000 crocodiles here, some 10,000 of them at the La Boca breeding farm, which, unfortunately, is the spot most visited by tourists who come to this region.

Other places of particular beauty are hidden in this marshland. Surrounded by an immense lake called Laguna del Tesoro, and accessible only by boat, the Guamá islands tourism and hotel complex is another option, with its open-air museum consisting of sculptures of the Taïno Indians, the first inhabitants of this area. La Salina, an isolated and hard-to-reach zone, is a gathering place for thousands of pink flamingoes. All told, however, one day should be enough to get to know this area, unless you are an ornithologist or a very devoted nature lover. You may, of course, decide to spent a night in one of Guamá's rustic huts.

Quite apart from the exotic natural beauty, history shares the stage with the beaches and spectacular underwater treasures of Playa Larga and Playa Girón. These two coastal villages are situated along the Bay of Pigs, made famous around the world after an invasion by American-backed paramilitary forces in 1961. A big propaganda billboard at the entrance to Playa Girón proclaims to visitors that here "American imperialism lost its first war in Latin America." After visiting the museum dedicated to this victory by Cuban revolutionary forces under the command of Fidel Castro, your attention will naturally be drawn to the area's beaches. The relaxed atmosphere of the little settlement of Playa Girón makes this a lovely spot to visit.

Heading east you come to Cienfuegos, capital of the province of the same name, with its many attractions and its rich history. The province of Cienfuegos has an area of 4,151 square kilometres (1,601 mi^2), dominated by the Escambray mountains whose highest peak is Pico San Juan (1,140 m). Although the sugar industry is the mainspring of the province's economy, tobacco and coffee are also grown in the mountainous areas.

The old waterfront city of Cienfuegos is a magnificent showcase of neocolonial architecture. A colonial castle, fine public squares and a handful of extravagant turn-of-the-century residences are some of the architectural highlights that once made Cienfuegos the "pearl of the Caribbean". Parque Martí is superb, and the town's 19th-century buildings are remarkably well preserved. The Paseo del Prado, lined with columned houses, leads to the fashionable Punta Gorda district, with its splendid seaside mansions. At the mouth of the bay, the Castillo de Jagua recalls Cienfuego's historical and commercial prominence. Nearby, the Rancho Luna beaches and the Escambray mountains make for excellent day excursions. It is well worth spending for a night or two in Cienfuegos.

The winding road from Cienfuegos to Trinidad runs near the majestic Escambray mountains, which are clearly visible on the horizon. The scenery is superb and, on a clear day, the mountains beckoning in the distance are hard to resist. About 40 kilometres from Cienfuegos, the Base de Campismo de Guajimico has excellent reefs as well as many hiking trails and several grottos.

Trinidad is located in the province of Sancti Spíritus, where the Taïno Indians lived before they were exterminated by the Spanish. The area's economy is dominated by sugarcane production.

Upon arriving in Trinidad, tucked away in the foothills of the Escambray mountains, you are immediately plunged into the atmosphere of the Spanish colonial era. With its narrow streets of paving stones, brightly painted houses, wrought-iron or sculpted wooden gates, and Spanish- or Arab-style roof tiles, this little town remains suspended in time. It is worth staying at least two nights in beautiful Trinidad. The town has become increasingly popular with tourists, however, so be sure to get an early start before the fleets of tour buses arrive from Havana or Varadero. At dusk, after the tour buses have

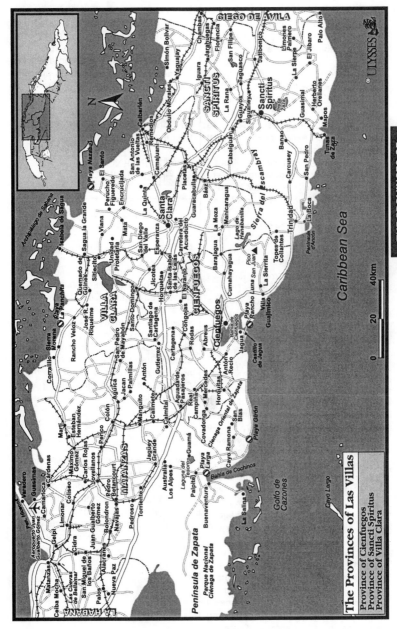

THE PROVINCES OF
LAS VILLAS

The Provinces of Las Villas
Province of Cienfuegos
Province of Sancti Spiritus
Province of Villa Clara

returned from where they came, Trinidad becomes remarkably calm. You will find excellent museums, good restaurants and a lively nightlife.

Trinidad has the added advantage of being near the fine white-sand beaches of Playa Ancón and the picturesque coastal village of La Boca. The magnificent Valle de los Ingenios, close by, is worth a half-day excursion. This valley used to be one of the main areas of sugar production and slavery. Today you can visit the biggest colonial-era plantation as well as buildings once inhabited by masters and slaves.

Accessible from Trinidad or Cienfuegos, the Sierra del Escambray is the country's second-highest mountain range. The village of Topes de Collantes, perched on these high mountains, has many hotels and a health spa. The trip there is delightful and leads along a winding road past countless valleys lined by steep mountains. There are good hiking and rafting opportunities and lovely plants and wildlife to observe.

At the eastern edge of this proposed itinerary is the town of Sancti Spíritus, capital of the eponymous province, well worth a few hours or a full day. The old part of Sancti Spíritus, classified as a national monument, has a peculiar labyrinthine urban layout, designed to foil pirates' attempts to capture the town. Nowadays, visitors amuse themselves by getting lost in these winding alleyways. There are several museums, some fine colonial mansions and, unfortunately, noisy traffic in places.

Santa Clara, capital of the province of Villa Clara, is bigger than the other cities on this tour. The city is an important economic centre, but it also has a lively cultural scene with interesting museums, including some dedicated to Che Guevara.

Very close to Santa Clara is the ancient village of Remedios, with imbued old-fashioned colonial charm. Fortunately, Remedios has not yet been spoiled by tourism, giving it an advantage over Trinidad. You can explore its peaceful little streets without being hassled by *jineteros*. Some people may want to spend an entire day here, while others may dream of staying for the rest of their lives!

 FINDING YOUR WAY AROUND

Ciénaga de Zapata

By Bus

Ciénaga de Zapata has no direct bus service from Havana or Varadero. You must get a ticket to Cienfuegos and get off at the town of Jaguey Grande, from where a few local buses run to the national park. You'll probably have better luck hiring a private driver in Jaguey Grande, however, which should not cost more than $10 for the trip to Ciénaga de Zapata. Hitchhiking is another option.

By Car

From Havana, take the Autopista Nacional west, heading south of the Central Australia exit located at Kilometre 140. From Varadero, the shortest route goes via Cárdenas, Jovellanos, Colón and Jaguey Grande, where there are some very pretty country roads. These tend to be poorly marked, however.

Bay of Pigs

Car Rental

You can rent all kinds of vehicles, including an all-terrain vehicle to reach **La Salina**, at the **Havanautos** offices in **Villa Playa Girón** (☎4123). **Transautos** also has an office at Playa Girón (☎4-126).

Cienfuegos

By Train

The delightful Cienfuegos railway station (*Calle 49, between Calle 58 and Calle 60*, ☎5495) is located near the centre of town and is easy to reach on foot if you don't have heavy baggage.

To Havana: Departure twice a day: 11:10pm (arrival: 6:25am, fare: $11) and 10:15am (arrival: 8:33pm, fare: $9.50).

To Sancti Spíritus: Departure twice a day: 4:30am (arrival: 10:01am, fare: $5.20) and 2pm (arrival: 8:13pm, fare: $5.20)

By Bus

Right next to the railway station, the **Estación de Omnibus Nacionales** (*Calle 49, between Calle 56 and Calle 58*, ☎5720) has many departures and a wide choice of destinations. Although the fares in pesos are very economical, buying tickets can be quite an experience. If luck is smiling on you, you may have to reserve only a few days in advance. As elsewhere in Cuba, American dollars will make the purchase of intercity bus tickets far easier.

There are five buses a day to **Havana**, at 6am, 12:30pm, 3:10pm and 11:50pm. Tickets to Havana cost $14. Buses are also the most economical way of getting around within the region to places such as the Rancho Luna beaches, the Hotel Pasocaballo, or the town of Trinidad.

To Camagüey: Departure: 8am (odd-numbered dates). Fare: $13.

To Paso Caballos: Departures: 8am, 10am and 3pm. Fare: $1.

To Rancho Luna: Departures: 5:10am and 5:40pm. Fare: $1.50.

To Santa Clara: Departures: 5am and 9am. Fare: $2.50.

To Santiago de Cuba: Departure: 5pm (even-numbered dates). Fare: $20.

To Trinidad: Departures: 9:25am and 5:55pm. Fare: $3.

By Boat

Boats going to the Castillo de Jagua and the Hotel Pasocaballo leave from the pier at the corner of Calle 25 and Calle 46, with daily departures at 7am, noon and 5pm. The fare is minimal; only one peso. These boats cross Cienfuegos bay, and are certainly the most scenic way to reach the Castillo de Jagua. You can also take the boat back to Cienfuegos once your excursion is over. It is best to check locally to confirm return times.

Car Rental

Havanautos has an office of the Hotel Rancho Luna (☎48120 to 23). **Transautos** has offices at the Hotel Jagua (☎27-982) and at the Hotel Rancho Luna (☎5929).

By Taxi

Turistaxi cars are usually parked in front of the Hotel Jagua in the Punta Gorda district. However, if you are in the central area of Cienfuegos, why not try the economical and picturesque horse-drawn carts at least once?

Trinidad

By Plane

There are very few flights to Trinidad. **Cubana de Aviación** *(Carretera de María Augural, Ancón,* ☎*2296)* has offices at the **Aeropuerto de Trinidad** *(*☎*2296)*, near the Ancón beaches a few kilometres from Trinidad. This new airport opened in 1998, offering better access to the lovely city of Trinidad. Below is the schedule in effect at press time:

Trinidad-Havana: departure at 12:25pm
Trinidad-Varadero: departure at 9:40am
Trinidad-Cayo Largo: departure at 9:25am
Trinidad-Cayo Coco: departure at 8am

Each of these 40- to 50-minute flights (depending on the destination) costs $50 one way and $100 return, except for the one to Varadero, which costs $45, or $90 return.

By Bus

The **Estación de Omnibus Nacionales** *(Calle Piro Guinart No. 224,* ☎*2404)* is located in the very heart of the old part of Trinidad. You can get there easily on foot from nearby hotels. Tickets may be bought at the bus station just before your departure, but it is always preferable to reserve ahead, especially if you are going to Havana.

Víazul runs to Havana and Varadero daily. The **Havana**-bound bus leaves at 1:50pm and arrives in the capital at around 8:35pm; the fare is $25. The bus to **Varadero** leaves Trinidad at 1:25pm and reaches Varadero at around 8:25pm. The fare is also $25. These coaches are much more comfortable, with air conditioning and seats that provide more room.

To Cienfuegos: Departures: 8am and 1:30pm. Travel time: 2 hours. Fare: $5.

To Havana: Departure: 1:30pm. Travel time: 5 hours 30 minutes. Fare: $21.

To Sancti Spíritus: Departures: 3am, 5am, 9am, 11:30am, 1:30pm, 4pm and 6pm. Travel time: 2 hours. Fare: $5.

To Santa Clara: Departure: 5:15pm. Travel time: 3 hours. Fare: $6.

To Topes de Collantes: Departure: 10am. Fare: $1.

Car Rental

In Trinidad, you can rent a car from **Havanautos** *(*☎*6100)*, located at the Hotel Costa Sur. At the Ancón beaches, go to the **Transautos** *(*☎*4011)* office at the Hotel Ancón.

By Taxi

It usually isn't necessary to take taxis in Trinidad. The town is easy to explore on foot, with little need for motorized transport, unless you're heading out of town to the Ancón beaches or for an excursion to the Valle de los Ingenios. **Transtur** cars are usually parked in front of the Hotel Ancón *(*☎*4011 or 5314)*.

Sancti Spíritus

By Train

The **Sancti Spíritus railway station** *(Avenida 26 de Julio No. 92,* ☎*24790)* is near the Puente de Yayayabo, Cuba's oldest bridge.

To Havana: Departures: 9:45pm. Fare: $24.

To Cienfuegos: Departures: 4:30am and 2:08pm. Fare: $6.

To Santa Clara: Departure: 4:30am. Fare: $4.

To Tunas de Zaza: Departures: 9:17am, 12:34pm and 7:41pm. Fare: $1.

By Bus

The **Estación de Omnibus** *(*☎*24142)* is located at the edge of town, at the intersection of the Carretera Central and the highway to Trinidad.

To Trinidad: Departures every hour. Fare: $3.

To Havana: Departure: 2:35pm. Fare: $15.50.

To Santa Clara: Departures: 5am and 10am. Fare: $3.50.

To Camagüey: Departure: 7am (alternate days). Fare: $7.

To Ciego de Avila: Departure every two hours. Travel time: 3 hours. Fare: $3.

Santa Clara

By Train

The Santa Clara railway station *(Calle Maceo, Parque de los Mártires,* ☎*27783)* is right in the centre of town. Ticket sales and reservations are made across from the station, on the other side of the Parque de los Mártires, at the **Agencia de Reservaciones y Venta de Boletines** *(Calle Luis Estevez, Parque de los Mártires,* ☎*27783)*. During my visit, the Santa Clara station was one of the few in the country that was still selling tickets to foreign tourists in pesos.

To Havana: Departures: 12:10am, 2:53am, 4:58am, 6:10am and 8:28am. Fare: $10 to $12.

To Sancti Spíritus: Departures: 7:18am and 5:29pm. Fare: $3.

To Cienfuegos: Departure: 5:27pm. Fare: $5.

To Camagüey: Departure: 11:27pm. Fare: $11.

To Santiago de Cuba: Departure: 8:48pm. Fare: $24.

By Bus

The **Estación de Omnibus Nacionales** *(Carretera Central,* ☎*92114)* is located near the Plaza de la Revolución, some distance from the centre of town, near the Motel Los Caneyes.

To Havana: Departures: 2pm and 11:50pm. Fare: $12.

To Matanzas: Departure: 12:20pm. Fare: $8.

To Varadero: Departure: 8:10am. Fare: $8.

To Ciego de Ávila: Departure: 2:20pm. Fare: $6.50.

To Morón: Departure: 7:40am. Fare: $7.50.

To Santiago de Cuba: Departure: 7pm. Fare: $27.

To Holguín: Departure: 6:30pm. Fare: $22.

To Trinidad: Departure: 1:20pm. Fare: $6.

To Sancti Spíritus: Departures: 7:30am and 12:30pm. Fare: $3.50.

To Cienfuegos: Departures: 7:10am and 11:20am. Fare: $2.50.

Car Rental

You can rent cars from the **Havanautos** office at the Motel Los Caneyes (*☎4512 to 15*).

PRACTICAL INFORMATION

Ciénaga de Zapata

Ciénaga de Zapata is a rather isolated spot with only a few restaurants and a single hotel. For medical care and other essential services, head to Playa Girón or Cienfuegos.

Playa Girón

All services such as laundry, the post office and so on are located on the street running perpendicular from the Villa Playa Girón hotel. For medical help, ask to see the hotel nurse.

Cienfuegos

The **Hotel Jagua** offers tourist information, currency exchange and postal service, all quite efficiently.

Medical Care

For medical help, the **Clínica Internacional** *(Calle 37 No. 202, facing the Hotel Jagua, Punta Gorda, ☎7008, ☎8959)* is reserved exclusively for foreign visitors and offers personal 24-hour service. This medical clinic is part of the Servimed national network. If you are not insured, a medical appointment costs about $25 and an X-ray between $12 and $25. The clinic's pharmacy is exceptionally well stocked. Ambulance service is available from the same telephone number.

Trinidad

Trinidad has a **Clínica Internacional** *(Calle Linos Pérez No. 130, corner of Calle Reforma, ☎3391, ☎33-5071)*, also part of the Servimed national hospital network. Conscientious medical care and good pharmacies characterize these clinics, established to meet the needs of foreigners.

Sancti Spíritus

The post office is near the Estación de Omnibus Nacionales *(Calle Guiteras No. 3)*.

Santa Clara

The **Santa Clara Libre** *(Parque Vidal)* hotel has a tourist office, a medical clinic and a telephone communications centre.

 EXPLORING

Ciénaga de Zapata ★★

Marshes, marshes and more marshes! Ciénaga de Zapata is a paradise for hunting and fishing, and is also popular spot with biologists, ornithologists and photographers.

This whole area was once one of the poorest and most isolated regions in the country. Before the Revolution, there was no highway access, and local residents had neither running water nor electricity. However, the Bay of Pigs skirmish in 1961 would soon transform living conditions here. Because of its isolation and the lack of easy road access, this area was a choice landing spot for paramilitary forces made up of Americans and Cuban exiles seeking to overthrow the Castro regime. The aim of these counter-revolutionaries and of the CIA was to set up a provisional government for a few days and then to request military aid from U.S. troops. Castro's military camp was set up on the Australia sugar plantation, along the road leading to Ciénega de Zapata and Playa Girón.

The plantation, called **Central Australia**, is open to the public, and has a museum recalling the actions of Castro and his revolutionary forces. To thwart further attacks in the area, and to improve living conditions for residents, a good highway was built; economic development and of tourism soon fol-

lowed. Simple monuments, set up in honour of the young militia members who perished in battle, lie along the stretch of highway leading to Playa Girón.

Parque Nacional Ciénega de Zapata ★★, with an area of 300 square kilometres (115 mi²), is recognized by the United Nations as a biosphere reserve. At the entrance is **La Boca**, a tourist complex that draws numerous tour buses from Havana and Varadero. Restaurants, bars and other facilities have been built to receive visitors, but don't expect to find anything inexpensive. Before the economic crisis of the early 1990s, this spot was very popular among Cubans.

Celia Sánchez

The first facilities in the Parque Nacional Ciénaga de Zapata were built in 1961 on the recommendation of Celia Sánchez, a close friend of Fidel Castro.

A unique population of animals attracts many visitors: crocodiles. About 10,000 of these reptiles can be seen in a 13-hectare (32-acre) enclosure, where they are raised commercially for their meat and their skin. The latter is turned into handbags, belts and shoes (this does not threaten the survival of the species). Observing these creatures, four to seven metres in length, can be both spellbinding and frightening.

La Boca is also the departure point for boats which cross the marshes through a canal, about six kilometres long, leading to **Laguna del Tesoro** ★ and **Guamá** ★. Two types of boat are available. A fairly big boat runs between La Boca and Guamá four times a day, at 8am, 10:30am, 1pm and 3pm. A more

THE PROVINCES OF LAS VILLAS

exciting option are the speedboats that leave whenever you are ready, although they cost a few dollars more. If you plan to stay overnight in Guamá, you will have to pay a supplement to be picked up the next day.

To reach Guamá, boats follow a long, narrow canal to Laguna del Tesoro (Treasure Lake). With an area of about eight square kilometres (3 mi^2), this lake is teeming with fish and is a popular spot for angling. Besides trout and carp, the lake is home to a unique species, *manguari*. This creature has most of the characteristics of a fish except for its head, which resembles that of a crocodile.

The lake got its name from the story of the Taíno Indian chief Guamá who, according to legend, sought refuge here with his people while fleeing Spanish attacks on their villages in the eastern provinces. They brought gold, silver and jewels with them, or so the story goes, and when the Spanish arrived here the Taínos threw their treasure into the lake to prevent it from falling into enemy hands.

The reconstituted village of Guamá, on the far share of Laguna del Tesoro, is a sort of modern reproduction of what a Taíno village may have looked like. Built on a series of marshy little islands, this tourism and hotel complex obviously has little to do with a native village apart from a certain architectural inspiration and the use of numerous canals linking the cabins to one another. The view from these rustic cabins, which stand out on the horizon, is quite interesting. Built according to traditional methods and topped by palm fronds, some cabins serve as guest rooms, while the bigger ones are used for a restaurant and a nightclub. Unfortunately, the nightclub does detract somewhat from the tranquil, natural surroundings, unless you're lucky and it's closed.

To get the most out of Guamá, spend at least one night here. After the boats and their busloads of tourists leave in the early afternoon, nature's preeminence restored. A walk along the many trails and numerous wooden bridges through the marshes is a fine idea. And why not rent a canoe and paddle on the canal's quiet waters or beneath the bridges, arriving at the dock in front of your hut? Canoes are the most common form of transportation among the workers at Guamá, and they are the best way to mix the practical and the enjoyable. Your canoe trip *($2 an hour)* will be accompanied by the silence and enchantment of dusk, or the musical serenade of birds at daybreak.

Awake to Nature!

To witness the spectacular spectacle of nature's awakening at Guamá, get up before the crack of dawn while most other humans are still asleep.

Guamá is also the site of Cuba's only open-air museum, **Aldea Taína** (Taíno Village), set on a small island with 25 sculptures portraying Taíno Indians carrying out various tasks. These are the work of Cuban sculptress Rita Longa. Walking along the museum grounds, you can explore traditional huts where some of the sculptures are hidden. The museum makes for a quick excursion, and the superb natural surroundings are irresistible.

Bay of Pigs ★

The beaches of **Playa Larga**, a few kilometres east of Ciénega de Zapata on the Bay of Pigs, are longer and sandier than those of Playa Girón. This peaceful spot thankfully has only one beachfront hotel.

Playa Girón might be an ordinary little coastal village were it not for the historic events which took place here in 1961 (see p 22). This is where Fidel Castro's forces trounced American mercenaries and Cuban exiles. Along the main road next to the beach, you can see some little houses hit by shells, maintained in that state to recall the events. The **Museo Girón** *($2; every day 9am to noon and 1pm to 5pm)* houses a permanent exhibit with period photos and pieces of artillery. This rather simple museum explains the conflict from a Cuban point of view. If you don't read Spanish, you may want to consider hiring a guide.

Playa Girón has a little beach which, unfortunately, is split by a long concrete wall extending into the sea. Called the Malecón de Playa Girón, there is nothing very charming about this wall, but it does at least reduce the currents and waves in the small bay. Apart from the pretty little village, worth visiting simply for the chance to take a walk and meet some of the residents, the real attractions in Playa Girón are the spectacular underwater formations, which draw divers from the world-over.

Cienfuegos ★★

Capital of the province of the same name, the city of Cienfuegos was founded in 1819 by a Frenchman named Louis de Cluet, who settled here with about 40 French families and named the village Fernandina de Jagua, *jagua* being a native word for beauty. The city is still known as the "beauty" or "pearl" of the south. Ten years after the founding of Fernandina de Jagua,

its name was changed to Cienfuegos, after the governor. Because of its geographic location on Cienfuegos Bay, the city thrived commercially. The narrow mouth of the bay offers natural protection against both the whims of the sea and pirate attacks.

The southern beauty still merits its nickname, although it has become somewhat industrialized. Visible in the distance, on the west side of Cienfuegos Bay, is a thermo electric plant, whose construction, in collaboration with the former Soviet Union, was delayed following the collapse of the Soviet empire in 1990. The city's industrial orientation remains alive; fortunately, it has not spoiled the beauty of the old neighbourhoods.

Arriving from the west, from Havana or Playa Girón, the highway leads directly to the **Paseo del Prado**, the longest promenade in Cuba. This avenue is lined with old colourful columned houses, some of them dating back to the city's founding in 1819.

Head west on Avenida San Carlos, also known as Avenida 56, until you reach **Parque Martí**, at the heart of the city. This big, peaceful square is charming, and the 19th-century buildings surrounding it are remarkably well preserved. The plaza itself is dominated by a statue of José Martí, which dates from 1902. A commemorative plaque in front of the statue marks the exact spot where the city was founded. The arch behind the statue was a gift from the workers of Cienfuegos to the nascent republic in 1902.

Parque Martí is one of the few public squares in Cuba to have kept its *glorieta*, a pavilion where local musicians would give concerts and residents would dance *La Retreta* on holidays.

La Retreta

La Retreta is a traditional dance in which men and women circle in small groups in opposite directions to music performed by the town band, bringing lovers and couples together. This tradition, unfortunately, has been lost over the years, though some groups are trying to revive it.

North of the square is the former **Escuela San Lorenzo**, built in 1927. This school had a religious orientation prior to the Revolution, and since then it has been a high school. You will recognize it by its faded sky-blue walls. Next door, the **Teatro Thomas Terry** occupies a handsome building, with a colonnaded, terraced entrance. This theatre, where Enrico Caruso and Sarah Berhardt once performed, has excellent acoustics and a magnificent decor. West of the plaza, the **Casa de la Cultura** is in a blue-tinted palace, which looks rather out of place in this setting. Cultural events are held here regularly, and you can pick up a schedule of upcoming events inside.

South of the plaza, the **Fondo de Bienes Culturales** *(free admission; every day 8:30am to 8pm; Avenida 54, ☎3400)* promotes contemporary artists and artisans from Cienfuegos. This building dates back to 1891 and served as the provincial museum during the Revolution.

The neighbouring **Museo de la Ciudad** *(\$2; Tue to Sat 11am to 7pm, Sun 9am to 1pm; Avenida 54 No. 202, ☎9722)* opened in its current location in 1995. Built in the late 19th century, this building once housed the Spanish Casino, a social club. The permanent exhibit features 19th-century furniture, al-

though several of the galleries are still closed due to the recent move.

Commonly called "El Bulevar" Avenida 56, between Parque Martí and the Paseo del Prado, is reserved for pedestrians, and is lined with shops and cafés.

From the Malecón to Punta Gorda

The neoclassical style dominates the Paseo del Prado as you approach the **Malecón**, which follows the long and rather gloomy shore of the Bahía de Cienfuegos. The houses and little parks to the left are rather uninteresting, but come dawn or nightfall, residents both young and old throng to Cienfuegos' longest avenue to enjoy a bit of fresh air, as well as a certain sense of freedom, no doubt.

It is worth taking a long stroll along the bay through the **Punta Gorda ★★** neighbourhood to see the lavish old vacation homes, most of which have wooden façades influenced by American architectural styles. At sunset, the reflections on these brightly coloured houses inspire playfulness in children and romance in their elders, who embrace one another with endless enthusiasm.

The Western Shore of the Bahía de Cienfuegos

The best way to reach the western shore of the Bahía de Cienfuegos is to take a boat from Cienfuegos (see p 169). The excursion offers some interesting scenery and leads right to the **Castillo de Jagua ★**. Built in the 18th century by the Spanish, this castle once guarded the entrance to the bay. Today it is being renovated to house a museum. The pretty little

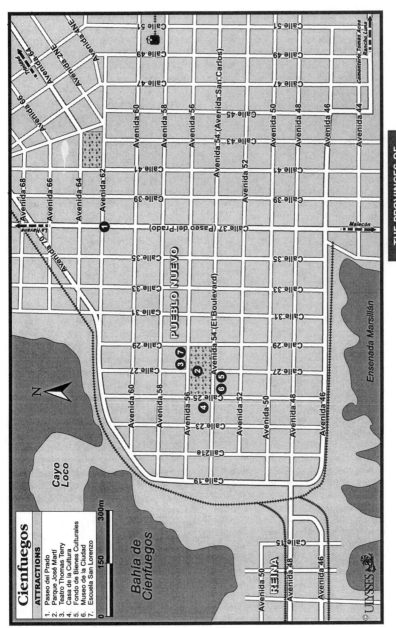

Cienfuegos

ATTRACTIONS

1. Paseo del Prado
2. Parque José Martí
3. Teatro Thomas Terry
4. Casa de la Cultura
5. Fondo de Bienes Culturales
6. Museo de la Ciudad
7. Escuela San Lorenzo

coastal village here charms visitors with its peaceful atmosphere. Unfortunately, however, the enormous Hotel Pasacaballo on the opposite shore detracts somewhat from the view. Behind the castle is a rather dreary hillside town built for the workers from the thermoelectric power plant.

Excursion to Rancho Luna

The **Rancho Luna** region is a good destination for a daytrip. Beaches, orchards and mountain hikes provide something for everyone. To get there, take the Carretera de Rancho Luna, which runs perpendicular to the Paseo del Prado, near the Malecón; the same road also leads to the town of Trinidad.

Along the way, the **Cementerio Tomás Acea** has an impressive façade, inspired by the Pantheon in Athens. Classified as a national monument, this large cemetery was built in 1902 with funds donated by Tomás Acea, a wealthy Cienfuegos personality. On the whole, this cemetery merits a visit; do not miss the imposing monument to the September 5 combatants.

The **Finca la Isabela** *(Carretera de Rancho Luna Km 4, ☎7606)* is an extremely curious place. This typical house, which once belonged to a Cuban farmer, is now much more than just a restaurant. A small group of trained dogs puts on an amusing show each day. The agility of these dogs is extraordinary. You can also ride a bull or a horse and ask to see a cockfight in the ring set up for this purpose. The congenial Rolando Hernández trains all of the animals.

Turn right at the first intersection just past the cemetery. The **Hotel Punta La Cueva** organizes boat trips on the Bahía de Cienfuegos *($8-$10; Tue, Thu and Sat at 9am, ☎3956)*, which covers

82 square kilometres (32 mi²). The trip, lasting 2.5 hours, includes stops on two little islands in the bay. The Carretera de Rancho Luna then leads through a fruit-producing region, whose produce includes coconut and mango.

Just outside the city, the **Jardín Botánico** displays more than 2,000 plant species, including one of the biggest collections of palm trees (more than 300 types) in the world. This botanical garden was purchased by Harvard University in 1917 from an American sugarcane grower there. With the Revolution, however, the garden came under the authority of the ministry of agriculture and then of the Cuban Academy of Science.

Trinidad ★★★

Founded in 1514 by Diego Velásquez on land once inhabited by Taïno Indians, Villa de la Santísima Trinidad became Cuba's third *villa*, following Baracoa and Bayamo. Trinidad's architectural heritage is the best preserved of Cuba's three oldest towns. Isolated in the south by mountains that surround it, Trinidad fell into economic decline as sugar plantations sprang up elsewhere in Cuba.

A short stroll here is like being transported to another era – one that still resounds from the age-old walls. Trinidad is one of very few colonial Latin American cities that has preserved almost its entire architectural heritage. With residences from another time appearing just around the corner of a simple cobbled street that follows its ancient, winding course, Trinidad is full of surprises, and wonderment blends with the sublime when, on a clear day, the high Escambray mountains rise proudly on the horizon.

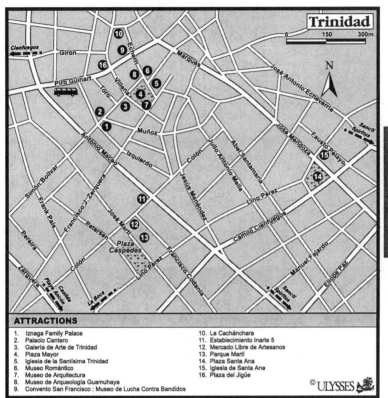

ATTRACTIONS

1. Iznaga Family Palace
2. Palacio Cantero
3. Galería de Arte de Trinidad
4. Plaza Mayor
5. Iglesia de la Santísima Trinidad
6. Museo Romántico
7. Museo de Arquitectura
8. Museo de Arqueología Guamuhaya
9. Convento San Francisco : Museo de Lucha Contra Bandidos
10. La Cachánchara
11. Establecimiento Inarte 5
12. Mercado Libre de Artesanos
13. Parque Martí
14. Plaza Santa Ana
15. Iglesia de Santa Ana
16. Plaza del Jigüe

© ULYSSES

However, nothing is perfect in this world. Wealthy tourists and the economic crisis afflicting Cuba have led to a profligation of begging, of which it may be said that Trinidad is the capital (it competes for this title with Old Havana and Varadero). It is hard to take even a few steps in the town, especially near the central plaza, with being the object of repeated entreaties from children and their mothers asking for a dollar, or a ballpoint pen, or a stick of chewing gum... and on and on if you dare to refuse initial requests. In many cases a veritable mob will throw themselves in front of you as soon as you arrive. Avoid getting out of your rental car on the Plaza Mayor, which is crowded with *jineteros*.

Recognized in 1980 as a national monument and then in 1990 as a UNESCO World Heritage Site, this old town has a fascinating history as evidenced by its architectural treasures. Trinidad's first commercial activity was gold mining. Indians living in the area were submitted to forced labour, and the rivers and mountains were exploited for many years until they yielded no more ore. Starting in 1540, the population of Trinidad dwindled slowly but surely, with the natives returning to repopulate the town. In 1573, however, the Span-

Trinidad

ish showed renewed interest and the town's wealth was then derived from livestock, tobacco and the contraband trade with France, England and Holland.

Attacked and destroyed a number of times by pirates, Trinidad suffered its final attack in 1702, when the construction of Trinidad as we see it today really began. Between 1724 and 1755, there were only 50 houses of mortar and stone built. Little by little, sugarcane grew in importance, becoming Trinidad's main source of wealth.

Slavery also grew in importance. The first Africans landed in 1514 as house-hold slaves. In 1789 the buying and selling of slaves became legal in Trinidad for the first time. Prosperity in the sugar industry created a slave boom in 1846; during that year alone, between 2,000 and 3,000 slaves were brought here. However, the growth of sugar production elsewhere in the country, and above all the destruction of sugar plantations during the wars of independence (Trinidad supported the Spanish) brought about the town's economic decline. In the **Valle de los Ingenios**, Trinidad's real bread basket where black slaves formed a majority, the situation became explosive and numerous rebellions broke out.

The town of Trinidad is best explored on foot. The old town's street layout is twisting and difficult to negotiate by car.

Chinas Peladas

Cobbled streets dominate the town of Trinidad. These stones, popularly called *chinas peladas*, were installed in 1820 at the initiative of the townsfolk.

From Calle Simón Bolívar to the Plaza Mayor

The 19th-century mansion of the Iznaga family (see p 185) is located along **Calle Simón Bolívar**, which leads to the Plaza Mayor. One of Trinidad's wealthiest families, the Iznagas owned many slaves and sugar plantations. Family members still live in the yellow-and-brown former palace, which has apparently been left to ruin. This is a pity, for it is one of the town's architectural jewels. The interior is not open to visitors.

Across the street, the **Palacio Cantero** ★ *($2; Sun to Fri 9am to 4:45pm)* is worth a visit. Built in the mid-19th century, its facade was recently restored to its original white colour, a project that involved the removal of ten coats of paint. The interior of this former palace is quite simply magnificent, and many original paintings have been preserved intact. Several period objects can be found in the pretty interior courtyard; a stairway leads to a tower from which a superb view of Trinidad and the Escambray mountains can be had.

The **Galería de Arte de Trinidad** ★ *(free admission; every day 8am to 5pm)* occupies an 1809 house with ochre walls and wooden window frames painted a striking sky-blue at the corner of Calle Simón Bolívar and the Plaza de la Catedral. It was once occupied by the *regidor* (the town governor). Today it houses Trinidad's biggest collection of contemporary art. Exhibitions of work by artists from Trinidad and from around Cuba are presented in three galleries. Gatherings with artists are held on the last Thursday of each month.

The **Plaza Mayor** ★★★, also called the Antigua Plaza de Trinidad, is the focal point of a visit to the town. Restored colonial mansions, sumptuous and brightly coloured, surround one of the finest public squares in Cuba and the entire Caribbean. The square as we see it today was laid out in 1856 with materials brought from Philadelphia. Well before this date, however, the Plaza Mayor was central to the history of Trinidad and of Latin America as a whole, for it was from here that the *conquistador* Hernán Cortés set out in 1518 to conquer the New World. A sculpture on the plaza portrays the Muse of Dance, and two bronze hounds stand guard at the entrance.

Construction of the **Iglesia de la Santísima Trinidad** ★★ began in the mid-19th century. It is unique in that it is the only cathedral in Cuba, and one of the few in the world, that does not have a clocktower. Visiting hours are rather limited, with doors open only from 11:30am to 12:30pm. Mass is celebrated each evening at 7pm.

The town's best museums are found around the Plaza Mayor. The **Museo Romántico** ★★★ *($2; Tue to Sun 8am to 6pm, ☎4363)* has an excellent permanent collection; the colonial mansion that houses it, built in 1740, is one of the finest in Trinidad. The interior courtyard is superb, with its yellow hues and its green wood trim. One of the museum's collections displays original furnishings from 19th-century Cuban bourgeois residences. Living rooms, dining rooms, bedrooms, kitchens and bathrooms are all represented. The high, magnificently carved cedar ceiling of the main drawing room dates from 1774, and has been remarkably well preserved considering the area's tropical climate.

At the entrance to the museum, the **Galería de Arte de la UNEAC** (same opening hours as the museum), the gallery of the Cuban union of artists and writers, presents a small temporary exhibition of works by contemporary Cuban artists.

The **Museo de Arquitectura** ★★ ($1; every day 8am to 5pm; Plaza Mayor, ☎3208) boasts one of the best designs of all Cuban museums. Dedicated to the architecture of the colonial era, it has eight exhibition halls displaying a collection of metal grillwork, period doors and construction materials, with pertinent explanations of the way houses were built. One interesting gallery is devoted to sugar plantations and to architecture during the era of slavery. Behind a closed gate in the charming, peaceful interior courtyard is hidden the museum's most original item: a steam bath. Don't forget to ask someone to show you this eccentric and ingenious turn-of-the-century tub.

Also on the Plaza Mayor, the **Museo Arqueológico** ★ ($1; Sun to Fri 9am to 5pm; ☎3420) is the least visited museum in Trinidad, but this lack of interest is in no way a reflection of the refinement of the archaeological collection it houses. The museum has three exhibits. The first presents objects, instruments and skeletons of Siboney Indians, including a necklace from 3000 BC. The second exhibition hall is dedicated to the Taïno Indians, who came to the eastern part of the island from northern Venezuela. The display includes ceramic items dating from the 10th and 11th centuries AD. Finally, a few European ceramic objects from the colonial era are presented in a much smaller room. The building itself is also worth lingering over. This former residence was built in 1732 and enlarged in 1835. It belonged to the Padro family which, on March 14, 1801, welcomed none other than the famous German biologist and traveller, Baron Alexander von Humboldt, for dinner.

Trinidad's symbolic **convent of San Francisco** ★★ is an ochre building facing a charming little square of the same name on Avenida Guitart. Construction began in 1731, with further work undertaken from 1810 to 1813 to complete it. Today, the convent little more than its clock tower remains from this era, the rest having been constructed later. The cupola was rebuilt in 1930 following its collapse. You can climb to the top of the clocktower: the view of the town and of the Escambray is stupendous. The San Francisco convent now houses the **Museo de Lucha Contra Bandidos** ★ (Museum of Anti-Bandit Struggle) ($1; Tue to Sun 9am to 5pm; Calle Fernando Hernández Echerre, Plaza San Francisco, ☎4121), which traces the history of the revolutionary struggles leading to the overthrow of Batista in 1959. It also recounts the combats waged by revolutionaries after 1959 against armed groups in the Escambray mountains. The exhibits include weaponry, boats that belonged to the CIA, pieces of spy planes and period photos.

Just past the entrance, on your right, are stairs that go up to the top of the **tower**. This spot offers the best **panorama** of the city and its old districts, but reaching it means climbing a rickety

The *Cachánchara*

The *cachánchara* became famous during the second war of independence when General Máximo Gómez arrived at this house to rest and replenish his energy. The hotel-keeper offered him the only thing he had to drink, a beverage based on *aguardiente* (a raw sugarcane liquor) with honey, lemon juice and water. Refreshed and satisfied, the general asked what he had just drunk. His host replied, "Oh, that was just a *cachánchara!*"

staircase — not recommended for those suffering from vertigo. The bell tower's structure seems to be more and more afflicted by the weight of the years — and not coping well, judging by the number of cracks. Indeed, you will be asked not to touch the huge cast-iron bells, most likely because using them could well cause the whole structure to collapse. You will have to content yourself with breathing the fresh air and admiring the mountains on one side and the sea on the other. The view of the tiled roofs for which the city is famous is particularly impressive. Upon leaving the tower, you will have a whole new perspective on the city.

Heading down Avenida Guitart, you will come to a lovely little square called **Plaza de Jagüey**. It is named after the tree found there, beneath which the Villa de Trinidad was founded and where the first mass was celebrated. Of particular note is the fact that this mass was pronounced by Fray Bartolomé de Las Casas, an ardent defender of native rights during the colonial era. He was the first to take stock of and denounce the horrors committed by the Spanish against America's aboriginal peoples.

Calle Rubén Martínez Villen leads to **La Cachánchara** *(free admission; ☎4345)*, a cultural centre where many musicians from Trinidad gather. This 18th-century house, with its *mudéjar* (Arab-Spanish) architecture, has a particular historical significance as the birthplace of a local cocktail called the *cachánchara.* Among other local drinks to try are *guarapito*, a mixture of sugarcane juice and rum or *aguardiente*, and *saoco*, prepared with coconut water and *aguardiente* and served in the coconut shell.

The little **Establecimiento Inarte 5** cigar factory *(free admission; Mon to Fri 7:30am to noon and 1pm to 4pm; Calle Maceo No. 403, corner of Calle Colón)* is a good place to observe the work and dexterity of tobacco craftspeople. You are free to photograph the men and women rolling cigars by hand, provided a throng of tourists hasn't gotten in ahead of you. Here, as elsewhere in Trinidad, early birds will be rewarded with an elbow-free visit. You can buy cigars right on the spot, although some aficionados may be disappointed by the very limited choice of good stogies.

Turn right on Calle Colón and head to Trinidad's **Mercado Libre de Artesanos**, a charming spot enlivened by its many colourful and tenacious vendors. The locals in Trinidad call this market *la cadonga*, a term supposedly derived from an Angolan word meaning "where the merchants are". Although it has been moved several times by the municipal authorities, this open-air market seems finally to have found a permanent site on Calle Cadahia, between Colón and Proscopio streets. It is open every day from 9am to 4pm. There is a

Fray Bartolomé de Las Casas

Fray Bartolomé de Las Casas, an ardent defender of native people's rights, was born in Seville in 1474 and became the first bishop in America. His father had been one of the navigators who accompanied Christopher Columbus on his first voyage to the Americas. After having been sent to America, this priest quickly became a wealthy landowner and master of many Indian slaves. But Bartolomé de Las Casas gave up his property to devote himself to the cause of the natives, whose rights were flouted by the Spanish colonists.

He appeared at the court of King Ferdinand the Catholic and before the regent of Cuba, arguing in their defence. Appointed Protector of the Indians, he undertook measures that proved fruitful when enslavement of natives was prohibited.

Las Casas wrote *Historia de las Indias*, his major work in which he presented a critical picture of the abuses inflicted on natives: "The Indians receive worse treatment than the manure dropped on the plazas," he wrote. He also denounced "those who, through their greed, make Jesus Christ the most cruel of gods and turn the king into a wolf ravenous for human flesh." In his proposals for freeing the Indians from slavery, he suggested that Africans and Moors be imported to America, showing that even Las Casas could be mistaken in his judgments.

Las Casas would become the first bishop of Chiapas, in what is now Mexico. Generally spurned by his contemporaries, Fray Bartolomé de Las Casas is regarded today as the first defender of the Amerindian cause.

wide choice of clothing, sculptures and handicrafts.

Around Old Trinidad

Although not as busy as Trinidad's old sector, **Parque Martí** (1909) does impart a special charm. A walk beneath its flowery arches, in the shade of a profusion of leafy plants, is a welcome haven from the tourists and the *jineteros* who don't miss a chance to ask you for some spare change. Parque Martí is much more a meeting-place for Trinidad residents who come to discuss what's happening in sports or politics. In this regard, it is livelier than its famous counterpart, the Plaza Mayor. Each November, Parque Martí hosts Trinidad's cultural week. These festivi-

ties, which are intended more for the locals than for tourists, consist of dance, folk music, handicrafts and local cuisine, and aim to preserve Trinidad's cultural and historical heritage among local residents. In June, carnival festivities are also held in this park.

The buildings of the municipal assembly and the municipal theatre, around the Parque Martí, display what may best be called *spaghetti western* architecture. Take Calle Camilo Cienfuegos on your left (heading northeast) to the **Plaza de Santa Ana** ★, where you can admire the only statue raised in homage to Fray Bartolomé de Las Casas. You can also see the **Iglesia de Santa Ana**, one of Cuba's oldest churches. Built between 1712 and 1812, it began falling into ruins but is now being rebuilt.

Here, you can either head toward Sancti Spíritus or toward Valle de los Ingenios, one of best preserved sites on the history of slavery in Cuba.

El Valle de los Ingenios ★★

There is no road sign for Valle de los Ingenios. You have to take the road north of the highway for Sancti Spíritus. Two kilometres north of Trinidad, a little dirt road leads to the **Mirador de la Loma ★**, from where you can appreciate the full extent of this sugarcane-growing valley. The road then drops down into the valley, whose rich plantations supported Trinidad's economic growth in the 19th century. This wealth was created, however, at the expense of the forced labour of thousands of black slaves. Many rebellions broke out in this valley and, in the confusion that ensued, some of these slaves managed to flee, hiding in the folds of the Escambray mountains.

The history of masters and slaves is presented poignantly at the **Hacienda de Iznaga ★★**, 15 kilometres from Trinidad, in the Valle de los Ingenios. Across the sugar cane fields, on your left, the **Torre de Iznaga ★★** is unmistakable. This observation tower was erected in 1820 by the Iznaga family (one of Trinidad's wealthiest) at **Caserío Manaca Iznaga**, a little farming village on the hacienda's vast lands. Even today it provides spectacular views. At 43.5 metres it allowed the masters to keep watch over slaves at work, to prevent them from fleeing, and to ward off any rebellions at a time when slaves were sacking and setting fire to plantations.

According to a legend surrounding the construction of this tower, two Iznaga brothers accepted a challenge from their father to decide which of them

would obtain the hand of a woman they both wanted to marry. One of them was to dig a well and the other to build a tower. The father would give the young woman's hand to whichever of the two achieved the greatest feat. However, both achieved the same result: one dug a well 43.5 metres deep, and the other built a tower 43.5 metres high. This legend doesn't tell us what happened to the young woman who was sought after by these two wealthy pretenders.

The family's old colonial house, built in 1750, remains the key attraction on the hacienda. The house is superb: blue wood trim and a spacious interior attest to the Iznaga family's wealth and splendour. The house's "four winds" architecture dictated a placement of windows and rooms such that, no matter where in the house occupants found themselves, cooling breezes could reach them to relieve the discomfort of the tropical heat. The cedar ceilings, beams and doors date from that early period. Add the original ceiling lamp, and the entire house is a veritable jewel. Oddly, Don Iznaga's bedroom window is the only one in the house without metal bars. Rumour has it that the master would select a female slave during the day and then have her brought to him at night. The residence has been fully restored, and today houses a restaurant and historical interpretation centre.

Even if the head of the Iznaga family had a fondness for female slaves, history has been kind to him, and he is remembered as one of the more benevolent masters. He is also the only one to have built real houses, an infirmary and a school for his slaves, as well as the only slave cemetery in all of Latin

America. Moreover, he made sure they washed each day to avoid dangerous illnesses such as cholera.

La Boca

The little village of **La Boca** ★, three kilometres south of Trinidad along the coast, is a popular bathing spot for Trinidad residents even though the beach is not very sandy. This spot has a friendly atmosphere and is remarkably devoid of tourists, though it can get quite crowded with locals who do not have access to nearby Ancón beach (if you are travelling by car or by bicycle, it is easy to get to the Ancón beaches from La Boca). The sunsets at La Boca are quite wonderful, as twilight settles over the sea and fishermen's lanterns glow ever brighter in the distance. The picturesque port is a great place to meet local fishermen and find rooms in private homes.

Sancti Spíritus ★★

Sancti Spíritus evokes the charm and the rhythm of a provincial town, though the layout of the streets, crossed by the Carretera Central with its heavy truck traffic, sometimes causes jams in the dense, noisy traffic flow. With its turbulent past, its ubiquitous colonial architectural legacy and its unusual urban plan, Santi Spíritus is one of those wonderful places that is best explored without any particular itinerary in mind.

Established in 1514 by Diego Velásquez, Sancti Spritus was the fourth *villa* founded early in the Spanish colonial period. The capital of the province of the same name, Sancti Spíritus used to be part of the province of Las Villas, one of the three provinces that

supported the independence movement in the 19th century.

Calle Independencia is the city's main artery, with many shops and plenty of people walking about. The **Galería de Arte Oscar Fernández Morera** *(free admission; Calle Independencia No. 35)* bears the name of Sancti Spíritus's greatest painter, and the gallery's large rooms hold some of his works. The charm of the gallery, however lies in its colonial patio at the rear, which connects the former with the Museo Provincial, on Calle Céspedes.

The small **Museo Provincial** *($1; Tue to Sat 8:30am to 5pm, Sun 8:30am to 12:30pm; Calle Céspedes No. 11, ☎27435)* is in a colonial house that once belonged to a brewer. Its 19th-century façade, however, hides an interior that you will probably find more attractive than the museum's collection, which consists of items tracing important events in the history of the city and province of Sancti Spíritus, from the pre-Columbian era up to the present day. The *caoba* wood ceilings at the entrance and in the dining room are especially beautiful. Many cultural activities are presented on the patio, including concerts on the third Thursday of each month.

Sancti Spíritus's **Parque Central** lies at the heart of the city, but unfortunately it falls victim to the trucks that destroy the calm that once presided here. However, it is surrounded by several fine buildings, including a movie theatre, the **Cinema Conrado Benítez**, and a library, the **Biblioteca Provincial Rubén Martínez** *(Mon, Wed, Fri 8am to 5pm; Tue, Thu 8am to 9pm; Sat 8am to 4pm)*; both establishments can provide refuge and a certain degree of peace.

On the west side of the Parque Central, the **Museo de Historia Natural** *(50¢; Tue to Sat 8:30am to 5pm, Sun*

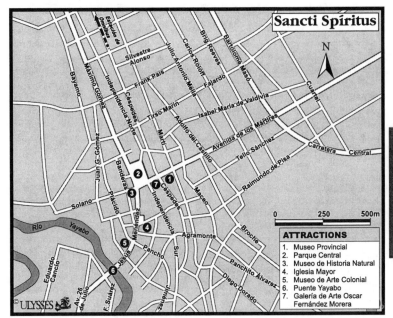

Sancti Spíritus

N

| 0 | 250 | 500m |

ATTRACTIONS

1. Museo Provincial
2. Parque Central
3. Museo de Historia Natural
4. Iglesia Mayor
5. Museo de Arte Colonial
6. Puente Yayabo
7. Galería de Arte Oscar Fernández Morera

© ULYSSES

THE PROVINCES OF LAS VILLAS

8:30am to noon; Avenida Máximo Gómez, ☎26365) is a small museum dedicated to the natural history of Sancti Spíritus province. Obviously intended for students from around the area, it has four small rooms, one devoted to geology and the others to zoology. Take the time to visit the planetarium, one of the few in Cuba and the oldest one in the country; it was designed in East Germany.

Heading south along Avenida Máximo Gómez, you will discover a charming little colonial plaza at the centre of which stands an early vestige, the **Iglesia Mayor**. Erected in 1522 and rebuilt in the 17th century after pirates destroyed it, this ochre church is very popular with local residents. In front of the church, little sidewalk cafés and wandering vendors create a lively atmosphere.

Close by, a colonial house from the first half of the 18th century now houses one of the city's greatest treasures, the **Museo de Arte Colonial de Sancti Spíritus** (*$1; Tue to Sat 8:30am to noon and 1pm to 5pm, Sun 8:30am to noon; Calle Plácido No. 74, ☎25455).* Its 12 galleries are dedicated to Cuban decorative arts of the colonial era. Every room from this period, from bedroom to dining room, is recreated in this sumptuous mansion, set up to reflect the residences of the 19th-century Cuban aristocracy. The treasures of this little museum are a joy to behold. The colonial patio provides a lovely backdrop for numerous cultural activities, including concerts presented toward the end of each month.

If you follow Avenida Jesús Menéndez, you will come upon Cuba's oldest bridge, the **Puente Yayabo**, crossing the little river of the same name. A few

The Hands of Che

In 1997, 30 years after his death in Bolivia, the remains of Che and a few of his soldiers who died in combat have finally been repatriated and buried at the foot of a monument erected in his honour. Cuban anthropologists, who had been leading the investigation for many years, finally succeeded in finding the remains of the real hero of the Cuban Revolution. His remains, it is said, were easily identified due to the skeleton's missing hands. Rumour has it that Castro was only truly convinced of his *Commandante*'s death when his hands were delivered to him!

metres beyond the bridge is the Sancti Spíritus train station.

Santa Clara ★★

The capital of the province of Villa Clara, Santa Clara was founded in 1689 as San Juan de los Remedios. This city has a rather intriguing history. It was founded by people from the neighbouring town of Remedios who, according to one version of the story, settled in Santa Clara to develop the economy, to breed livestock and to escape from pirates. Another version, however claims that their reasons were actually diabolical. The well-known Uruguayan poet and historian Eduardo Galeano, whose works include the best-selling book *Las venas abiertas de America Latina* (The Open Veins of Latin America), relates how the inhabitants of Remedios were pressed to leave their town by the local priest, who was also the parish inquisitor. He had extracted from a slave, who was possessed of a demon, the warning that "Remedios would be swallowed up" by the will of the devil. Some followed the priest, while others stayed at Remedios.

Santa Clara is the Cuban city that most reveres Che Guevara. The **Plaza de la Revolución** ★ is dedicated to the famous Argentine guerrilla who fought fiercely with Fidel Castro to overthrow Batista in the late 1950s. A gigantic statue of Che Guevara dominates this plaza, the site of major political and cultural rallies in Santa Clara. Built in 1988 to commemorate the Battle of Santa Clara led by him, this seven-metre high bronze sculpture is the work of the Cuban artist Delana; the gigantic stone pedestal upon which it rests is more than 10 metres high. Although the monument is impressive, the plaza itself is somewhat gloomy, like the majority of public squares in Cuba.

Below this monument, anyone interested in this almost mythical Argentine guerrilla will not want to miss the **Museo Memorial Nacional Comandante Ernesto Che Guevara** ★ *($2; Tue to Sat 9am to noon and 2pm to 7pm, Sun 9am to noon; ☎5878)*. Inaugurated on December 28, 1988, it traces Che's life from his childhood up to his death, including his trips through Latin America, his stay in Mexico, where he met the exiled Fidel Castro, the landing on the *Granma* on the Cuban coast, and his revolutionary experience in the Sierra Maestra. The museum is well documented, and displays a number of Che's personal items, including his uniforms, hand-written letters and many photos. Ask to see the 9-milli-metre video on the life of Che Guevara presented in a hall near the museum exit.

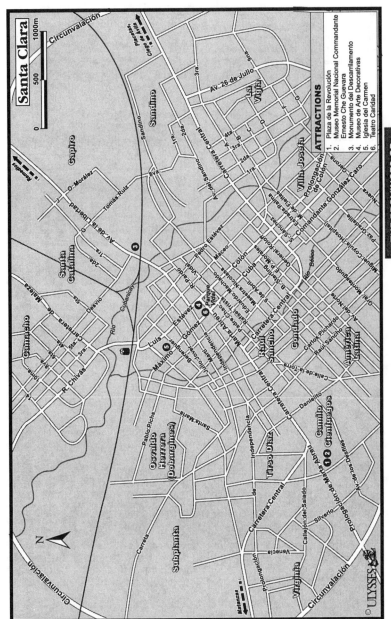

Following Che Guevara's steps in Santa Clara also requires a visit to the **Monumento de Carilamiento, Acción y Toma del Tren Blindado** ★ *($1; Tue to Sat 9am to 5:30pm, Sun 8am to noon; Carretera de Camijuani, between Linea and Puente, ☎22758)*, which recounts the decisive battle led by Che Guevara against an armoured train carrying Batista's forces on December 28, 1958. The reinforcements aboard this train were sent by Bastista to help his army in the centre of the country finish off the rebels. After leaving Havana, the train arrived in Santa Clara on December 24. Che arrived on December 28 and settled in at the University of Santa Clara, where he made clandestine requests for equipment with which he could derail the train. He managed to obtain a bulldozer and, during the night, he breached the railway line leading toward Havana. The ensuing attack from atop a hill, prompted the train's crew members to back up and attempt to return to Havana... and the rest is history. Four of the train's 22 cars can be viewed at the monument.

Of course, Santa Clara offers more to the visitor than just monuments in memory of Che Guevara. The **Museo de Artes Decorativos** ★★ *($2; Mon, Wed and Thu 9am to noon and 1pm to 6pm, Fri and Sat 1pm to 6pm and 7pm to 10pm, Sun 6pm to 10pm; Parque Vidal No. 3, ☎5368)* occupies a magnificent colonial house built around 1740. Transformed over the centuries, it was restored in 1820 and again in 1980. The furniture exhibited here comes from several homes in Santa Clara and is displayed in chronological order, with a series of rooms presenting various decorative art ensembles from the 17th century up to the 20th century. In the baroque tradition, the rooms are very heavily decorated. This custom goes back to the inferiority complex felt by members of the Cuban aristocracy toward Spain. To prove their wealth, they filled their rooms and walls. The museum has some extraordinary items, including an armoire built without nails and a washbasin from the days prior to running water. Hire a guide to get the most out of your visit.

Finally, be sure to feast your eyes on the **Iglesia del Carmen**, dating from 1756, and at the **Teatro Caridad**, built in 1885.

Remedios ★★

Some 43 kilometres northeast of Santa Clara, the lovely town of Remedios offers authentic vistas of Cuba around every corner. Thanks to a bizarre turn of events in its history, Remedios has so far managed to escape the torments of tourism. What bizarre turn of events, you ask? The local priest and inquisitor, a prophet of doom, who managed to persuade many of his parshioners to flee the town because it was about to be "swallowed up by the will of the devil" (see p 188), was not entirely wrong.

Remedios suffered repeated pirate attacks, but it could at least boast for a time that it was never swallowed up by flames. Ironically, it was the Spanish themselves who set fire to their town to impose once and for all the King of Spain and of the Captain-General of Cuba's order that the town was to be evacuated. Captain Pérez de Morales arrived in 1691 to burn the town and the devil, who was hiding there. The following day, some inhabitants of Remedios, who remained skeptical about the devil's presence in their town and who noted that there was no odour of sulphur or of charred devil's flesh, set about rebuilding their town. This romanticized tale is told by the poet and historian Eduardo Galeano in his

Las Parrandas

Every year over the Christmas period, the El Carmen and San Salvador districts build huge allegorical monuments on the Parque Central; a fireworks competition that has become quite ritualized follows. At nine o'clock in the morning, the fireworks begin, and the creativity of the pyrotechnists gets better year after year. From nine in the evening until four in the morning, the two districts continue the competition by setting off fireworks every half-hour. Just imagine the spectacle! Finally, from four o'clock until sunrise, the two teams end the ceremonies with the greatest fireworks of the competition. The winner is decided by popular vote.

book *Memoria del Fuego* (Memory of Fire).

Today, Remedios is a sleepy little town that is a pleasure to simply stroll about aimlessly. The **Parque Central ★★** is one of the loveliest colonial plazas in Cuba. Lined by numerous buildings from that era, this vast square is unique in Cuba in that two churches face it. The bigger of the two, the **Iglesia Parroquial San Juan Bautista**, has a stylish classical façade. Unfortunately, an irregular and limited schedule affords few opportunities to visit its interior.

The **Museo Alejandro García Caturia** *($2; Tue to Sat 8am to noon and 1pm to 5pm, Sun 9am to noon)*, facing the Parque Central, is a small museum dedicated to a famous Remedios musician. Unless you are a lover of learned music, you won't find much of interest, although the house has been classified a national monument.

Nearby, the little **Galería de Arte** *(free admission; Tue to Sat 8am to 5pm, Sun 9am to 1pm)* exhibits several works by contemporary Cuban artists.

The **Museo de las Parrandas Remedianas ★★** *($2; Tue to Sat 9am to noon, Sun 9am to 1pm; Calle Máximo Gómez No. 71, between Calle Alejandro del Río and Calle Andrés del Río, ☎5400)* tells the living story of the festival that is the town's pride and joy. *Las Parrandas* is a sort of carnival in which Remedios's two main neighbourhoods have competed since 1820. The museum presents sculptures, costumes, streamers, musical instruments, photos and a model. Don't forget to go upstairs, where much of the collection is located.

Calle Maceo, a winding colonial street, makes for a very pleasant stroll. At number 56 is the **Museo de la Historia**, exhibiting a small collection on the history of the town. Unfortunately, this museum is often closed and does not seem to observe a regular schedule. At number 25, you can enter the offices of **UNEAC** (the National Union of Cuban Writers and Artists). You will be greeted by friendly people at almost all hours of the day and night. Poetry readings are often held here.

La Hanabanilla ★★

Lago Hanabanilla is 57 kilometres south of Santa Clara and 19 kilometres from Manicaragua. With a surface area of 32 square kilometres and a depth of about 40 metres, this lake used to be known for its high waterfalls. However, the building of a hydroelectric dam and the subsequent flooding have changed things considerably. Fidel Castro himself ordered the construction of the hotel that now overlooks the lake. At first it served only Cuban tourists, but the hotel is gradually welcoming a greater number of foreigners.

The spot is pleasant and well suited for excursions on the lake and its surroundings. However, the hotel itself is rather noisy during the day, with music blasting from loudspeakers around the pool. The music will probably be much too loud for some, though some Cubans seem to enjoy it.

A good way of escaping this racket is to take an excursion on the boat that heads across the lake to **Río Negro** *($16 per person, including lunch at Río Negro; departures at 10am and 11am).* These excursions are organized each day at the reception desk of the Hotel Hanabanilla. A trip of several kilometres takes you across the lake. Little farm houses perched on the mountainside ceate an enthralling backdrop; the boat actually stops at one of these houses in the course of the tour, enabling you to meet a farm family, to see the many animals roaming freely on their little island, and to taste the coffee they grow themselves. This spot is obviously well adapted to international tourism, to the point where the family seems more interested in collecting a few dollars for the coffee and trying to sell some bottles of Coca-Cola than in explaining the lives of Cuban farmers. Goodbye, spontaneity; hello, tourism industry! It is worth visiting anyway, if only to play with the friendly pigs and turkeys. The next stop is a waterfall where more courageous passengers can bathe and slide along the smooth rocks to a spring-fed pool. Then the moment you've been waiting for: the Río Negro restaurant, perched on a hillside; this spot serves up good food and has an excellent atmosphere.

The flooding of this area has transformed the way of life for local farmers, who now get around by boat. If you don't like organized tours, it is possible to take the boat used by local people. Not only is it cheaper (just a few pesos), but there is also nothing to stop you from pitching your tent right on the shore or from seeking lodgings with a real farm family, one not jaded by tourism. Several trails run along the mountains near the lake, and some of them are great for hiking. To take the boat used by the local people, go to the dam, a few hundred metres before the Hotel Hanabanilla. Ask about return schedules; if not, you risk spending several days on a nearby beach, which isn't such a terrible thing if you have the time.

  PARKS AND BEACHES

The **Parque Nacional Ciénaga de Zapata**, designated a biosphere reserve by UNESCO, has an area of 300 square kilometres (see p 173).

In the province of Cienfuegos, the **Rancho Luna** area offers a lovely, but small, beach. To get there, take the Carretera de Rancho Luna, perpendicular to the Paseo del Prado near the Malecón in Cienfuegos. This is the same road that goes to Trinidad (see p 178). Excellent hiking trips in the Escambray mountains are organized in this area.

Some 15 kilometres east of Cienfuegos, the **Base de Campismo de Guajimico** offers many trails overlooking the sea and running along high cliffs. You can also visit superb grottos; a white owl has its nest in the biggest of them, the **Cueva de la Virgen**, and upon our arrival this superb creature took off and swept past right above our heads. Guajimico is an ideal spot in which to enjoy the natural setting. There is also good diving here; the almost pristine underwater formations are quite exceptional. A boat is available to tourists for excursions and for deep-sea fishing.

Near Trinidad, the **Península de Ancón** ★★ has superb white sand beaches. People come here from to relax and enjoy the facilities of the area's two hotels, far from major tourist resorts. This area has especially beautiful underwater formations, making it an excellent spot for divers.

The 172-square-kilometre **Topes de Collantes** ★★ natural park lies in the highest reaches of the Sierra del Escambray. This area delights biologists, ornithologists and nature-lovers generally. Many ecological trails cross the high mountains of this area, including **Pico San Juan** (1,140 m).

This area can be reached by road, either via Cienfuegos or via Trinidad. However, in some places the road from Trinidad to Topes de Collantes is the subject of frequent rockslides and mudslides. Both roads are scenic, running next to the mountains in spectacular fashion and surrounded by lush tropical vegetation. Along the way you will doubtless find some coffee growers. The cool climate (it can turn quite cold at night), is a wonderful escape from the torrid heat in the rest of the country.

 OUTDOOR ACTIVITIES

 Bird-watching

A bumpy little 10-kilometre dirt road between Playa Larga and Playa Girón (the trip is easier in an all-terrain vehicle) brings you to **La Salina** ★★, one of the most extraordinary spots in the area. Little known and hard to get to, this saltwater lagoon is home to hundreds of pink flamingoes, parrots, hummingbirds, and so on. To get the most out of this place, which offers no services for visitors, it is best to arrive very early in the morning and to be sure to bring along all the water and food you'll need for the day.

  Diving and Snorkelling

Playa Girón

Playa Girón is noted for its underwater formations, including several types of corals and sponges, and attracts divers from the four corners of the globe. The **Villa Girón** (☎4118) diving school offers boat dives for $25 if you are an accredited diver. Playa Girón is one of the few spots in Cuba where week-long diving courses are offered, leading to international accreditation.

Along the seaside road, eight kilometres east of Playa Girón, is **Caleta Buena** ★, an isolated little bay and an excellent spot for snorkelling that does not require a boat. A multitude of colourful tropical fish are visible from the water's edge. Take your snorkelling mask, or rent one here; all the necessary equipment for snorkelling is available at Caleta Buena. There is an admission fee of $1 for use of the facilities, and a small cafeteria where you can buy water and soft drinks. During peak tourist season, a bus leaves Villa Girón bound for Caleta Buena each day at 10am. You can also rent a scooter or bicycle. Along the way, you can stop at some small and nearly deserted beaches.

Hotel Ancón has its own dive shop, which offers free lessons in the pool for all levels, as well as sea outings every morning at 9am. One dive costs $30, while two go for $50. The diving sites are more spectacular during the dry season, when the river bed doesn't swamp the sea bed. Remember that (PADI) certification is required to practise this sport.

Cienfuegos

The **Base de Campismo de Guajimico**, 40 kilometres east of Cienfuegos, is popular with hikers. It also offers nearly pristine underwater formations and its numerous grottos thrill spelunkers.

 Hiking

Topes de Collanes

Several excursions are offered by the Hotel Los Helechos. As its name suggests, the *Rambotour* excursion *($30 including lunch and transport)* is more of an expedition than a mountain hike. A walk along and swim across a river lead to the Salto del Rocío waterfalls. It is something of an adventure, after which you will enjoy a copious meal at the Casa La Gallega restaurant.

Exploring the **Hacienda Codina** *($30 including lunch and transport)* is certainly less perilous and consists of a two-kilometre mountain hike along a trail that lets you observe the area's flora and fauna. It includes a visit to a farm where coffee was once produced, an orchid garden with more than 40 species, the Cueva del Altar, a grotto, and a lookout.

 Fishing

Ciénega de Zapata

The marshes here are noted for the quality of the fishing, especially for trout, carp and *manguari*, a fish with a head resembling that of a crocodile. It is better to spend the night at the **Villa Turística Guamá** (see further below) or to organize a day excursion from Playa Larga or Playa Girón.

Sancti Spíritus

Lago Zaza, noted for trout fishing, lies in the Sancti Spíritus area along the highway to Havana. The Hotel Zaza (see p 198) dominates the landscape.

 ACCOMMODATIONS

Ciénega de Zapata

The **Villa Turística Guamá** *($35-$45; ≈, pb, ℜ, ≈; ☎2979)* has 44 thatched huts spread over about 20 little islands. The huts are accessible by canoe (each hut has its own pier) or by crossing the many wooden footbridges. The rooms are rather dark, but they are pleasant and well maintained. Although the water is potable, the quality is dreadful, and it has an unpleasant metallic taste; if you take a shower, you will smell of rust for the rest of the day. The poor state of the plumbing here is responsible for this phenomenon. Be sure to stock up on bottled water before coming to Guamá.

Playa Larga

Villa Playa Larga *(☎7225)* offers the same rates and roughly the same conditions as its counterpart in Playa Girón (see below).

Playa Girón

Villa Playa Girón *($30-$45; ≡, tv, pb, ≈, ℜ, ⊗, ℝ; ☎94110)* has a series of bungalows with direct access to the beach, and private entrances and terraces. It has an air of tranquillity and comfort. The houses are particularly spacious and bright.

Cienfuegos

Hotel Perla del Sur *($10; ≡, pb, ℜ; Avenida 62 between Calle 37 and Calle 35, ☎21531)* is the most economical choice in Cienfuegos. This establishment is clean, and the staff are courteous and hospitable. It is nevertheless a good idea to bring your own sheets or a sleeping bag. The hotel is near the entrance to the Paseo del Prado, and all the points of interest are within walking distance.

The biggest hotel in Cienfuegos, the **Hotel Jagua** *($70; ≡, ≈, pb, ℜ, ctv; Calle 37 No. 1, between Calle 0 and Calle 2, Punta Gorda, ☎3021 to 3025, ➔66-7454)* is located at the end of the Malecón, at the entrance to the stylish Punta Gorda district. This establishment was built in the late 1950s by Batista's brother and completed during the Revolution. It has all the facilities you would expect in a four-star hotel, and most rooms offer sea views. As a whole, however, the hotel seems to have been somewhat neglected over the years, and its four stars are not fully deserved. The rooms are comfortable, nevertheless.

Around Cienfuegos

Several quality hotels lie along the Rancho Luna road. However, it is becoming more common for travellers to take rooms in private homes. Fine country houses are frequently offered discreetly for rental; you can approach occupants of the houses located between the Hotel Rancho Luna and the Faro Maya, the lighthouse that marks the entrance to the Bahía de Cienfuegos. The usual asking price is $5 per day per house.

At the far end of the Rancho Luna road, **Hotel Pasacaballo** *($30; ≡, ℜ, ℝ, tv, ≈; Carretera Rancho Luna km 23, ☎96212)*, inaugurated on July 26, 1976, was the first hotel built here after the Revolution. Unlike other establishments in the area, this one is open to Cubans, who come in large numbers. The balconies on the higher floors offer stunning views of the entrance to the Bahía de Cienfuegos and the Castillo de Jagua. A boat *(0.40 peso; 10am, 3pm and 6pm)* runs between the castle, Cienfuegos and the hotel. Ask for a room on the upper floors. The hotel nightclub is very popular with Cubans, and is a good place to meet some islanders.

Located on the Rancho Luna beaches, **Hotel Rancho Luna** *($42-$52; ≡, ≈, ℜ, pb, tv)* offers all the advantages of a good hotel. Although small, the hotel's beach will be of interest if you are thinking of spending a few days in the area. The tourist office here offers many excursions to the Escambray mountains.

Right next to the Hotel Rancho Luna, **Hotel Faro Luna** *($50; ≡, hw, ≈, ℜ, pb, ctv, ☎162 or 165, ➔33-5059)* offers a small private beach. This establishment is considerably quieter and more exclusive than its Rancho Luna counterpart. Mountain trips are organized jointly by the two hotels.

Hotel Punta La Cueva *($50; ≡, pb, ≈, ℜ; Carretera Rancho Luna km 3, ☎3956 to 3959)* has a very pretty pool facing the Bahía de Cienfuegos. This new hotel is located midway between Rancho Luna beach and Cienfuegos. This pleasant establishment is surrounded by gardens. Boat excursions on the Bahía de Cienfuegos are available.

Trinidad

Until just recently, *casas particulares* were still prohibited in Trinidad, but are now legal, which is great for travellers wishing to get closer with the people of Cuba and farther away from the major hotels. This involves staying in someone's home and sharing in their daily routine. Moreover, this option is much cheaper: for $10 to $25, you get a room, a private or shared (but always clean) bathroom, and you may even get to dine with your host family.

The little coastal village of **La Boca**, about three kilometres from Trinidad, also offers excellent houses and rooms at modest prices.

Maytta Marín Calderón *($15-$25; Avenida Martí 422, between Calles Fidel Claro and Santiago Escobar, ☎3516)* will welcome you into her home with open arms. Request a room at the back if you are sensitive to noise. If by some chance the room is already taken, she will refer you to one of her friends who offers the same services.

A similar place is the **Casa Muñoz** *($15-$25; on the other side of the street, a little farther along Avenida Martí)*. It is well situated, clean and the owners are pleasant.

Recently reopened after renovations, **Hotel La Ronda** *($22; Calle Martí 238, between Calles Colón and Lino Perez, ☎2248)* has a lot going for it and, though far from being a luxury hotel, it is the best situated, only a stone's throw from the old district. A lounge has been set up on the second floor, with balconies and a small bar, which liven up at night. There is also an interior courtyard overflowing with plants on the main floor. This establishment is a great base from which to explore Trinidad on foot.

🐝 In a quiet, bucolic setting, the 20 charming bungalows of the **Finca Maria Dolores** *($27; 3 km before Cienfuegos on Carretera del Sur, ☎3851)* offer tourists a real getaway. There is a small, inexpensive restaurant as well as a bar, so guests can enjoy a quiet stay without having to go into town. A *río* skirts the estate and guests can make an excursion to the mouth of the river, near Playa Ancón. The other activities offered are all more appealing than the last: evening shows put on by *campesino* farmers (revival of traditions and the Cuban rural way of life) and horseback riding on the trails of the surrounding hills *($5/hour)*. Walking to town takes scarcely an hour, but you can always rent a car. Thus, with the city nearby, this place has all you need for a pleasant stay. Be sure to reserve in advance, because the *finca* is very popular with visitors. In addition to the addition of a swimming pool, 30 more bungalows should be built in the near future. Come enjoy fresh air while sipping a *mojito* and watch sheep grazing in the pasture!

Some distance away, on the Santa Ana hill overlooking Trinidad, **Motel Las Cuevas** *($45; ≡, tv, ≈, ℜ; Calle Finca Santa Ana, ☎4013 to 19)* has several little houses with terraces. This establishment is pleasant and quiet, and the centre of town is within walking distance. This motel has a very special history: it was destroyed by the rebels in 1958, but once they got into power, the revolutionaries had it rebuilt.

Near the Hotel Ancón, the **Costa Sur** *($45; ☎6174, ⇝6173)* describes itself as that establishment's equivalent (see below). It is quite a bit smaller, and provides a friendly welcome. Even if the beaches are not as beautiful as those of the Hotel Ancón, the underwater formations are far superior, especially for snorkellers. Bicycles can be rented. There are also bungalows for rent on the beach.

Hotel Ancón *($58; ≡, tv, pb, ℜ; ☎4011, ⇝7424)*, on the Ancón peninsula about 12 kilometres from Trinidad, is a big seafront hotel with an architectural style common to a number of Cuban establishments. The hotel has magnificent beaches. The rooms are clean but small, nearly all facing the sea. Tennis courts are available, and several types of boats can be rented.

The **Trinida del Mar** should be completed by press time and will be the most luxurious hotel in the Playa Ancón area. This will make it easier for tourists to find accommodations, because the hotels on the Costa Sur and Playa Ancón are usually full (even in low season). The new establishment will be located just before Ancón and should charge between $80 and $100 a night.

Topes de Collantes

Several hotels are located up in the Topes de Collantes, most of them reserved for holidaying Cuban military personnel. However, it should be possible to get rooms there, as long as luck is with you and you persevere with the receptionists. Room rates are quoted in pesos and are thus very affordable.

The **KurHotel Escambray** *($30-40; pb, ≡, ℜ; ☎40288)* describes itself as a national and international health tourism centre, but looks more like an enormous hospital than like a hotel. Walking along the corridors, we were quite surprised to see the entire clientele, the patients, wearing identical green uniforms at all hours of the day, accompanied by doctors and nurses. If you don't like hospitals, don't go to the KurHotel! Little green men wandering through the corridors aside, the rooms are impeccable and modern. Service is very attentive, and everything appears spotless. The restaurant (also full of little green men) looks like a hospital cafeteria, although this takes nothing away from the quality of the food served here. The breakfasts are good, and this is one of the few spots in Cuba where whole-grain bread is served.

Only a minute away from the Kurhotel is the **Villa Caburni**, which offers the same services and level of comfort as its neighbour and is managed by the same organization.

Hotel Los Helechos *($38; ≡, pb, tv, ☎40180 to 189)* offers better furnished rooms providing greater comfort and hot water, which is important here since the temperature sometimes drops quite abruptly at night. The restaurant is decent, and the rooms have balconies.

Sancti Spíritus

In addition to being the best budget option, accommodation in private homes (*Casas Particulares*) offer a better quality stay than do the downtown hotels.

Adventure-seekers should head for the **Hotel Colonial** *(8.60 pesos; ≡, cold* water only; *Avenida Máximo Gómez No. 43*, ☎*25123)*, tucked away at the northwestern edge of the Parque Central and quieter than its counterparts. Take note, though, this one really is for adventurers only. This establishment is reserved for Cuban tourists, although nothing prevents you from trying to persuade those in charge to rent you a room. As at most establishments of this type in Cuba, try to use your own sheets or your sleeping bag, and ask to check the room before.

Among the *casas particulares*, the **Hospedaje Colonial Los Zamoras** *($15; ≡, sb; Calle Independencia Sur 56,* ☎*2-3046)* has two comfortable, air-conditioned guestrooms.

A similar establishment, **Los Richars** *($15; ≡, sb; Calle Independencia Sur 28)*, rents out second-floor rooms with a view of the sometimes noisy, bustling central square. This place is less sombre that the above, and the hosts are most congenial.

Hotel Perla de Cuba was just about to be sold to the Cubanacan group, according to the latest rumours. If the deal goes through, this old building, which is presently closed, will undergo extensive repairs that will lead to its reopening in 2000.

Facing the Parque Central, **Hotel Plaza** *($20; ⊛, ℜ, pb, cold water only; Calle Independencia No. 1,* ☎*27102)* is centrally located, but the heavy truck traffic creates a real racket. Since the rooms don't have air conditioning, you have to keep the windows open when it's warm, so forget about peace and quiet! Despite everything, this is the best option if you want to be right in the city centre.

The best hotels in Sancti Spíritus are a few kilometres out of town, along the Carretera Central heading toward Ha-

vana. If you have a car, do not hesitate to choose one of these establishments. Their presence seems to have held back hotel development in the city centre, so you may as well take advantage of the chance to be a little closer to nature.

The busiest of these more secluded establishments is the **Hotel Zaza** *($45; ≡, pb, ≈, ℜ; Finca San José, Lago Zaza,* ☎*26012,* ⌐*66-8001)*, a big 128-room hotel located at the edge of a lake. The natural surroundings will please most travellers. Many of the guests stay here for the fishing.

Villa Rancho Hatuey *($60; Carretera Central, Km 384,* ☎*26015)* once belonged to the former owner of the famous brewery that produces Hatuey beer in Sancti Spíritus. Located two kilometres from Sancti Spíritus, along the Carretera Central, this establishment has several simple but well arranged cabins, as well as a good restaurant (see p 201).

Santa Clara

The **Santa Clara Libre** *($27.50; ≡, tv, ℜ; Parque Vidal No. 6,* ☎*27548)* is the only decent hotel in the city centre. This rather gloomy-looking high-rise has obviously come down a few notches over the years. However, as far as downtown hotels go, this establishment is worth its weight in gold. The rooms are decent, and it is more than chance that leads many Cuban honeymooners to choose this spot: some of the rooms have big beds, something quite uncommon in Cuba.

Motel Los Caneyes *($40; ≡, pb, ℜ, ≈; Avenida Eucaliptus,* ☎*4512)* is ideal for those with rental cars. It is set in a modernized reproduction of a native village and has many huts spread over a large wooded area. It is pleasant to walk among the huts and explore the lush vegetation. The pool is surrounded by a bar and a cafeteria, so you can spend the day in the sun. The rooms are rather dark and poorly ventilated, however. Employees come regularly to spray insect repellant; ask to see and "smell" your room before settling in. The restaurant has good food (see p 201), especially when the buffet is available. There is also a generous selection of fruit for breakfast.

Far from the concrete jungle and the exhaust of diesel engines is the **Villa Granjita** *($50-$55; Carretera de Maleza, Km 5.5, ☎2-8190, ⌐2-8192)* and its 75 little bungalows dispersed over a large property full of trees and shrubs that invite relaxation. The interior design of the octagonal-shaped straw-roofed cottages is both luxurious and sobre. The huts combined with the bar, restaurant and pool look like a small village – the only thing missing is the sea!

 RESTAURANTS

Cienfuegos

Right near No. 1819 along the *Prado* are a host of *paladares*, which offer cheap fast food in a quintessentially Cuban setting.

The **El Buzo** *paladar ($; Avenida 42 No. 4109, near Calle Tacón)* offers a good selection of seafood-based dishes. This spot has a pleasant tropical decor and a relaxed atmosphere.

Facing Parque Martí, **El Palatino** *($; ☎7811)* is an excellent spot to sample some Cuban rum or have a cold drink or a cup of coffee. The rum is especially cheap: a glass of Havana Club Extra Dry is only 35¢! Sandwiches and

fried chicken are also served. This spot is lively all day long thanks to a musical trio that performs Cuban tunes. El Palatino occupies a colonial house built in 1840. The first bar and cafeteria opened its doors here in 1919. The high blue-trimmed wooden ceilings and the colonial decor lend this establishment a picturesque touch.

In the heart of Cienfuegos, in a dilapidated colonial building, lurks **Restaurante 1819** *($; Paseo del Prado 5609, between Calles 56 and 58)*, a surprisingly luxurious restaurant. Despite the high-quality food served here, the limited choice of dishes is deplorable. But the "authentic" colonial decor is appealing. The *Criollo*-style food (chicken or fish with rice and beans on the side) is of better quality than average.

One of the best eating spots in Cienfuegos, and also one of the least expensive, is the **San Carlos 38** *paladar ($; Avenida 56, formerly Calle San Carlos, between Calle 19 and Calle 21, ☎6795)*, a family-run restaurant two blocks west of Parque Martí. The dining room occupies a pleasant upstairs verandah, and the food has a Creole slant, based mostly on pork or fish. The owners, Felix Sr. and Felix Jr., will make your visit a pleasant one and can advise you on places to visit in the area. If you are looking for a room in a private home, this is a good place for information.

La Cueva del Camarón *($$; ☎8238)*, facing the Hotel Jagua (see p 195), offers a seafood-based menu.

Restaurant La Verja *($$; Avenida 54 No. 3335, ☎6311)*, very popular with local people, offers a rustic atmosphere that suits this Boulevard establishment well. With its colonial furniture and subdued lighting, you could well be in

THE PROVINCES OF LAS VILLAS

another era. The menu consists mostly of pork-based dishes.

Restaurante Palacio de Valle *($$$; Calle 37 between Calle 0 and Calle 2, near the Hotel Jagua, ☎3021)* occupies one of the most architecturally eclectic mansions in town. This Arab- and Spanish-inspired palace, built between 1903 and 1917, verges on kitsch. A wealthy Spanish Muslim lived here for several years, but Papo Batista, brother of dictator Fulgencio Batista, bought the palace to turn it into a casino, grandiose plans which were stopped short by the Revolution. The restaurant is superb, and the change of scenery is dramatic. Seafood dishes are the house specialty. A grand piano dominates the dining room, and if you are lucky you may see and hear the eccentric bolero singer Carmen Iznaga Guillén, niece of the celebrated Cuban poet Nicolás Guillén. She sings several of her uncle's poems.

Rancho Luna

The **Finca de Isabela** *($$; Carretera de Rancho Luna km 4, ☎7606)* describes itself as a typical Cuban peasant's house. Its natural setting is charming, and what with the dog circus, the bull, the horse and the cockfights, you're bound to have a good time. The restaurant specializes in Creole cuisine.

You can also try **La Casa del Pescador** *($$$; Carretera Rancho Luna km 25)*, magnificently located on a little beach facing the Bahía de Cienfuegos, near the Hotel Pasacaballo. This rustic house used to belong to a fisherman. Fish and seafood dishes top the menu. This is a good spot to enjoy the bay's scenery and a light midday meal.

Trinidad

There are several good restaurants in Trinidad, but most are expensive. Trinidad is one of the few places in Cuba where *paladares*, small family-run restaurants, are officially prohibited. In the past, they created "unfair" competition for the big national tourism chains by offering quality menus at cheap prices in a healthy family atmosphere, as elsewhere in Cuba. This official attitude is unfortunate. However, you should not believe that there are no *paladares* in Trinidad. They abound, but in secrecy. If budget is your main concern, don't hesitate to ask around for a *paladar*. Someone will no doubt show you the way.

To eat at a *casa particulare*, inquire within. Indeed, you don't have to stay with a family to enjoy a meal with them. Just be sure to give them advance notice (generally in the morning) so they can buy the necessary ingredients at the market. Your hosts will generally ask you which Cuban specialty you prefer. Expect to pay about $10 per person for generous portions.

After catching an impromptu street performance on Calle Toro, where the band *Los Pinos* often plays Cuban tunes, you can drop by the superb **El Mesón del Regidor** *($; Calle Bolivar 424, at Calle Toro)*. The typical, quality fish- and chicken-based cuisine here can be enjoyed in a relaxed ambiance amidst a polished decor. While the front of the restaurant faces the street and the park nearby, a pleasant interior courtyard at the back exudes a quiet ambiance. For those who merely wish to quench their thirst, there is also a bar next door.

Open all day, the restaurant of the **Hotel La Ronda** *($; see Hotel La Ronda,* *p 196)* features a menu with a good choice of dishes. Despite its lack of charm, the place is very cheerful.

Restaurant Las Begonias *($; Calle Maceo, corner of Calle Simón Bolívar)* offers an original fish- and seafood-based menu. The house specialty, fish of the day with begonias, is stuffed with vegetables and covered with melted cheese, a true delight. This restaurant also has a good wine selection.

The two superb restaurants of **Plaza Santa Ana** *($-$$$; Calle Santo Domingo, corner of Santa Ana, Plaza Santa Ana, ☎3523)* occupy what was once a former colonial-era prison, the Cárcel Real. Now a magnificent enclosure for tourists, this place contains a seafood restaurant, a cafeteria and a souvenir shop. The spot is enchanting, and you will not want to miss visiting the bar, set on a lookout. The ceilings have their original wooden beams, and all the furniture is made of precious wood. When you add the rooftop terraces, the folk music groups that perform as of 9pm, and the stunning view of the town, the result is a fine evening out on the town.

Restaurant Manacas Iznaga *($$; ☎7241)* is the only restaurant in the Valle de los Ingenios. It occupies the former residence of the wealthy Iznaga family (see p 185). Besides sandwiches, pizzas and spaghetti, Creole meals are served here. The house specialty is *cerdo a la Iznaga*, a pork dish prepared with sour orange, garlic and white wine and slow-cooked in an oven.

Sancti Spíritus

The least expensive meals in Sancti Spíritus are found in the very pictur-esque setting of the **Mercado Agropecuario**, on Calle Céspedes near the Museo Provincial. Here you won't see many tourists but rather merchants and local residents taking their meals served in cardboard boxes. The Creole-style dishes are based on pork, rice, beans and a little lettuce or fresh tomato, and should not cost more than a dollar per person.

You can also try **El Conquistador**, a very friendly restaurant and cafeteria near the Plaza de Fundación.

Restaurante El Mesón *($; Avenida Máximo Gómez No. 34)* is rather gloomy and dirty (especially the toilets). However, this establishment is located in the old town, and it occupies a fine house with a big dining room and colonial decor. We can hope that improvements will come with time. El Mesón specializes in Creole dishes.

Like the best hotels, the best restaurants in Sancti Spíritus are found outside the city, along the Carretera Central. For good cooking, head to the restaurant of the **Villa Rancho Hatuey**, two kilometres from Sancti Spíritus along the Carretera Central heading toward Havana.

Santa Clara

There are few good restaurants in Santa Clara. Ask local people if there is a *paladar* worth going to. Otherwise, **Colonial 1878** *($; Calle Máximo Gómez, between Calle Independencia and Parque Vidal)* offers decent Creole dishes.

The restaurant of the **Motel Los Caneyes** (see p 198) serves good food. If the buffet is available, check first to see what there is before digging in.

THE PROVINCES OF
LAS VILLAS

There is usually a good choice of fruit at every meal.

  ENTERTAINMENT

Cienfuegos

The only nightlife in Cienfuegos is at the bars and nightclubs of hotels, which are not much frequented by Cubans. Those looking to mingle with the locals should head out to the park where people meet around dusk to chat, play chess, or have a beer.

The **Cinema del Prado** *(Paseo del Prado, corner of Calle 54)* usually shows good films, including Cuban productions, for just a few pesos. For live theatre, try your luck at the **Teatro Luisa** *(Paseo del Prado between Calle 52 and Calle 51)*.

The **Punta Gorda** area is generally quite lively at night. At the far end, well beyond the little rotunda in front of the Hotel Jagua, the **Centro Recreativo La Punta** *($1; Avenida 35)* is an outdoor bar pleasantly located in a little park on the shore of the Bahía de Cienfuegos. This establishment draws a young, noisy crowd at dusk. If disco and dance music are your thing, give it a try.

The recently inaugurated danceclub of the **Hotel Jagua** (see p 195) draws a large crowd every evening. A $5 cover charge is payable at the door.

The **Fondo de Bienes Culturales** *(free admission; open every day 8:30am to 8pm; Avenida 54, ☎3400)* promotes contemporary artists and craftsmen from Cienfuegos. It also organizes the occasional fashion show. Musical improvisation events are presented on the last Friday evening of each month. All the items exhibited in this gallery are for sale, and you will find a good selection of handicrafts, sculptures, paintings and stylish clothing.

The **Galería de Arte** *(free admission; Tue, Thu and Sat 1pm to 10pm, Wed and Fri 8am to 4pm, Sun 8am to noon; Calle 54 No. 3310 between Calle 33 and Calle 35, ☎8307)* exhibits works by Cienfuegos artists. Cultural events are held every Wednesday and Saturday.

Trinidad

The town of Trinidad is enlivened by the presence of many musical groups. Various charming locales stay busy all day up until nightfall in a picturesque colonial setting. The **Casa de la Trova** *(free admission; Tue to Sun 8am to 4pm; Calle Echeri No. 29)*, south of the Plaza Mayor, describes itself as the mecca of traditional Cuban music in Trinidad. In the small interior courtyard of the colonial residence that houses this well known musical institution, trios play all day long, to the great delight of tourists who wander in. There is a bar offering cocktails at competitive prices. This place is ideal for a break from a long day walking in the sun. On Friday, Saturday and Sunday evenings, the Casa de la Trova hosts more elaborate shows, starting at 9pm.

Right in front, toward the Plaza Mayor, you may have a chance to see the **Conjunto Folklórico de Trinidad** perform. This Afro-Cuban folk music and dance group prepares its shows in the exterior courtyard of its school; the rhythmic sound of its *bata* drums announces these practice sessions which usually take place between 10am and 1pm. Don't hesitate to go inside and find your way to a corner of the courtyard to sit down and enjoy a free show.

Sancti Spíritus

The **Cine Principal** *(Avenida Máximo Gómez near the Puente Yayabo)* presents films and also the occasional live play. Schedules of upcoming shows are only available here.

There is also another **cinema** on the south side of the central park. Because the program is irregular, you will have to go there to check the schedule.

The **Casa de la Trova** *(Máximo Gómez No. 26)* is the best spot to hear traditional and modern Cuban musical groups.

Santa Clara

The **Casa de la Trova**, on Parque Vidal, regularly presents concerts of Cuban music.

To dance to the sounds of salsa or disco, head to the danceclub in the **Motel Los Caneyes** (see p 198), which is growing in popularity among locals and visitors.

The **Museo de Artes Decorativos** *(Parque Vidal No. 3)* offers concerts of classical music. The museum is recognized as Santa Clara's most important centre for classical music. Soloists and a chamber orchestra perform in the museum hall almost every Sunday at 5pm.

The **Casa de la Cultura Juan Marineyo** *(Parque Vidal No. 5, ☎27181)* is Santa Clara's community cultural centre. At the entrance, a small art gallery exhibits works by contemporary artists from the region. This beautiful house, built in 1927, is the site of many cultural activities. Shows and concerts are held here regularly. A noticeboard in front of the

Casa de la Cultura announces the schedule of activities. The people in charge of this spot are friendly and apparently will organize a show upon request. Dance, music and crafts courses are also offered here.

 SHOPPING

Cienfuegos

You will find many little shops serving local residents along El Boulevard, the pedestrian street *(Avenida 56)*. Among them is a bookshop, the **Librería del Oro**. For anything related to photography, head to **Photo Service** *(every day, 8am to 10pm)*.

Glamour *(Calle 35, corner of Calle 56)* boutique has a good selection of imported clothing for men and women, as well as exclusive designs.

Casa Mimbre *(Calle 35, corner of Calle 60)* also has a good selection of clothing and footware. Both this and Glamour (see above) display their prices in U.S. currency. If you enjoy shopping, check out the two stores, they are two of a kind in Cuba.

Trinidad

The **Centro de Arte Amelia Pelaez** *(Calle Simón Bolívar)* has many handicraft items.

Trinidad's **Mercado Libre de Artesanos** *(every day, 9am to 4pm)* is especially charming and is enlivened by its many colourful and tenacious vendors. This outdoor market is located on Calle Cadahia, between Calle Colón and Calle Proscopio. It has a vast selection of clothing, sculptures and local handicrafts.

Sancti Spíritus

The **Fondo de Bienes Culturales** has a shop in Sancti Spíritus *(Calle Independencia No. 55 between Agramonte and Honorato, ☎27106)* that generally has a good selection of local handicrafts.

Santa Clara

Shopping is a rare diversion in this region of the country, but head anyway to **Calle Independencia**, open only to pedestrians starting at Calle Maceo. Most of the shops are intended for local residents, including Santa Clara's biggest bookshop, **Librería Vietnam** *(Avenida Independencia No. 106).*

THE ARCHIPELAGO Of
CAMAGÜEY AND HOLGUÍN

he central part of the country has many attractions, especially along the northern coast. It is there that you will find the heavenly little islands of the Archipelago of Camagüey and Santa Lucia, with its long, fine-sand beaches washed by emerald waters.

Except for Camagüey, the small inland towns in the central provinces are not the most interesting in Cuba, and most travellers simply pass through them on their way to the region's beaches and fishing and hunting areas. Day and night, trucks and cars pass through Ciego de Ávila on their way across Cuba, for the town is located right in the centre of the island, almost equidistant from the two major Cuban cities (469 km from Santiago de Cuba and 426 km from Havana).

To the north lies Morón, a small rural town graced with numerous neoclassical houses with columned façades. It could easily be called the "City of Columns" if that title hadn't already been bestowed upon Havana. All in all, you can spend about half a day visiting Morón, which is a good base from which to explore the Archipelago of Camagüey.

Cayo Coco, the largest island in the Archipelago of Camagüey, lies 60 kilometres from Morón. It is 36 kilometres long and boasts nearly 22 kilometres of beaches. Its smaller neighbour, Cayo Guillermo, is a pleasant place to spend half a day or so. Together, these two little islands form a natural paradise that has spawned a thriving tourist industry.

After Ciego de Ávila, the Carretera Central straightens out, running through sugarcane and fruit plantations and passing from the province of Ciego de Ávila, Cuba's leading producer of exotic fruit, into the province of Camagüey.

Florida is a sleepy little town whose main attraction is its hunting ground, the Coto de Caza Florida. It has a good hotel, which is a perfect place to stay if you're driving across the island and prefer the countryside to urban areas. Florida is the second-largest town in the province of Camagüey, and the principal economic activity here is sugarcane production.

The town of Camagüey, located 108 kilometres from Ciego de Ávila, is the oldest town in central Cuba and the region's main cultural attraction. If you only have time to visit one town in this area, make it Camagüey and spend a day or two. It will capture your heart with its numerous architectural attractions, winding streets and relaxing atmosphere, which make it a perfect place to stroll about. Founded in 1515 under the name Santa Maria de Puerto Principe, it was the fourth of seven *villas* established by the Spanish. Camagüey means "son of the tree" in the language of the local natives.

Seventy-six kilometres northwest of Camagüey, the superb beaches of Playa Santa Lucia delight vacationers from all over the world. This little seaside resort boasts nearly 20 kilometres of fine white sand, protected by a coral reef that stretches 32 kilometres. The underwater scenery is magnificent, and many divers come here to observe the marine life, especially the grey sharks in the channel of the bay (on the other side of the reef!).

Points of interest on the north shore of the province of Holguín include the beaches of Guardalavaca and the old town of Gibara, located on the celebrated Bahía de Bariay, where Columbus landed on October 27, 1492. Here, the flat land of the middle of the province gives way to a rolling landscape, heralding the high mountains in the eastern part of the country.

The capital of the province of the same name, Holguín is the third-largest city in Cuba. Founded in 1752 by Captain García Holguín, the city still boasts some colonial architecture, as well as a few good museums and a lively cultural scene. Overlooked by most travellers, Holguín will appeal to those who like to venture off the beaten path.

Toward the north coast, the road leads into a mountainous zone, the Sierra de Crystal, where traditional houses with palm roofs lie nestled in the valleys. Royal palms, the national emblem of Cuba, reign over this 54-kilometre stretch of road, which is a veritable feast for the senses.

Parque Natural Bahía de Naranjo, a few hundred metres before Guardalavaca, is a good place from which to set out on a sea excursion. A visit to its aquarium and a swim with the dolphins are well worth your while. Meanwhile, Guaralavaca is a seaside resort with lovely beaches, magnificent underwater scenery and modern hotel complexes.

Halfway between Holguín and Guardalavaca, there is a detour to the forgotten colonial town of Gibrara. To the east lies one of the country's most extraordinary nature reserves, Cayo Saetia, a paradise for game hunters and shutterbugs. The island is home to an unusual assortment of animals, most imported from Africa: zebras, buffalo, antelope and wild boars.

 **FINDING YOUR WAY AROUND**

Ciego de Ávila

By Plane

With the development of the tourist industry on Cayo Coco and Cayo

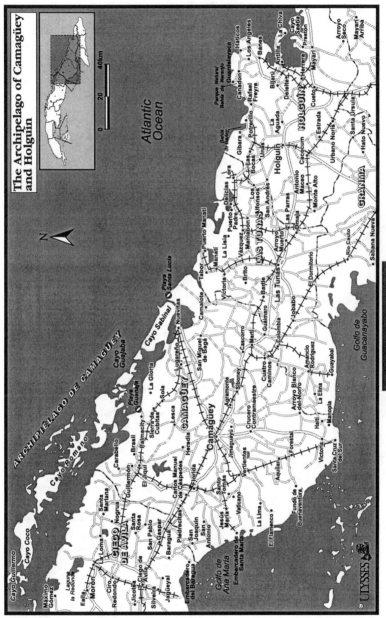

The Archipelago of Camagüey and Holguín

ARCHIPELAGO OF
CAMAGÜEY & HOLGUÍN

Guillermo, there has been a sharp increase in the number of international flights to and from the **Aeropuerto Máximo Gómez** *(☎2-5717)*, located east of downtown Ciego de Ávila. In the near future, however, this facility will once again be limited to domestic air traffic, since a new airport is scheduled to be built on Cayo Coco.

There are two flights per week heading to **Havana**. Departures are Wednesdays and Fridays at 5pm *($50; one way)*.

Airline Office

Cubana de Aviación *(Calle Chicho Valdés No. 83, at the corner of Calle Maceo, ☎2-5313)*.

By Train

Estación de Trenes *(Calle Van Horne, ☎2-3313)*.

To Havana: Departures: 12:10pm, 1:44am and 5:50am. Travel time: 9 hours. Fare: $18.

To Santiago de Cuba*: Departure: 11:13pm. ~~Travel~~ time: 7 hours. Fare: $18.

To Camagüey: Departures: 2:26am, 4:18am, 2:25pm and 7pm. Travel time: 3 hours. Fare: $4.

To Santa Clara: Departure: 8am. Travel time: 4 hours. Fare: $5.

To Morón: Departures: 10:47am and 9:41pm. Travel time: 1 hour. Fare: $1.

* The train to Santiago goes to **Guantanamo** *($20)* and **Holguín** *($13)* every other day.

By Bus

The **Estación de Omnibus Nacionales** *(☎2-5109)*, on the Carretera Central, is very busy.

To Havana: Departures: 4am, 9:25am, 6:25pm, 8:25pm and 10pm. Fare: $20.

To Santiago de Cuba: Departure: 6am. Fare: $18.

To Holguín: Departure: 4pm. Fare: $14.

To Camagüey: Departures every hour. Fare: $4.

To Santa Clara: Departures: 9:50am and 7pm. Fare: $7.

To Sancti Spiritu: Departures every two hours. Fare: $3.

To Cienfuegos: Departure: 8:05am. Fare: $11.

To Matanzas: Departure: 9:20am. Fare: $14.

Car Rental

Havanautos *(Hotel Ciego de Ávila, ☎2-8013)*.

By Taxi

Transautos *(Hotel Ciego de Ávila, ☎2-8940)*.

Morón

By Train

Numerous stained-glass windows adorn the ceiling of the handsome, dusty **Estación de Trenes** *(Avenida Martí, ☎3683)*, right in the centre of town.

To Ciego de Ávila: Departures: 12:55am, 6:30am and 7:13pm. Fare: $1.

To Camagüey: Departures: 3:13am and 1:32pm. Fare: $4.

To Santa Clara: Departure: 5:55am. Fare: $5.

To Nuevitas: Departure: 6:20am. Fare: $5.

By Bus

Morón's **Estación de Omnibus** is located across from the train station on Avenida Martí. It is best to reserve your seats several days in advance; however, if you give the employee at the ticket booth a small tip in U.S. currency, you'll have no trouble getting a ticket the day of your departure.

To Havana: Departure 7pm (every other day). Fare: $20.

To Santa Clara: Departure: 12:30pm. Fare: $8.

To Camagüey: Departure: 6:45am. Fare: $6.

To get to Cayo Coco, you can take the workers' truck from the tourist station in front of the Estación de Omnibus in Morón. It leaves early in the morning, around 6am.

Camagüey

By Plane

The **Aeropuerto Internacional Ignacio Agramonte** (*☎6-1000*) is located four kilometres northeast of Camagüey.

Havana is well serviced from Camagüey, which has two flights daily at 4:20pm and 5:55pm, except for Tuesdays (5:25pm) and Saturdays (10:40pm). The trip takes an hour and a half (*$72; one way*).

Airline Office

Cubana de Aviación (*airport, ☎6-1020; Calle República No. 400, ☎9-1338*).

By Train

The train station is located just north of downtown.

To Havana: Departures: 10:23pm; 7:13pm; 3:48am. Fare: $22; $19.50; $19.50 (respectively).

All three trains to Havana stop in **Ciego de Ávila** (*$3.50*), **Las Tunas** (*$4.50*), **Santa Clara** (*$9*) and **Matanzas** (*$16*).

To Las Tunas: Departures: 5:40am and 1:15pm. Fare: $4.50.

To Santiago de Cuba: Departures: 12:54am and 3:10am. Fare: $11.50.

By Bus

Estación de Omnibus Interprovinciales (*Carretera Central, near the Hotel Camagüey*). It is wise to check the schedule beforehand as these hours vary considerably.

To Havana: Departures: 6am and 9:40pm. Fare: $27.

To Ciego de Ávila: Departures: 7:40am, 1:55pm and 7:20pm. Fare: $4.

To Cienfuegos: Departure: 3:30pm (every other day). Fare: $13.

To Las Tunas: Departure: 8:30am (every other day). Fare: $5.

To Santiago de Cuba: Departure: 9:30am (every other day). Fare: $13.

There is daily bus service to **Playa Santa Lucia** *(2 pesos; departure 8am, return 4pm)* from the **Estación de Omnibus Provinciales**, near the Estación de Trenes.

Car Rental

Havanautos *(Hotel Camagüey, ☎7-2015).*

Playa Santa Lucia

Car Rentals and Taxis

Cubacar *(Hotel Cuatro Vientes, ☎3-6317).*

Holguín

By Plane

Travellers are greeted at the **Aeropuerto Frank País** *(☎46-2512 or 4-3934)* by a big propagandist fresco showing the heros of the world's communist revolutions. The airport is located southwest of town and linked to Holguín by a road. The schedule is not exactly regular, but there is at least one flight a day to **Havana** every day except Sunday, between 2:45pm and 9:45pm. On Saturdays, one flight leaves at 3:40pm; Sunday departures are at 6:55pm and at 9:30pm *($82; one way).*

Airline Office

Cubana de Aviación *(Calle Libertad, corner of Calle Martí, Edificio Pico de Cristal, ☎42-5707, ⊷46-8111).*

By Train

The **Estación de Trenes** *(Calle Terminal de Ferrocariles, between Calle Maceo and Calle Manduley)* is a handsome and very busy train station. It is crammed with pedestrians and cyclists, with vendors strolling about capitalizing on all the activity.

To Havana: Departure: 6:15pm. Fare: $31.

To Las Tunas: Departure: 9:05am. Fare: $7.

To Camagüey: Departure: 6:15pm. Fare: $9.

To Santiago de Cuba: Departure: 2:35pm. Fare: $5.

By Bus

Estación de Omnibus Nacionales

To Havana: Departure: 7am (every other day) and 8pm. Fare: $30.

To Camagüey: Departures: 5:30am and noon. Fare: $6.

To Ciego de Ávila: Departure: 6am (every other day). Fare: $10.

To Santiago de Cuba: Departure: 7:30am (every other day). Fare: $5.

To Guantanamo: Departure: 6:30am (every other day). Fare: $12.

Renting a Car

Havanautos *(Aeropuerto Frank País, ☎46-2512).*

Transautos *(Hotel Pernik, ☎48-1011).*

Guardalavaca

By Bus

There are several buses from the small local **Estación de Omnibus** to **Banes** *($1; 6:25am, 12:25pm and 5:55pm)* and **Holguín** *($2; 9:50am, every other day)*.

Car Rental

All the hotels rent out cars and scooters. The latter are a popular and inexpensive means of exploring the area.

PRACTICAL INFORMATION

Camagüey

Pharmacy *(Calle Ignacio Agramonte No. 447)*.

Holguín

Medical Care

Centro El Quinqué *(Carretera Central Vía Bayamo, 776 km, Los Pedernales, ☎46-2480, ⊷33-5301 ext.4105)*.

Guardalavaca

Medical Care

Clínica Internacional Guardalavaca *(☎30291, ⊷33-5073)*, a clinic for foreign tourists, is located in the eastern part of Guardalavaca.

EXPLORING

Ciego de Ávila

As the Carretera Central runs right through **Ciego de Ávila**, many travellers pass through on the way to exploring the rest of the country. The town has little to speak of in terms of tourist attractions, and is often viewed simply as a place to wait for a bus or a train connection. You can nevertheless take a stroll through town, and let your curiosity be your guide.

Parque Martí is the town's central square. It lost its colonial character when a number of government buildings were erected here between the 1950s and the 1970s, and is presently undergoing a major overhaul. You can still relax in the shade beneath one of the many trees, however.

Calle Independencia, the commercial artery of Ciego de Ávila, is flanked by several period houses and a number of shops which cater to local residents.

The **Museo Provincial** *($1; Tue to Sat 8am to 5pm, Sun 8am to noon; Calle José-Antonio Echevarria No. 25, between Calle Independencia and Calle Libertad)* is slightly removed from the centre of town, but is nonetheless within walking distance via Calle Independencia. This large museum is housed in a former preparatory school and has very large galleries. Unfortunately, however, the permanent collection isn't big enough to fill up all the space! The museum serves an educational purpose, and is frequented by local students. It contains a few interesting pieces, including the shrunken head of a native and several archaeological vestiges from the Punta Alegre region, on the north coast of the prov-

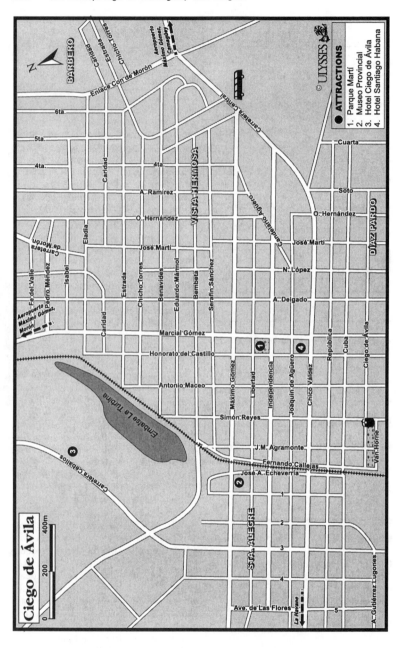

Ciego de Ávila

0   200   400m

ATTRACTIONS

1. Parque Martí
2. Museo Provincial
3. Hotel Ciego de Ávila
4. Hotel Santiago Habana

© ULYSSES

ince. There is a small room dedicated to Afro-Cuban religions, which displays articles donated to the museum by a *santero*, a priest in the Afro-Cuban tradition.

Morón ★

Morón is a peaceful little rural town also known as the "Ciudad del Gallo", the City of the Rooster. Upon arriving in Morón, you'll see a modern bell tower topped by a rooster in front of the Hotel Morón. Former dictator Fulgencio Batista inaugurated the tower during a visit to the region. The rooster thus became a symbol of his power and was removed from its base when the revolutionaries came to power; they were having problems with the local population, who viewed the new government unfavourably for the first few years. The present rooster dates from the 1960s. The rooster tradition actually originated in the Spanish town of Morón de la Frontera.

The most interesting part of Morón is the area around **Avenida Martí**, which is lined with slightly run-down neoclassical houses. You are sure to attract the attention of the locals, who are unaccustomed to seeing foreign tourists, and won't hesitate to interrupt their peaceful and apparently carefree existence to approach you and find out what brings you to these parts. All sorts of vendors are stationed along the town's main street, and you can enjoy a sweet, black *cafe cubano* for less than a peso at one of these strolling salesmen's makeshift tables.

Take Calle Castillo to the **Museo Municipal de Morón** *($1; Tue to Sat 8am to noon, 1:30pm to 5:30pm; Calle Castillo No. 164)*, which presents a very simple exhibition on the history of the town. This place has an educational slant, and is mostly frequented by local students. There are five galleries covering the history of Morón from the pre-Columbian era to the present day. The gallery devoted to Afro-Cuban religion is particularly interesting, since it contains numerous objects related to this blend of African faiths and Catholicism.

Camagüey ★★

Camagüey is the most interesting town in central Cuba. Founded by Diego Velásquez in 1515, it was originally named Puerto Príncipe and located by the water at Punto del Guincho, near Nuivitas. The following year, however, the residents decided to move it to the banks of the Río Caonao, where natives soon attacked and destroyed it. Finally, the townspeople opted for the present location near the native village of Camagüey, hence the name.

In the following century, the notorious pirate Henry Morgan attacked Camagüey (1668), attracted by legends of hidden treasures. He succeeded in capturing the town, but never found any treasure here. In 1679, the town underwent another pirate raid, this time at the hands of François Gramont.

To ward off these kinds of attacks, Camagüey adopted a labyrinthine layout. That way, any pirates who ventured into the town would get lost and find themselves caught like mice in a trap. Today, there is nothing more pleasant than losing oneself in this town, which is best explored on foot. In many ways, Camagüey is still like a small European town from the 18th century, with winding, pebbled streets and squares reminiscent of Italian or Spanish villages.

Large terracotta urns known as *tinajones* are the symbol of Camagüey.

ARCHIPELAGO OF CAMAGÜEY & HOLGUÍN

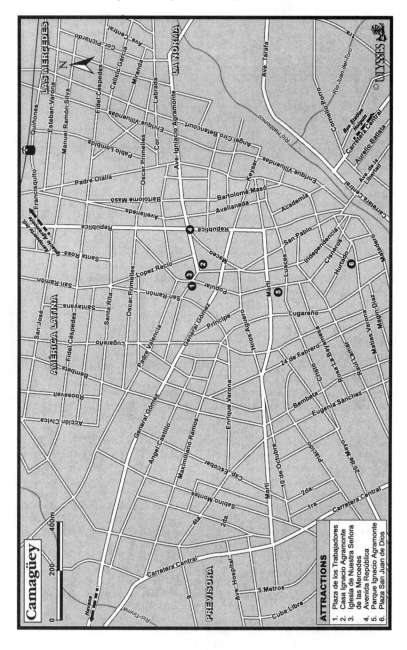

Camagüey

ATTRACTIONS

1. Plaza de los Trabajadores
2. Casa Ignacio Agramonte
3. Iglesia de Nuestra Señora de las Mercedes
4. Avenida República
5. Parque Ignacio Agramonte
6. Plaza San Juan de Dios

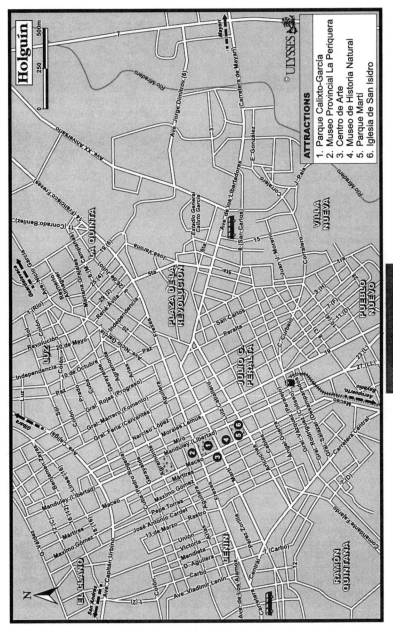

Holguín

ATTRACTIONS
1. Parque Calixto-García
2. Museo Provincial La Periquera
3. Centro de Arte
4. Museo de Historia Natural
5. Parque Martí
6. Iglesia de San Isidro

© ULYSSES

ARCHIPELAGO OF
CAMAGÜEY & HOLGUÍN

In the colonial era, these urns were used to collect rainwater and store oil and basic foodstuffs. The tradition of using *tinajones* is so entrenched that according to a 1974 count, there were some 18,000 in the town of Camagüey alone! In order to see a few, you'll have to venture onto the patios of colonial houses.

Start off your tour of Camagüey at the central square, **Plaza de los Trabajadores**, where you'll find the **Casa Ignacio Agramonte ★** *($1; Tue to Fri 9am to 6pm; Sat and Sun 8am to noon; Calle Ignacio Agramonte No. 459, ☎97116)*, home of the celebrated 19th-century hero of Cuban independence, who was captured and killed in combat. The house has been converted into a small historical museum.

On the opposite side of the square stands the **Iglesia de Nuestra Señora de las Mercedes ★★**. Built in 1748, it is the largest church in Camagüey and houses some truly precious pieces of sacred art, including the Holy Sepulchre to the left of the altar. Executed by a Mexican artist in 1762, this sarcophagus is one of the most important religious pieces in the country. Twenty-three thousand silver pieces had to be melted in order to cover it. A former monastery, built in the colonial style, lies behind the church in an inner court shaded by tall trees and guarded by an owl, which nests in the church tower.

While you're at the church, make sure to visit **Las Catacumbas ★** *(free admission; every day 8am to 6pm)*. Up until the 18th century, there was no cemetery in Camagüey, and the deceased were buried under the church. To get to the catacombs, you have to walk under the altar. At the entrance, there is a small museum displaying sacred objects. Next, you'll pass through a series of vaults, which have been re-constructed using brick to enable them to withstand the weight of the marble altar. Here, you will find two open tombs containing mortal remains from the 18th and 19th centuries. You can clearly see the bones and hair of the deceased, as well as the sacred objects with which they were interred and what is left of their clothing.

Avenida República, Camagüey's commercial artery, is a good place to take a walk, stop for an ice cream or a tropical fruit *batido* (milkshake) or poke about in an old bookstore. The vast majority of the little stores cater to Cubans. Stopping in at these places, far off the beaten tourist track, offers the chance to feel you've participated in day-to-day Cuban life.

The **Parque Ignacio Agramonte ★★**, with its convivial atmosphere, is one of the most pleasant squares in town. Take the time to relax in the shade of a tree and watch the passers-by. The neoclassical-style houses here are a bit run-down, giving the place a pleasantly antiquated ambiance. You'll get a feel for the real Cuba here, for the coming and going of life in Camagüey. The Casa de la Trova (see p 230) and a few cafés face onto the square.

Architecturally speaking, **Plaza San Juan de Dios ★★** is the most harmonious square in Camagüey. With its colonial buildings, it has retained all the charm of yesteryear. To get there, cross a number of narrow streets; once you reach the pebbled pavement, you'll find yourself in the heart of the labyrinth that makes up Camagüey. Here, the old colonial houses still have their original colouring. The **Iglesia San Juan de Dios ★★** occupies one whole side of the square. Built in 1728 and restored in 1941, it has lost none of its panache.

Head over to the **Restaurante La Campanas de Toledo ★** (see p 229), located on the square, to enjoy a bit of shade and see the pretty colonial house it occupies. Erected in the 18th century, it belonged to a wealthy Spaniard from Toledo. An old bell in the middle of the patio is used to announce the arrival of visitors.

Holguín

Start off your tour of Holguín at **Parque Calixto-Garcia**, a square flanked by a number of art galleries and the little **Museo Provincial La Periquera** *($1; Mon to Fri 9am to 5pm, Sat 9am to 1pm; Calle Frexi No. 198, between Calle Maceo and Calle Libertad, Parque Calixto Garcia, ☎46-3395)*, the former home of a wealthy local merchant named Francisco de Ruldán. Built between 1860 and 1868 by black and Chinese slaves, it now contains three galleries devoted to the history of the town and province of Holguín.

The **Centro de Arte** *(Calle Maceo No. 180, between Calle Frexi and Calle Martí)* has a large gallery devoted to work by contemporary artists from the Holguín region.

As you leave the square, take Calle Maceo, which is a pedestrian zone here. The neoclassical houses and laid-back atmosphere make this one of the most interesting streets in Holguín. The tiny **Museo de Historia Natural** *($1; Sun to Thu 9am to 5pm, Sat 1pm to 5pm; Calle Maceo No. 129)*, with its elegant turn-of-the-century façade is worth a quick look, mainly for its collection of shells.

Parque Martí and the **Iglesia de San Isidro** lie at the end of the pedestrian street. Parque Martí is home to numerous little shops. The church was built in

1720, and its classical façade is presently being restored.

The **Loma de la Cruz San Andres ★**, the little mountain overlooking Holguín, is topped by a cross and is a popular pilgrimage site. It offers a beautiful view of the town and the Sierra de Crystal, which stands out against the horizon. In a small tower, the little **La Galeria de Arte Pilgrim** *(Mon to Sat 8am to 5pm)* displays and sells paintings by members of the UNEAC (Union of Cuban Writers and Artists).

To get there, you can either climb the 458 steps from Calle Manduley or drive up the road that winds around the mountain to the cross.

Guardalavaca ★

Located 54 kilometres from Holguín, the two fine sandy beaches of Guardalavaca attract more and more travellers each year. Large Canadian and Spanish chains have erected hotel complexes on two separate beaches. One Spanish chain has built two superb hotels, the **Río de Luna** (see p 227) and the **Río Mares** (see p 227) on **Playa Esmeralda ★**.

This crescent-shaped beach, isolated by a small, gently sloping cliff scattered with luxuriant tropical vegetation, is perfect for swimming and other water sports, including scuba diving. Every day, novice divers plunge into the sea from here, and more experienced ones climb aboard a boat that takes them out to the coral reef. Come nightfall, a cocktail and a romantic stroll along the beach will quickly chase all your worries and troubles away.

The other beach, in **Guardalavaca**, two kilometres farther east, is considerably longer and thus scores more points with tourists who enjoy lengthy, bare-foot walks in the sand. Here, too, the water is good for swimming and other water sports. Numerous hotels line the beach, and promenades have been laid out beneath the palm trees. The night-life is particularly lively.

The east end of Guardalavaca is also worth a visit, on foot along the beach or by scooter on the main road (head toward the sea at the intersection near Banes). A small dirt road lined with little wooden houses winds its way along the shore, forming a striking contrast with the tourist complexes and enabling visitors to see and appreciate the peaceful lifestyle of the local resi-dents, most of whom are fishermen. There is very little traffic on this road, which is only a few hundred metres long. Aside from the beach, there is little to see in the area. Adventurous visitors (that means you, of course!) can explore the little village of Guardalavaca.

An excursion to the little village of **Banes**, about 30 kilometres southeast of Guardalavaca, is a pleasant way to spend half a day. If the spirit moves you, the town is easily reached by car, or even by scooter. Banes is a peaceful fishing village located off the tourist track. The **Museo Indocubano** *($2; Tue to Sat 9am to 5pm, Sun 8am to noon)* definitely merits a visit. Its superb col-lection of artifacts includes ceramics, jewellery and, most importantly, a small gold statue dating from the pre-Colum-bian era. These objects illustrate the importance of these vanished pre-Co-lumbian civilizations.

Gibara ★★

A picturesque little seaside town west of Guardalavaca, Gibara is not to be missed. Its colonial architecture has

been beautifully preserved, and its location, about 50 kilometres from Holguín, makes it a perfect stopping place for visitors who would like to learn a bit about the "real" Cuba, whether they're touring the country or staying in Guardalavaca. To get there from Guardalavaca, retrace your steps to Holguín, then head northeast.

Christopher Columbus discovered this region on October 29, 1492, during his first voyage to the New World, and named it Río de Mares. There is still a great deal of controversy among histori-ans as to exactly where the celebrated navigator first landed, Baracoa or Gibara. But don't ask the residents of Gibara, who have no doubt that the honour should be attributed to their town.

Apparently, Columbus was detained in Gibara for about 12 days, due to bad weather. He seized the opportunity to become acquainted with the local na-tives. In his account of the voyage, he describes a mountain shaped like a saddle: the Silla de Gibara, which is still visible in the distance.

As early as 1737, pirates began attack-ing this community. The town was actually founded on January 16, 1817, with the construction of the **Bateria Fernando Septimo ★** *($; every day 8:30am to 4:30pm)*, a fortress de-signed to protect the area from pirates and corsairs. There are all sorts of festivities to commemorate the event during Gibara's cultural week, which starts on January 16.

Over the years Gibara became prosper-ous as the local bourgeoisie supplied the town of Holguín with shipped mer-chandise. During the wars of independ-ence in the second half of the 19th century, Gibara's wealth and its alle-giance to the Spanish crown made it necessary to build more fortifications, including a wall around the town. Aside from Havana, Gibara is the only fortified town in the country.

From the top of the **Loma de la Vigia ★★**, the little mountain that rises up behind the town, you can see a little fort dating back to that era, along with the remains of the wall. A trip up to the lookout is a must, since it offers a unique view of the sea and the town, with its colonial houses topped by Mediterranean-style tiled roofs.

Due in part to the fortifications, it took 30 years of wars and fighting for the *mambices* (independentists) to take Gibara, which they finally succeeded in doing on July 25, 1868. However, with the construction of the Carretera Central, which runs east-west across the country, the town became isolated and fell into economic decline. This economic isolation has undoubtedly allowed Gibara—to my personal delight—to preserve its original layout along with several colonial and neoclassical houses. Fortunately, the picturesque historic section of Gibara remains unaltered by the tourist industry, so you can stroll about the town at your leisure, discovering all its little treasures on your own.

Start off your tour at the former Plaza de Armas (parade ground), **Parque Calixto-García**, then take Calle Independencia, which runs through the heart of the old town. Here, you'll find the pretty **Museo de Historia Natural ★** *($; Tue to Sat 8am to noon and 1pm to 6pm, Sun 8pm to noon; Calle Independencia No. 23, at the corner of Calle J. Peralta, ☎3-4222)*, which contains an impressive collection of stuffed fish and birds. The highlight: the skeletons of a whale and a dolphin.

It is worth stopping in at the little art gallery next door, the **Salón Municipal de Artes Plásticas** *(Calle Independecia*

No. 19). The **Museo Municipal** *(free admission; Tue to Sat 8am to noon and 1pm to 5pm, Sun 8am to noon, Calle Independencia No. 19, ☎3-4405)*, at the same address, contains nothing of great interest. This house, however, is where the independentist general Calixto García set up residence after taking possession of the town.

Continue to the Malecón, which runs along the waterfront. At the end, to the southeast, near Parque Calixto-García, lies the **Plaza del Fuerte ★★**, where you'll find the **Bateria Fernando Septimo**, the first fortification built in Gibara in the colonial era (see p 218). A little beach is accessible by cutting through the **Restaurante El Faro ★** (see p 229), which has small changing rooms.

PARKS AND BEACHES

Archipelago of Camagüey

Cayo Coco ★★

One of the largest islands in the Archipelago of Camagüey, Cayo Coco is gradually becoming one of Cuba's principal tourist regions. The main attractions of this island off the Atlantic coast are its white sand beaches and crystalline waters ranging in colour from blue to turquoise.

A spectacular 17-kilometre stretch of road runs through the marshes to Cayo Coco. In order to lay the road in 1991, the swamps had to be filled with stones and dirt, and the local residents are very proud of that feat. The entire way, visitors can observe the region's abundant marine life and relish the sensation of making a pilgrimage into a natural paradise.

ARCHIPELAGO OF CAMAGÜEY & HOLGUÍN

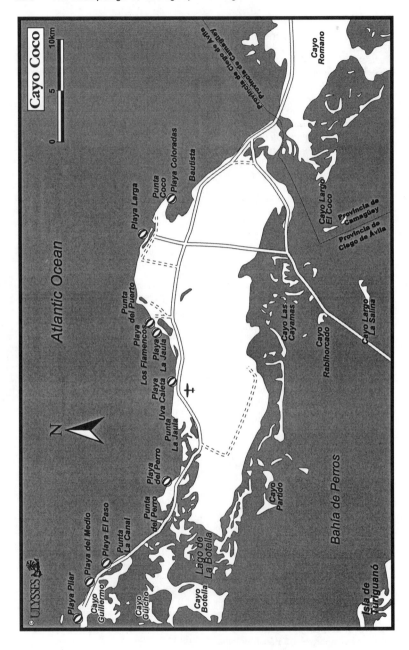

Cayo Coco is a fast-expanding tourist ghetto—a "ghetto" because except for those who work at the tourist complex, Cubans are forbidden access to the island. Consequently, you won't meet any Cubans here, and to get to know the country, you'll have to make a trip to Morón. Although there are legends about this region having been a pirate haunt, Cayo Coco looked like a desert island before the tourist industry began developing in the early 1980s. Its superb beaches, emerald waters and marshy landscapes make for a worry-free stay that is sure to leave you well rested.

The development of the local tourist industry worries environmentalists, however. The construction of numerous hotel complexes is bound to have an impact on the fragile ecosystem of this nearly pristine territory. To learn more about this subject, you can venture off the tourist track and visit the **Centro de Investigación de Ecosystems Costeros**, located at the entrance to Cayo Coco, near the kiosk. Administered by the Cuban Ministry of Science, this centre studies Cayo Coco's ecosystem in order to ensure its protection. On the centre's advice, it has been agreed that only four percent of the territory will be developed for tourism. A nature centre will probably be opened for visitors in 1997. In the meantime, it is worth stopping by to meet the team of scientists working here.

Cayo Guillermo ★

Cayo Guillermo is a little island only 13 kilometres long, located northwest of Cayo Coco. A magnificent road leads all the way to this tiny natural paradise. The beach is not as long as Cayo Coco's, but the place is a little less touristy, and perhaps a little more charming as a result.

Playa Santa Lucia ★

From Camagüey, head northeast on the road to the Aeropuerto Ignacio Agramonte. This 86-kilometre stretch of road leads into a farming region, with the little Sierra Cubita mountain range visible in the distance. At the first major intersection, turn right. The road then passes through a large stockbreeding area.

A 19-kilometre stretch of white sand, the **Playa Santa Lucia** is unquestionably one of the most beautiful beaches in Cuba. Large shells lie in the shallow water, and if you have a mask and snorkel, the hours can just slip away. Protected by a 32-kilometre coral reef, the beach is washed by calm, crystalline waters. The excellent facilities and magnificent underwater scenery make this a scuba diver's paradise (see p 223).

The travel agencies in the various hotels arrange excursions to the incredible beaches of **Cayo Sabinal ★★**. Skeptics won't believe their eyes: there really is a heaven on earth, and you'll find it on Cayo Sabinal!

Holguín

Parque Natural Bahía de Naranjo ★

The **Parque Natural Bahía de Naranjo**, on the road to Holguín, a few hundred metres from Guardalavaca, is an undeveloped bay. The main attraction here is the aquarium, superbly located on a little island about 10 minutes by boat from the park entrance. This modern facility has been designed to accommodate the hordes of tourists who come here from Guardalavaca. A series of foot bridges link each little island to the next, leading to different points of interest: a place where visitors can go swimming with the dolphins *($15 for a 15-min swim with these charming mammals)*, sea-lion shows, a restaurant, etc.

To get to the aquarium, make your way to the wharf at the park entrance. Boats shuttle passengers back and forth regularly, and you can climb aboard when you want. You can also visit the home of an old fisherman named Mongovinia. The Parque Natural Bahía de Naranjo is the perfect place to stretch your legs and explore the area on the numerous trails leading into the lush tropical vegetation that blankets the surrounding hills. There are several bike paths to scout out as well, if you have a chance.

Cayo Saetia ★★

A paradise for game hunters (see p 223) and shutterbugs alike, Cayo Saetia is a 42-square-kilometre island located in the Bahía de Levisa, north of the village of Mayari, 120 kilometres from Holguín. The road is particularly bad from Mayari on. The major hotels in Guardalavaca, Varadero and Santiago de Cuba offer helicopter flights to Cayo Saetia for excursions of a day or longer. To give you an idea of the prices, a day-trip from Guardalavaca costs $99, including meals, transportation and guide.

Pristine beaches with steep 10-metre-high cliffs rising above them, ring the island of Cayo Saetia, 65 percent of which is covered in lush vegetation. Wildlife from Africa, including buffalo, antelopes, zebras and wild boars have been introduced to the island and roam about freely. To make the most of your visit, take a ride in a 4-wheel drive vehicle. Enthusiastic guides lead you across steep, bumpy terrain in Soviet-made former Cuban-army WAZ vehicles that have been converted for tourism.

 OUTDOOR ACTIVITIES

Morón and Cayo Coco

The hotels in Cayo Coco and Cayo Guillermo offer a number of outdoor activities. *Seafaris ($55)* and excursions to the **tobacco plantation** in Boquerón are organized, and water sports equipment can be rented.

 Horseback Riding

Ciego de Ávila

Finca Oasis, 19 kilometres east of Ciego de Ávila, is right on the Carretera Central.

Playa Santa Lucia

The **King Ranch** *($30; every day 9am to 4pm)* is located on the road to Camagüey, about 10 kilometres from Playa Santa Lucia. Most of the hotels around the beach offer excursions here.

Holguín

Eight kilometres south of Holguín, the **Villa Mirador de Mayabe** *($5 an hour; ☎4-22160)* offers riding trips around the Mayabe valley.

 Fishing and Hunting

Ciego de Ávila

The **Coto de Caza Florida** *($100; one day, including two hunting trips, ground transportation, boat, guide, hunting equipment and accommodation at the Hotel Florida, ☎5-3011)* is located along the Carretera Central, about 106 kilometres east of Ciego de Ávila. There are three lakes where you can go fishing, as well as hunting for ducks and wild geese. The best time to go is between October and March.

Morón and Cayo Coco

The hotels on Cayo Coco and Cayo Guillermo arrange outdoor activities such as seafaris *($55)* and excursions to a **tobacco plantation** in Boquerón, near Morón, and also rent out the necessary equipment for various water sports.

For trout fishing, people go to the **Laguna La Redonda**, a 24-square-kilometre stretch of water along the road to Cayo Coco, 12 kilometres from Morón. You can take a 45-minute boat trip here for $5. The rates for fishing are $35 for half a day and $70 for a full day, boat and guide included. There is a small restaurant by the shore. Don't forget to bring along insect repellent; otherwise, you'll get eaten alive by mosquitoes.

Cayo Saetia

If you've always dreamed of going on a real safari, the kind Ernest Hemingway would have approved of, go to the game preserve at Cayo Saetia. Not everyone will be able to afford this expedition, but those who can will have some impressive trophies to show their friends. The prices are as follows: $1300 for an antilope; $300 for a buffalo and $250 for a wild boar.

 Scuba Diving

Playa Santa Lucia

Even the most demanding divers will be satisfied by what they find here: a coral reef nearly 32 kilometres long, with 34 dive sites, including the wreckage of three ships (one dating back to 1896) and a shark habitat. You can snap some great pictures while the instructors feed the grey sharks.

The **Sharks Friends** diving centre, on the beach between the Villa Coral and Cuatro Vientos hotels, offers a wide range of diving excursions and packages *(introductory course: $50, 1 dive; $95, 2 dives; SSI and PADI certification courses, $365)*.

"Frequent diver" rates are available. For example, 2 to 5 dives cost $30 each; 6 to 10, $28 each; 11 and over, $25 each.

 Snorkelling

Playa Santa Lucia

Hotel Cuatro Vientos *($19; Tue, Thu, Sat 9am; 4-hour excursion; transportation and equipment included)*.

 Sea Excursions

Playa Santa Lucia

The **Villa Coral** *($300 for 4 passengers, including lobster lunch)* arranges sailing trips along the coral reef.

ACCOMMODATIONS

Ciego de Ávila

The *casa particulares* here don't seem to stand out as much as in other cities. It may take a bit of walking around in order to find and recognize the triangular blue-and-white logo affixed on the entrance of the residences. If you stroll through the central park, however, you are almost guaranteed to be approached by a child who will guide you to the doors of one of these *casa particulares*, in return for a commission from the proprietor. Check the level of noise and for cleanliness and a functional bathroom before renting the room. Also, try not to pay over $20.

María del Carmen Perez *($20; ≡, pb; Edificio 1, Apartamento 14, Calle Honorata del Castillo at the corner of Av. Independencia)* rents two rooms, equipped with a kitchen, right across from the park. The owners actually live in another building, so they don't reside in with their guests.

Located three kilometres from downtown, the **Hotel Ciego de Avila** *($24-30; ≡, ≈, pb, ℛ, ctv, ☎; Carretera de Ceballo, 2.5 km, ☎2-8013)* has an outmoded façade and a run-down interior that is definitely quaint, and will only attract those looking for hunting and fishing holidays. Fortunately, the large pool and many palm trees seem to breathe some life into this rather dreary picture, as if to compensate for its lack of style. Some tourists spend the night here while waiting to get to Cayo Coco.

The **Hotel Santiago-Habana** *($34; ≡, pb, tv, ℛ, ℛ; Calle Honorato del Castillo, at the corner of the Carretera Central, ☎2-5703)*, the most centrally located hotel in Ciego de Ávila, lies near the train and bus stations, just a few blocks from Parque Martí. It has a pleasant restaurant and a cabaret on the top floor.

Morón

The **Hotel Cubanacán Morón** *($36; ≡, pb, ℛ, ≈, tv; Avenida Carafa, ☎3901)* is just the place for travellers who are not staying on Cayo Coco or Cayo Guillermo. It has a lovely swimming pool, and the luxuriant vegetation in its courtyard reaches all the way to the top floors of the building. The outstanding service is provided by the students of one of the best hotel management schools in the country under the supervision of their instructors.

Cayo Coco

Cayo Coco's recent tourist boom took off after several large hotel complexes were built here, complete with all the necessary amenities for a pleasant stay: shops, restaurants, bookstores, nightclubs and bars. These comfortable places make it easy to kick back and relax. The only thing that could use some improvement is the food, which can be a bit bland at times.

The **Tryp Cayo Coco** *($92-132 fb; ≡, ctv, ≈, ℛ; ☎30-1311, ⊷ 30-1386)* is the loveliest hotel on Cayo Coco. Its lovely Mediterranean-style architecture is sure to capture your imagination. The service is somewhat impersonal, both at the restaurant and the reception desk, but a few words in Spanish will win you a genuine smile.

Surrounded by crystalline water and white sand dunes, **El Senador** *($120; ≡, ⊘, ℛ, ≈, △, ▣ from Toronto, ☎416-601-0343, ⊷601-0346, www.cubanacan.cu)* is named after the former star defenseman and general manager of the Montréal Canadians hockey team, Serge Savard. This Spanish colonial-style four-star hotel is set in the midst of lush vegetation. Situated about 80 kilometres from Máximo Gómez Báez Airport and only 10 kilometres from the future Cayo Coco International Airport, the hotel will open in October 1999 and offer all-inclusive vacation packages. There are 400 impeccable rooms and lodgings, 36 of which are individual *cabañas* raised up on piles with balconies overlooking a splendid saltwater lagoon, a refuge for exotic flora and fauna. Among the services offered are a 24-hour medical services. Bicycles, watersports equipment, windsurfing boards, catamarans, motorbikes and cars can be rented, and there are tennis and volleyball courts.

On Cayo Guillermo, the **Villa Cojimar** *($130 fb; ≡, ctv, ℜ, ≈; ☎30-1712, ⇔33-1727)* is the oldest place in the area. Unpretentious and a bit outdated, it consists of a series of little waterfront bungalows. Friendly staff.

Florida

The pleasant, comfortable **Hotel Florida** *($40; ≡, tv, ≈, ℜ, ℝ; ☎5-3011)* is where all the game hunters from Coto de Caza Florida stay. The restaurant, naturally, specializes in game dishes.

Camagüey

The **Hospedaje Casa Colonial** *($15; ≡, sb; Calle Independencia No. 251, ☎9-4606)* is a stunning example of Cuba's *casas particulares*. Located in an old colonial edifice, its balconies offer a feast for the eyes with a view overlooking the Plaza Maceo. The livingroom, furnished with period pieces, a television and stereo, be-

comes a meeting place for guests in this three-room building. The rooms are comfortable and decorated in a colonial style, blending harmoniously with the rest of the building. This is a popular place, so it is best to make reservations ahead of time.

Within walking distance, the casa of **Noemi Fernandez** *($15; ≡, pb; Av. Ignacio Agramonte No. 439, between Calles Maceo and Independencia)* also offers rooms with air conditioning and private bathrooms. The quiet ambience and Ms. Fernandez' exceptional hospitality make for a worthwhile stay, even though the rooms here are perhaps less impressive than those of the Casa Colonial (see above).

On Avenida República, a few blocks from the train station, the **Hotel Colón** *($22; ≡, pb, ℜ, ⊚; Avenida República, between Calle San José and Calle San Martín, ☎8-3380 or 8-3346)* is a converted colonial house dating from 1827. The place has a unique style, with its high ceilings and long corridors awash with natural light. The rooms are attractively furnished. The *especiales* rooms are equipped with air conditioning and a minibar, and are considerably larger than the others. The inner patio is covered with trees and plants, making it the perfect spot to relax, read or write a few postcards.

If the Hotel Colón is full, head over to the **Hotel Isla de Cuba** *($17; ≡, pb, ℜ; Calle San Esteban No. 453, at the corner of Calle Popular, ☎9-1515)*, whose sole attraction is its rates.

🏨 The most centrally located hotel in Camagüey, the **Gran Hotel** *($29; ≡, pb, tv, ≈, ℜ, ℝ; Calle Maceo No. 67, between Calle Ignacio Agramonte and General Gómez, ☎92093)* has a turn-of-the-century charm.

A handsome, colonial-style building, the **Hotel Plaza** *($30; ≈, pb, ℜ; Calle Van Horne No. 1 between Calle Avellanada and Avenida República, ☎8-241)* is well located near the train station. It is best to ask for a room that opens onto the inner patio, as the others are rather noisy. A bit outmoded but comfortable on the whole.

Following three years of intensive renovations, Camagüey's most central hotel now has simple, comfortable rooms that are stylishly furnished. The most remarkable addition is the beautiful pool where you can cool off after a stroll through the *muy calientes* streets of the city. The charming building was also well restored during the renovations, preserving its colonial style. Without a doubt, the best price to quality ratio in Camagüey.

Playa Santa Lucia

The **Villa Tararaco** *($50; ≈, ℜ; Carretera Santa Lucia, ☎3-6222, ⊷36-5126)* is the least expensive place around Playa Santa Lucia. Located at the northwest end of the beach, it is a small, 31-room hotel with a friendly staff. The beach directly in front of it is not the best in the area, but the prettier spots are just a few minutes' walk away (some people prefer this stretch of beach, however, as it is less crowded with tourists).

The **Villa Coral** *($65; ≈, ≈, ℜ; Carretera Santa Lucia, ☎3-6429, ⊷36-5153)*, the oldest hotel on Playa Santa Lucia, is attractively laid out and has a relaxing atmosphere. It is run by a Dutch company, as is the **Hotel Caracol** *($72; ≈, ≈, ℜ; Carretera Santa Lucia, ☎3-6402)*, a lovely, modern complex of little houses with Mediterranean-style tiled roofs. A few rooms offer a view of the sea.

Surrounded by palm trees, the **Hotel Cuatro Vientos** *($70, $110 ½b; ≈, ≈, ℜ; Carretera Santa Lucia, ☎3-6140)* is a small grouping of traditional Cuban bungalows.

Holguín

Casas particulares in Holguín are scattered about here and there, and, without an address in hand, the lack of signs can make it a bit difficult to find accommodation. A good bet is **El Chino** *($15; ≈, sb; Calle Frexes No. 166, between Calles Morales Lemus and Narciso Lopez)*, who rents out convenient though basic rooms himself, with a livingroom where you sit and read. If there is no vacancy, he will direct you to other commendable places.

As a last resort, there is almost always room at **Haydée Torres Marrero** *($26; ≈, sb; Calle Narciso Lopez between Av. Frexes and Marti, ☎42-4721, ⊷4-25347)*. Looking more like a garage turned into a house, this hotel does not win any prizes for hospitality. It is, however, a good spot to sleep in. A piano at the entrance has potential to warm up the ambience, and, of course, the garage is open for visitor parking.

The **Villa Mirador de Mayabe** *($26; ≈, ≈, ℜ; ☎42-2160, ⊷42-5347)* is perched on a mountain overlooking the Mayabe valley, eight kilometres south of Holguín. It has a pretty view and a rural ambiance, which is occasionally disrupted by loud disco music. Guests stay in rustic but fairly comfortable little cabins. Suites can be rented for $50, everything included.

The **Villa El Bosque** *($27; ≈, tv, pb, ≈, ℜ; Avenida Jorge Dimitrov, near the Hotel Pernik, ☎48-1012)* stands on a wooded property near the centre of town. Its rustic bungalows and natural setting create a pleasant, relaxed ambiance. This is definitely your best option in Holguín, and is more conducive to rest and relaxation than the Hotel Pernik.

The **Hotel Pernik** *($32; ≡, pb, ≈, ℛ; Avenida Jorge Dimitrov, ☎4-81011, ⇝33-5301)* is the largest hotel in Holguín. The rooms are comfortable, but the service is impersonal and the quality of the restaurant's food is inconsistent.

Guardalavaca

Although there are no inexpensive hotels at this seaside resort, you can rent a room or even a small house right on the beach, at the east end of Guardalavaca, where the main road ends and then heads toward Banes (turn left toward the sea at the intersection). A number of local residents rent out their little wooden houses to visitors. You'll have to inquire at random.

Guests of the **Hotel Atlántico** *($92; ≡, pb, ctv, ≈, ℛ; ☎30188)*, in the eastern part of Guardalavaca, have access to a long, gorgeous beach. The hotel has all the necessary facilities to ensure a pleasant stay. The rooms are spacious and comfortable, and a number of them offer a view of the sea.

The **Villa Turey** *($101; ≡, pb, ctv, ≈, ℛ; ☎30195)* has a series of bungalows set near the sea. The atmosphere is pleasant, but the quality of the rooms and the service is not quite in keeping with the high rates.

The **Hotel Delta Las Brisas** *($150 everything included; ≡, pb, ctv, ≈, ℛ; ☎30218)* is one of the largest hotels in the region. Run by a Canadian hotel chain, it offers impeccable service and

top-quality rooms. It is an imposing place, but somewhat lacking in charm.

Isolated to the west of Guardalavaca, on Playa Esmeralda, the **Río de Luna** and the **Río de Mares** *($200 fb; ☎30102)* are both magnificent and very inviting, with all the ingredients necessary for an enjoyable stay. The spacious, comfortable rooms have a Mediterranean charm, and the various restaurants offer a wide variety of dishes.

Gibara

The tiny, little **Hotel Bello Mar** *(18 pesos; pb, ⊗; Calle Ricardo Sartorio Leal No. 125, ☎3-4206)* only has 12 rooms. The amenities are few, but the place is clean and the service is friendly. The clientele consists mainly of Cuban tourists.

 RESTAURANTS

Ciego de Ávila

The **Moscú** *($; Thu to Tue 6pm to 10pm; Av. Chicho Valdés No. 78, ☎2-5989)* is a pleasant, if rather sombre, bar-restaurant. It is a good spot for evening drinks, but its name has nothing to do with the food: only Cuban cuisine is served.

Closer to the central park, **La Romagnola** *($; every day 6pm to 10pm; ☎2-5386)* is an Italian restaurant offering various pasta dishes at a good price. Spaghetti and pizza are the specialty of the house, and other typical Italian fare is served as well. The interior is simple but tastefully decorated.

The loveliest restaurant in Ciego de Ávila contrasts with the rest of the town. With its pretty wooden doors and colonial-style roof, the **Restaurant Don Pepe** *($$; Calle Independencia No. 103, ☎3713)* has a relaxed atmosphere that is hard to resist. The prices were still listed in pesos when we visited, but the owners were considering switching to U.S. currency, which would up the bill. Creole cuisine.

The restaurant in the **Hotel Santiago-Habana** *($$; Calle Honorato del Castillo and Carretera Central, ☎2-5703)*, is popular with visitors; it is pleasant, but no more. The menu lists a variety of Creole and Italian dishes.

The **Restaurante Solaris** *($$; Parque Martí)* is located on the 12th floor of the tallest building facing onto Parque Martí. The food is somewhat bland, but the panoramic view of the city makes this a good place for drinks before dinner.

The **Finca Oasis** *($$)* lies in the countryside along the Carretera Central, on the way to Camagüey, 19 kilometres east of Ciego de Ávila. Here, guests dine on traditional *campesino* food in a rustic house. A more affordable cafeteria menu (fried chicken, sandwiches, etc.) is also available. The food lacks zing, but the service is friendly. You can also come here to go horseback riding in the fruit plantations.

Morón

Opposite the train station, next to the Estación de Omnibus, the **Paladar La Rueda** *($; Avenida Martí No. 414, ☎3008)* is a small family restaurant where you can have a full meal for about $1 — usually Creole chicken served with rice and black beans. The staff is friendly and convivial, but the menu is very limited.

Camagüey

One of the few places to have preserved its pre-Revolutionary charm, **La Casa de Ron Cuba El Cambio** *($)* faces onto Parque Ignacio Agramonte. This little café is set up in an old turn-of-the-century house, where lottery tickets and rum were once sold. When lotteries were banned in 1960, the place was forced to change with the times; its walls still bear witness to those bygone days, however. The café serves casual fare like hamburgers and sandwiches. You'll also find a very good, reasonably priced selection of Cuban rums here.

For ice cream, head to the **Heladeria Coppelia** *(Calle Maceo No. 161)*.

There are two centrally located pizzerias in downtown Camagüey, both of whose prices are listed in Cuban currency. The typically Cuban **Restaurante La Piazza** *($; until 6pm; Calle Maceo, facing the Plaza de Gallo)* is located on the second floor of an old, slightly rundown building. Its balcony is clearly visible from the Plaza del Gallo, and its tiny little entrance is on Calle Maceo. This place is patronized mainly by locals, and its appeal lies more in its atmosphere than the quality of its food.

A few metres away, **La Regazza** *($; noon to 7:30pm; Calle Maceo, between Calle Ignacio Agramonte and Calle General Gómez)* is a little restaurant with a big, rather neglected-looking terrace. It serves pizza, but toppings are often in short supply.

The restaurant in the **Gran Caribe Hotel** *($$; Calle Maceo No. 67, between Calle Ignacio Agramonte and Calle General Gómez)* is an extremely charming place to have dinner in town. Located on the fifth floor of this turn-of-the-century hotel, it offers a lovely view of the faintly lit city below. Creole cuisine.

The **Restaurante La Campanas de Toledo** *($$; ☎9-5888)* occupies a pretty colonial house on the Plaza San Juan de Dios. When you hear the church bell, you'll know you're in the right place. Most of the tables are set up beneath a series of arches; others are on the patio. The ambiance is very agreeable and the service is courteous. This region is renowned for the quality of its cattle, and the house specialty is *Boliche de Mechado*, a beef dish prepared according to a traditional local recipe.

Holguín

Holguín has two family-style Creole restaurants, the **Pepezón** *($; Calle Miró, between Calle Martí and Calle Luz Caballero)* and **El Colonial** *($; Calle Maceo, between Calle Agramonte and Calle Garallalde)*. Both *paladares* are pleasant and well-located downtown, offering visitors a chance to get off the beaten path and enjoy some good food at reasonable prices.

La Begonia *($; Calle Maceo No. 176, between Calle Frexi and Calle Martí)*, located adjacent to Parque Calixto-García, is a charming little snack bar with a flowery terrace.

Head to **La Magía** *($; 5pm to 11pm, closed Mon; Av. Luz Caballero No. 64)* for the best fish and seafood in the city. Generous portions of dishes with tantalizing flavours are served in a homey decor.

Pizzería Roma *($; Calle Maceo and Av. Agramonte)* offers slices of pizza at unbeatable prices. It is, however, bad pizza – but empty stomachs and wallets will get their money's worth!

Hamburger lovers should not miss the **Taberna Pancho** *($; noon to 4pm and 6pm to 10pm; Av. Jorge Dimitrov, near the Plaza de la Revolución, ☎48-1868)*. Beer is also available, as the name implies, making an excellent accompaniment to any hamburger. Oddly, the Taberna Pancho is located near the high-end hotels, so it is a bit out of the way from the downtown core.

Gibara

Restaurante El Faro *($$; Plaza del Fuerte; ☎3-4596)* is the perfect place to have lunch during a daytrip to Gibara. It has an attractive seaside terrace and a small private beach. The menu consists of cafeteria fare (hamburgers, pizza, etc.), Creole cuisine and a few fish and seafood dishes.

  ENTERTAINMENT

Ciego de Ávila

The **Casa de la Trova** *(4pm to 2am; Calle Libertad No. 130, at the corner of Calle Simón Reyes)* presents *trova*, bolero and jazz concerts.

The **Museo Provincial** *(last Thu of every month; Calle José-Antonio Echevarria No. 25, between Calle Independencia and Calle Libertad)* organizes a cultural festival called La Cachanchara, after a cocktail made with *aguardiente* (a liquor distilled from cane juice), honey and water. On the agenda: traditional music, dancing, history and, of course, *cachancharas*.

The cabaret in the **Hotel Santiago-Habana** *(free admission; every day*

8:30pm to 1:40am; Calle Honorato del Castillo, at the corner of Carretera Central, ☎2-5703) is one of the few places in Ciego de Ávila to go after dark. Unfortunately, you won't hear much Latin music here.

The **Teatro Principal** (Calle Joaquin de Aguero, at the corner of Calle Honorato del Castillo) puts on a series of plays.

Morón

The **Casa de la Trova** (free admission; Tue to Sun, from 2pm on; Calle Libertad No. 74, at the corner of Avenida Martí, ☎4158) presents live traditional Cuban music. It also displays a few typical instruments and photographs of musicians.

The **Casa de la Cultura Haydee Santa-Maria** (free admission; Tue to Sun, Avenida Martí No. 218, ☎4309) regularly hosts performances of folk and Afro-Cuban dance. The group Renacer Haitiano puts on voodoo dance shows rooted in Haitian culture.

The little **Galeria de Arte** (free admission; Tue to Sun; Avenida Martí No. 151) opposite the Casa de la Cultura displays painting by local artists.

Camagüey

Camagüey's **Casa de la Trova** (free admission; every night from 8:30pm on; Calle Cisneros, Parque Ignacio Agramonte) is particularly charming. This institution of traditional Cuban music lies hidden behind the big wooden door of a colonial house with numerous arches.

The **UNEAC** (Calle Cisneros No. 159), the Cuban writers' and artists' union, has a small crafts shop where all sorts of cultural activities are held.

On Avenida República, you'll find many small theatres that show video movies. Most of the films are American with Spanish subtitles.

Holguín

The local **Casa de la Trova** (Calle Maceo No. 174, between Calle Frexi and Calle Martí, Parque Calixto-García), which presents live traditional and popular music, is a pleasant place to enjoy some late-afternoon entertainment.

At nightfall, the **Cafe Cantante** (Calle Frexi No. 194, at the corner of Calle Libertad) livens up to the sounds of Latin music.

Next door, the **Casa de la Cultura** (Calle Maceo No. 172, between Calle Frexi and Calle Martí, Parque Calixto García, ☎42-2084) has a small art gallery that shows films on video.

Guardalavaca

La Dulce Vida, the nightclub in the Hotel Delta Las Brisas, is especially lively at nightfall.

The outdoor nightclub **La Roca**, located right on Playa Esmeralda, is the perfect place to enjoy a great night out under the stars. The tropical ambiance puts everyone in a festive mood, and die-hard fun-lovers keep the place open until the wee hours.

SHOPPING

Morón

Libreria Moderna Poesia *(Avenida Martí No. 314)*.

Fondo de Bienes Culturales *(Avenida Martí No. 264)* has a small selection of crafts from this region and other parts of Cuba.

For imported foodstuffs, wine and beer, go to the **Mercado los Balcones** *(Avenida Martí No. 284)*.

Artex *(Avenida Martí No. 358)* sells posters, music and books.

Photo Service *(Avenida Martí No. 364)*.

Camagüey

The **UNEAC** *(Calle Cisneros No. 159)* has a small crafts shop and an art gallery. The **Fondo de Bienes Culturales** *(Avenida Caridad)* also sells crafts.

Photo Service *(Calle Ignacio Agramonte No. 430)*.

Holguín

The **Fondo de Bienes Culturales** *(Mon to Sat 10am to 5pm; Calle Frexi No. 196)*, in the house adjacent to the museum, has a large array of crafts produced in the province of Holguín.

ARCHIPELAGO OF CAMAGÜEY & HOLGUÍN

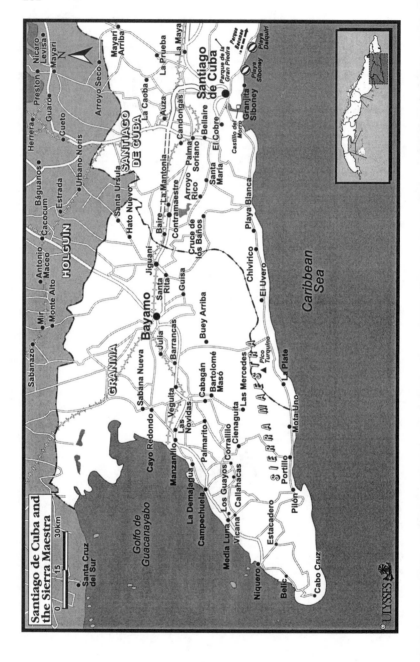

Santiago de Cuba and
the Sierra Maestra

0   15   30km

SANTIAGO DE CUBA
AND THE SIERRA MAESTRA

he capital of Afro-Cuban culture in the country, Santiago de Cuba is a city that sizzles in the noonday sun and rocks into the wee hours of the morning. Day and night, the distant rhythm resonating through the steep, winding streets of Santiago is an invitation to dance and a promise of discovery. Santiago is to Cuba what New Orleans is to the United States or Bahia to Brazil. Cultures intermingle here, creating an enthnic diversity unique in this country. Over the centuries, the Africans, the French, the Spanish, the Chinese and even the natives have developed a culture that has influenced the rest of the island. The cradle of *son*, the rhythmic base of Cuban music, Santiago de Cuba is the most exotic yet also most typical of the country's major cities.

July 24, 25 and 26 are the most important days of Santiago's Carnaval, which honours Santiago Apóstol (St. James the Apostle). It is at this time of year that the town is most true to itself, when residents from all different neighbourhoods joyfully take to the streets of old Santiago.

Santiago de Cuba lies between the lofty mountains of the Sierra Maestra and the sea. Its geographical location on a large bay led to the rapid development of the city, which was at one time the country's capital. Founded in 1515 by Diego Velásquez, it prospered thanks to copper mining and the huge fortunes that passed through here on their way to Spain.

Hernán Cortés, who orchestrated the conquest of Mexico, was Santiago's first mayor. The enormous wealth that he and Diego Velásquez amassed helped finance the numerous treasures of colonial architecture that can still be admired here today. For many years Santiago de Cuba seemed destined for a brilliant future, until Havana, better located on the shipping route, gained favour. In less than 40 years, Santiago would lose its status as the capital of Cuba.

Santiago de Cuba has earned a place in history as the "birthplace of the revolutionaries". The great generals who fought for Cuban independence in the 19th century were born here in the wake of numerous popular uprisings. Carlos Manuel Céspedes and Antonio Maceo Grajales were two of the principal architects of these battles. It was here, too, that Fidel Castro first became politically active—and we all know what that led to! In 1953, with Frank País and the other members of the *Grupo Generaciones*, he tried to seize the Cuartel Moncada, a military barracks. This unsuccessful attempt landed Castro in jail. Upon being released, he went into voluntary exile in Mexico. When he returned aboard the *Granma* with Che Guevara and a number of other rebels, he chose to land in this region.

Santiago de Cuba, the capital of the province of Santiago, is now the second-largest city in the country, with nearly 400,000 inhabitants. Its economy is based chiefly on agriculture and a few small industries.

The province of Santiago has many parks along the Sierra Maestra. There are hiking trails on the Gran Piedra, a 1,200-metre-high mountain east of the city, and right nearby, in the Siboney region, a number of excellent beaches lead to the sea. Furthermore, the biggest park in the country, Parque Bocanao, lies some 50 kilometres east of Santiago de Cuba.

There are a number of excursions to be enjoyed around Santiago de Cuba, including a trip to La Caridad del Cobre, about 15 kilometres northwest of Santiago. Thousands of pilgrims come to this temple in the countryside to honour the patron saint of Cuba, the Black Virgin of La Caridad del Cobre. It is worth spending half a day to visit the place.

How many days should you spend in Santiago de Cuba? It is difficult to say, but no matter how long you stay, you'll always be a little sad to leave this city. If only you could linger a bit longer and mingle with the warm, vibrant people here and lose yourself forever in the picturesque neighbourhoods.

Granma, west of Santiago, is traversed by the legendary Sierra Maestra mountains and is the most mountainous province in the country. Among these lofty summits, you can climb Pico Turquino, the highest peak in the country, and visit the Comandancia de la Plata where Fidel Castro set up his command post in the 1950s, when the fighting between his guerilleros and the Cuban army reached its peak.

For many years, this region was the private territory of the Revolutionary Armed Forces, but it has fortunately begun opening up to foreign tourism. These valleys were the birthplace of the Castroist revolution, for it is here that the rebels hid out after sailing to Cuba aboard the *Granma* in 1956. Today, visitors can relive the country's recent history while taking in some magnificent scenery.

Finally, it is worth spending a day or two exploring Bayamo and Manzanillo, the two main towns in the province of Granma.

Have you visited our web site?
www.ulysse.ca

FINDING YOUR WAY AROUND

Santiago de Cuba

By Plane

Santiago de Cuba is well served by the Cubana de Aviación airline. The **Aeropuerto Internacional Antonio Maceo**, located five kilometres south of town, is modern and well run; with its tourist offices, car rental service and taxis, it has kept up with the country's growing tourist industry. The taxi ride into town costs about $10. There are a number of buses you can take as well, although they don't follow a regular schedule. If you want to hitchhike into town, go to the Carretera del Morro, a few hundred metres from the airport.

Cubana de Aviación and **Lacsa** are two airlines offering flights from Santiago de Cuba to other cities in Cuba. There are three flights a day to **Havana** *($160 return, $90 one way).* For the same price, departures leave once a day for **Varadero**. Call the airport to check current schedules *(☎9-1014).*

Airlines

Cubana de Aviación: Aeropuerto Internacional Antonio Maceo, ☎9-1014 ext. 2019; 671 Calle Felix Peña, between Calle San Basilio and Calle Heredia, ☎2-0898, 2-2290 or 2-4156.

Aerotaxi: Aeropuerto Internacional Antonio Maceo, ☎9-1410 ext. 2019.

By Train

The train is a popular means of travelling between Havana and Santiago de Cuba. It is a picturesque trip, as the railway crosses the island from west to east, stopping in a number of towns and villages along the way. The train is relatively comfortable, and few people regret having spent 16 hours in one of the cars of *tren especial no.1*. Although there are frequent delays, the situation has improved greatly since 1995. Watch out, though: the train occasionally leaves early! Bring along some sandwiches and water. There is cafeteria service on board, but it has a strange schedule. Sometimes coffee is served, other times, sandwiches; if you miss one or the other, you have to wait an hour or two for the next sitting.

The **Estación de Trenes de Santiago** *(Avenida Jesús Menéndez, ☎2-2836)* is bustling with activity all day long. This station surpasses all others in the country. It was completely rebuilt in 1997 in a grand style that equals the famous stations of Europe. In fact, it almost looks like a modern airport, but unfortunately, the trains have yet to be modernized and are as ancient as ever. The archaic locomotives entering a modern platform are a strange spectacle. When you get to Santiago, you'll be assailed by taxi (*particulares*) drivers and Santiagueros offering you rooms in private homes. If you have a backpack or can carry your baggage easily, however, go ahead and walk into town.

The black market for train tickets is very well organized in Santiago, and you can easily purchase tickets at ridiculously low prices. Go to the departure platform, then climb the little staircase. Admission tickets for places all over town, especially tourist attractions, are available on the black market; *particulares* drivers are in the best position to find such tickets.

To Havana: Departure: 4:35pm. Travel time: 16 hours. Fare: $35.

SANTIAGO DE CUBA & THE SIERRA MAESTRA

To Camagüey: Departure: 10:30pm. Travel time: 7 hours 30 min. Fare: $11.50

To Holguín: Departure: 9am. Travel time: 4 hours. Fare: $5.

To Manzanillo: Departure: 5:25pm. Travel time: 6 hours. Fare: $5.75. The 408 train also stops at **Bayamo** *(4 hours; $4)*, **Jiguani** *(3 hours 30 minutes; $3)*, and **Contramestre** *(3 hours; $2.50)*.

By Bus

The **Estación de Omnibus Interprovinciales**, on Avenida de los Libertadores (near Avenida de Las Américas), is usually packed. You can easily purchase tickets for Guantánamo or Bayamo on the day of your departure. For other destinations, however, it is better to buy your tickets a few days in advance unless you show up to purchase a ticket directly from **Víazul**.

To Havana: Departure: 7:30pm. Fare: $42.

To Matanza: Departure: 3:20pm (every other day). Fare: $37.

To Cienfuegos: Departure: 4pm (every other day). Fare: $25.

To Santa Clara: Departure: 4pm (every other day). Fare: $22.

To Camagüey: Departures: 2:30pm and 6:30pm. Fare: $35.

To Banes: Departure: 7am (every other day). Fare: $9.

To Moa: Departure: 7:20am (every other day). Fare: $12.

To Manzanillo: Departure: 8am. Fare: $9.

To Bayamo: Departures: 6am, 10:50am, 1:20pm and 3:30pm. Fare: $6.

To Guantánamo: Departures: 5:20am, 11:20am, 12:45pm and 5:15pm. Fare: $3.

To Holguín: Departure: 1:30pm (every other day). Fare: $7.50.

Víazul only runs to **Havana** from Santiago. Departures are every afternoon at 4pm. The trip takes about 16 hours and costs $51, which is admittedly more expensive than the train or the regular bus, but is infinitely more comfortable. In fact, the Víazul fleet is known for its air-conditioned buses and padded reclining seats. It may also be cheaper to take the route via **Holguín, Camagüey, Ciego de Avila** or **Santa Clara.**

By Taxi

Cabs belonging to the **Turistaxi** fleet are usually parked in front of local hotels.

Turistaxi: Aeropuerto Antonio Maceo, ☎9-2245; Hotel Balcón del Caribe, ☎9-1011; Hotel Casa Granda, ☎8-6107; Hotel San Juan, ☎4-2474.

By Taxi *Particulares*

The less expensive *particulares* taxis are usually unauthorized, although a new regulation went into effect in 1996, enabling more and more drivers to obtain their taxi license. These drivers usually wait outside the **Estación de Trenes**, on Avenida La Alameda, and the **Estación de Omnibus Interprovinciales.** Plaza Martes is another good place to find *particulares*.

The fares vary greatly depending on the driver and how you look. Remember that most drivers try to charge tourists at least twice the standard fare so be prepared to bargain. Within city limits, don't pay more than $3 per car during daytime and $5 per car in the evening or at night.

A ride to the beaches in **Daïquirí** and **Siboney**, east of town, should be $12 per car. You'll need the driver to take you back into town as well, so ask him to wait for you outside the tourist facilities on the shore. Cubans are not permitted on these beaches; so if you'd rather invite your driver to come with you instead of having him wait, you'll have to buy him a $5 guest pass.

An excursion to **La Caridad del Cobre** takes half a day and costs about $12 per car (return).

Car Rental

Cubacar: Carretera Autopista, Km 2.5, ☎4-1787 or 4-2714.

Havanautos: Aeropuerto Internacional Antonio Maceo, ☎9-1873;
Hotel Las Américas, ☎4-1338;
Motel San Juan, ☎4-1121.

All the hotels on the beaches east of Santiago offer car rental services.

By Bicycle

The Hotel Las Américas rents out bicycles for $1 an hour. However, Santiago de Cuba is very hilly, so cycling is not the easiest way to get around here. The old sections are best explored on foot.

Bayamo

By Plane

The **Aeropuerto Carlos Manuel de Céspedes** is located on the road to Holguín, four kilometres from downtown Bayamo. This little airport offers a few flights to **Havana** *($82; Mon and Thu, 10:45am departure; every other Fri, 4:15pm departure; every other Sat and every other Sun, 11am departure)*.

By Train

Estación de Trenes: Calle Linca, between Plaza Luis Ramirez Lopez and Calle Figueredo.

To Santiago de Cuba: Departures: 9:50am and 4:10pm. Fare: $4.

To Havana: Departure: 11:10pm. Fare: $26.
To Manzanillo: Departures: 6:20am, 10:24am, 2:32pm and 6pm. Fare: $2.

To Camagüey: Departure: 4:20am. Fare: $6.

By Bus

Estación de Omnibus Provinciales: Carretera Central, Via Santiago No. 395.

To Manzanillo: Departures: 6:30am, 9am, 2pm and 5:30pm. Fare: $1.80.

To Holguín: Departures: 6:10am and 3:10pm. Fare: $2.

To Bartolmé Masó: Departures: 7:40am and 5:10pm. Fare: $1.30.

The **Estación de Omnibus Nacionales**, a few metres away on the same side of the Carretera Central Via Santiago, offers bus service to the major Cuban cities.

To Havana: Departure: 8pm. Fare: $36.

To Santiago de Cuba: Departures: 6:20am and 2pm. Fare: $5.

Guantánamo: Departure: 7:50am. Fare: $16.20.

Manzanillo

By Plane

The Manzanillo airport offers one weekly flight to **Havana** *($82; Mon, 2:35pm; every other Sun, 11am)*.

By Train

Trains run from the **Estación de Trenes de Manzanillo**.

To Santiago de Cuba: Departure: 2:10pm. Fare: $5.75.

To Havana: Departure: 9pm. Fare: $28.

To Bayamo: Departures three times a day. Fare: $1.70.

By Bus

Buses run from the **Estación de Omnibus Nacionales**.

To Santiago de Cuba: Departure: 2:20pm. Fare: $7.50.

To Havana: Departure: 8pm. Fare: $39.

To Bayamo: Departures: 6am, 9am, 3pm and 4:30pm. Fare: $1.70.

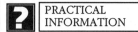

PRACTICAL INFORMATION

Tourist Information

The **Infotours** *(every day 8am to 8pm; Calle Heredia, at the corner of Calle San Pedro, ☎2-2222)* tourist office is located on Plaza de la Catedral.

Currency Exchange

The **Banco Financiero Internacional** *(Calle Felix Peña, one block east of Parque Céspedes)* offers the best rates for converting your money into American dollars. The rates at the local hotels are generally competitive as well.

Medical Care

Clinica Internacional de Santiago de Cuba : Calle 13 at the corner of Av. 14, reparto Vista Allegre, ☎4-2589, ☎33-5015 ext.3011.

Hopital Saturnino Lora: Avenida de Los Libertadores.

Policlínico Camilo Torres: Calle Heredia, at the corner of Calle Valientes.

Safety

Santiago de Cuba has not escaped the resurgence of crime that has recently marked the country, especially in large towns and resort areas. Although there is no cause for alarm, make sure to take the usual precautions.

Jineteros are also on the prowl in Santiago. These local youths find ingenious ways of extracting a few dollars from tourists, claiming they need money to care for their ailing mother, or offering a box of cigars in exchange. This practice is relatively common in Santiago, though not nearly as widespread as in Havana. The methods are more subtle here, and most *jineteros* will try to get what they want by befriending you. Certain ill-intentioned individuals manage to use their friendly nature to exploit the country's economic problems. Unfortunately, unpleasant situations commonly arise between tourists and Santiagueros. You may well be robbed once you start feeling too much at ease and forget to keep a close eye on your belongings.

 EXPLORING

Santiago de Cuba ★★★

The natural place to start exploring Santiago de Cuba, which has preserved more of its typical colonial wrought-iron balconies and doors than any other town in the country, is **Parque Céspedes ★★★**. The monument in the centre of this former parade ground is dedicated to the park's namesake, Manuel Céspedes, considered the "father of the country". A major 19th-century landowner and sugar producer, he freed his slaves and then joined his country's struggle for independence.

Towering over Parque Céspedes is the **Santa Iglesia Basílica ★★**, one of the oldest cathedrals in Cuba, built in 1522 and restored in 1932. This classical cathedral is topped by a superb sculpture, the *Angel of the Annunciation*, which stands between two tall, domed bell towers. The interior is made entirely of carved wood and houses an ecclesiastical museum where several manuscripts dating from the early days of colonization are on display.

On the west side of the square, the **Hotel Casa Granda ★★**, with its charming raised terrace, beckons to travellers at all hours of the day and night. Sitting here with a cigar in one hand and a seven-year-old *ron añejo* in the other, you can relive the era when Graham Greene stayed at the hotel to write part of *Our Man in Havana*.

On the east side of the square, the **Casa Diego Velázquez ★★★** *($1; Mon to Fri 9am to 1pm; Calle Felix Peña No. 610)*, a veritable masterpiece of colonial architecture, was erected in 1515 for Diego Velásquez and has withstood the ravages of time. The extraordinary interior boasts the original carved-wood furnishings, ceiling and balconies, while warm pastel tones on the walls and an abundance of luxuriant plants on the patio add to the delightful surroundings. The house is now home to the **Casa Museo Ambiente Histórico Cubano**, a museum that recreates various colonial interiors using period furniture and decorations.

The **Museo Del Carnaval ★★** *($1; Tue to Sun 9am to 5pm, Sat until 9pm; Calle Heredia No. 303, at the corner of Calle Pío Rosado)*, set up inside an 18th-century house whose walls, roofs and floors have all been maintained in their original state, retraces the history of Santiago's Carnaval. This 400-year-old annual festival was once known as the *Fiesta de Mamarchos*. The first room in the museum is devoted to the colonial era, and contains some magnificent masks and costumes and a number of period photographs. Another room displays all the instruments traditionally used during the celebrations (*tumba francesca, conga, corneta china*, etc.). A visit to this museum is sure to make you feel like returning to Santiago for the Carnaval itself!

Next, walk up Calle Carniceria, one block north, then take Calle Aguilera

SANTIAGO DE CUBA & THE SIERRA MAESTRA

Making Rum

In the old Bacardi factory in Santiago de Cuba, now known as the Ron Caney, the first step in making rum is to extract the molasses from sugar cane. This molasses is fermented to produce a liquid with an alcohol content of 95%, which is then diluted with distilled water in copper barrels. Next, the alcohol is decanted into another set of copper barrels and mixed with almonds and caramel to give it its characteristic flavour and colour. This blend is decanted yet again, this time into barrels made of Canadian white oak and aged for one to 25 years. Afterward, it is filtered and sampled, then left to settle for 15 days in copper barrels to make sure there will be no sediment in the finished product. Finally, the rum is bottled, thus becoming the favourite companion in both joy and sorrow of the Cuban population.

south to the **Museo Provincial Emilio Bacardi Moreau ★★★** *($2; Tue to Sat 9am to 9pm, Mon 3pm to 9pm, Sun 9am to 4pm, Calle Pío Rosado, at the corner of Calle Aguilera, ☎2-8402)*. This art museum is a legacy of the well-known rum-maker Emilio Bacardi. The first mayor of Santiago under the Republic of 1902, he used his fortune to acquire numerous objects of historical interest, works of art and archaeological artifacts. Founded in 1899, the Museo Bacardi is considered the oldest museum in Cuba. The present building was begun in 1920 and inaugurated in 1927. On the ground floor are there is a collection of historical objects dating from the Spanish conquest up to the war of 1895; on the second floor are a collection of paintings from Europe and Santiago and sculptures and artifacts found on Cuban, Central American and Egyptian archaeological sites. Most memorable, however, is the amazing outdoor replica of a street in colonial Santiago, which looks like a movie set; this little lane leads to a patio and a well behind the museum. In many ways this is one of the best museums in the country.

Natural science buffs can stop by the **Museo Tomás Romays** *($1; Tue to Sun 9am to 5pm, Sun 9am to 1pm; Calle Enramada no. 601, at the corner of* *Calle Barnabás, ☎2-3277)*, a sizeable museum with one room entirely devoted to Cuban flora and fauna. The *Centro Oriental de Ecosistemas y Biodiversidad*, whose offices are located in this building, organizes regular excursions to the Sierra Maestra (see p 249) and will also do so on request.

La Alameda

The Avenida Jesús Menéndez, better known by its former name, La Alameda, runs past the port and the train station. It is always very busy, as cyclists compete with cars and trucks for a piece of the road.

Most of the buildings along it date from the end of the previous century and house various enterprises typical of Santiago, the most famous being **Ron Caney** *(free admission; Avenida Jesús Menéndez, between San Antonio and San Ricardo, ☎2-5576)*, where Bacardi rum was produced. You can tour this factory with a guide who will explain how rum, that quintessentially Cuban beverage, is made. A lot of tour groups come here in the morning, and joining up with one is a good way to visit the premises. This factory produces nine million litres of rum a year, 70% of which is exported.

Cubans are crazy about cars, and pre-1959 "American Beauties" like this one can still be seen on the streets.
- *Tibor Bognar*

An old man and his cat enjoying a tranquil siesta in the sun.
- *Jean Terroux*

The cigar industry is one of the mainstays of Cuba's economy.
- *Denis Drolet*

Motorcycles, like this one in front of the Museo Histórico de Guanabacoa, are a popular means of transportation in Cuba.
- *Jean Terroux*

In the province of Pinar del Río, huts with palm-thatched roofs dot the endless pastures. - *Tibor Bognar*

The 1950s are still alive in Cuba thanks to cars like this one from the days when Elvis was "King". - *Denis Drolet*

The Valle de Viñales, in the province of Pinar del Río, a verdant landscape of *mogotes* and quaint wooden houses. - *Tibor Bognar*

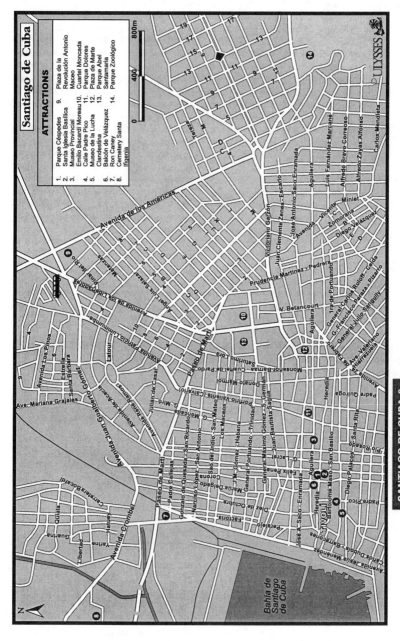

Santiago de Cuba

ATTRACTIONS

1. Parque Céspedes
2. Santa Iglesia Basílica
3. Museo Provincial
   Emilio Bacardí Moreau
4. Calle Padre Pico
5. Museo de la Lucha
   Clandestina
6. Balcón de Velázquez
7. Cementery Santa
   Ifigenia
8. Ron Caney
9. Plaza de la
   Revolución Antonio
   Maceo
10. Cuartel Moncada
11. Parque Dolores
12. Plaza de Marte
13. Parque Abel
    Santamaría
14. Parque Zoológico

Bahía de
Santiago
de Cuba

© ULYSSES

You can also visit the **Fábrica de Tabacos César Escalante** *(free admission; Mon to Sat 7:30am to 11:30am and noon to 4pm; Calle Jesús Menéndez, between Calle Aguilera and Calle Aduana)*, located in front of the clock that rises up in the middle of La Alameda. Here, you can watch craftsmen making the cigars for which Cuba is renowned. There is also a small sales outlet where all different types and brands of cigars can be purchased.

A few hundred metres northwest of La Alameda lies one of the most famous cemeteries, listed as a national monument. Founded in 1878, the **Cementerio Santa Ifigenia** *($1; every day 8am to 8pm; Calle Raúl Perozo, ☎3-2723)* contains the tombs of some of Cuba's best known personages, including José Martí; Mariana Grajales, mother of independence fighter General Antonio Maceo; Carlos Manuel de Céspedes; Emilio Bacardi and Miguel Matamoros, creator of *son*, the rhythm on which all Cuban music is based. During a long walk in this vast cemetery, far from the hubbub of the city, you can enjoy some peace and quiet and admire monuments in various architectural styles ranging from neoclassical to Art Deco. Guided tours are available.

Calle Padre Pico ★★

Calle Padre Pico is Santiago's most typical street. In a series of curves and hills, it plunges into the working-class neighbourhood of Tivolí via a long flight of stairs, the local children's favourite playground. This area was founded and inhabited by French settlers who arrived in Santiago de Cuba starting in 1791. It has served as the setting for numerous films and is a hot spot during Carnaval.

Climb the stairs to Calle Santa Rita, where you'll spy the **Museo de la Lucha Clandestina** ★★ *($1; Tue to Sun 9am to 5pm; 1 Calle General Rabi, ☎2-4689)* at the top of a hill, housed in a superb, early-18th-century colonial residence that was lived in by a succession of wealthy Santiago families. It served as a police station from 1951 to 1956, during which time it was attacked by the rebels of the *Movimiento 26 de Julio* under Frank País, thus earning it a place in Cuban history. The rebels' goal was to ensure the safe landing of the *Granma*, the yacht carrying Fidel Castro, Che Guevara and the other revolutionaries, by diverting the attention of the Cuban army. The museum, which opened in 1976, is dedicated to the rebels of the *Movimiento 26 de Julio* and displays photographs, uniforms and an assortment of other objects. Frank País's life story, from his birth right up until his death in 1957, is also recounted in great detail.

It is pleasant to stroll about in the Tivolí area, exploring the winding streets and taking in scenes of day-to-day life here. Amateur photographers will be thrilled by all the local activity, the dilapidated old houses and the antiquated air of the place, which gives it its own subtle charm. Retrace your steps from the Museo de la Lucha Clandestina, but don't go back down the stairs. You'll come to Calle Bartolomé Masó, a typical pebbled street, and then, right nearby, the **Balcón de Velásquez** ★ with its arched entryway. This lookout commands a view of the bay and once served as a watchtower to monitor the comings and goings of ships.

From Avenida Las Américas to the Cuartel Moncada

One of the largest avenues in Santiago de Cuba is flanked by the buildings of the Universidad de Oriente, the

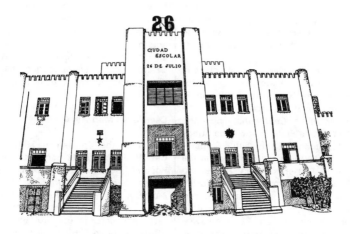

Museo 26 de Julio

Instituto Superior de Constucción, the Villa Panamericana and the Estadio de Vasebal Guillermo Moncada, which can hold about 25,000 spectators. The neighbouring Teatro Heredia, the biggest and most modern theatre in the country, was built in 1991, has a seating capacity of nearly 2,500 and is used primarily for variety shows.

Opposite the Teatro Heredia lies the vast **Plaza de la Revolución Antonio Maceo ★**, where the region's major political and cultural gatherings are held. An imposing statue of Cuban freedom fighter General Antonio Maceo occupies the place of honour on the square. This equestrian monument is surrounded by 23 machetes, a reference to March 23, 1878, the date when the struggle for independence was resumed. An eternal flame burns atop one of the columns behind the statue. The **Sala de Exposición Holográfica** *($1; Mon to Sat 9am to 5pm; Sun 9am to 1pm; at the corner of the Carretera Central and Avenida Las Américas)* beneath the monument presents a collection of holograms of

guns, uniforms and various objects related to the rebellions that led to the Revolution of 1959.

Follow Avenida de los Libertadores, which is lined with busts of the principal freedom fighters in the Latin American wars of independence. The statues were put here in 1995 to replace the busts of well-known members of the Santiago bourgeoisie, which were removed from their pedestals when Castro claimed victory. The first of these monuments is located towards the rear of the famous **Cuartel Moncada ★★**, easily recognizable by its yellow and red walls. The building is now known as the Ciudad Escolar 26 de Julio and houses the **Museo 26 de Julio** *($1; Mon to Sat 9am to 5pm; Sun 9am to 1pm; Avenida Moncada, at the corner of Calle General Portuondo, ☎2-0157)*. Built by the Spanish in 1859, the fortress originally bore the name Reina Mercedes and served as a prison and barracks. Once the Republic was established at the turn of the century, it was renamed the Cuartel Moncada after a general who was imprisoned here during the war of independence. Destroyed by fire in 1936, it was reconstructed under Batista, who was the head of the Cuban army at the time.

The Cuartel Moncada took its place in modern Cuban history on July 26, 1953 when it was attacked by an as yet unknown political group, the *Generación del Centenario*, under the orders of one Fidel Castro. The attack was launched while the city's Carnaval was in full swing. At 5 o'clock in the morning, 120 armed men, all wearing Cuban army uniforms, spread confusion amongst the prison guards. The real army, however, responded swiftly; 6 rebels were killed and 55 others were apparently tortured and assassinated the same day inside the fortress. Castro managed to flee eastward, but was captured a few days later in the **Granjita Siboney** (see p 246). Since 1959, the Cuartel Moncada has been used as a school, which explains all the children running about the grounds. Smiling and playful in their red and white uniforms, they often outshine the museum, which focuses on Cuba's periods of conflict, from those involving the country's indigenous peoples in the colonial era right up to the present day, with particular emphasis on the history of the Cuartel Moncada. Many original documents and photographs are on display, along with bloodied uniforms and some of the rebels' personal belongings.

There is one monument in **Parque Abel Santamaria**: a fountain topped by a large, concrete block bearing the images of José Martí and the park's namesake, a Santiago rebel assassinated by the Cuban army while he was preparing for the Revolution. The park itself has been somewhat neglected, but the **Museo Abel Santamaria** *($1; Mon to Sat 9am to 5pm, Sun 8am to 2pm;* ☎2-4119) lies behind it, in the former hospital where Castro gave his famous speech, *La Historia Me Absolverá*. The museum contains a small number of photographs and presents historical data on the period leading up to the Revolution, elucidating Castro's views on education, health care, the economy and poverty.

Castillo del Morro ★★

Begun by the Spanish in 1640, the **Castillo del Morro de San Pedro de la Roca** *($1.50; Mon to Fri 9am to 5pm, Sat and Sun 8am to 4pm; Carretera del Morro, Km 7,* ☎9-1569) was used to protect the city of Santiago from pirates and corsairs up until the early 18th century. In 1662, while it was still under construction, it was attacked by the English. Assisted by Jamaican corsairs, the head of the English fleet, Christopher Myns, took possession of the fortress for a month before he withdrew from Santiago. The English attempted to recapture the castle in the 18th century, but their efforts were in vain.

One of the finest fortresses in Cuba, the Castillo del Morro features a blend of medieval and Renaissance styles. Its beauty is set off by its natural surroundings; the sea and the mountains. The overall effect is quite impressive. The fort is also the perfect spot from which to take in the magnificent spectacle of the sun setting over the Caribbean. The Spanish chose this site because it lies at the mouth of the bay, 70 metres above sea-level on a hill that serves as a natural fortification. During the wars of independence in the 19th century, the Castillo was used as a prison. Among the *mambises* incarcerated here were General Flor Crombet and Emilio Bacardi, the founder and owner of the *ronera* bearing his name.

The Castillo saw its final moments of glory on July 17, 1898, when the famous naval battle between the American and Spanish fleets in the Bahía de Santiago was fought here. Following this conflict, the Spanish lost both Cuba and Puerto Rico, the last of their colonial territories in the Americas. The fortress fell into the hands of the Americans, who maintained control over it until January 25, 1904, at which point it was returned to the Cuban artillery. From 1920 until the Revolution, the fort was completely abandoned. Restorations were begun in the 1960s, but it wasn't until 1978 that the **Museo de la Piratería ★** *(same hours as the Castillo)*, located inside the castle, was opened to the public. The museum presents a relatively thorough overview of the history of corsairs and pirates in the Caribbean and Latin America. Maps, drawings and a few relics serve to illustrate the tale of these adventurers who once ruled the roost in this part of the world. The written commentary is all in Spanish; you should take a guided tour to fully appreciate the exhibition.

To get to the Castillo del Morro, take the Carretera del Morro, the same road that leads to the airport. There are several hills on this road, and the local kids regularly hold bike races here. Many of them lie flat on their stomachs on their bicycles in order to go as fast as possible. Another option is to take the Carretera Ciudad Mar, a scenic highway that runs alongside the Bahía de Santiago. Off in the distance, you'll see Isla Granma, a small island inhabited by fishermen and formerly known as Cayo Smith, the name of the American who used to own it.

El Cobre ★★

The **Sanctuario Nacional a Nuestra Señora de la Caridad del Cobre** is the most revered pilgrimage site in the country. There is something magical about the way this pastel-coloured church suddenly springs into view as you make your way along the road about 15 kilometres northwest of Santiago. Graced with two bell towers, it stands proudly atop a verdant hill. A symbol of the region, it attracts large numbers of pilgrims from all over the country. The object of all this devotion is the Black Virgin of the Caridad del Cobre, the patron saint of Cuba. There is a statue of her in a small display case above the altar (no photographs allowed). Her legend dates back to the early days of colonization, when she appeared to some local fishermen. The Black Virgin is worshipped fervently, for she is believed to have miraculous healing powers. At the entrance to the church, you'll see all sorts of objects, such as crutches, souvenirs from the war in Angola and, oddly enough, a few articles owned by members of the Revolutionary Armed Forces. The building itself has simple, classical architecture and a bare interior with wooden confessionals and balustrades and some marble decoration.

A stroll around the area offers some excellent photo opportunities of the church. Upon your arrival, you'll be swarmed by children trying to give you gifts of small stones. Of course, they expect some change in return. Getting out of your car under these conditions can prove to be quite a feat of acrobatics!

East of Santiago

The scenic road that runs along the east coast of Santiago is a visual feast of mountain- and seascapes. It leads to the Gran Piedra, a perfect mountain for hiking (see p 250), and to the beaches of Siboney, Daïquirí and Baconao (see p 248). Along the way, you'll see numerous monuments dedicated to the

SANTIAGO DE CUBA & THE SIERRA MAESTRA

Sanctuario Nacional a Nuestra Señora de la Caridad del Cobre

rebels who perished in this region while beating a retreat after the failed attack on the Cuartel Moncada on July 26, 1953.

The **Granjita Siboney** *($1; every day 9am to 5pm; Carretera de Siboney, Km 13.5, ☎3-9836)*, located 16 kilometres from Santiago de Cuba, is the house where the rebels gathered before the assault on the Cuartel Moncada, and where they hid their weapons and uniforms. Although the attack was unsuccessful, a few of the rebels, including Fidel Castro, managed to return here safe and sound. It was from this house that they fled into the mountains, where they were captured six days later. The Granjita contains photocopies of genuine documents from that period, as well as cars, weap-

ons and uniforms used by the rebels. You can also see the well in which the weapons were hidden.

The **Valle de la Prehistoria** *($1; every day 9am to 5pm)* is a park containing lifelike concrete replicas of dinosaurs. This place will thrill youngsters and fans of the Jurassic period.

The **Acuario de Baconao** *($3; Tue to Sun 8am to 5pm; ☎3-5145)* is an aquarium that presents dolphin and sea-lion shows for tourists staying in the hotels along the coast. Two dolphins perform flips to Hawaiian music. There are three shows a day, at 10:15am, 11:30am and 2:45pm. Visitors can also observe sharks and dolphins from a 30-metre-long glassed-in tunnel under the pool. To round things out, there is a small marine museum. A sure hit with children.

The Sierra Maestra

Bayamo

One of the oldest *villas*, or towns, in Cuba is now nicknamed the "city of carriages", since local residents never stopped using these vehicles and hundreds of them can be seen peacefully winding along the streets. Bayamo was founded in 1513 by the Spanish conqueror Diego Velásquez. It has a rather complex layout, since it was designed like a labyrinth to ward off pirate attacks, even though it is located too far from the sea to have been in any real danger.

Over the centuries, Bayamo's residents prospered by smuggling in finished products from France and Holland, obtained in exchange for meat and leather up until the 17th century. The town then experienced a relatively uneventful period until the wars of independence, when it became a hub of nationalist conspiracy. In fact, it was a local musician, Manuel Muñoz Cedeño, who wrote Cuba's national anthem. Bayamo can also pride itself on being the first town in the country to abolish slavery (December 17, 1868). Unfortunately, only a few colonial buildings remain, because General de Céspedes ordered the nationalists to set fire to the town before relinquishing it to the Spanish on January 12, 1869. Today, you can start off your tour of Bayamo at the former Parque Céspedes, now the **Plaza de la Revolúcion**; a statue of the general stands in the middle. This square is extremely pleasant, beckoning to passers-by to relax on a bench in the shade of an old tree.

On Calle Maceo, in front of the park, the **Casa Natal Carlos Manuel de Céspedes** *(free admission; Tue to Sat 9am to 5pm, Sun 9am to 1pm)*, the general's birthplace, has been converted into a museum. Unfortunately, the building itself has not been kept up. Nevertheless, you can see a few of Céspedes's personal documents, including a copy of the *Cubano Libre*, the newspaper he published after taking possession of the town.

In the neighbouring house, the **Museo Provincial Granma** *($1; Tue to Sun, 8:15am to 6pm; Calle Maceo)* contains a small collection of objects related to the history of the province of Granma. It was in this house that Manuel Muñoz Cedeño composed the Cuban national anthem.

Follow Calle Maceo to the baroque **Iglesia San Salvador de Bayamo**, which has been destroyed several times over the centuries. The present structure dates from the 18th century and stands near the **Plaza del Himno**, which is graced with the most beautiful colonial architecture in Bayamo. Here you'll find the pretty, white **Casa de la Nacionalidad**, the residence of Bayamo's official historian who will be happy to guide you through the town's maze of streets. The house has several lovely rooms and a small yard that looks out onto the Río Bayamo.

Slightly removed from the historic section, on the banks of the Río Bayamo, the **Museo Ñico Lopez** *($1; Tue to Sat 9am to 5pm; Calle Aviqail)* is devoted to one of the revolutionaries who helped the Castroist cause, and focuses on the attack he led on this building, a former military barracks.

SANTIAGO DE CUBA & THE SIERRA MAESTRA

Manzanillo

After Bayamo, the road leads through endless fields of sugar cane and runs alongside the mountains of the Sierra Maestra, where you can head south to Bartolomé Masó and Fidel Castro's former hideout (see p 250). Located 60 kilometres from Bayamo, Manzanillo presents a spectacular sight from the top of the hill where the road starts plunging down toward the sea; the tiled roofs of the houses spread out like a mosaic below.

Manzanillo was founded around 1513 near the Río Yara, the longest river in Cuba (370 km), which was navigable in the 16th century. It was already an important town in the 16th century, since its port was used to bring in smuggled goods bound for Bayamo. In 1570, however, pirates and corsairs began to harass local residents. According to historical records, a French pirate named Filibert Giron attacked the town in 1600 and held the parish priest for ransom. Things turned around, however, when the townspeople managed to liberate the prisoner and capture the villain. In the 19th century, Manzanillo was attacked by pirates yet again; then, in 1882, the last cargo of slaves passed through its port. Sugar production in the area was stepped up, and the town prospered as a result of its commerce with Bayamo. Manzanillo is also where the first Cuban work of literature, *Espejo de la Pasión*, was written by Silvestre de Balboa in 1792.

Today, Manzanillo is a small, peaceful town where you can enjoy a pleasant stroll along typical little streets, wandering wherever your curiosity leads you. In Parque Céspedes, the central square, the **Museo Historico Municipal** *($1; Tue to Sat 8am to noon and 2pm to 6pm, Sun 8am to noon; Calle Martí No. 226)* has four galleries. It retraces the history of Manzanillo and exhibits several pre-Columbian artifacts.

The **Glorietta** ★ in the centre of Parque Céspedes was inaugurated on June 24, 1924. The symbol of Manzanillo, this little pavilion of Moorish inspiration is an almost exact replica of the one on the Patio de los Leones in Granada, in Andalusia. The local *malecón*, or boardwalk, is by no means the prettiest one in the country, but it leads to the old parts of town.

Twenty kilometres southwest of Manzanillo lies the **Parque Nacional Demajagua**, where Carlos Manuel de Céspedes freed his slaves on October 10, 1868, so that they could join in the battle against the Spanish. It is now home to a small museum dedicated to that era. Outside, you'll see a cogwheel from the old sugar factory.

PARKS AND BEACHES

Santiago de Cuba

A huge sign on the highway indicates the entrance to **Playa Siboney**, which is frequented mainly by local residents. The beach is not very sandy, so bring along a pair of sandles.

A 200-metre mountain trail leads from the Hotel Daïquiri to **Playa Daïquiri ★★**, also known as Playa Bibijagua. One of the prettiest beaches in the region, this is a snorkeller's paradise.

Playa Bucanero ★ is a small, isolated beach on a bay. Not only is it hard to find a place to lie down here during the high season, but the swimming conditions are not the best.

A quick, simple and inexpensive way to reach this area is to hire a *particular* taxi in Santiago (see p 236).

Laguna Baconao ★

Located about 100 kilometres east of Santiago de Cuba, at the end of the road that leads past the beaches in the Siboney region, is the **Laguna Baconao ★**. Fresh water and salt water blend in this large lagoon, attracting an unusual assortment of wildlife, including crocodiles. Baconao means "son of the tree" in the language of the Taïnos, who inhabited this region before the Spanish arrived. Today, the lagoon is a favourite spot for fishing expeditions; packages are available at the tourist offices in the local hotels.

The Laguna Baconao is part of the Parque Baconao, the country's largest nature reserve, which stretches across the mountains of the Sierra Maestra. The lagoon is not, however, the best starting point from which to explore the park's main attractions, such as the Pico Turquino and the Comandancia de la Plata (see p 250). East of the Laguna Bacanoa, an unfinished, poorly maintained road leads to Guantánamo.

The Sierra Maestra

The province of Granma is the starting point for some of the most extraordinary mountain outings that Cuba has to offer. The **Villa Santo Domingo** (see p 254), at the end of the road south of the village of Bartolomé Masó, can be your base camp. The road there leads through a series of magnificent mountain landscapes: south of Bartolomé Masó, you'll pass through picturesque little villages where women casually wash clothes in small streams and young shepherds go about their daily

chores. This is an entirely different side of Cuba, no doubt the one the revolutionaries knew better than anyone else, since it is here that they set up camp, taking advantage of the silence and the cooperation of these isolated rural folk.

The first and longest excursion is the trip up **Pico Turquino ★★★**, the highest peak in the country. See the "Hiking" section for more details, p 250.

A trip through the Alto del Naranjo provides an opportunity not only to explore some beautiful countryside but also to see a part of Cuban history. The Comandancia de la Plata is a veritable pilgrimage site for some. See the "Hiking" section (see below) for more information.

OUTDOOR ACTIVITIES

Hiking

Santiago de Cuba

The **Centro Oriental de Ecosystemas y Biodiversidad** *(Museo Tomás Romays, Calle Enramada No. 601, at the corner of Barnabás, ☎2-3277)* organizes excursions in the Sierra Maestra on request, and also provides specialized guides, transportation, accommodations, and anything else necessary for scientific expeditions in the mountains near Santiago de Cuba. Even ordinary travellers can embark on this type of expedition. You can also go to the centre simply to ask for advice or information.

The **Finca Juan Gonzalez** *(20 km west of the city, on the Carretera Mar Verde)* makes for a lovely day of walking not far from Santiago. Pretty fields lie along the hills of the Sierra Maestra. You may even end up eating in the company of some farmers, although it is recommended to bring food along since they don't always have any. It would be hard to find a more enchanting place in which to have a picnic. If you can't make it to the Pico Turquino, this little daytrip is nevertheless very rewarding.

Parque de la Gran Piedra ★★

The Parque de la Gran Piedra is one of the few easily accessible places in Cuba where you can go hiking in the mountains. The exit for the Gran Piedra is well signed out on the Carretera de Siboney, about 15 kilometres east of Santiago. You can drive almost to the top of the mountain (1,200 m), which is traversed by hiking trails. The park contains several old French coffee plantations and offers some lovely general views of the region. Although you won't need more than a day to explore the mountain, you can camp here overnight if you like.

The Sierra Maestra

This 13-kilometre climb up **Pico Turquino** ★★★ is best undertaken in two days. A number of rustic cabins halfway up the mountain are at hikers' disposal; it is wise to spend the first night here and then make the rest of the trip the following morning, leaving everything but absolute essentials behind. Hikers are also strongly advised to hire a guide at the Villa Santo Domingo (see p 254).

A trip to the Alto del Naranjo and the **Comandancia de la Plata** ★★★ is a real thrill for anyone with an interest in the Cuban Revolution. A veritable pilgrimage site for communists from around the world, especially members of Cuba's Communist Youth Movement, this region offers visitors a chance to plunge into the jungle on the same dirt trails used by Fidel Castro,

Che Guevara and Camilo Cienfuegos in the late 1950s. The best way to go is to enlist the services of Rubén, now 58, who joined in the Revolution at this very spot when he was only 18. He can tell you all sorts of historical anecdotes about the heros of the Revolution. You'll find him at the Villa Santo Domingo, where he is the groundskeeper.

It is best to drive the last five kilometres of the road, which climbs very steeply after the Villa Santo Domingo. It is then a relatively easy three-kilometre hike to the Comandancia de la Plata. On the way, at a point where the mountainside trail takes an unexpected turn, Rubén told me about the time when he went to the Comandancia de la Plata with Che Guevara. *"It was nighttime and Che's mule was stuck in the mud. In his efforts to get the animal moving, Che fell straight into the gully and the mule stayed put on the trail. After climbing back up, Che said, 'You see, the mule is much smarter than I am!'"*

After hiking for one kilometre, you'll reach the first stop on the itinerary, the **Campamento Medina** ★★. This was once a peasant's home where Castro asked permission to leave a few wounded men, including Che Guevara, who had injured his foot, while he built his camp two kilometres farther. Today, it is a military surveillance post — you will have to leave any camera equipment you have with you. Take a few moments to relax on the pleasant terrace looking out onto the valley before embarking on the last leg of the journey.

The trail continues and suddenly becomes much steeper as you head to a section that has remained unchanged since the Revolution. A staircase made of tree trunks stuck into the ground leads up to the Comandancia de la

Plata. Fidel Castro's house, concealed by lush tropical vegetation, is made of wood and is firmly planted on the mountainside. I'll let you find your own way to its secret door and then inside, where you'll see Castro's bed, his little kitchen and of course the makeshift table where he wrote out the orders which were transmitted all over the country. You'll certainly recognize the latter from the countless historic photographs seen the world-over in the not-so-distant past.

While you're here, you can also visit a small museum that provides an overview of the fighting that occurred in this region, venture over to the first *Radio Rebelde* station and explore a number of other houses in the paramilitary camp.

Snorkelling

Playa Daïquirí is the perfect place to take in some great underwater scenery. Don't forget to bring your own equipment, though.

Scuba Diving

The **Hotel Balneario del Sol** (*2-5949*), is about 50 kilometres east of Santiago, and charges $35 per dive.

ACCOMMODATIONS

Santiago de Cuba

Two downtown hotels are currently undergoing renovations. The **Libertad** (*Av. Aguilera No. 656, Plaza Marte*) is a mid-range hotel located in the downtown's east side, across from a park. The **Impérial** (*Av. Enmerada No. 251,* between Calles Felix Peña and Carniceria, *2-8917*) is being upgraded to become a high-class hotel whose prices should be similar to those of the Casa Grande once renovations are completed. The biggest challenge will be to conserve the colonial façade. Both hotels should reopen before the year 2000.

The **Hotel Rex** (*$18; ≡, pb, ℜ, ctv, ☎; Av. Victoriano Garzón No.710, second floor, nearby Parque Marte, *2-6314 or 5-3507*) is a ten minutes' walk from the cathedral, and offers an excellent price for accommodation. In fact, it has something of a reputation with foreign travellers who flock here. Rooms are bright, clean, comfortable and cheap, and the staff is friendly. Guests, which consists of a good mix of Cubans and foreigners, often meet up around the small bar on the first floor.

The capital of eastern Cuba abounds with commendable *casas particulares*. Two of them are especially noteworthy. First, that of **Armando Carballo Fernández** (*$20; ≡, sb; Calle Hartmann, also named San Felix, No. 306, between Av. J.M. Gomez and G. Portuondo, *2-8643 or 2-4961*). Unfortunately, it is often full, unless you make reservations a few days ahead. Armando and his wife, both of whom are doctors, are wonderful hosts who know how to put guests at ease, serving up a refreshing margarita as a welcoming drink. The impeccably clean, white rooms are bit reminiscent of a hospital, but are more comfortable and have air conditioning. Another excellent casa is that belonging to **Magdalena Grau Carbonell** (*$15; ≡, sb; Calle Aguilera No. 772, between Av. Pizarro and Trocha*), close to the Parque Marte. The location is not as central, but the cozy rooms and homey atmosphere make for a lovely stay. The house is close to the park, on one of Santiago's many hills.

Originally a hotel for Cubans, the **Hotel Venus** *($30; Calle Hartmann, also named San Felix, between Avenidas Aguilera and Heredia, ☎2-2178)* has sparsely furnished rooms of rather dubious cleanliness. You might be able to stay here if you are low on money and don't look like a tourist, which means putting away both travel guide and camera! Note that this place, in the heart of sweltering Santiago, does not have any air conditioning, so be ready to deal with a few discomforts in order to save a few pesos.

Balcón del Caribe *($35-$42; ≡, ≈, pb, ℜ, ctv, ☎; Carretera del Morro 7.5 km ☎9-1011)* attract legions of travellers to this idyllic setting only a few metres from the fortifications of the *Castillo del Morro*. The 72 rooms in 22 bungalows are soberly furnished and uncluttered, although in need of some decorating. To make up for this, there is a splendid pool surrounded by palm tree at the back of the hotel, right on the Caribbean Sea. The promontory offers a grand view. Complementing the whole is a delightful bar and restaurant (see p 255). Those wishing to avoid the bustle of Santiago can certainly find refuge here.

There are many houses and rooms for rent in Santiago de Cuba. Head over to the **Casa de Tamara** *(118 Calle Jaguey, between Calle 10 de Octubre and Calle Padre Pico, ☎2-0550)*, whose owner will help you find a place to stay or give you a tour of her charming house.

The **Hotel Las Américas** *($50-$67; ≡, ctv, pb, ℜ, ≈; Avenida Las Américas, at the corner of Calle General Cebreo, ☎4-2011, ⌐86075)* is popular with people who are travelling on a shoestring budget and prefer to stay in a hotel rather than a private home. The clientele consists largely of young travellers and Latin American tourists. The service is generally friendly and the atmosphere is pleasant and relaxed. The place is clean, and the rooms are small and simple. It is well located just a few minutes' walk from the historic centre. The hotel nightclub, the Havana Club, gets quite crowded at night. Pricewise, this is a good deal, although the breakfasts are a bit expensive.

The **Villa Gaviota** *($50-$55; ≡, ctv, ℝ, ≈; Avenida Manduley No. 502, between Calles 19 and 21, Vista Alegre, ☎4-1368)* is slightly removed from the centre of town, in the chic neighbourhood of Vista Alegra. This motel also has a group of lovely houses, an excellent option for groups or families.

The **Villa San Juan** *($53-64; ≡, ≈, pb, ℜ, ctv, ☎; Carretera to Siboney 1.5 km, ☎4-2478 or 4-2490)*, located just between the city and the coast, is a peaceful sanctuary. Obviously, its distance from downtown Santiago means you must take a taxi in order to get around, unless you have a car handy. Each room has a little balcony with a view of the trees stretching to the horizon. The villa is a beautiful building with good-sized rooms, and, even though it is not directly facing the sea, the large pool and welcoming 24-hour bar help ensure a wonderful stay nonetheless. Furthermore, various services are available for guests, such as $10 massages offered by a university graduate!

The appealing **Hotel Versailles** *($68-$80; ≡, ctv, ℜ, ℝ, pb, ≈; Carretera del Morro, Km 1, ☎9-1016 or 9-1504, ⌐8-6145)*, near the airport, has 60 rooms; the bungalows are especially popular with travellers. This peaceful place is surrounded by greenery, offering a compromise between the city and the countryside. The rooms, with their red-brick walls and ceilings made of precious wood, are pretty, but try to avoid the ones overlooking the road to the airport, which can be noisy.

The **Hotel Casa Granda** *($70-$90 bkfst incl.; ≡, pb, ctv, ℛ; Calle Heredia No. 201, corner of Calle General Lacret, ☎86-600, ≈86-035)* will set romantic hearts aflutter and seduce you with its colonial charm. Located in the middle of the historic district, at the edge of Parque Céspedes, this is the oldest hotel in Santiago and has a turn-of-the-century elegance. The Casa Granda has been completely renovated, and its two terraces, one on the ground floor, the other on the fifth, offer splendid panoramas of the city and the bay. The restaurant is refined, and serves delectable desserts (see p 255). The rooms are comfortable, with modern bathrooms. The best rooms have balconies facing the Parque Céspedes.

Unrivalled in Santiago, the 302-room **Hotel Santiago de Cuba** *($89-$113; ≡, ctv, pb, ≈, ℛ, minibar, ⊘, ⌂; Avenida Las Américas, corner of Calle M, ☎42634, ≈86-170)* contrasts architecturally with the rest of the city. The furnishings aren't aging well, and the place is somewhat impersonal on the whole. On the other hand, this hotel has all the amenities necessary for a comfortable stay, including a gym, a game room, a nightclub, a hairdressing salon, a sauna, three swimming pools and a bar with a panoramic view on the 15th floor.

East of Santiago

Foreign tourists are definitely in the minority at the **Camping Playa Larga** *(15 pesos; every day in Jun, Jul and Aug; Fri to Sun in winter)*, which is the perfect place for bargain hunters. You can either rent a bare, rustic cabin or set up your tent by the sea. The beach is not the best, and the unpredictable currents make it unsuitable for children. You can, however, walk over to **Playa Verraco**, a decent beach for swimming.

The campground staff organize a variety of activities, including excursions to the Juarnica grotto.

About 50 kilometres from Santiago, on the east tip of Baconao, the **Hotel Balneario del Sol** *($40; ≡, ℛ, pb, ctv, ≈; ☎2-5949 or 39-8113)* is a member of Canada's Delta hotel chain. Although it is located by the sea, it has no beach. Guests do, however, have access to a swimming pool and a natural pond. The hotel also offers scuba diving excursions.

The **Villa Daïquirí** *($41; ≡, ≈, ℛ, pb; Carretera Baconao, Km 8.5, ☎5-4016 or 2-4849)* is located right near a pretty beach where iguanas roam about, waiting with their legendary patience for you to give them a bit of food. The rooms are well-kept and the food is good. One of the best deals in the beach region.

The **Lookéa Carisol** *($50; everything included; ≡, ℛ, pb, ☎, ctv, ≈; ☎2-8519)* is also situated near the Laguna de Baconao. It is comprised of 100 rooms spread over 4 two-storey buildings set around a swimming pool, as well as 44 suites found in 11 cabins scattered through the park. There is always lots going on here, for young and old alike.

Nearer Santiago, the **Club Amigo Bucanero** *($134, everything included; ≡, ctv, ℛ, ≈; Carretera Baconao, Km 4, ☎2-7126 or 2-8130)* faces a small, isolated beach in a sandy bay flanked by a steep cliff. The place is magnificent, but has a few disadvantages: when the hotel is full, you'll have a hard time finding a spot to lie down on the beach, and the rocks make it dangerous to swim if the sea is the least bit rough. The hotel itself is comfortable and well run. All water sports (windsurfing, sailing, etc.) are included in the price of the room.

The Sierra Maestra

Bayamo

The **Hotel Sierra Maestra** *($18-41; ≈, pb, ≈, ℜ; Carretera Central Via Santiago)*, the only hotel in Bayamo, has a pleasant atmosphere, decent food and comfortable rooms.

Bartolomé Masó

The **Villa Santo Domingo** *($18 everything included; pb, ℜ)* is located at the end of the road south of the village. Hidden away in a valley, this hotel is made up of a series of bungalows and has recently begun welcoming foreign tourists. It is the ideal base camp for mountain excursions into the extraordinary Sierra Maestra. Guides can be hired here for hikes up Pico Turquino (see p 250) and to the Comandancia de la Plata (see p 250).

Manzanillo

The only good hotel in Manzanillo is the **Hotel Guacanayabo** *($27; ≈, pb, ≈, ℜ: Avenida Camilo Cienfuegos, ☎5-4012)*, located at the edge of town on a hill overlooking the sea. This is a comfortable place with a friendly staff. It is very popular with Cubans, and is thus a good place to meet some locals. The old parts of Manzanillo are within walking distance; keep in mind, however, that you'll have to climb back up the hill after your day in the sun.

 RESTAURANTS

Santiago de Cuba

For obvious reasons, the only *paladars* mentioned here are those officially registered. Two are particularly friendly, in the heart of Santiago: the **Restaurante Las Gallegas** *($; open evenings; Av. Bartolomé Masó between Calles Hartmann, also named San Felix, and General Lacret)* and the **Restaurante Doña Nelly** *($; open evenings, Av. Carniceria No. 412, between Calles Juan Bautista Sagarra and Sanchéz Hechavarría, ☎5-2195)*. Both serve Cuban cuisine, which usually consists of rice, salad, beans, fish or chicken, in a family atmosphere. It is the perfect occasion to experience the "real" Cuba for those who aren't staying in *casas particulares* and who wish to discover, not to mention taste, what Cuba has to offer. It is best to drop in during the day to let them know of your arrival in the evening.

If you are ravenous and craving familiar, American-style sustenance, head to the *Cafetería* of the **Hotel Las Americas** *($; always open; Av. Las Americas and Calle General Cebreco, ☎4-2612)* for food like pizzas and fried chicken. Plain and unoriginal decor.

Steps away from the Balcón del Caribe (see below), the **San Pedro del Mar** *($$; noon to 9pm; Carretera del Morro 7.5 km, ☎9-1287)* has a beautiful location. A massive cliff overlooks the sea where you can witness a different sunset every evening. The interior decor, much like the cuisine, is characterized by the establishment's proximity to the sea. A wonderful place to feast on fresh fish and to enjoy the sea breeze.

The **Restaurante Balcón del Caribe** *($$; 7:20am to 9:30pm; next to the Castillo del Morro, ☎9-1011)*, in the hotel bearing the same name, offers excellent *criolla* and international cuisine. The sunsets on Santiago Bay are particularly magnificent here, providing the perfect backdrop for the Castillo del Morro. Service is excellent and the massive wooden chairs add style.

Three new restaurants have sprung up alongside Parque Dolores this year. They are all pleasant and beautifully decorated, and the atmosphere of each corresponds to the type of cuisine featured on the menu. Together, they form a sort of gastronomical emporium. **Don Antonio** *($$)* serves Creole cuisine in a colonial-style dining room. Pork gets top billing on the menu, and the *bisteck ahumado* (grilled ham steak) is the most popular dish.

La Perla Del Dragon *($$)*, whose *table d'hôte* costs less than $6 per person, boasts a superb decor; the waiters wear costumes that will transport you to far-off places. At the time of my visit, an Italian restaurant was about to open, thus completing this trio of restaurants.

The renowned **1900** *($$; Calle Basilio No. 354, ☎2-3507)* is the best restaurant in town. It is set up inside Emilio Bacardi's former home, and the chance to see unusual, baroque and grandiose decor alone is worth the hefty bill you will be served at the end of your meal. The Creole cuisine is succulent, especially the pork dishes, but seafood is also available.

The restaurant in the **Hotel Casa Granda** *($$$; Parque Céspedes)* serves varied cuisine in an elegant colonial setting. The desserts are especially appreciated by travellers who have been in Cuba for a long time; flambéed pears and crème caramel are rare commodities in this country.

If you're staying in the Vista Alegre district, try the **Restaurante Tocororo** *($$$; Avenida Manduley No. 159, corner of Calle 7, Vista Alegre)*. Although it is relatively expensive, it serves quality Creole specialties.

The Sierra Maestra

Bayamo

The *paladar* **Chiquil** *($; Plaza del Hymno)* is set up inside a charming colonial house and has a pleasant, family-oriented atmosphere. Guests have the choice of dining inside or on a pretty patio. The Creole *tables d'hôte* cost about $2.

For ice cream, go to the terrace of the **Tropi-crema** *(Plaza de la Revolución)*.

Manzanillo

Ice cream can also be had at the **Heladeria El Jardín** *(Avenida 1 de Mayo, at the corner of Calle Sariol)*, which has a terrace near Parque Infantil. The neighbouring **Restaurante El Golfo** *($; Avenida 1 de Mayo)*, located by the sea, is an alternative to the restaurant in the Hotel Guacanayabo.

The restaurant in the **Hotel Guacanayabo** *($$)* is the only place in town with a decent selection of quality dishes. It is a favourite with the inhabitants of this region, who come here to celebrate weddings and other family events. These customers are charged in pesos, unlike foreign travellers, who must pay in U.S. dollars.

ENTERTAINMENT

Santiago de Cuba

Under the sun or under the stars, Santiago de Cuba will surely enchant you with all it has to offer. Strolling about this city at night, you need only follow the sound of music to find some entertainment, day or night. Santiago is home to the best known **Casa de la Trova** *(Calle Heredia, between Calle Carniceria and Calle San Felix)* in the country. It was no mere fluke that *son*, the rhythm underlying much Latin music, originated here. The traditional decor features photographs of famous and forgotten musicians who came here to improvise rumba or cha-cha-cha tunes. Musicians and artists gather here all day long, and one group after another entertains the crowd. Not to be missed.

La Isabelica *(Calle Calvario, between Calle Aguilera and Calle Heredia, Parque Dolores)*, a traditional Cuban cafe, is a friendly place with tons of character, the perfect spot to savour a real Cuban coffee, served black and sweet. While you're at it, take the opportunity to dip the tip of a cigar in your coffee then enjoy a leisurely smoke while reading a good book. In the evening, an unusual crowd gathers here, mostly young people, including a few of Jamaican ancestry.

The **Bar El Marqués**, by Parque Dolores, is set on a charming patio, El Patio del Amor... Located beside the Don Antonio restaurant, it is a pleasant place to go for drinks.

The **Buró de Información Cultural** *(free admission; 24 hours a day; Plaza de Marte, Calle Pérez Carbó No. 5, ☎2-3302)* has a pleasant little inner courtyard that serves as a venue for live music, a bar and a cafeteria. Known as the Patio de los Abuelos (Grandparents' Patio), it is adorned with a sculpture of two old men, one black and one white, symbolizing the ancestors of modern-day Santiagueros. The place showcases live traditional Cuban music every night *($2; starting at 10:30pm)*. The atmosphere is friendly and extremely lively, and the drinks are affordable; a beer, for example, costs $1.20. Sandwiches are also served here.

On weekend afternoons, the **Museo Del Carnaval** *($1; Tue to Sun 9am to 5pm; Sat until 9pm; Calle Heredia No. 303, at the corner of Calle Carniceria)* presents live music and dancing of the kind that characterizes Santiago's Carnaval, offering a foretaste of the atmosphere that pervades this festive event.

Espantasueños *(Hotel Santiago, Avenida de Las Américas, ☎4-2656)* is the only danceclub in Santiago worthy of the name. An unusual decor, lots of dance music and a bit of salsa: fans of this kind of music will find all they need for a good time.

In the fashionable neighbourhood of Vista Alegre, the **Centro Cultural Africano** *(free admission; Mon to Sat 9am to 5pm; Avenida Manduley No. 106, at the corner of Calle 15, ☎4-2487)* presents live Cuban folk music every Friday at 7pm, as well as displaying a few African works of art.

The **Cabaret Tropicana** *(☎4-3036)* is located near the *circumvalación*, on the way to Baconao and the airport, at the corner of the Autopista Nacional. Affiliated with Havana's famous cabaret, this venue presents shows with elaborate tropical sets and costumes.

The **El Colibrí** *($10; 9am to 11pm; Playa Daiquíri, ☎2-4735)* is right on the beach and a good spot to spend the day or just take a walk. It is also safe for swimming. Overall, the El Colibrí looks a bit like a ranch. Musicians play traditional music here every night.

The Sierra Maestra

Bayamo

The **Casa de la Trova** *(Calle Maceo, near the Plaza de la Revolución)* features the folk group Grupo Horabuena. On some days, this group performs a show recounting the history of Cuba's national anthem on the Plaza.

 SHOPPING

Santiago de Cuba

The **Libreria Internacional** *(9am to 7pm; Calle Heredia)*, beneath the cathedral, has a fairly good selection of new books and records. You can occasionally find novels in foreign languages (mainly English) here as well.

The **Bazar Raices** *(Calle, 8, between Calle 11 and Calle B)* has a good selection of crafts.

Art Galleries

A few steps from the Hotel Casa Granda, by Parque Céspedes, the **Galeria d'Oriente** *(free admission; Tue to Sun 10am to 8pm; Calle Lacret No. 653, ☎53857)* displays works by Santiago painters. It has a very good selection of contemporary art. The building, erected in 1900, used to be a casino; while you're there, take a look at the magnificent inner patio.

The nearby **Casa Municipal de Cultura** *(San Pedro No. 653, between Calle Heredia and Calle Aguilera, ☎25710)* houses a small art gallery where all sorts of cultural activities are held. Concerts *($2)* are presented every weekend on the rooftop terrace. Definitely worth checking out!

From Parque Céspedes, head west on Calle Heredia, where you'll find a large number of colonial houses, as well as the **Galeria la Confronta de la Uneac** *(free admission; Mon to Fri 10am to 6pm, Sat 10am to 2pm; Calle Heredia No. 268, between Calle Carniceria and Calle San Felix)*. Here, you can see artwork by members of the Santiago branch of the **Uneac** (Union of Cuban Writers and Artists). The patio is an extremely pleasant place to have a drink.

The **Galeria de Arte Universal** *(free admission; Tue to Sun 9am to 5pm; Calle 1, between Calle M and Terrazas, ☎4-1198)*, right near the Hotel Las Américas, sells works by contemporary Cuban artists. Most of the pieces are of good quality, and it is definitely worth stopping by if you're a fan of contemporary art.

On the road to Siboney, the **Taller Cultural** *(316 Calle 11, between Calle 12 and Calle C, Carretera de Siboney, ☎4-2384)* is both a studio and a gallery.

The Sierra Maestra

Bayamo

The **Libreria la Literaria** *(Plaza de la Revolución)* sells local crafts and has a small selection of books on art.

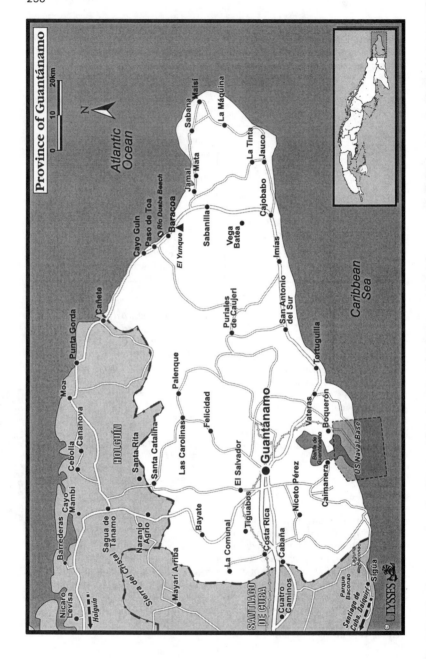

Province of Guantánamo

Atlantic Ocean

Caribbean Sea

0   10   20km

N

Nicaro
Levisa
Holguín
Barréderas
Cayo Mambí
Sagua de Tánamo
Sierra del Cristal Tánamo
Naranjo Agrio
Mayarí Arriba
Cebolla
Cananova
HOLGUÍN
Santa Catalina
Santa Rita
Moa
Punta Gorda
Cañete
Cayo Guín
Paso de Toa
Río Duaba Beach
Baracoa
El Yunque
Sabanilla
Vega Batea
Jamal
Mata
Sabana
Maisí
La Máquina
La Tinta
Jauco
Cajobabo
Imías
San Antonio del Sur
Puriales de-Caujerí
Palenque
Felicidad
Las Carolinas
El Salvador
Bayate
La Comunal
Tiguabos
Costa Rica
Cabaña
Cuatro Caminos
SANTIAGO DE CUBA
Niceto Pérez
Guantánamo
Caimanera
Bahía de Guantánamo
US Naval Base
Vateras
Boquerón
Tortuguilla
Parque Baconao
Santiago de Cuba Daiquirí
Laguna Baconao
Sigua

ⓒ ULYSSES

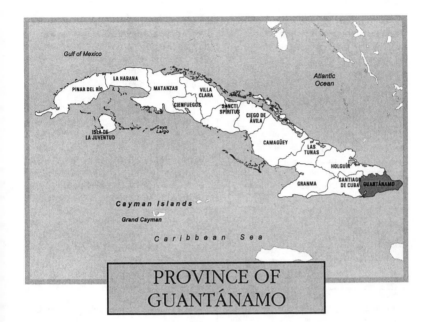

PROVINCE OF GUANTÁNAMO

Now the capital of the province of the same name, Guantánamo was once part of the former Province of Oriente. This large region has since been divided into five provinces, including Guantánamo, which is the easternmost part of the country. The name Guantánamo is known the world over, because of the U.S. naval base located about 40 kilometres east of the capital.

Although the town of Guantánamo itself has little to offer in terms of tourist attractions, the 158-kilometre stretch of road between Guantánamo and Baracoa is positively breathtaking. The eastern coast of Cuba looks like the end of the world. Over the years, it has been sculpted by "Foens", a wind caused by the warmth of the sea. This air-current creates a desert-like microclimate in which cacti thrive. The road crosses the steep mountains, zigzagging through stunning landscapes all the way to Baracoa.

For the residents of Baracoa, this road across the mountains which passes little houses amidst cacao plantations is "like an endless branch that someone has hung in the sky".

Baracoa is a magical town. Here, myths and legends go hand in hand with historical facts. Baracoa was the first *villa*, or town, founded by the Spanish in Cuba (1511), and its name means "presence of the sea" in the language of the Arauca Indians. Since the colonial architecture has suffered the effects of time, Baracoa's charm is difficult to pin down. Does it lie in the unique character of the local residents, who live in a town that has been forgotten over the centuries? Or is it the natural surroundings, the mountains and the sea? Or perhaps it is the spirit of the many natives who once inhabited this land, a few of whose descendants can still be found on the island...

The "spirit" of Baracoa is no doubt a combination of all of these things, as well as the feeling that this is where it all started, for this was one of the first places where Christopher Columbus set foot on Cuban soil in 1492, when the Americas first began to take shape in the European imagination.

It is worth spending anywhere from two to seven days in Baracoa, which can serve as a base for exploring rivers, beaches and small communities of cacao farmers in the surrounding mountains.

 FINDING YOUR WAY AROUND

Guantánamo

By Plane

Cubana de Aviación flies once a day from Havana to Guantánamo *($100 one way; Mon, Tue, Thu, Fri, Sat, Sun 8:40am; Wed noon)* and leaves very early in the morning (be at the airport for 7am), except Saturdays when it leaves at 4pm.

The return flight to Havana leaves Guantánamo the same day *($100 one way; Mon, Thu, Sat, Sun 11:55am; Tue to Fri 2:05pm; Wed 3:05pm)*.

Airline Office

Cubana de Aviación *(Calle Calixto Garcia, near the central square, ☎3-4533)*.

By Train

The **Estación de Trenes** *(Calle Perez, ☎32-5518)*, located north of Guantánamo's central square, is more attractive than practical. The trains for Santiago de Cuba follow an erratic schedule.

In theory, there should be one every day. There are several departures every day for the other small towns bordering Guantanamo Bay. Show up at the terminal at least one hour prior to departure in order to purchase tickets.

By Bus

The **Estación de Omnibus Interprovinciales** is located just west of Guantánamo on the Carretera de Santiago de Cuba *(Km 1, ☎32-3830)*. If you are leaving the same day, you can purchase your ticket at the station. For reservations, go to the **Agencias de Omnibus Nacionales** *(Carretera, between Martí and Pedro A. Perez)*.

To Baracoa: Departures: 7am and 2pm. Fare: $5.

To Havana: Departure: 7:30pm. Fare: $46.

To Santiago de Cuba: Departures: 6:30am, 9am, 11:20am and 3pm. Fare: $4.

To Camagüey: Departure: 7:30am (every other day). Fare: $16.

To Holguín: Departure: 1pm. Fare: $11.

To Bayamo: Departure: 1pm. Fare: $8.

By Car

The 86-kilometre highway between Santiago de Cuba and Guantánamo is one of the best in the country. A multilane highway that is usually empty, it was probably built to protect the country in case the Americans were to launch an attack from their base at Guantánamo.

Car Rental

Havanautos has a branch at the Cupet gas station in Guantánamo.

Baracoa

By Plane

There are three flights per week from Havana to Baracoa *($108 one way; Tue and Fri 9:45am; $116 Sun noon)*.

The flights back to Havana are on the same days *(Tue and Fri 2:05pm; Sun 2:25pm)*.

By Bus

Estación de Omnibus *(1 Calle Martí, ☎4-2239)*.

To Santiago de Cuba: Departure: 1:20pm. Fare: $9.

To Guantánamo: Departure: 5:30am. Fare: $5.

To Havana: Departure: 7:30pm (every other day). Fare: $53.

To Camagüey: Departure: 8am (Mon and Fri). Fare: $21.

You can also buy a ticket to Guantánamo with a rail connection to Santiago de Cuba.

Car Rental

Havanautos: Hotel Porto Santo *(☎4-3606)*.

0By Horse-drawn Carriage

You can rent a horse-drawn carriage, driver and all, for a peso or two at Parque de la Victoria.

PRACTICAL INFORMATION

Guantánamo

Tourist Information

At the tourist office in the **Hotel Guantánamo** you can sign up for a variety of excursions (to the Mirador de Malones, for one) and make airplane reservations.

Post Office

The reception desk at the **Hotel Guantánamo** provides mail service.

Medical Care

Guantánamo General Hospital *(☎32-6013)*.

Baracoa

The tourist offices of the **Hotel Porto Santo** provide a variety of services (mail service, tourist information, nursing care and pharmaceuticals).

EXPLORING

Guantánamo

The town of Guantánamo has few attractions, and some visitors will be disappointed to learn that the U.S.

naval base is not visible from the capital. In order to see it, you have to go to Caimanera (see below).

Guantánamo's architecture shows a clear Soviet influence; prefabricated and concrete structures are the norm here. The **Plaza de la Revolución Mariana Grajales** is a perfect example. Inaugurated on July 26, 1985, it was named after the mother of several *mambises*, including the celebrated general Antonio Maceo Grajales who fought for Cuban independence in the 19th century.

A few kilometres northwest of Guantánamo, the **Zoológico de Piedra** *(free admission)* is laid out on a coffee plantation on the property of Angel Iñigo, a self-taught sculptor. It's an unusual zoo; all the animals are made of stone.

The **Mirador de Malones** lies on the only border zone on the island of Cuba. Located 40 kilometres east of Guantánamo, on the road to Baracoa, this lookout faces the U.S. naval base. To go there, you must have authorization from the Puesto de Mando de Guantánamo. The best way to arrange a visit is through the tourist office in the Hotel Guantánamo. Admission to the lookout is $5 per person.

Caimanera is a small village adjacent to the naval base. It has a good hotel and is the best place from which to view the base, located on the other side of the bay. Visitors can sit back and reflect on the strained relations between the United States and Cuba while sipping a nice, cold Cuba Libre. There is supposed to be daily train service from Guantánamo to Caimanera, but the schedule is notoriously erratic. Another option is to rent a car in Guantánamo and drive the few kilometres to Caimanera.

The **Guantánamo Naval Base** was founded in 1903. Covering an area of 110 square kilometres and is home to 8,000 Americans. A 100-year lease was signed in 1933, and the contract stipulates that the arrangement will only be terminated if both countries are in agreement. The odds are low that the United States will want to remove this thorn from Castro's side. The American government still pays $4,000 a year to lease the territory, but Castro refuses to cash the cheques.

Golf courses, McDonald's, five movie theatres... the soldiers, civilians and their families have everything they need to feel right at home. However, this microcosm of American society took on an unusual appearance during the Cuban *balsero* crisis.

In mid-August 1994, the naval base took in over 22,000 Cuban refugees after Bill Clinton decided to place them in camps rather than allowing them into the United States. All those Cubans who had risked their lives by setting out for Florida aboard makeshift rafts suddenly found themselves in camps right back where they started. Ironically, a number of refugees tried to swim across the Bahía de Guantánamo to get back home. According to American authorities, over 350 of them succeeded. Many others, however, were swept away by the currents in these snake-infested waters. On average, about 100 Cubans manage to swim to the base every year to take refuge on American territory.

At present, it is not possible to visit the base from Cuba. As a result of the Cold War, you must first obtain special permission from the United States and make the trip from Norfolk, Virginia aboard an American military plane.

La Guantanamera

La Guantanamera is the most popular of all Cuban songs. The melody was composed in the 1940s by Joseito Fernández for a radio show, in which he used songs to report the gossip of the day. The tune became so famous that it was made the musical symbol of Cuba. Today, a poem by José Martí accompanies the melody.

Chorus

Guantanamera, guajira
Guantanamera (repeat)

Yo soy un hombre sincero
De donde crece la palma

Y antes de morirme quiero
Echar mis versos del alma

Chorus

Con los pobres de la tierra
Quiero yo mi suerte echar
El arroyo de la sierra
Me complace más que el mar

Chorus

No me pongan en lo oscuro
A morir como un traidor
Yo soy bueno y como bueno
Moriré de cara al sol

Translation

Guantanamera, country lass,
Guantanamera

I am a sincere man
From the place where the palm tree grows
And before I die I want
To pour forth the verses from my soul

With the poor of the earth
I want to play out my destiny
The mountain stream
Suits me better than the sea

Don't cast me into the darkness
To die like a traitor
I am good, and like a good man
I die facing the sun

Baracoa ★★

Baracoa is a long, narrow town hidden in the mountains near the **Ensenada de Miel**, a narrow-mouthed ("pouch") bay. Baracoa was the first *villa*, or town, founded by the Spanish in Cuba on August 15, 1511. Its character can be summed up by the following saying: "I may always be the smallest town in Cuba, but I'll always be first".

The neighbouring bay, Porto Santo, lies one kilometre north of Baracoa and earned a place in the history of the New World on November 27, 1492. Some people claim that this is where Christopher Columbus first set foot on Cuban soil, for his travel log describes *"a squarish mountain that looks like an island"*. This mountain, **El Yunque**, stands out against the Baracoa sky. Certain doubting historians, however, assert that Columbus was not describing Baracoa but rather Gibara. This issue is still a common subject of debate in Cuba.

Starting in 1791, many French men and women fleeing the Haitian independ-

PROVINCE OF GUANTÁNAMO

ence movement settled in the Baracoa area. These people left an indelible mark on Cuban culture, introducing the violin, the piano and a variety of dance steps, as well as exerting a major economic influence on their newly adopted society.

Although it was already in decline by that time, the town of Baracoa did play a role in the 19th-century wars of independence. Every year on April 1 at sunrise, local residents celebrate the arrival of one of the heroes of independence, General Antonio Maceo Grajales, in remembrance of how the people of Baracoa took to the streets to welcome their liberator and back him in his struggle.

Isolated from the rest of the country, the people of Baracoa were mostly poor and uneducated at the time of the Revolution of 1959. A charming anecdote illustrates the changes that took place here back then. During the first years of the Castro regime, when the national literacy campaign was in full swing, the children living in the mountains around Baracoa were brought down to the town. Most of them had never seen a town before, much less electric lighting. They were heading down to Baracoa at night, and one of them asked, "What's that village with all the low stars?"

Baracoa's history is full of mythical figures and legends. You will certainly meet some interesting people in your travels, and historian, poet and storyteller Miguel Angel Castro is definitely one of the most extraordinary individuals now living in Baracoa. He loves his town like no one else, and shares his passion for it with others. You'll find him at the Fuerte Matachín, where he works as a guide. He will be glad to show you around town, wherever his feet lead him.

Among the historical figures who have sought refuge from the rest of the world here in Baracoa, "El Pelu" is surely the most mysterious. According to Miguel Angel Castro, El Pelu, whose photograph is displayed in the museum in the Fuerte Matachín, was a prophet of doom. History has made him the scapegoat for all the catastrophes that have befallen Baracoa.

El Pelu had long hair and a long beard and wore shell necklaces. A hippie ahead of his time, he was spurned by the local townspeople at the end of the last century. He fled into the mountains, pronouncing the following curse, known as *la maldición del Pelu*, on Baracoa: "The people here are so uncivilized that this town will never prosper".

More recently, Magdalena, commonly known as "La Rusa", left her stamp on the town. An opera singer and the daughter of one of the Tsar's officials, she fled socialism in Russia and settled in Baracoa, where she opened a hotel in the early 1950s. But the socialist movement followed her all the way here! Nevertheless, she decided to take part in the resistence movement known as the *Movimiento 26 de Julio*. When the revolutionaries triumphed over their opponents, she donated $25,000 to the new government. Fidel Castro and his brother Raúl came to Baracoa and stayed at the **Hotel La Rusa** (see p 268). La Rusa died in 1978, but she remains forever immortalized in the history of Baracoa and in *La Consécration du Printemps*, a novel by celebrated Cuban writer Alejo Carpentier.

Baracoa is one of the few towns in Cuba that still has its original layout. Paradoxically, the architecture of its buildings has been considerably modified over the centuries. Calle Martí, Baracoa's main street, runs from one

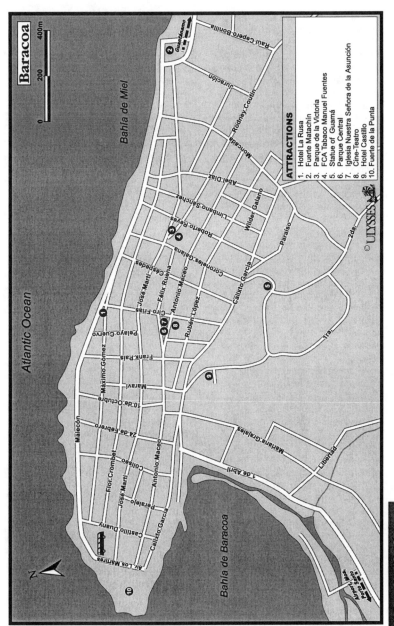

Baracoa

0 200 400m

Atlantic Ocean

Bahía de Miel

Bahía de Baracoa

© ULYSSES

ATTRACTIONS

1. Hotel La Rusa
2. Fuente Matachín
3. Parque de la Victoria
4. FCA Tabaco Manuel Fuentes
5. Statue of Guamá
6. Parque Central
7. Iglesia Nuestra Señora de la Asunción
8. Cine-Teatro
9. Hotel Castillo
10. Fuente de la Punta

end of the little town to the other, linking two coastal fortresses.

The quieter Malecón runs alongside the sea, and also spans the entire town. Unfortunately, this waterfront area has been spoiled by the construction of numerous housing projects with typically socialist architecture. This blunder in urban planning mars the beauty of the setting, but a simple paint job would put a bit of colour back into the place.

The **Fuerte Matachín** *($1; Calle Martí, at the corner of Juración)* is one of three fortifications in Baracoa. Located at the edge of town, in front of Parque Maceo, this fort now serves as the town's museum of history. It contains numerous original documents, sketches and photographs. Here you can meet Baracoa's spiritual guardian, Miguel Angel Castro, known simply as "Castro", who works here as a guide and knows the secrets and mysteries of Baracoa better than anyone else. In front of the fort, a statue of Christopher Columbus commemorates the celebrated navigator's stop in Baracoa in 1492.

Parque de la Victoria is a pretty little Y-shaped plaza where the local carriage-drivers congregate. It is a very lively place, due to the presence of numerous second-hand shops catering to the local population. Next door to the Centro de los Veteranos, a senior citizens' residence, the **FCA Tabaco Manuel Fuentes** *(free admission; Mon to Sat 8am to 5pm)* cigar factory is open to the public, although it is not really geared to tourism. Inside, you can watch artisans rolling cigars by hand.

You can take refuge from the sun beneath the many trees in **Parque Central**, the most attractive square in town. Right nearby stands the **Iglesia Nuestra Señora de la Asunción ★★**, which dates from 1805. This church may not be an architectural masterpiece, either inside or out, but it does house the **Cruz de la Parra**. This cross was supposedly brought to Cuba from Europe and erected in Porto Santo by Christopher Columbus on his first voyage to the Americas. Much later, it was placed inside this church in order to protect it; apparently, fishermen had been cutting off pieces of it to make talismans. The remainder of the cross, which was originally nearly two metres high, is now displayed in a small glass case. The Iglesia Nuestra Señora de la Asunción usually opens very early in the morning.

In front of the church is an imposing bust of **Hatuey**, a famous native chief who rebelled against the Spanish and was burned alive by the Catholic church in Baracoa during the colonial era. The positioning of the bust, facing the church, is thus very symbolic. Many people consider Hatuey one of the first rebels in the Americas.

Also near Parque Central is the **Ciné-Teatro**, the largest house in the area. Built in 1931, it contains several works of art, and films are presented here regularly. The Ciné-Teatro has a certain old-fashioned charm, but has unfortunately been neglected. The handsome orange-coloured building adjacent to Parque Central is the **Ayuntamiento**, the Town Hall. Erected in the 1930s, it has a pretty patio, open during office hours, where you can take in some fresh air and admire the peaceful surroundings.

This is where Avenida Maceo opens onto Parque Central. The cultural artery of Baracoa, Avenida Maceo still boasts a few vestiges of colonial architecture.

Calle Calixto-García leads to the **Hotel Castillo** (see p 269). This former for-

El Tibaracón

In Baracoa, the sand prevents the **Río de Miel** and the **Río Duaba** from emptying straight into the sea. This phenomenon, referred to by Baracoa residents as "El Tibaracón", forces the two rivers to skirt round the sand banks and drain out a few hundred metres farther along.

The Río de Miel, which dodges the sandbanks in the little bay of Ensenada de Miel, becomes more beautiful with the arrival of the *tétis*, small transparent fish that suddenly appear here once a year, usually in August or September, when the new moon is just a sliver in the sky.

There is also a legend surrounding the Río de Miel. Supposedly, the Spanish conquistador Diego Velásquez was staying in Baracoa and bathed in the river before getting married in town. It is thus said that those who bathe in the Río de Miel will marry in Baracoa.

tress, built between 1739 and 1742, stands on a hilltop overlooking Baracoa. It offers a unique view of the town, I Yunque, the Bahía de Baracoa and the mouth of the Río de Miel. The terracotta tiles on the roofs of the houses reveal French and Spanish influences. Make sure to come here in the morning to watch the sun rise over the sea, a truly spectacular sight.

 PARKS AND BEACHES

It is definitely worth spending at least half a day at the beach at the mouth of the **Río Duaba ★★**. It lies on the former site of a native village, where a few archaeological vestiges still lie scattered about on the ground. This long, sandy beach, overlooked by most tourists, is one of the places where you can witness the natural phenomenon known as the "Tibaracón" in all its splendour.

To get there, turn right in front of the little school in Alto del Pino, north of Baracoa. You'll know you're in the right place when you see the bust of General Maceo and the two cannons in front of the school. The general set up an ambush for the Spanish army here during the wars of independence. The short dirt road leading to the mouth of the Río Duaba is lined with royal palms, the symbol of Cuba. There are a few rough spots along the way, but you can still drive to the beach without too much trouble.

Near the sea, turn right and continue for about one kilometre. At the end of the road, you'll be greeted by a handful of picturesque little houses. Go to the last house, which belongs to Carmen and Jiménez and is a veritable museum. Jiménez, an old fisherman, has a large collection of sculptures, most of which were thrown into the sea by Haitian fishermen during religious ceremonies. You can also see a few archaeological artifacts the couple found on their land. While you're there, Carmen and Jiménez might even invite you to sample their crab with coconut sauce, which they prepare behind their house.

OUTDOOR ACTIVITIES

Hiking

You can set off on an expedition to the top of **El Yunque**, the famous mountain that Christopher Columbus supposedly saw when he landed in Cuba in 1492. A small, backcountry campground has been cleared at the very top of the mountain. It takes about 13 hours to hike to the summit, and the last leg of the journey is rather difficult. Those interested in making the trip should enlist the services of a mountain guide. Ask Castro, the guide at the Fuerte Matachín, to go with you or inquire at one of the local hotels.

ACCOMMODATIONS

Guantánamo

The motel-style **Villa La Lupe** *($23-$29; ≡, tv, ℝ, ℛ, pb, ≈; Carretera El Salvador)*, located four kilometres from Guantánamo, regularly caters to groups of kids on organized trips. It is a little far from town, but the setting is peaceful and pleasant, albeit somewhat bare. The surrounding playing fields have been neglected. The name of the motel refers to the title of a song by General Juan Almeida Bosque, a member of the Central Committee of the Cuban Communist Party.

The **Casa de los Ensueños** *($25.35; ≡, tv, vcr, ℝ, pb, ℛ; Calle Ahogado, at the corner of Calle 15 Norte, ☎32-6304)* is without question the best place to stay in Guantánamo. It is a modern house with three bedrooms and a terrace on the second floor. The service is friendly, and the atmosphere almost homey. The restaurant is definitely the pride of this establishment. The Casa de los Ensueños has the same management as the nearby Hotel Guantánamo, and guests of the former enjoy access to the swimming pool and all other amenities of the latter.

You can stay at **Brasil** *(30 pesos; Calle Calixto García near the Parque Martí)*, which is the only "pesos" hotel in the city. They generally don't accept foreigners, although some basic Spanish skills just may get you in if you are short on funds.

The big **Hotel Guantánamo** *($31-$35; ≡, tv, vcr, pb, ℛ, ≈; Calle 13 Norte, at the corner of Calle Ahogado, ☎32-6015)* is identical to a number of other hotels in the country, since most Cuban hotels built in the 1960s and 1970s followed the same architectural model. The service is friendly on the whole, and the swimming pool is well maintained. There are also a nightclub and a cabaret on the premises.

In Caimanera, the **Hotel Caimanera** *($40; ≡, pb, ℛ, tv; ☎9-414, ☎6-2294)* is renowned as one of the only hotels outside the tourist resorts that fully deserves its three stars.

Baracoa

Each hotel in Baracoa has a charm all its own, and the jury's still out on which is the best. One thing is certain, though: there's something for everyone.

The least expensive of Baracoa's three hotels is also the oldest. At the foot of the Malecón, right in the heart of town, the little **Hotel La Rusa** *($18-22; ≡, ℛ, pb; Avenida Máximo Gómez No. 161, ☎4-3011)* is easily recognizable, thanks to its yellow walls. This hotel used to belong to La Rusa, an opera singer of Russian origin. Fidel Castro and his brother Raúl were among the distinguished guests of this hotel following the victory of the Revolution. To this day, local artists get together here for evening drinks. The place is a little outdated, and scores more points for character than for comfort. The rooms are small, even cramped, but they all offer a view of the sea. The service is friendly and the clientele mainly Cuban; foreign visitors tend to opt for the considerably higher standards of comfort offered by the other hotels in town.

Many people claim that no other hotel in Cuba offers better value for your money than the **Hotel Castillo** *($25-30; ≡, ˜tv, ℝ, pb, ℛ, ≈; Calle Paraíso, ☎4-2103)*. A converted colonial fortress, the hotel stands on a hilltop overlooking Baracoa. It was completely restored in 1990, at which time a superb lookout was added to the colonial structures. The panoramic view of the town and its surroundings is positively stunning. And then there's the pool, set in the centre of a little square inside the fortress! In the rustic rooms, you can still see the old castle walls, and your eye will naturally be drawn to the windows, which look out onto the sea and the town of Baracoa. Don't miss the sunrise, a veritable feast for the eyes from this vantage point. The loveliest and most spacious rooms are numbers 101 and 201.

Then again, some travellers prefer the **Hotel Porto Santo** *($28-35; ≡, pb, ≈, ℛ; Carretera Aeropuerto, ☎4-3590)*, which stands on the very spot where Christopher Columbus supposedly first set foot in Cuba in 1492, and where he erected a cross to mark the spot. Located near the sea two kilometres north of Baracoa, this hotel is the perfect place for travellers who are looking for peace and quiet and can't resist the call of the wild. It has an attractive pool, a good restaurant and relatively large, comfortable rooms.

 RESTAURANTS

Guantánamo

The **Paladar** *($; Calle Martí, at the corner of Crombet)*, near Parque Central, is very popular with the residents of Guantánamo. It serves Creole cuisine, with pork as the house specialty, in a homey atmosphere.

Many people consider the restaurant in the **Casa de los Ensueños** *($; Calle Ahogado, at the corner of Calle 15 Norte, ☎32-6304)*, near the Hotel Guantánamo, to be the finest in town. The one real advantage here is that guests can create their own personalized menu, provided that they place their order several hours in advance. Another plus is the outdoor terrace on the second floor. The breakfasts are particularly copious.

Baracoa

During your stay in Baracoa, you will no doubt want to try out a family restaurant where you can mingle with the local residents. The **Casa de Walter** *($; Calle Rubén López No. 47, at the corner of Coroneles Galano)* is a typical, inviting *paladar*. The family lives in a comfortable old house. Try the *pierna adobada* (stuffed pork); the lamb is also succulent. The portions are very generous, and all the dishes are served on platters.

The **Hotel Castillo** *($$; Calle Paraíso, ☎4-2103)* is known for the quality of its restaurant, which specializes in Creole cuisine. What with the colonial setting and the lookout at the top of the fortress, this is sure to be a memorable evening.

  ENTERTAINMENT

Guantánamo

Near the central square, head to the **Casa de la Cultura**, one of the few places in Guántanamo where a fun evening is guaranteed.

Baracoa

The **Casa de la Trova** *(Calle Maceo, near the church)* is a good place to take in some live folk music and *descargas* (improvisations) by amateur musicians. The Casa de la Trova is frequented mainly by locals, which makes it a perfect place to meet Cubans. As the night wears on and the rum starts working its magic on the customers, the place gets livelier and livelier—perhaps a bit too much so for some people. Ask to see Pedro Garrino, the friendly manager of the place.

The **Casa de Cultura** *(free admission; Mon to Fri 8am to noon and 2pm to 6pm; Calle Maceo No. 174)* exhibits works by local artists and occasionally offers art classes.

The **Sala de Teatro de la Casa de Cultura** *(free admission; every day 9am to 5pm; Avenida Maceo No. 126)* displays a few works of art and regularly hosts concerts, dance shows and plays in the early evening.

 SHOPPING

Baracoa

The **Fondo de Bienes Culturales Galeria Yara** *(free admission; every day 8am to noon and 2pm to 6pm; Avenida Maceo No. 120, ☎4-2637)* has a vast selection of local crafts, including works by Ramón Domínguez, who created the sculpture of Guamá on Calle Coroneles Galano.

While you're at it, why not stop in and see Ramón Domínguez at home, in his studio? To do so, take Calle Calixto-García, which runs parallel to Avenida Maceo. This street affords some good views of the bay and the port. You access **Ramón Domínguez**'s humble home *(Calle Calixto-García No. 43)* through a small patio. Some real treasures are hidden away here, mostly sculptures of native and African faces. Certain pieces are clearly intended for the tourist market, but that does not detract from the artist's talent nor from the quality of his work, which has earned him several provincial prizes.

ISLA DE LA JUVENTUD AND CAYO LARGO

Next to the island of Cuba itself, the Isla de la Juventud (Isle of Youth) is the biggest in the country. It measures 2,200 square kilometres and has a population of about 90,000. Over the centuries, it served variously as a pirates' refuge and a Cuban penal colony before being transformed into a centre for Communist youth — hence its name. It offers beautiful, remote beaches and spectacular ocean depths. It's less expensive than Cayo Largo and its residents are friendly and young at heart. Plan to spend between three and six days on Isla de la Juventud, exploring its natural attractions and its capital, Nueva Gerona.

Despite the recent construction of numerous hotels and a huge influx of tourists, Cayo Largo, part of the Los Canarreos archipelago, remains a genuine natural paradise. An oasis rising from the ocean, it boasts picture-perfect beaches that will delight anyone who likes seaside holidays. Note, however, that Cubans aren't allowed on Cayo Largo, so it's not the place to go if you want to mix and mingle with locals. One day is enough time to see Cayo Largo itself, and a second day will suffice to explore the surrounding islets. Still, if you're into lounging around on beaches, you'll find Cayo Largo very much to your taste.

 FINDING YOUR WAY AROUND

Isla de la Juventud

Entrance Formalities

Arriving on Isla de la Juventud by plane or boat, you'll probably have to show your passport, so don't leave it behind in Havana or Varadero, even if you're planning only a one- or two-day visit.

By Plane

Isla de la Juventud is a mere 45-minute flight from Havana. Numerous flights depart from Havana every day for Nueva Gerona's airport.

Cubana de Aviación and **Lacsa** offer daily departures to **Isla de la Juventud** from Terminal 3 of José-Martí airport in **Havana**. At press time, Lacsa's flight schedule was more regular. It leaves Havana daily at 11:25, lands at Nueva Gerona at 12:05pm, refuels and heads back to the capital at 12:20pm *($50 one way, $100 return)*. If Cubana's irregular schedule isn't too much of a hassle, its several daily flights will take you to the beautiful Isla de la Juventud for half the price, at $25 for a one-way trip and $50 return. Furthermore, this option allows you to make daytrips if you are pressed for time but still want to see the island. Departures are early in the morning and evenings.

Aerotaxi, a charter airline, offers flights from Varadero, Havana and Santiago de Cuba to the Sigüanea airport, near the Hotel Colony's marina.

The Nueva Gerona Airport

The airport is about 5 kilometres from Nueva Gerona and 46 kilometres from the Hotel Colony, the most popular lodging on the island among foreign tourists. Public buses run between the airport and Nueva Gerona and at one peso are the cheapest way to get into town. To get to the Hotel Colony, you can use the hotel's courtesy car (it's usually waiting in front of the airport). If you haven't booked a room at the Colony, climb in anyway and negotiate a price (if you say you're a guest at the hotel, the ride is free). You can also take the public bus into Nueva Gerona. To get to the Colony once you're in the city, either hail a *particular* taxi (don't pay more than $15 per car for the ride)

or wait for a bus of workers at the end of their working day.

Airlines

Cubana de Aviación has two offices on Isla de la Juventud. One is in Nueva Gerona *(1415 Calle 39, between Calle 16 and Calle 19, ☎2-2531 or 2-4559)*. The other is at the Aeropuerto Cabrera Mustelier *(Carretera de la Fé km 35, ☎2-2690 or 2-2184)*.

Aerotaxi

Aeropuerto de Nueva Gerona: ☎2-2300 or 2-2690.
Aeropuerto de Sigüanea: ☎9-8282 or 9-8181.
Hotel Las Codornices: ☎2-4969 or 2-4981.

By Ferry or Hydrofoil

The Isla de la Juventud is linked to the island of Cuba by a ferry and by a high-speed hydrofoil. Departures are from the port of **Surgidero de Batabanó**, roughly 70 kilometres south of Havana.

The ferry from Surgidero de Batabanó to Isla de la Juventud *($10 one way; Wed, Fri and Sun 7:30pm)* runs on the schedule for the return trip from the dock in Nueva Gerona *(Calle 31, between Calle 22 and Calle 24)*.

Commonly called *la cometa*, the hydrofoil is more comfortable and faster than the ferry. Departures from the port of **Surgidero de Bataban** are at 10am and 4pm *($15 one way)*. The return trips leave at 7am and 1pm, in the direction of **Nueva Gerona**. At the ticket office in Nueva Gerona (on the arrivals and departures dock), you can reserve bus tickets to get from Surgidero de Batabanó to Cuba's main cities.

Cigar-smoking street vendors selling flowers or produce are common sights in Cuba.
- *Jean Terroux*

The Convent of San Francisco in the mountains of Trinidad. - *Tibor Bognar*

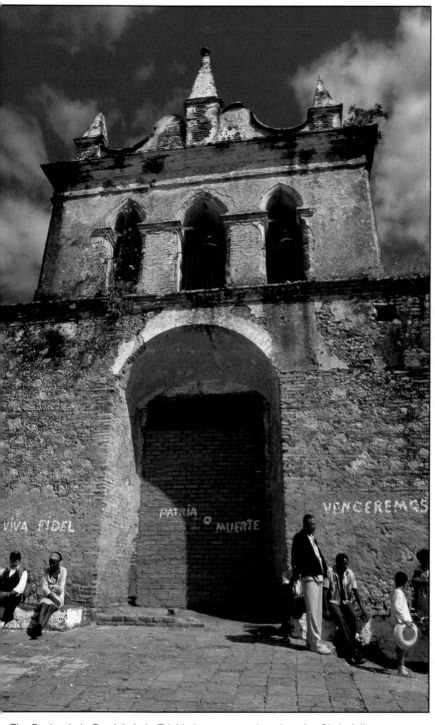

The Ermita de la Candelaria in Trinidad was a meeting place for Che's followers, as attested to by the revolutionary graffiti on its walls. - *Tibor Bognar*

The facade of a bourgeois residence from a more prosperous era. - *Jean Terroux*

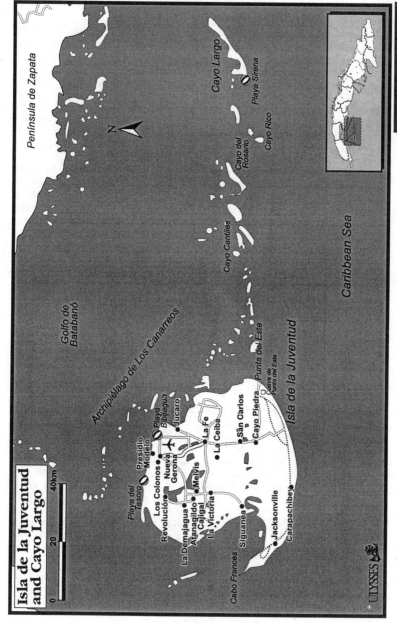

Isla de la Juventud and Cayo Largo

By Car

Isla de la Juventud's road network is good; renting a car lets you see the island's many attractions while saving precious time. Public transport is more reliable than elsewhere in Cuba, but bus schedules are generally limited to rush hour.

Also, a few *particulares* operate in Nueva Gerona, although they are less numerous than in the rest of the country. Negotiate with the drivers beforehand, and be firm. Alternately you can hitch-hike, an activity made easy by the *amarillos*, the police officers clad in yellow who are stationed on the roads during rush hour. They encourage carpooling by stopping state-owned vehicles and asking them to take on other passengers.

Car Rentals

Havanautos (☎9-8181 or 9-8282) and **Transautos** (☎9-8281) both have offices at the Hotel Colony.

By Taxi

Transtur (☎33-5212 or 9-8281), whose offices are in the Hotel Colony, offers both taxi services and minibus rentals on Isla de la Juventud. It also operates a shuttle service between Nueva Gerona's airport and the hotel, and between the hotel and the Marina Sigüanea.

Cayo Largo

Entrance Formalities

Bring your passport to Cayo Largo, even if you're only staying for a day.

By Plane

Flights depart from Terminal 3 at Havana's Aeropuerto José-Martí. **Aerocaribbean** offers several flights daily from Havana or Varadero to Cayo Largo. Most travel agencies in Varadero and Havana hotels offer one-day excursions for about $100, a price that includes lunch. Some of **Aerocaribbean**'s planes are old DC-3s, aviation legends for more than 50 years.

The charter airline **Aerotaxi** also offers numerous daily flights to Cayo Largo, mainly from Havana and Varadero. Flying in their quaint 12-passenger biplanes, you'll probably be reminded of Humphrey Bogart in *Casablanca*! You can reserve a seat or a group of seats, or even charter an entire plane. The return trip between Havana and Cayo Largo costs $533 for a group of 12.

Lacsa airline has daily flights between **Cayo Largo** and Cuba's major tourist destinations. Flights never take more than an hour.

Havana-Cayo Largo: departures at 6am and 1:15pm *($60 one way, $120 return)*.

Cayo Largo-Havana: departures at 10:20am and 2:20pm.

Cayo Largo-Varadero: departures at 7:45am and 3:15pm *($55 one way, $110 return)*. The return trips are at 6:45am and 2:15pm.

Cayo Largo-Trinidad: one departure only, at 7:05am *($50 one way, $100 return)*. The plane returns from Trinidad at 9:20am.

Airlines

Aerocaribbean:
Calle 23, at the corner of P, Vedado, Havana, ☎33-4553, ◦33-5016.
Aeropuerto Internacional Juan Gualberto Gómez, Varadero, ☎33-7093 or 53-616.

Cubana de Aviación:
Aeropuerto Internacional de Cayo Largo, ☎79-3255 or 79-3215.

Aerotaxi:
Aeropuerto Internacional de Cayo Largo, ☎79-3255 or 79-3215.
In Havana, ☎32-8127, ◦33-2621.

By Yacht

If you're arriving on a private boat, you have to use the Yucatán Canal. Call **Cuba Náutica** for more information *(☎53-5-4-8220, ◦4-8221)*.

By Car

With only 15 kilometres of roads, Cayo Largo is easy to explore by car. Public transport consists of tourist buses that run between the hotels and the airport. A small, colourful cart pulled by a tractor takes tourists to Playa Sirena.

Car and Scooter Rentals

If you want to rent a car, contact **Transautos** *(☎33-3156)*, which has offices in the Pelícano and Cayo Largo de Sur hotels.

Scooters are the cheapest and most practical way to get around Cayo Largo. Rentals are available at all hotels.

PRACTICAL INFORMATION

Isla de la Juventud

Post Office

The Nueva Gerona post office is on Calle 39, at the corner of Calle 18. If you want faster, more efficient service, try the telecommunications counter at the Hotel Colony.

Medical Care

The **Policlínico** is on Calle 47, at the corner of Calle 18.

Cayo Largo

Tourist Information

Small tourist information counters are found in all Cayo Largo hotels, but they're usually not all that helpful since their main purpose is to sell tours to Havana, Trinidad and Pinar del Río. You can purchase an air ticket without having to buy a package tour. If you're spending several days on Cayo Largo, consider flying to the island of Cuba.

Mail and Telecommunications

The **Centro de Comunicaciones** *(every day, 8am to 8pm)* offers photocopy, telephone and postal services.

Water

Cayo Largo's drinking water isn't the most pleasant, since it tastes rather salty and sulferous.

EXPLORING

Isla de la Juventud ★★

During his second voyage to the New World in 1494, Christopher Columbus came across Isla de la Juventud and named it La Evangelista. However, aboriginal paintings in grottos in the Punta de l'Este region indicate that indigenous peoples lived there some 3,000 years ago, well before the arrival of the Europeans. You can view those paintings today on Isla de la Juventud, in what is considered the "Sistine Chapel" of aboriginal mural art in the Americas.

Isla de la Juventud failed to pique the interest of the Spanish Crown during the colonial era. Left to itself, the island was favoured by pirates because of its water supply. Legend has it that they also hid untold treasures here. By the 17th century, the island had become known as Treasure Island. In fact, this island inspired Robert Louis Stevenson's famous novel of the same name. John Hawkins, Francis Drake and Henry Morgan were among the notorious pirates who hung out here. Eventually, however, the pirates were forced to cede the island to the Spanish, who began colonizing it in the mid-1800s.

The island took on yet another role during Cuba's struggle for independence. It was renamed Reina Amalia Colony and then Isla de los Deportados (Isle of the Deported) after the Spanish began sending nationalist prisoners here.

After Cuban independence, the American administration postponed a decision on the political status of the island. At the time, many assumed the island would come under U.S. control, so 300 Americans settled there. Traces of this period can still be seen today, particularly in the architecture of some of the houses in Nueva Gerona. In 1926, the island officially became Cuban territory and construction of the enormous Presidio Modelo prison marked a return to its past as a penal colony. In the years that followed, there were times when prisoners made up the majority of the population. Fidel Castro, arrested during the attack on the Cuartel Moncada, was himself among the prisoners who served a sentence in what was, in effect, Cuba's Siberia.

The island was successively renamed Isla de la Cotorras (Isle of Parrots), Isla de los Pinos (Isle of Pines) and, in 1978, Isla de la Juventud (Isle of Youth), after Castro's government decided to populate the island and create a unique model of socialism there. The island was transformed from a penal colony into one big school whose students were guests from poor countries around the world. Coddled by the regime, this Eden for the world's youth was sheltered from Cuba's economic crisis in the early 1980s. Supplied with abundant provisions, Isla de la Juventud avoided the shortages that plagued the rest of the country. The major economic activities were the cultivation of citrus fruits (mainly grapefruit), plus marble mining, fishing and tourism. The highest mountain, La Cañada, is 332 metres and makes for a good day trip.

Nueva Gerona ★

Tranquil, typical Nueva Gerona is the biggest city on Isla de la Juventud. Much of the architecture is in the American West Coast style, a result of the island's belated settlement and the presence of so many Americans here at

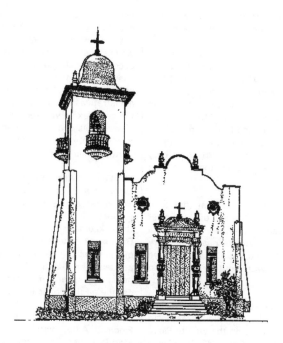

Isla de la Juventud cathedral

the turn of the century. Wandering around, you can't help but be reminded of a town in a western, especially around the harbour. Nueva Gerona has changed over the years, most dramatically since 1978, when it was transformed into a welcome centre for students from around the world. Although the influx of foreign students is no longer what it once was, this place has retained its cosmopolitan ambiance.

Nueva Gerona's central square, the **Parque Guerrillero Heroíco Ernesto Che Guevara**, is named after the legendary Argentinean guerrilla who was such a potent symbol for Cuban youth. The square is relatively large but not as interesting as some others in Cuba. The old city hall, now an economics school, is worth checking out, as is the former Nueva Gerona military barracks, now

the Escuela de Artes *(Calle 39)*. The Iglesia Católica at the corner of Calle 39 and the square is a charming church built in 1929 and typical of that era.

Attractive colonial houses line **Calle 39**, whose official name is José-Martí but which locals persist in calling Calle 39. Although you can only view it from the outside, the house that serves as the headquarters of the *Poder Popular* (Popular Power: government) is particularly representative of the colonial era. Nueva Gerona's most attractive and popular restaurants are also situated on Calle 39. The **El Cochinito** and **El Corderito** (see p 284) restaurants are located in the only houses on the street that have been repainted and restored to their former beauty. Small as Nueva Gerona is, it has an outstanding cultural scene as you can see for yourself in the many art galleries along this Calle.

The **Museo de la Lucha Clandestina** *($1; Tue to Sun 1pm to 9pm; Calle 24, between Calle 43 and Calle 45)* show-cases a collection of artifacts and photographs that retraces the preparations for the Revolution in the '50s, including the activities of the Movimiento 26 de Julio cell. This museum is worth at least a brief visit to learn something about Isla de la Juventud's political past.

The *Barco Pinero*, the boat that took Castro back to the island of Cuba after he was freed from prison on Isla de la Juventud, is moored near the ferry dock, by the Río Las Casas. If you're going by car, watch out for the holes in the road.

The remains of the old prison, **Presidio Modelo ★★**, lie four kilometres north of Nueva Gerona, on the way to Playa Bibijagua *(take Calle 32 in Nueva Gerona and follow the Río Las Casas)*. Built during President Machado's regime, between 1926 and 1931, and modelled after a jail in Joliet, Illinois, it's a good illustration of Isla de la Juventud's former role as a penal colony. The site is awesome: at first glance, you'd never guess the purpose of the five massive, circular, five-storey buildings that make up the complex. You can go inside one to get an idea of the prisoners' harsh living conditions. Fidel Castro and the other unfortunates involved in the failed 1953 attack on the Cuartel Moncada were luckier than most, for they were imprisoned in the infirmary. It was from his cell there that Castro clandestinely circulated his famous pamphlet, *La Historia me absolverá* (History Will Absolve Me). The tiny cells, which held two men apiece, had no bars inside the prison. From his fortified watchtower in the middle of the prison, a guard could watch for any prisoner leaving the confines of his cell. The complex is now in ruins, although the roofs and walls still stand. You can also view the access tunnels to the watchtower, designed so that jailers couldn't be seen by the prisoners. Today, the administrative buildings at the entrance to the complex serve as a high school. All in all, this is one of the country's most extraordinary sites — a must for every visitor to Isla de la Juventud.

The **Finca El Abra** *($1; Tue to Thu 9am to noon and 1pm to 5pm, Carretera Sigüanea)*, a museum displaying some of José Martí's personal effects, lies three kilometres southwest of Nueva Gerona. Martí was the firebrand leader of the rebellion that led to Cuban independence in 1898. He lived in this house for several months in 1870 to escape all the political turmoil and rest up for a while. The Sardá family, whose descendants still live in the Finca El Abra, were close friends of Martí's father. The farmhouse is colonial in style and its grounds feature an imposing tree, a *ceiba*, that was planted in 1945 to commemorate Martí's departure from the island on December 8, 1870. This museum merits a visit to see how rural Cubans live and learn about the life and work of José Martí.

The typical village of **La Fé** lies southwest of Nueva Gerona. La Fé once drew visitors for its medicinal waters and still has a special charm about it. Take the time to make the small detour to this village before heading to the Punta del Este nature park (see p 280).

Cayo Largo ★★

Measuring 38 square kilometres, Cayo Largo is just 200 metres wide at its narrowest point. Small though it is, it boasts nearly 25 kilometres of long, white-sand beaches that are among the most beautiful in the country. Its reef stretches many kilometres out from the lengthy southern shoreline, to the delight of divers and water sports aficionados.

Cayo Largo, 180 km from Havana and 170 kilometres from Varadero, is part of the string of 350 small islands that make up the Los Canarreos archipelago southwest of Cuba. Before tourism arrived, its visitors consisted mostly of a few lonely fishermen from the Cayman Islands. At other times, pirates used Cayo Largo as a base. Naturally, some believe they must have hidden some of their booty on the island. Treasure-hunter Cyrus Wicker, for one, spent a fortune searching for loot and came up empty-handed. The climate is superb, with an average temperature of around 26°C. With 270 days of at least 8 hours of sunshine, the water is warm year-round too.

For the growing number of tourists looking for a peaceful, sunny haven by the sea, Cayo Largo and its neighbouring islands are delightful discoveries. Other visitors will be less thrilled, because tranquillity, sun, sand and water are basically all Cayo Largo has to offer. If you want culture, or museums, or to meet Cubans, give this island a miss. Everything sells in dollars and is more expensive than anywhere else in Cuba, but that's the price a lot of visitors are willing to pay for a hassle-free vacation on long, sun-baked, white beaches.

Isla del Sol, the only village on Cayo Largo, is where all the tourist-industry workers live. Packed in like cattle, sometimes living eight to a room, they hardly enjoy the same living conditions as visitors. Still, they're not truly deprived, since living on the island has certain advantages for them, like being able to go home with precious American dollars. In the village, which locals call *El Pueblo*, the Marina Porto Sol consists of several tourist boutiques, restaurants and a dock that serves as the starting point for daily scuba-diving trips and sight-seeing cruises to neighbouring islands.

Many of the surrounding islands are worth a visit, especially if you're planning to spend a week or two on Cayo Largo. **Cayo Iguana**, as its name suggests, is home to scores of iguanas. On **Cayo Rico** and **Cayo Cantele**, the Cuban government is raising monkeys and various other animals destined for pharmaceutical research labs in Havana; also, honey is produced on both islands. **Cayo Rosario** and **Cayo Los Pájaros** occasionally attract hunters, but people who prefer to do their shooting with cameras are welcome year-round. Opposite Cayo Largo, three islets called **Cayos Ballenatos** are small mountains that look like three whales (*ballenatos*) cruising along the horizon.

PARKS AND
BEACHES

Isla de la Juventud

Playa del Tesoro ★★

The Playa del Tesoro, one of the most extraordinary beaches in Cuba, lies secluded on the Cabo Francés point, where the sand is white and the water shallow. To go there is to experience what Christopher Columbus must have felt when he came across this island.

The Playa del Tesoro is well-equipped for divers and their companions, with lounge chairs, a restaurant, a bar and picnic tables – everything a visitor needs. The restaurant is at the end of a long pier where the dive boats tie up.

Both the dock and the restaurant have recently been renovated after being damaged in a hurricane. The menu is pretty basic, generally offering either fish or pork, plus appetizer and dessert, for about $15 per person.

There are some mosquitoes in the area, especially in the shade of small palm trees, so bring along insect repellent.

To get to Playa de Tesoro, you have to catch a boat at the Marina Sigüanea, two kilometres from the Hotel Colony. The vessel departs at 9:15am daily and returns in the late afternoon. The round-trip cost is $15 per person.

You can also get to Playa del Tesoro in an all-terrain vehicle; it takes about two hours to travel 28 kilometres of rough, unsurfaced road. There are no service stations en route and no car traffic; in the event of a breakdown, you'll just have to pray that someone else comes along the road that day!

Playa Bibijagua

Playa Bibijagua's black-sand beaches aren't the best on Isla de la Juventud. More gray than black, and often poorly maintained, these beaches are nevertheless the pride of locals. And they are indeed striking when you first see them: the black sand, unrolling for several hundred metres, is in marked contrast to the rest of Cuba's beaches. Furthermore, Playa Bibijagua lies in an exceptional natural setting, isolated between hills and rimmed with Isla de la Juventud's characteristic dense vegetation. It is therefore worth a visit and, unless you decide to base yourself there, makes for a good half-day excursion.

To get there, you'll have to rent a car or hire a *particular*. If you're staying at the Hotel Colony, a car is cheaper and more pleasant than a taxi. If you're starting out from Nueva Gerona, head east on Calle 32. Take the opportunity to visit the nearby Presidio Modelo prison (see p 278). The entrance to Playa Bibijagua is well-marked by large signs on the road.

Punta del Este ★★

Punta de l'Este, a remote region that is difficult to get to, is in the southwest part of Isla de la Juventud. It features magnificent scenery, hills that slope down to the ocean, crystalline waters and long beaches. Hidden in the coastal grottos of this practically pristine nature park are the oldest paintings not only in Cuba, but in all of the Caribbean. Painted by the Siboney Indians more than 3,000 years ago, they were discovered at the turn of the century by the famous Cuban ethnologist Fernando Ortíz, whose many books are for sale just about everywhere in Cuba.

In addition to long, deserted white-sand beaches, and places to go scuba diving and snorkelling, the Punta de l'Este region has marshlands and crocodiles. The area is worth a full day's visit, to see Isla de la Juventud's flora and fauna. Bring along drinking water, food and insect repellent.

Cayo Largo

Cayo Largo's beaches need no introduction. Several of them, however, deserve a special mention. **Playa Sirena ★★**, the most famous beach on Cayo Largo, is featured on the island's postcards. This idyllic beach is shaped like a drop of water. To get there, go to the Marina Porto Sol, seven kilometres from the Pelícano Hotel. Twice a day, a bus makes the tour of all of Cayo Largo's main hotels and then heads for the Marina Porto Sol *($2; Hotel Pelícano, departures at 9am and 10:30am, return trips at 3pm and 5pm)*. The entire trip takes 15 minutes. At the beach, a bar, a restaurant and a tourist office cater to visitors. You can also rent sea-doos and windsurfers.

Playa Paraíso is another of Cayo Largo's charming little remote beaches. A cart pulled by a tractor runs between the Hotel Pelícano and this beach, at no charge *(every day at 9am)*.

 OUTDOOR ACTIVITIES

 Scuba Diving

Isla de la Juventud

A veritable paradise for scuba diving, the Cabo Francés offers 56 dive sites within an area of about three nautical miles. Multi-coloured coral, sponges, grottos and shipwrecks make this one of the Caribbean's most popular diving areas. Staff at the Centro Internacional de Buceo are pleasant and professional.

If you're not certified, you can take a diving course there, although the courses aren't recognized elsewhere.

To get to the dive sites, drop in at the Hotel Colony offices of the Centro Internacional de Buceo. If you're not staying at the hotel, you can go directly to the Marina Sigüanea, scarcely two kilometres from the hotel. A car leaves the hotel for the marina daily at 9am. The boats for Cabo Francés set out at 9:15am *($15 for the day, transportation by boat only)*. The 16-nautical-mile crossing takes about 50 minutes.

Non-divers accompanying divers will find plenty of diversions at **Playa del Tesoro**, one of the most remote and remarkable beaches in the country (see p 279). The coral barrier reef is about 200 metres from shore, so you can snorkel from the beach or the dock. Be careful, though, because the barrier is virtually impassable for swimmers.

All necessary diving equipment can be rented at the Marina Sigüanea. You can get to Cabo Francés by boat or by land (see above).

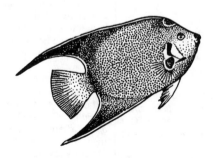

Angelfish

Cayo Largo

Cayo Largo offers some of the most beautiful underwater scenery in the Caribbean — even, some fans say, in the world. In addition to sponges, the area is renowned for its huge variety of soft coral. Veterans rave about the underwater cliffs, more than 1,000 metres deep, around Cayo Largo.

The **Dive-in** *(Marina Porto Sol, ☎54-8214)* dive shop is run by an Italian firm. It offers various ocean trips, equipment rentals *($20)* and diving courses.

One-day excursion: $60, plus $5 for an Italian buffet lunch; two dives; 8:30am to 5pm.

Half-day excursion: $35; one dive; 8:30am to 11:30am.

Non-divers whose companions dive can go along for the boat ride. The cost for them is $20 for the day-long trip and $10 for the half-day trip.

Sailing

Cayo Largo

Cuba Náutica *(Marina Porto Sol, ☎4-8220, ⌐4-8221)* offers yacht and catamaran rentals as well as organized cruises. A day trip in a catamaran or yacht to see the coral barrier and surrounding islands costs $65 *(including lunch, refreshments and coffee; departure at 8:30am, return at 5pm)*. You can make a reservation at any of the hotel's tourist offices or at Cuba Náutica. The firm also arranges customized trips and sunset cruises.

Marine Life Watching

Cayo Largo

Cuba Náutica offers a one-hour trip *($19; departures at 11am and 2pm)* aboard a semi-submarine – a boat with a glass bottom through which passengers can view the ocean floor and tropical fish. It's sort of an upside-down aquarium, and you have to wonder sometimes who's watching whom...

ACCOMMODATIONS

Isla de la Juventud

Nueva Gerona

The **Hotel La Cubana** *($10-$15; ≈, pb, ℜ; 1415 Calle 39, between Calle 18 and Calle 14, ☎23512)*, a friendly little place that's good value for the money, is located in the middle of Nueva Gerona. At the desk they may tell you that the hotel is only for Cuban tourists, but don't give up right away. Start out by asking if there's a room available, since that way you are more likely to get in. An increasing number of foreigners are able to obtain accommodation this way. It seems the exclusive national tourist regulations have slackened over the years.

Just two kilometres from the Nueva Gerona airport, **Las Codornices** *($11-$18; ≈, ℜ, ≈; Antigua Carretera La Fé km 4.5, ☎2-4981)* is an old *hacienda*, a ranch at the edge of a small river. The tranquillity of the setting is generally respected, although the music around the pool is sometimes a bit loud. The welcome is warm and the staff are good-natured. *Parrilladas* (barbecues) are frequently held here.

The **Rancho Tesoro** *($15-$20; pb, ℜ, tv; Carretera La Fé,* ☎2-4069) has just reopened its doors after undergoing renovations. The 60-room hotel is well furnished, but its main attraction is its location in the middle of a forest, within walking distance of Río Las Casas.

The **Villa Gaviota Isla de la Juventud** *($35; ≡, tv, pb, ℜ, ≈; Autopista Nueva Gerona-La Fé km 1,* ☎23256 or 23290) is the best lodging on the island after the Hotel Colony, offering spacious rooms and all the amenities of a good hotel. The loud techno music may not be to everyone's liking, so it's a good idea to bring along earplugs.

Playa Bibijagua

The **Campismo Arenas Negras** *(13 pesos; pb)* operates full-time in June, July and August; the rest of the year, it is only open on weekends. This campground has rustic and rather dark little cabins along one of the black-sand beaches typical of the area. In summer, it's crowded with young Cubans. You can make campfires for cooking. The facilities are generally well maintained, but there is no hot water.

Midway between Playa Bibijagua and the Presidio Modelo, the **Villa Paraíso** *(20 pesos; ≡, pb;* ☎2-5246) is situated on Playa Bibijagua's prettiest beach, and offers a warm welcome and plain but comfortable rooms. Its appealing little restaurant opens out onto the ocean.

Nearby, the **Villa Bibijagua Arenas Negras** *(17 pesos; ≡, pb;* ☎2-5290) is open year-round but is busy only in summer. This tourist complex features lots of rooms and several houses. The houses can be rented *(20 to 80 pesos)*; the best are equipped with a gas stove, a refrigerator and a TV.

With just three rooms around a small restaurant, the **Villa Gaviota** *($30; ≡, pb, ≈, ℜ;* ☎2-5230) is a small establishment. The beach isn't as well maintained as the one at the nearby campground, but the comfortable rooms are definitely superior.

The **Hotel Colony** *($70; ≡, tv, ≈, ℜ, pb; Carretera de Sigüanea km 41,* ☎9-8290 or 9-8282), an international diving centre, stands alone in the southwest of the island and caters only to international visitors. The water off the beach is so shallow that swimming there is difficult. Head for the pool instead, or sign up for one of the daily excursions to the superb Cabo Francés beach, which depart from the Marina Sigüanea. The food at the restaurant is adequate but the menu varies little, as you'll soon realize if you're spending longer than a few days at this hotel.

Cayo Largo

The most economical way to stay on Cayo Largo is to rent a cabin on board one of the yachts at **Cuba Náutica** *($20;* ☎4-8220, ⊷4-8221) in the Marina Porto Sol. The drawback is that you have to leave early every morning and take all your personal effects with you, since the boats are usually rented out for the day. You can come to an arrangement with Cuba Náutica's Quebecois director, Joey Roussel.

All hotels on Cayo Largo are modern and comfortable and their rooms are air-conditioned. Prices are pretty much uniform. Two reception desks represent all the hotels on the island. The largest is located in the lobby of **Complejo Hotelero Isla del Sur** *(☎/⊷4-8160)*. It's basically a reservation service for the following hotels: the Isla del Sur, Villa Capricho, Villa Soledad, Villa Iguana and Villa Coral. The counter is very easy to find; it's at the end of the road, in front of the only rotunda there. All these hotels stand on a long, magnificent beach that rings Cayo Largo's entire south coast.

The **Villa Capricho** *($70-84)* is Cayo Largo's most popular hotel, offering typical chalets with rustic rooms much admired by travellers for their exotic flavour. On the other hand, this is the only hotel on Cayo Largo that doesn't have a pool; guests use the pools at other hotels. The quality of the rooms is rather uneven. Ask for a room that's numbered between 1001 and 1038, so you can enjoy an ocean view. Along with the Villa Capricho, the neighbouring **Villa Iguana** *($70-84)* has the lowest room rates on the island. Nudism is common on the section of the beach that faces this hotel.

The **Hotel Isla del Sur** *($77-93)*, the **Villa Coral** *($77-93)* and the **Villa Soledad** *($77-93)* all offer similar amenities and fall in the same category. The three comfortable hotels are neighbours, and all have an excellent location right on the Caribbean.

The **Hotel Pelícano** *($102; ≡, ≈, ℛ, pb, tv; ☎4-8333, ☎4-8166)* has its own reception area. It's located between the airport and the Isla del Sur complex. This superb hotel occupies a particularly pretty section of Cayo Largo's long beach. Rooms are spacious and comfortable. The hotel's two restaurants are pleasant and offer a varied buffet. This luxurious esta-blishment attracts many Europeans.

RESTAURANTS

Isla de la Juventud

Coppelia *(Calle 37, near the central square)* offers excellent ice cream. Young and not-so-young alike congregate here.

Nueva Gerona's two best restaurants stand side by side on Calle 39. Both have been completely renovated and proudly display the prettiest colours in the city. They cater to locals and their prices are in pesos. As its name suggests, **El Cochinito** *($; Calle 39)* serves up pork-based Creole dishes. The other restaurant, **El Corderito** *($; Calle 39)*, specializes in lamb-based dishes. Both have a relaxed ambiance and decent service.

The restaurant at the **Hotel Colony** *($$)* offers good food, notably a buffet that is wide-ranging but unchanging. There is also an à la carte menu, if you care to spend a fortune on Creole pork dishes. If you're staying at the hotel for a while, you'll begin to crave variety. The restaurant's ambiance is rather cold, largely because of the neon lights on the ceiling.

Cayo Largo

Rock lobster is abundant on Cayo Largo. The variety and quality of the food are generally superior to what you find elsewhere in the country, which means that the prices are higher, too. Besides Cayo Largo's hotel restaurants, there are several establishments at the Marina Porto Sol.

The **Taberna del Pirata** *($$$)*, at the entrance to the marina, is a popular place, especially between 3pm and

4pm, when vacationers on one-day tours from Havana and Varadero gather here to have one last snack while waiting to be taken to the airport. The menu consists mainly of seafood dishes (crayfish, shrimp, fish), but offers chicken as well. The house specialty is a plate of *ostiones* (oysters) marinated in a tomato sauce spiced with garlic and Tabasco.

Nearby, **El Criollo** *($$$)* serves up typical Cuban fare. The dishes are pork-based, accompanied by rice, manioc and plantain. While the food is a tad greasy, the atmosphere is pleasant and relaxed.

  ENTERTAINMENT

Isla de la Juventud

The **Complejo Juvenil Parque Ahao** *(Carretera de Chacón, Km 1)* boasts an excellent danceclub. Cabaret shows are staged here periodically and the place is hopping from Friday to Sunday. It's a popular hangout for locals, but visitors often check it out too. It's just past the bridge over the Río Las Casas, east of Nueva Gerona's central square.

Cayo Largo

Other than the hotel discos, **La Chusmita** is the best nightspot on Cayo Largo. Located behind the Marina Porto Sol, in the village of Isla del Sol, it's popular with Cayo Largo's Cuban tourist-industry workers, providing a good opportunity to get to know some of the locals.

 SHOPPING

Isla de la Juventud

Cubalse, the biggest boutique and the biggest supermarket in Nueva Gerona, is full of imported goods. It's on Calle 39, behind the Coppelia, near the central square.

The **Libreria Frank País** *(Calle 22, at the corner of 39)* sells a few books in Spanish.

The **Centro de Desarollo de las Artes Visuales** *(free admission; Tue to Sun noon to 10pm; Calle 39, at the corner of Calle 26, ☎2-3770)* showcases attractive exhibitions of paintings, ceramics and sculpture by local artists. Much of the artwork carries a very reasonable price tag and some of it is priced in pesos. The building next door houses the **Fondo de Bienes Culturales**, which offers a limited selection of local arts and crafts.

GLOSSARY

Several tips on Spanish pronunciation in Latin America.

CONSONANTS

b Is pronounced **b** or sometimes a soft **v**, depending on the region or the person: *bizcocho* (biz-koh-choh or viz-koh-choh).

c As in English, *c* is pronounced as **s** before *i* and *e*: *cerro* (seh-rroh). When it is placed in front of other vowels, it is hard and pronounced as **k**: *carro* (kah-rroh). The *c* is also hard when it comes before a consonant, except before an *h* (see further below).

d Is pronounced like a soft **d**: *dar* (dahr). *D* is usually not pronounced when at the end of a word.

g As with the *c*, *g* is soft before an *i* or an *e*, and is pronounced like a soft **h**: *gente* (hente). In front of other vowels and consonants, the *g* is hard: *golf* (pronounced the same way as in English).

ch Pronounced **ch**, as in English: *leche* (le-che). Like the *ll*, this combination is considered a single letter in the Spanish alphabet, listed separately in dictionaries and telephone directories.

h Is not pronounced: *hora* (oh-ra).

j Is pronounced like a guttural **h**, as in "him".

ll Is pronounced like a hard **y**, as in "yes": *llamar* (yah-mar). In some regions, such as central Colombia, *ll* is pronounced as a soft **g**, as in "mirage" (*Medellín* is pronounced Medegin). Like the *ch*, this combination is considered a single letter in the Spanish alphabet, and is listed separately in dictionaries and telephone directories.

ñ Is pronounced like the **ni** in "onion", or the **ny** in "canyon": *señora* (seh-nyo-rah).

qu Is pronounced **k**: *aquí* (ah-kee).

r Is rolled, as the Irish or Italian pronunciation of **r**.

s Is always pronounced **s** like "sign": *casa* (cah-ssah).

v Is pronounced like a **b**: *vino* (bee-noh).

z Is pronounced like **s**: *paz* (pahss).

VOWELS

a Is always pronounced **ah** as in "part", and never *ay* as in "day": *faro* (fah-roh).

e Is pronounced **eh** as in "elf," and never *ey* as in "grey or "ee" as in "key": *helado* (eh-lah-doh].

i Is always pronounced **ee**: *cine* (see-neh).

o Is always pronounced **oh** as in "cone": *copa* (koh-pah).

u Is always pronounced **oo**: *universidad* (oo-nee-ver-see-dah).

All other letters are pronounced the same as in English.

STRESSING SYLLABLES

In Spanish, syllables are differently stressed. This stress is very important, and emphasizing the right syllable might even be necessary to make yourself understood. If a vowel has an accent, this syllable is the one that should be stressed. If there is no accent, follow this rule:

Stress the second-last syllable of any word that ends with a vowel: *amigo*.

Stress the last syllable of any word that ends in a consonant, except for **s** (plural of nouns and adjectives) or **n** (plural of nouns): *usted* (but *amigos*, *hablan*).

GREETINGS

Goodbye	*adiós, hasta luego*
Good afternoon and good evening	*buenas tardes*
Hi (casual)	*hola*
Good morning	*buenos días*
Good night	*buenas noches*
Thank-you	*gracias*
Please	*por favor*
You are welcome	*de nada*
Excuse me	*perdone/a*
My name is...	*mi nombre es...*
What is your name?	*¿cómo se llama usted?*
yes	*no*
no	*sí*
Do you speak English?	*¿habla usted inglés?*
Slower, please	*más despacio, por favor*
I am sorry, I don't speak Spanish	*Lo siento, no hablo español*
How are you?	*¿qué tal?*
I am fine	*estoy bien*
I am American (male/female)	*Soy estadounidense*
I am Australian	*Soy autraliano/a*
I am Belgian	*Soy belga*
I am British (male/female)	*Soy británico/a*
I am Canadian	*Soy canadiense*
I am German (male/female)	*Soy alemán/a*
I am Italian (male/female)	*Soy italiano/a*
I am Swiss	*Soy suizo*
I am a tourist	*Soy turista*
single (m/f)	*soltero/a*
divorced (m/f)	*divorciado/a*
married (m/f)	*casado/a*
friend (m/f)	*amigo/a*
child (m/f)	*niño/a*
husband, wife	*esposo/a*
mother	*madre*
father	*padre*
brother, sister	*hermano/a*
widower widow	*viudo/a*
I am hungry	*tengo hambre*
I am ill	*estoy enfermo/a*
I am thirsty	*tengo sed*

DIRECTIONS

beside	*al lado de*
to the right	*a la derecha*
to the left	*a la izquierda*
here	*aquí*
there	*allí*
into, inside	*dentro*
outside	*fuera*
behind	*detrás*

in front of	*delante*
between	*entre*
far from	*lejos de*
Where is ... ?	*¿dónde está ... ?*
To get to ...?	*¿para ir a...?*
near	*cerca de*
straight ahead	*todo recto*

MONEY

money	*dinero / plata*
credit card	*tarjeta de crédito*
exchange	*cambio*
traveller's cheque	*cheque de viaje*
I don't have any money	*no tengo dinero*
The bill, please	*la cuenta, por favor*
receipt	*recibo*

SHOPPING

store	*tienda*
market	*mercado*
open	*abierto/a*
closed	*cerrado/a*
How much is this?	*¿cuánto es?*
to buy	*comprar*
to sell	*vender*
the customer	*el / la cliente*
salesman	*vendedor*
saleswoman	*vendedora*
I need...	*necesito...*
I would like...	*yo quisiera...*
batteries	*pilas*
blouse	*blusa*
cameras	*cámaras*
cosmetics and perfumes	*cosméticos y perfumes*
cotton	*algodón*
dress jacket	*saco*
eyeglasses	*lentes, gafas*
fabric	*tela*
film	*película*
gifts	*regalos*
gold	*oro*
handbag	*bolsa*
hat	*sombrero*
jewellery	*joyería*
leather	*cuero, piel*
local crafts	*artesanía*
magazines	*revistas*
newpapers	*periódicos*
pants	*pantalones*
records, cassettes	*discos, casetas*
sandals	*sandalias*
shirt	*camisa*
shoes	*zapatos*
silver	*plata*
skirt	*falda*
sun screen products	*productos solares*
T-shirt	*camiseta*
watch	*reloj*
wool	*lana*

MISCELLANEOUS

| a little | *poco* |

a lot	*mucho*
good (m/f)	*bueno/a*
bad (m/f)	*malo/a*
beautiful (m/f)	*hermoso/a*
pretty (m/f)	*bonito/a*
ugly	*feo*
big	*grande*
tall (m/f)	*alto/a*
small (m/f)	*pequeño/a*
short (length) (m/f)	*corto/a*
short (person) (m/f)	*bajo/a*
cold (m/f)	*frío/a*
hot	*caliente*
dark (m/f)	*oscuro/a*
light (colour)	*claro*
do not touch	*no tocar*
expensive (m/f)	*caro/a*
cheap (m/f)	*barato/a*
fat (m/f)	*gordo/a*
slim, skinny (m/f)	*delgado/a*
heavy (m/f)	*pesado/a*
light (weight) (m/f)	*ligero/a*
less	*menos*
more	*más*
narrow (m/f)	*estrecho/a*
wide (m/f)	*ancho/a*
new (m/f)	*nuevo/a*
old (m/f)	*viejo/a*
nothing	*nada*
something (m/f)	*algo/a*
quickly	*rápidamente*
slowly (m/f)	*despacio/a*
What is this?	*¿qué es esto?*
when?	*¿cuando?*
where?	*¿dónde?*

TIME

in the afternoon, early evening	*por la tarde*
at night	*por la noche*
in the daytime	*por el día*
in the morning	*por la mañana*
minute	*minuto*
month	*mes*
ever	*jamás*
never	*nunca*
now	*ahora*
today	*hoy*
yesterday	*ayer*
tomorrow	*mañana*
What time is it?	*¿qué hora es?*
hour	*hora*
week	*semana*
year	*año*
Sunday	*domingo*
Monday	*lunes*
Tuesday	*martes*
Wednesday	*miércoles*
Thursday	*jueves*
Friday	*viernes*
Saturday	*sábado*
January	*enero*
February	*febrero*
March	*marzo*

April	*abril*
May	*mayo*
June	*junio*
July	*julio*
August	*agosto*
September	*septiembre*
October	*octubre*
November	*noviembre*
December	*diciembre*

WEATHER

It is cold	*hace frío*
It is warm	*hace calor*
It is very hot	hace mucho calor
sun	*sol*
It is sunny	hace sol
It is cloudy	*está nublado*
rain	*lluvia*
It is raining	*está lloviendo*
wind	*viento*
It is windy	*hay viento*
snow	*nieve*
damp	*húmedo*
dry	*seco*
storm	*tormenta*
hurricane	*huracán*

COMMUNICATION

air mail	*correos aéreo*
collect call	*llamada por cobrar*
dial the number	*marcar el número*
area code, country code	*código*
envelope	*sobre*
long distance	*larga distancia*
post office	*correo*
rate	*tarifa*
stamps	*estampillas*
telegram	*telegrama*
telephone book	*un guia telefónica*
wait for the tone	*esperar la señal*

ACTIVITIES

beach	*playa*
museum or gallery	*museo*
scuba diving	*buceo*
to swim	*bañarse*
to walk around	*pasear*
hiking	*caminata*
trail	*pista, sendero*
cycling	*ciclismo*
fishing	*pesca*

TRANSPORTATION

arrival	*llegada*
departure	*salida*
on time	*a tiempo*
cancelled (m/f)	*anulado/a*
one way ticket	*ida*
return	*regreso*
round trip	*ida y vuelta*

schedule	*horario*
baggage	*equipajes*
north	*norte*
south	*sur*
east	*este*
west	*oeste*
avenue	*avenida*
street	*calle*
highway	*carretera*
expressway	*autopista*
airplane	*avión*
airport	*aeropuerto*
bicycle	*bicicleta*
boat	*barco*
bus	*bus*
bus stop	*parada*
bus terminal	*terminal*
train	*tren*
train crossing	*crucero ferrocarril*
station	*estación*
neighbourhood	*barrio*
collective taxi	*colectivo*
corner	*esquina*
express	*rápido*
safe	*seguro/a*
be careful	*cuidado*
car	*coche, carro*
To rent a car	*alquilar un auto*
gas	*gasolina*
gas station	*gasolinera*
no parking	*no estacionar*
no passing	*no adelantar*
parking	*parqueo*
pedestrian	*peaton*
road closed, no through traffic	*no hay paso*
slow down	*reduzca velocidad*
speed limit	*velocidad permitida*
stop	*alto*
stop! (an order)	*pare*
traffic light	*semáforo*

ACCOMMODATION

cabin, bungalow	*cabaña*
accommodation	*alojamiento*
double, for two people	*doble*
single, for one person	*sencillo*
high season	*temporada alta*
low season	*temporada baja*
bed	*cama*
floor (first, second...)	*piso*
main floor	*planta baja*
manager	*gerente, jefe*
double bed	*cama matrimonial*
cot	*camita*
bathroom	*baños*
with private bathroom	*con baño privado*
hot water	*agua caliente*
breakfast	*desayuno*
elevator	*ascensor*
air conditioning	*aire acondicionado*
fan	*ventilador, abanico*
pool	*piscina, alberca*
room	*habitación*

NUMBERS

1	uno	80	ochenta
2	dos	90	noventa
3	tres	100	cien
4	cuatro	101	ciento uno
5	cinco	102	ciento dos
6	seis	200	doscientos
7	siete	300	trescientos
8	ocho	400	quatrocientoa
9	nueve	500	quinientos
10	diez	600	seiscientos
11	once	700	sietecientos
12	doce	800	ochocientos
13	trece	900	novecientos
14	catorce	1,000	mil
15	quince	1,100	mil cien
16	dieciséis	1,200	mil doscientos
17	diecisiete	2000	dos mil
18	dieciocho	3000	tres mil
19	diecinueve	10,000	diez mil
20	veinte	100,000	cien mil
21	veintiuno	1,000,000	un millón
22	veintidós		
23	veintitrés		
24	veinticuatro		
25	veinticinco		
26	veintiséis		
27	veintisiete		
28	veintiocho		
29	veintinueve		
30	treinta		
31	treinta y uno		
32	treinta y dos		
40	cuarenta		
50	cincuenta		
60	sesenta		
70	setenta		

INDEX

INDEX

INDEX

INDEX

Travel Notes

ORDER FORM

ULYSSES TRAVEL GUIDES

☐ Atlantic Canada	$24.95 CAN $17.95 US	☐ Lisbon	$18.95 CAN $13.95 US
☐ Bahamas	$24.95 CAN $17.95 US	☐ Louisiana	$29.95 CAN $21.95 US
☐ Beaches of Maine	$12.95 CAN $9.95 US	☐ Martinique	$24.95 CAN $17.95 US
☐ Bed & Breakfasts in Québec	$13.95 CAN $10.95 US	☐ Montréal	$19.95 CAN $14.95 US
☐ Belize	$16.95 CAN $12.95 US	☐ New Orleans	$17.95 CAN $12.95 US
☐ Calgary	$17.95 CAN $12.95 US	☐ New York City	$19.95 CAN $14.95 US
☐ Canada	$29.95 CAN $21.95 US	☐ Nicaragua	$24.95 CAN $16.95 US
☐ Chicago	$19.95 CAN $14.95 US	☐ Ontario	$27.95 CAN $19.95US
☐ Chile	$27.95 CAN $17.95 US	☐ Ottawa	$17.95 CAN $12.95 US
☐ Colombia	$29.95 CAN $21.95 US	☐ Panamá	$24.95 CAN $17.95 US
☐ Costa Rica	$27.95 CAN $19.95 US	☐ Peru	$27.95 CAN $19.95 US
☐ Cuba	$24.95 CAN $17.95 US	☐ Portugal	$24.95 CAN $16.95 US
☐ Dominican Republic	$24.95 CAN $17.95 US	☐ Provence - Côte d'Azur	$29.95 CAN $21.95US
☐ Ecuador and Galapagos Islands	$24.95 CAN $17.95 US	☐ Québec	$29.95 CAN $21.95 US
☐ El Salvador	$22.95 CAN $14.95 US	☐ Québec and Ontario with Via	$9.95 CAN $7.95 US
☐ Guadeloupe	$24.95 CAN $17.95 US	☐ Toronto	$18.95 CAN $13.95 US
☐ Guatemala	$24.95 CAN $17.95 US	☐ Vancouver	$17.95 CAN $12.95 US
☐ Honduras	$24.95 CAN $17.95 US	☐ Washington D.C.	$18.95 CAN $13.95 US
☐ Jamaica	$24.95 CAN $17.95 US	☐ Western Canada	$29.95 CAN $21.95 US

ULYSSES DUE SOUTH

☐ Acapulco	$14.95 CAN $9.95 US	☐ Cartagena (Colombia)	$12.95 CAN $9.95 US
☐ Belize	$16.95 CAN $12.95 US	☐ Cancun Cozumel	$17.95 CAN $12.95 US

ULYSSES DUE SOUTH

☐ Puerto Vallarta	$14.95 CAN $9.95 US	☐ St. Martin and St. Barts	$16.95 CAN $12.95 US

ULYSSES GREEN ESCAPES

☐ Cycling in France .... $22.95 CAN
$16.95 US
☐ Cycling in Ontario .... $22.95 CAN
$16.95 US

☐ Hiking in the .... $19.95 CAN
Northeastern U.S. $13.95 US
☐ Hiking in Québec .... $19.95 CAN
$13.95 US

ULYSSES CONVERSATION GUIDES

☐ French for Better Travel ..... $9.95 CAN
$6.95 US

☐ Spanish for Better Travel .... $9.95 CAN
$6.95 US

ULYSSES TRAVEL JOURNAL

☐ Ulysses Travel Journal ... $9.95 CAN
(Blue, Red, Green, Yellow, Sextant)
$7.95 US

☐ Ulysses Travel Journal ... $14.95 CAN
80 Days $9.95 US

TITLE	QUANTITY	PRICE	TOTAL

Name	Sub-total	
Address		
	Postage & Handling	$8.00*
	Sub-total	
Payment : ☐ Money Order ☐ Visa ☐ MasterCard		
Card Number	G.S.T. in Canada 7%	
Signature	TOTAL	

ULYSSES TRAVEL PUBLICATIONS
4176 St-Denis,
Montréal, Québec, H2W 2M5
(514) 843-9447 fax (514) 843-9448
www.ulysses.ca
* $15 for overseas orders

U.S. ORDERS: **GLOBE PEQUOT PRESS**
P.O. Box 833, 6 Business Park Road,
Old Saybrook, CT 06475-0833
1-800-243-0495 fax 1-800-820-2329
www.globe-pequot.com